Tomato Head

The Value Of An Examined Life

From frontier Texas to the epicenters of civilization,
a true life story

J.B. Garrett

TOMATO HEAD

Boulevard Press books may be purchased for educational, business, or sales promotion use. For information, please send email to www.TomatoHeadBook.com This web site also contains information on book sales and special arrangements with the author. Reviews of Tomato Head are encouraged at Amazon.com or TomatoHeadBook.com

ISBN 978-0-9832411-4-0

First Edition

Boulevard Press

www.BoulevardPress.com

For

Scott Edwin Garrett

August 30, 1964--December 14, 2011
You were warmth, adventure, humor, energy, joy and love.

AND FOR

Joan

For the first 49 years

And for

Jon, Terry, Jack, and Audrey

The love and spice in our lives.

And for

My brothers and sisters

TOMATO HEAD is a term of affection and humor, referencing a young boy with bright red hair. It was a name my aunts, uncles, and grandparents thought appropriate for a time when my hair was just that, with an unruly cowlick in front.

This story of my life so far is written in the same spirit of affection and humor.

The story is mine, but it is also about family and friends, the times we lived in, some of our concerns, and my conclusions. From it, our descendants will learn some things about themselves, and the genes they have carried forward.

"I" is central to autobiography, but the essence of the journey is how friends and family and the larger environment have shaped me, rather than how "I" have shaped and changed them.

—JBG—

Contents

BOOK FOUR   *New York Years: Joan, Scott & Jon*

BOOK FIVE   *Atlanta Years*

BOOK SIX   *New York, Connecticut, Harvard*

BOOK SEVEN *Saint Louis Years, International Business*

BOOK EIGHT *Connecticut And New/Old Beginnings*

BOOK NINE *California Years*

Photos

BOOK ONE
Foundation Years

Photo 1. In our "Sunday" garb. Me, Dad, Raby, Mom, Cal, outside my Grandmother Morris' house, 1939.

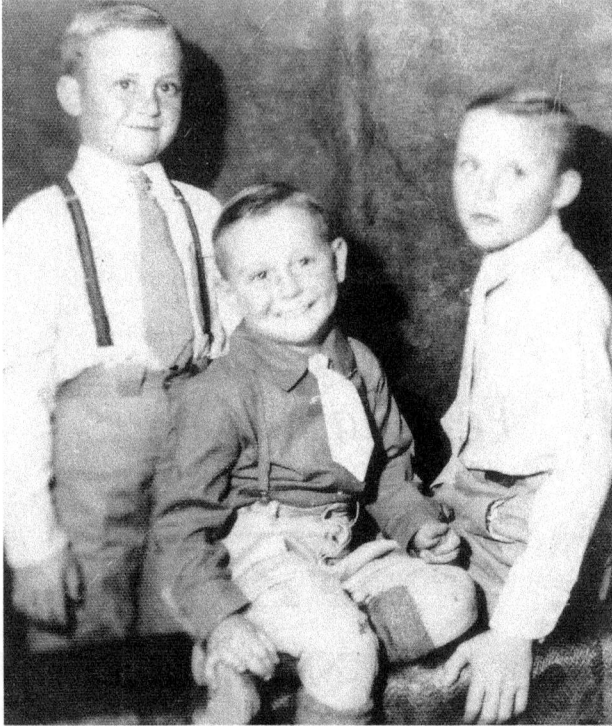

Photo 2. *My favorite picture with my older brothers, 1939, Flomot, in dress up. Raby, left, me, center, and Cal right.*

Photo 3. The same threesome, almost 70 years later, Raby left, Me center, and Cal right. Cal passed away in October of 2008.

THE EARLY YEARS

T he odds against being born in the tiny agricultural foothills of Flomot, Texas, on the Panhandle Plains, are greater than I can calculate, yet I was born there on July 4, 1933, in a isolated one-room tarpaper shack, a mile east of the little outpost village.

This dry land farm settlement was in the twin clutches of the dust bowl and the great depression, the former a direct result of homesteaders plowing under native grasses in a period of extreme draught, and the latter a paralysis of the economic system following the stock market crash of "29". Their concurrent curses on the Great Plains were seen by the faithful as evidence of God's wrath.

These crises scarred many lives forever, my parents among them. While the economic wheel refused to turn, almost no rain and high winds produced 60 to 70 killer dust storms each year, killing animals with silicosis, clogging every mammal orifice, and creating widespread fear and despair which placed the region's survival in doubt.

I was the third child and third son of Frank William and Dillie Dean Morris Garrett, both 27 at the time. My older brothers were Calvin Earl, born in October, 1928, and Raby Duane, born in June, 1930. Four sisters would come after me, all too young to remember living in Flomot. Shirley Dean, in 1941, Norma Jean, in 1942, Dora Bonita, in 1946, and finally, Sharon Ann, in 1950. Seven children from the same parents over a 22 year span seems odd in retrospect, but was not considered unusual at the time for farm families with room to expand, a need for extra hands, and scant knowledge of birth control.

This period in history was, to paraphrase then President, FDR, "a time which will live in ignominy". My mother was attended by one of her sisters, Annie Morris Washington. Dad was away earning one dollar for a 12-hour work-day, and rushed home when the news reached him in the field. The doctor showed only later to confirm that the birth had gone well.

Birthing at home was the norm for settlers in this accidental place, which was later destined to die gradually from the same forces of westward migration which first made it seem viable some 50 years earlier. It had sprung organically from the need to serve the original homesteaders and settlers. It died when these families moved on to larger towns with paved streets, electricity, water and sewer systems, better schools, better shopping, and fewer day-to-day hardships. This same downward spiral was the fate of hundreds of these stopover villages throughout the West. They had served their purpose and were no longer needed.

THE OUTPOST: SELF RELIANCE FOR SURVIVAL

Environment shapes character, attitudes, and expectations. Where we come from influences our opinions for life, therefore the need to understand the nature and values of the isolated community which launched my parents and my older brothers and me. Beyond the primary influence of inherited genes, our surroundings in early years shaped our emotions and intellect and set our bearings for the course of our existence. Witnessing and actually living the responsibility-for-self creed of our close relatives and friends in this community no doubt shaped forever our conservative political and economic convictions. West Texas today votes almost 80% conservative, a consistent record interrupted only by its sticking with Franklin Roosevelt during the depression and world war two years.

The pioneer frontier village of Flomot was formed in 1880 on the edge of civilization, just six years after warring Comanche Indians had been finally cleared from the Southern plains. The year 1933 was not yet one lifetime away from the time when savage Comanche bands fighting on horseback had routinely terrorized settlers intruding on their territory. Nomadic, and following millions of buffalo, they so thoroughly dominated the Llano Estacado (so named by Spanish explorer Francisco de Coronado) that all Anglo, Mexican, and Spanish settlers, as well as other Indian bands, feared for their lives daily.

THE SETTING

The dust bowl was a phenomenon wrought by disastrous government policy of rewarding homesteaders to cultivate and plow under the virgin soil holding native grasses. Flomot was on its eastern border, and, in the 30's, retained all the characteristics of a simple western trading post or stagecoach stop. Nearby Quitaque, 15 miles to the northwest, had in fact been such a stop.

In this remote place, qualified and accessible medical care was rare. The nearest doctor was 15-20 miles away. Specialists were unimagined even in larger towns. Healthcare of any type was primitive, resting almost entirely on home remedies. Penicillin, antibiotics, most vaccines that might have prevented common diseases like measles, mumps, pneumonia, tuburculosis, cholera, and whooping cough, hadn't yet been developed.

A stop-gap home treatment for childhood cough or severe sore throat was a "sugar tit" to suck on. This was devised by putting a spoon of sugar in a cloth, twisting it tightly, then infusing it with a drop or two of coal oil. The slowly released oil soothed the throat while the sugar served as a pacifier.

One of my Dad's favorite treatments for a deep chest cold was a "mustard plaster" spread over the chest and covered with hot cloths. As I remember, it was a mixture of Vick's VapoRub with starch as binder, perhaps actual mustard, heated to barely tolerable temperature, then lathered on. The smell was perhaps the cure.

Deaths hastened by common flue and "consumption" were frequent. The terror of polio was just gaining steam, and afflicted many in the community, including my mother's sister, Zula, who survived but suffered a permanently deformed leg and foot. The "Iron Lung", which kept polio victims breathing, was a nightmare conception to young minds. We were aware of TB around us. Cancer was not often identified as such, although it was certainly a killer even then.

As a newly walking toddler, I was severely burned when curiosity brought serious trouble. I tipped a container of boiling starch into my bib overalls, resulting in third degree burns over my chest and stomach area. This burns were treated at home over an extended period, without a doctor's advice, luckily escaping infection which could have been deadly. I carry the outline of the burn on my chest and stomach today, concealed by an inordinately dense crop of body hair.

Scarce water was pumped from scarcer wells, and many homes got drinking and wash water from open barrels or smaller containers hauled from neighbors, or from cisterns which collected gutter water from roofs. Hygiene was difficult, with little refrigeration, no indoor plumbing and no sewer system. Water contamination was inevitable.

There was only one indoor bathroom in the town, an oddity and subject of much speculation. Every other house had a "two holer" outhouse, stocked with "reading" material, and plenty of flies. My brother Raby jokes that some were too poor for a two-holer, and had only a path.

Raby contracted typhoid fever from hauled water at about age eight and very nearly died during a month's hospital stay in Turkey, Texas, 17 miles to the Northeast. The long-needled and painful immunizations my older brother and I suffered are still vivid memories.

Clean clothes and bodies were always a daunting challenge. One early memory is of my mother heating wash water with firewood, outdoors in a black iron pot, scrubbing clothes with homemade soap on a washboard, rinsing them in a galvanized tub with bluing (to whiten them), heating starch to stiffen them, and hanging them on a wire clothesline to dry in the dusty West Texas wind.

Bathing was once or twice weekly in the same tub used for rinsing clothes, or more simply with a wet washcloth. Dental hygiene consisted of rinsing with salt water or brushing with baking soda, if anything at all. Cheap dentures were a common appliance by middle age. My first dental checkup was age 12, in the town of Plainview, and ended with a molar being yanked out without anesthesia, while I held on to the dental chair for dear life.

Cuts and bruises were treated with rubbing alcohol or liniment and home made bandages.

There was no social safety net, no unemployment insurance, no food stamps, no medicare or medicaid, no walk-in clinics with nurses, no social security, and no credit cards. Soup lines and militant labor unions common in the urban East never found their way to the pioneer West, where plentiful land allowed space for animals and the growing of healthy foods. Crowding was never an issue, and disease was slower to spread as a consequence. But daily life was hard and lonely on the distant frontier, with family helping family, friend helping friend, neighbor helping neighbor, but more important than all of these, people helping themselves.

Gravel coated dirt roads were the only identifiable infrastructure, leveled infrequently by the county road grader. Smaller feeder roads were not passable after rains. Transportation was rudimentary, consisting mainly of farm pickups and horses and wagons. There was no rural electricity until the early 1940's, telephones were rare, and almost every form of communication was face-to-face or by letter. Coal oil lamps, carried from room to room, were standard in every home, replenished by a barrel of fuel stored outdoors.

Coal oil and later, butane gas stoves were used for home heating, supplemented by wood and coal. With electricity, a few families in town had radios, but television and computers were unimagined. The internet was still two generations into the future. Scratchy music was sometimes played on windup Victrolas , but music was more often made by family members who might also play at church socials or the occasional community gathering or rare square dance.

The county seat of Matador was 20 miles to the Southeast, near the headquarters of the famed Matador ranch, one of the largest ranches in the world. The Matador courthouse and jail served the need to hold and try serious law-breakers, record marriages, deaths, wills, and land transactions. The county had a sheriff but no other uniformed law. A gentleman named Robert I. Thomas, a local service station owner, was the appointed justice of the peace for Flomot, with unknown official duties. There was no speed limit other than common sense, no stop signs, and no known town rules for anyone to enforce. There was no bank. Most goods were bought and sold for cash or barter.

Most in the broader community lived on their own family farms, with houses perhaps a mile apart. They came to town by wagon or horseback or tractor when need arose for food items or spare parts or plow sharpening or to visit the post office or hardware store. If wet weather prevented working the fields, farmers and wives came to town to shop and exchange news, but there was no meeting hall or community gathering place except the mercantile or hardware store for such socializing. Al Clement's barber shop was busy on these days. Men talked about crops or weather or animals, but did not gossip.

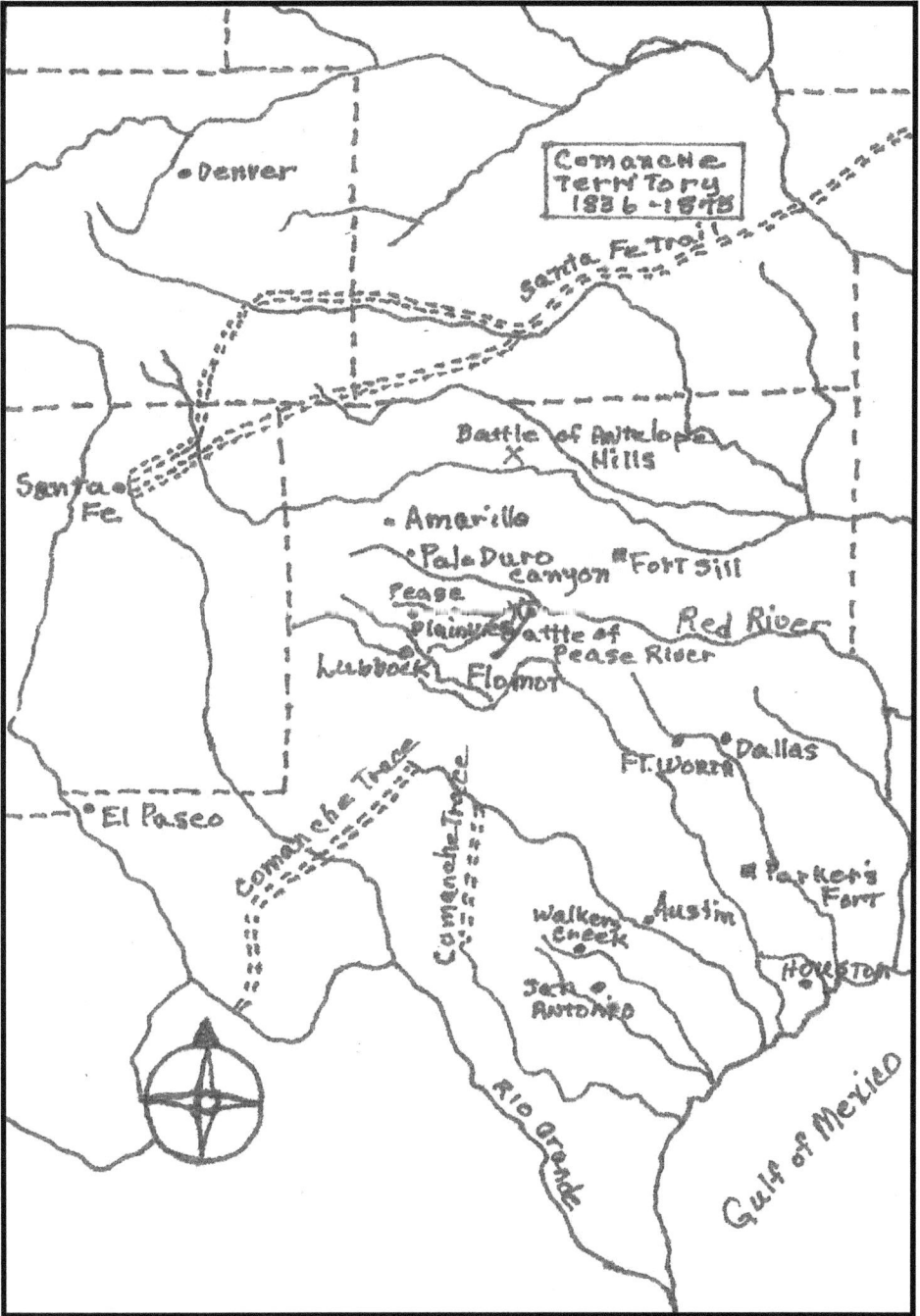

Photo 4. Geographic region of the dust bowl, which happens to coincide with the outlines of Comanche territory. Comanche bands dominated the region until the 1870's.

FINDING FLOMOT

The never incorporated town may be found on earth at coordinates 34 degrees, 13 minutes, and 37 seconds North, and 100 degrees, 59 minutes, and 19 seconds West. Anything west of 98 degrees was considered high risk Indian territory until the late 1870'.

Flomot was (is) 2 degrees north and 300 miles west of Dallas. It sat at the center of a triangle, with Quitaque 15 miles Northwest, Turkey 15 miles Northeast, and Matador 20 miles Southeast. Go there and view the remains of a once vital but never quite thriving homestead waypoint settlement which served as a way point in the government push to populate the West through the Homestead Act, offering 160 acres to male heads of household who lasted five years on their claim.

Importantly, it was also in the heart of Comanche Indian country, who, before their virtual extermination, had dominated the area for hundreds of years until the Mexicans and Europeans came to "discover" lands already occupied. In its determination to conquer and secure all the land, our government policy trumped morality, inhumanely and militarily eliminating an entire race of admittedly savage humans who defended their homes and families the only way they knew how.

The rolling grass and mesquite covered land lies some 800 feet below the escarpment known as the Caprock, above which laid the flat and windswept Texas plains, with their lack of natural shelter or adequate water for settler families and their cows, horses, and pigs. Though rain was rare below the featureless plains, enough water collected in draws and otherwise dry creek beds below the Caprock to assure survival of these hardy people, and the terrain itself provided a degree of protection from harsh elements.

Before beginning the difficult ascent up the sharp ridges some 10 miles to the west, those moving by wagon and horseback stopped here for rest and fresh supplies. The recent war with Mexico had reclaimed the land for Texas, and this part of the state had been freshly mapped into counties by the government in Austin. Homesteaders followed close on the heels of surveyors to claim their plot of land.

In the late 1874, just after the Comanche defeat at Palo Duro Canyon, just east of Canyon, Texas, a small group of adventuresome and high risk homesteaders put down roots here and began subsistence farming to feed themselves and their animals, building their own dwellings, and later, a school.

Small businesses began to be established in the early 1890's to serve the estimated 50 farm families. Henry (Putt) Gilbert opened a cotton gin. Leonard Crowell opened a hardware store, with hitching post. A. J. Hudson started a dry goods and mercantile store. A cafe opened on the dusty main street, and, of course, the barber shop offered cheap shaves and haircuts.

Much later, as gasoline vehicles and tractors gradually supplemented work horses and mules, two service stations (we called them filling stations) opened. In 1902, a Post Office opened on the county line between Motley and Floyd counties, and gave Flomot its name. A blacksmith serviced the need for sharpened plows and horseshoes, and to repair harness and hitches, but several farms had their own blacksmith shops to do these basics. In the 30's, two farm implement stores also opened, selling both horse drawn and later, tractor pulled plows and planters.

The impetus for Flomot and for exploring and claiming the entire West rested on the results of three major Federal government initiatives. First was the Louisiana purchase of 1803 which created the contiguous land mass connecting East to West. Second was the Mexican/American war of 1845/46, which added the western half of Texas, New Mexico, Nevada, much of Arizona, Utah, and all of California as United States territory. Finally, the concept of manifest or divine destiny permitted and even encouraged waging war to either obliterate or relocate the aboriginal hunter- gatherer and warrior Indians to make room for secure settlements by whites of European ancestry.

This particular slice of West Texas was the riskiest, wildest, least civilized, and hardest to tame. The Comanche bands, without hesitation, killed and scalped any and all settlers or other tribes who encroached on their hunting grounds, a practice effectively unchecked until well after the American Civil War. The Comanches adopted the Mustang pony from the Spanish, and were the first tribe to become expert horse mounted warriors. They had brutally defeated the Apaches, then the Mexicans and Spanish, the earlier invaders, using basically terrorist and guerilla tactics against conventionally uniformed foot soldiers advancing in lines with muskets. [1]

Texas had become an independent nation in 1836, with the defeat of Mexican general Santa Anna in the battle of San Jacinto, by General Sam Houston. Although terms of the victory named the Rio Grande as the new nation's southern boundary, Mexico never ratified this agreement, and the border remained in dispute until resolved finally by the Mexican/American war. The war was precipitated by Texas agreement to annexation by the United States in 1845, and President James Polk's determination to clear the path for settlement of the West.

PROFILE OF A SETTLEMENT TOWN

The businesses of Flomot served an area of perhaps 30 square miles, populated by migrating colonialists who had made their ways, successively, from Virginia, to the Carolinas, to Kentucky, Tennessee, and later, Oklahoma. They were white of British Isles ancestry, (Anglo-Saxon) but in this country long enough so that no trace

1. An excellent and carefully researched book detailing the history and ultimate defeat of the Comanche Indians is "Empire of the Summer Moon", by S.C. Gwynne. Scribner. 2010.

accents or sense of historical origins remained.

Names such as Martin, Morris, Turner, Bynum, Gilbert, Hudson, Spear, Washington, Garrett, Clements, Cloyd, Logan, Slover, Skinner, George, Fisher, Pope, Cromer, Tanner, Thomas, Gunn, Bourland, Webb, Preston, Moseley, Clay, Titus, Tibbits, Barton, True, Stapleton, Jones, Monk, Hunt, Amick, and Calvert confirmed their Anglo origins. Saxon Germans made their way to many parts of Texas founding towns like Fredericksburg, Southwest of Austin, and Nazareth in far West Texas.

In the old country, their great grandfathers were the landless peasants who came early to the colonies in search of a new life of equality free of the English class system.   Many, including the Garrett/Morris ancestors, had fought in the Revolutionary war, then moved southward searching for better farm land on which to stake claims. Seven generations earlier, clan grandfather Henry Garrett served in George Washington's army during the Revolutionary war and earned a government pension, before finally settling in Franklin, Tennessee, near Nashville. More about Henry later.

Their sons and daughters continued this migration as each generation sought independence and fresh land ownership.   Always attracted to the soil, most moved South and West ahead of the American Industrial Revolution, which first mechanized the textile industry centered in New England and brought waves of Irish, Polish, Czech and other middle and eastern European immigrants to man these new factories.

The Civil War divided and scattered them farther, and with the South in reconstruction, they moved on Westward.   My grandfather Alexander Shakespeare Morris, born in 1858 in Hendersonville, North Carolina, near Charlotte, was one of these.   At age 17, in 1875, he left home on horseback and gradually rode west , working as a cowboy, farm hand, and cable ferry operator, stopping in Montague county near Bowie, Texas. He married Lillie Grimes there in 1895, and together they continued west to Flomot, where they had eleven children and lived the rest of their long lives. Grandad Morris never saw his North Carolina family again, and had no contact with them until his oldest son Robert (Bob) established letter contact around 1920. More about Alexander and Lillie later.

Our forebearers were not, and never desired to be, labor for the industrial revolution in this country. Social conventions in urban settings were part of what they wanted to escape by moving westward and keeping their individualism, always with government urging to claim the entire continent.

But post Civil War expansion west into new territories was made more difficult by the Union army's preoccupation with restoring law and order in the South, and replacing the various confederate militias and authorities. Pioneers hoping for military protection from attacking Indians in their outposts in the West, took a back seat to this reconstruction priority. Many were forced to retreat from homesteads under constant threats from Indians, and killings of entire families by Indians were reported regularly. But the impulse to dig in and remain was strong, propelled by major enabling inventions in the East which aided the national ambition.

Key inventions of the 18th and 19th centuries supported and made possible this migration. These included the steel plow, the cotton gin, mechanical cotton spinning and weaving, the McCormick reaper (combine), the telegraph, the telephone and electric light bulb, steam powered ships and locomotives, plus the completion of the transcontinental railroad and opening of railheads in Kansas. Together, this infrastructure created ready and accessible markets for cattle ranchers, weapons, buffalo hides, and farm products from the West, and fueled the expansion. Our families rode this powerful yet treacherous migratory crest.

HIGH AGRARIAN SOCIETY

Culturally, Flomot was always a monolith. Virtually everyone made their living by dry land farming, almost everyone grew, slaughtered, and stored their own food. Quilting, cutting and sewing clothes, and canning vegetables for storage in cellars, were essential duties of women, often done cooperatively with extended family. My mother and her sisters would gather at each other's homes and gossip all day around quilting frames, pressure cookers, or baking pies, cakes, and cookies. The ability to talk farming and weather, livestock, cooking, quilting, sewing, baking, and child raising, with the Protestant faith as a backdrop to these chores associated with frontier life, placed one in the cultural center of Flomot.

There were no strangers in the community, and no racial, religious, or ancestral diversity. English with a western twang was the only language spoken. Everyone had the same color skin, with similar genomic heritage. We never heard any funny accents except during Fall when truckloads of migrant Mexicans were brought in from Mexican border towns to speed the cotton harvest. We did not have the challenge of wondering about Catholics, Jews, Muslims, or Buddhists, Athiests, or strange cults, because there were none.

We had never seen a live "Asian" and no conception of them beyond the hated "Japs" and the open racism widely prevalent throughout the country after their attack on Pearl Harbor in December 1941. We did not know any African Americans, and would not have known what the term meant. The rare black farm worker person we saw was known unashamedly by the term for blacks used commonly before political correctness changed the nation's speech and perceptions. The community was insular and homogenous with its own sort of social ecosystem. New ideas from other countries or cultures were late to come here.

Growing up with almost complete freedom to roam and explore with little supervision, we lived in a protected cocoon comprised of a large wheel of intermarried families and their offspring. There were no ethnic or off limits neighborhood, no gangs, no narcotics, very little exposure to alcohol (the county was officially dry), but smoking roll –your- own Dukes mixture or Bull Durham was a favorite of children and adults, some of whom also chewed tobacco. None of the Garrett/Morris extended family used much alcohol, but almost all used tobacco in its various forms.

The smoking vice aside, our lives were healthy and busy, with little to fear except infectious disease, the occasional encounter with poisonous snakes, falling from or being stepped on or kicked by a horse, or an accident involving farm machinery. There were a few horror stories about runaway tractors or horse teams in harness, Riley Turner lost an arm after being caught in the knives of a cotton gin. Ottie Hines was struck by lightning while driving a tractor, and was never "right" again. Limbs were broken and sometimes lost to mechanized power lifts and other unfamiliar machinery as new technologies gradually replaced horses and mules.

At age 11, plowing alone in my uncle Austin Tanner's field, riding a "go-devil" behind a team of two large horses, I very nearly became a statistic when the horses became tangled in harness while turning sharply at the end of a "row", and fell backwards on top of the plow, pinning me underneath. They could not get up while in harness, and I couldn't get out from under, my leg being pinned by an iron bar extending from the front to the back lever of the machine. I was trapped there perhaps ten to fifteen minutes, losing circulation in my right leg, when my Aunt Lillie Tanner accidentally happened by and came to the rescue. She had to completely unharness the horses before they could wrestle themselves upright, and pulled me out from underneath while the horses were struggling to get up.

We both were panicked, as were the horses, but circulation returned to my leg. We walked a half mile to the house, where she rubbed my thigh with liniment and put me to bed.   I never saw a doctor, and was afraid to mention the incident to my parents when they drove me home to town that night. (But Aunt Lillie did) To this day, there is a distinct crease in the flesh of my right upper thigh, not visible but easily felt, a hidden scar from 66 years ago, and a indelible reminder of the everyday dangers of child labor on farms.

My cousin Orville "Junior" Washington was always a daredevil, and a menace with Uncle Dick's big John Deere tractor. I was much younger but loved to visit their family more than any other, mainly because I worshipped my uncle Dick Washington from my earliest memory. But Junior would dare me to ride upfront above the engine and front wheels of the tractor, holding on to the exhaust stack for dear life, while he made the tractor rear up in front by releasing the clutch suddenly with the engine revved up. The action was much like a horse rearing up on its hind legs. It was terrifying, but I held on for fear of being called scared and afraid of dying if I didn't. It was potentially lethal for another reason! These John Deeres were known to do back flips during such maneuvers, especially if no plow was attached to stop the inversion.

On another occasion, Junior told me to hold the nozzle while he pumped kerosene fuel from a barrel into their model A pickup, the fuel intake for which was located just in front of the windshield. Dark was descending, so Junior instructed me to strike a match to see if the tank was nearing full, which I obediently did. Fortunately, the kerosene ignited but did not explode. I was not hurt, and we managed to smother the resulting fire with blankets. Both Junior and I were humiliated at our own stupidity, but uncle Dick said nothing about it. Thankfully, gasoline was rationed during the big war, so I owe my life to rationing.

Like Tom Sawyer with a fence to be whitewashed, Junior could sell the younger male cousins on doing almost anything he wanted, whether by daring them or using shrewd psychology. An example was the battery powered electric fence my uncle put up to keep the cows in their pasture and out of the maize crop. A game ensued which required us to take turns holding on to the live electric wire while Junior turned up the voltage. First person to let go was a piker!! We had no idea that we were getting electroconvulsive therapy before it was so named, or that our heart rhythms might be interrupted by this near electrocution.

My Mother and her ten siblings produced 41 first cousins. Together with 20 aunts and uncles, our family accounted for a good part of that protective web, and first cousins as playmates were always plentiful. Charles Tanner, Jimmy Purcell, Janice Pyron, Bobbie Morris, Betty Morris, Orville (Junior) Washington, were family regulars, complimented by a wide circle of indirect relations and friends. Cousins of all ages could be matched up with my brothers and me, and we all got along very well.

Buddy Riddle, part Indian, and Erwin Merritt, who's family owned the other dry goods store in town, were pals of mine. We hiked, rode horses, played games constantly. When we were about 8 or 9 years old, chasing each other in a pasture filled with mesquite trees with thorns, Erwin lost most of the sight in one eye when a thorn pierced his retina, and infection followed.

Soon after, Buddy's dad, Buck Riddle, was killed when he lost control of his pickup while descending the narrow gravel road curving down the Caprock, a few miles to the west of town. Rumors were that his brakes failed, and alcohol might have been involved, since Buck was known to take a drink. Young minds had difficulty imagining and coping with a loss of life that way, and I remember having dreams seeing the truck crash down the rocky canyon with Mr. Riddle inside.

Buck's wife, Merle Pyron Riddle, was a sister to my uncle Jack Pyron, who was married to my Dad's sister Lila, so we functioned much like a large circular family, interconnected with most families around us. My Aunt Irene was a Merritt who married my mother's brother John. Another brother, Audric, married Naomi Bynum of the large Bynum clan, and still another brother, Robert, married Minnie Turner from the large and respected Turner tribe. Mom's sister Annie married into the Washingtons, and my uncle Bud (Pinkney Henderson Morris) married Doris Washington, from another branch of that family. Another aunt, Bertie, married Harley Gunn of the local Gunn family. Uncle Boyd Morris married Joyce Fisher from a nearby farm. Cousins married Martins and Clays and Jones's, who in turn became like family to the rest of us.

Before World War two, nobody, young people included, seemed to move from the farm. Everybody married locally and stayed with their kind. Neither college nor marriage nor occupation took them far away. Marriage, like always, was to the girl or boy who was nearby and of the same circumstances. The wheel of relations just seemed to grow larger and larger, to the point that almost every family had blood connection with every other family.

In our closed time capsule, we functioned much like sheltered tribes from history, observing family and religious traditions, relying on and helping each other just as the aboriginals had done. Though not thought of as such, we followed what sociologists might describe as a closed stockade mentality, missing only the fence, suspicious of outsiders and narcissistically occupied with ourselves, just as every ethnicity and religion has in the history of man.

FAITH, SCHOOL, FUN, DECLINE

Most social interaction centered on Christianity and its Babtist, Methodist, and Church of Christ, traditional Anglican iterations. No Catholic churches, no Temples, and certainly no Mosques were to be found. "Faith" carried only one meaning in this cloistered town. The notion of a faith menu or a social agenda which might include no faith at all, was outright heresy and a mortal sin in itself. Two generations earlier, the native occupants of this land would have been incredulous at the Judeo Christian radical idea of worshipping one God. In the span of history, monotheism was a very new concept, and especially the idea that everyone should conform to it. The aboriginals paid tribute to many Gods and spirits, as their ancestors had done since the beginning of known time.

Virtually every family attended one church or the other regularly on Sunday morning and sometimes evening. A centerpiece of each service was the singing of traditional hymns followed by old fashioned morality sermons from the church's part time preacher who had to make ends meet with second jobs. The sermon was always followed by a "come to Jesus" call for sinners to come forward and be converted and saved through babtism, and the pressure on young minds to conform to this model of faith was considerable. Summer Bible schools at the Babtist or Methodist churches were filled with younger boys and girls. Indoctrination was early. Prayer before each meal was offered in most homes.

Travelling quartets, like the well know Stamps Baxter group, toured through and led "all night singings", which were quite popular. Local quartets or ensembles joined in carrying on through the night. Singing was a large and very important component of worship in these denominations. Churches were the community meeting halls.

Morally and ethically, the sermons probably were taken to heart. Most citizens seemed honest and sober in their dealings with each other. Relative to urban kids, teenagers and young adults appeared to have less opportunity for temptation, but inevitably managed experimentation with the same vices.

Many years ago, a case of adultery involving Mr. Clarence Washington and a Mrs. Preston, ended with Mr. Preston shooting Mr. Washington to death as he led the singing in the First Babtist Church Sunday evening service. No charges resulted! The community was just too close and too small to permit much infidelity, and that which surely happened did not reach the innocent ears and minds of my age group.

EDUCATION

The community school building housed all eleven grades in one small two-story structure, with elementary grades on the first level, and high school upstairs. Texas schools were still legally segregated; there were no blacks or Hispanics in the school, or in the community. The quality of education was highly suspect, especially in the high school grades. Learning by doing, akin to the apprenticeship system, was much respected. Science and math offerings which might have helped student admissions to good colleges were especially weak due to the shortage of qualified teachers for these subjects. Many teachers had only high school diplomas. During WW 2, male teachers went to war, as did many women, and the school district had to make do with the talent at hand.

Classrooms and teachers served double duty, with one half of the room devoted to one grade, and the other half to a different grade. Teachers would shift to one side of the room and teach a different subject to a different grade, then shift back. Classrooms were heated with a large coal fired stove in the corner, fed with buckets of raw coal nuggets hauled by student "volunteers" from bulk storage in the school basement.

School buses picked up farm kids, but during the war, some rode their own horses and hitched them at the school. Toilets were three hole outhouses well away from the main building.

Texas standardized on twelve grades during the 1943-44 school year, and Flomot accommodated this cleverly by simply allowing all students to skip a grade. Sixth graders were now called seventh graders, in spite of continuing to follow a sixth grade curriculum. When we moved from Flomot to the much larger town of Plainview, in the Spring of 1945, I transferred into the seventh grade, but teachers quickly realized that I had never been exposed to seventh grade work. So I was "put back" and caught up by repeating the 7th grade, finally graduating high school in the correct class.

In Flomot, there were no organized extra curricular activities or structured play, during or after school hours. The high school grades did have a basketball and six man football team, but sports before these grades were impromptu recess events. There were no band, choir, language, drama classes, or special interest clubs of any sort, but I do remember my cousin Bobby Morris and I singing a duet at a rare assembly.

Food was not provided by schools at any time. Lunches were brought in paper sacks or lunch boxes with thermoses. Most often, we walked a half mile home for lunch, or took a baloney sandwich to school with us.

School had traditionally taken a back seat to the priority of harvesting cotton in the early Fall. School closed for two weeks in September while students pulled "bolls" on family or neighboring farms, supplemented by the aforementioned Mexican temporary "bracero" labor. My parent's generation experienced far greater interruptions of schooling, often skipping a year or more in deference to the family need for farm labor. Consequently, a large percentage never completed high school, finally dropping out because they felt they were too old to continue. This same pattern held true since the birth of the country, especially in the rural South, and in the coal mines of Pennsylvania , West Virginia, and Kentucky.

RECREATION/LEISURE

A s young people growing up before the electronic age, our recreation was almost entirely out of doors, and included invented fun such as sliding down cotton burr piles on sheets of tin, climbing trees, building and walking on stilts, wrestling with cousins, hunting with BB guns or home made slingshots, riding horses bareback, (a favorite) follow the leader (with double dares), reading and exchanging comic books, riding double on tricycles, and later, bicycles; telling stories at night in dark rooms, jumping across rows of cotton bales stored outdoors in the gin yard, barefoot racing, playing guitars and singing, playing and trading marbles, spinning tops, playing Jacks with cousins and friends, hop-scotch, broad jumping, sleep-overs on quilt pallets with friends or cousins, touch football, impromptu swimming in small dirt playas and one quasi community pool owned by a farmer a few miles to the North of town.

Highest ranked was riding ponies bareback. My pied-piper uncle Dick was a kid magnet, and he owned a mustang/shetland mix, named Peanuts, who was especially stubborn. We were able to bridle him and swing up by his mane, but staying on was another matter entirely. He had a stay at home personality, and, at times, was almost impossible to persuade to leave the corral, even with a slap of the reins and repeated strong kicks. After being thrown off once or more, and finally winning the battle by getting him away from the barn, he became completely unpredictable in a run and might suddenly shift left or right, while the rider continued straight ahead.

Uncle Dick told the story that when he was a young man, he often visited on horseback a girl who lived 10 miles away.   At the end of the evening, in pitch dark, he would simply allow the horse to take him home. This trip often took a good part of the night, but the horse had great homing instincts and never failed to deliver him to the proper place. Many animals, I have since learned, have this inborn ability.

During our last couple of years in Flomot , we moved into a house in town next to our Morris grandparents. This, after a few months living briefly a couple of miles south of town on a small isolated farm which Dad had somehow acquired. He felt, I suppose, that the experience would be good for growing boys. The farm was not far from a mostly dry riverbed, isolated and without electricity or any means of communication. Dad would take the pickup to town for work during the day, leaving Mom and me basically stranded at the farm, while Cal and Raby went in by school bus. Weekends, my brothers and I gathered scrap iron from the place, mostly old rusty plows, to be sold to support the war effort. It was a bleak trial for a few months, and Mom soon insisted that it end.

While it lasted, Dad and I sometimes went quail hunting, which he loved. He could track blue quail through the snow, with me tagging along with my very cold feet wrapped in gunny or toe sacks for a degree of warmth. He shot left-handed with his Browning automatic, and always bagged several, which we cleaned at home and ate. I was about eight at the time, but took a turn shooting. The twelve-guage shotgun had plenty of kick and sometimes left me with a black and blue right shoulder.

Living back in town, we had a small pasture out back and a semblance of a couple of stalls, where we kept a roman-nosed full sized sorrel, and a paint shetland named Dolly. My brothers and I rode these horses, without saddles, over a range of several miles .

It was in this house that we discovered, in a dresser drawer, a good sized rattlesnake, when we returned home from a trip to my Grandad Garrett's in Durant, Oklahoma. Nobody was hurt, mainly because we could hear him rattling before we opened the drawer. Dad always thought a disgruntled customer might have planted the surprise. It was also here that we drilled a deep well in search of our own water supply, but the hole turned up dry.

Another fun competition was wrestling my cousins, Charles Tanner and Jimmy Purcell, evenings after dinner, by lamplight, in the cleared out living room of Uncle Austin Tanner's farmhouse. Uncle Austin encouraged these matches and delighted in them, and they continued until one pinned his opponent, no matter how rough or heated the sport became. Aunt Lillie would become concerned, but a match was never interrupted until completed. It was a test of strength and endurance.

We worked side by side with adults in fields pulling cotton, shocking feed, heading maize, feeding animals, milking cows, gathering eggs, turning the cream separator by hand, hunting jack rabbits or quail or possum. We were seldom bored, never tired, and always hungry. About age 10, I learned to drive a stick shift pickup, mainly to haul water in open barrels daily from my uncles farm a mile away, or to retrieve some vehicle which Dad had taken as barter for an unpaid grocery bill.

CULINARY CHOICES: EATING, NOT DINING!

Eating out in this town was unheard of, ever, in my family. Until I went away to college, we never ate in a restaurant as a family. Such a luxury was just not affordable. But we did eat with relatives often, and they ate with us even more frequently at our forever open house, sometimes bringing foods with them to share. Home slaughtered beef, pork, and chicken, and fresh vegetables from gardens including tomatoes, peas, green beans, onions, cucumbers, and lettuce were part of most meals. Watermelon and hand churned homemade ice cream were special treats for kids. Home baked cornbread or biscuits were regular treats, and pies and cakes, often shared with several families, were frequent desserts.

Two breakfast favorites were pork chops and eggs with flour gravy, accompanied by home made biscuits with lots of butter, and fresh fruit, or a plate of simple cooked white rice, covered with whole milk and lots of sugar stirred in. When we didn't have milk, Mom made gravy with just bacon grease and water.

We ate lots and lots of green beans, red beans and large butter beans, lots of black-eyed peas, together with so called "light' bread and cornbread, raw onions and many other raw vegetables such as radishes, cucumbers, raw and cooked squash, and corn, both creamed, canned, and on the cob. Tomatoes came from local gardens, or were canned for later use, along with beets, turnips, and other vegetables.

Our milk came fresh daily from our own cow. My brothers and I preferred it warm, fresh from the udders. Cream was churned by hand from whole milk, by use of a plunger moving up and down in a large crock until the butter congealed and formed large rounded mounds. Churning was a regular duty of mine at my grandmother Morris's house, and at all my aunt's houses. Pasteurization and homogenization had not reached these communities. If whole milk soured from age or lack of refrigeration, it congealed into "clabber", with the consistency of cottage cheese. Add salt and pepper and crumbled cornbread to clabber for a special treat.

All meals at home were served family style, in bowls or platters, with each person choosing what he wanted and the amount. The understood rule was this: You are not required to eat anything, but if you put it on your plate, plan on eating it all!

Photo 5. Frank and Dillie Garrett in their general store, Flomot, 1942.

THE MERCANTILE STORE

Store bought necessities were flour, salt, spices, baking powder, baking soda, sugar, and the occasional cold cuts for school lunches, but few paper goods including toilet paper, for which there was no demand. Thread, thimbles, needles, yard goods cut from bolts of cloth, patterns for cutting and sewing clothing, decorative ribbons, some condiments such as mustard, mayonnaise, and some seeds and rice were purchased at the store, frequently on credit. Kerosene and coal oil were bought in gallon or five gallon cans, or delivered to homes in barrels.

My Mom and Dad operated a general mercantile store in town from about 1936 to 1940, owned by Mr. A.J. Hudson, one of the town's founders. They shared the profit 50/50 with him until his death, at which time his heirs took over. My folks moved to a large three story stucco building across the street and installed their own store, both working behind the counter serving customers six days a week, early till late. They finally sold out to Tom Turner in early 1945, when the decision was made to move to Plainview in search of better schools. This move turned out to be prescient, and many others would soon follow.

In these pre-war years, self-service retailing had not been conceived, and at least had not reached farm communities. Customers simply asked Mom or Dad for a particular item, they went and retrieved it, often the length of the store, returned to the counter and asked what else the customer would like. Serving each customer took an extended time, as did ringing each item up on a primitive cash register with a pop out cash drawer.

A hand written itemized list was made, signed by the customer, and credit extended for an uncertain period, depending on when the customer sold some crop or other. It was a somewhat risky business, but most customers were honest, even if it meant paying grocery bills with musical instruments, old cars, an old tractor, or even a horse.

Periodically, I rode with Dad as he drove to various farms in his model A pickup to collect past due bills, and he sometimes accepted barter when cash could not be mustered. But every customer was valuable, and he tolerated slow pays as best he could, while becoming privately suspicious of preachers and those who were most pious.

About once each month, Dad would fill the covered pickup bed with a load of hogs from local farms, and, for a small fee, and take them to market in Plainview. He would then buy a load of supplies for the store to take back home. I went with him occasionally, and we often had to run down and catch the squealing fat hogs and carry them, slippery and writhing, to the pickup. While in Plainview or Matador on buying trips, he always saved time for a very thick chocolate malt at the local drugstore fountain, a special treat.

My Dad bought merchandise for the store from "drummers" who

came through town every week or so, taking orders which a truck would deliver a few days afterward. A lot of goods for the store, including bulk cold cuts, and sacks and flour and seeds and beans came from the Kimble Grocery company, in Plainview, about 50 miles away. The drummer on our account, a big, heavy man named Chunky Yates, was a well-liked, jovial gentleman who was also full of news and anecdotes.

I was a preschool age at the time, so was always in the store with my parents when Mr. Yates came through on his rounds. He made a big fuss over me, and I liked him a lot. He always asked me to go home to Plainview with him, where he had a daughter my age and a son a little older. Many years later, when we moved to Plainview, I developed a strong high school friendship with his daughter, Alice Ann, a very talented singer, and his son, Glenn, an excellent golfer.

At the time, we lived in the back of the store, which was basically a partitioned off warehouse. Bedrooms were defined by hanging sheets between poles. Again, there was no bathroom indoors, and the kitchen was primitive. When we needed more food, Mom simply walked to the front of the store and took food off the shelves. We ate lots of cold cuts during this period, because they were readily available in the store.

The store was run for the proceeds of the day, with no thought of accounting concepts like return on capital or investment. My parent's time and labor were never valued as costs. At the end of each day, what remained in the cash register after suppliers were paid was "counted up" as profit and taken home. It was elemental bookkeeping, but without knowing a better way, it worked fine.

Barter was common. The store was heated by a single kerosene stove in the back, vented by a long stovepipe through a tall 20 ft. ceiling. A fond winter time memory of age 4 or 5 was sitting near the warm stove on a upside down coke box with my legs inside an apple crate, looking through the Sears Roebuck or Montgomery Ward catalogues, and dreaming of owning the horses, saddles and boots those pages depicted.

Each night, the dusty concrete floors were swept with a wide broom, after being sprinkled with an oil impregnated saw dust mixture which keep the dust down.

HOME CHORES & WORK

Dishes were done always by hand, with older kids often assigned to wash and dry. Laundry duties were likewise shared by older siblings. Large families had plenty of cloth diapers, non-disposable. There were no paper diapers or diaper services. Everything went on the outdoor clothesline to dry. My grandmother Morris cooked all her meals and heated her irons on a wood stove. Steam irons modernized this drudgery somewhat, but the electric iron and indoor washers and dryers were still in the distant future.

Cleaning house, making and changing beds, some light ironing were expected chores and we helped out my Mom as much as possible, especially when the girls started to come along and she was busy with one baby after another. But a lot of emphasis was placed on work, and my brothers and I hired out to chop cotton, pull cotton, and do other jobs we could find. We worked alongside each other, with me trying to keep up. Cal and Raby were teenagers at this point. It was hard work for a 10 year old, but I was cut no slack that I remember, and pride motivated me to keep up and stay in the field as long as my older brothers.

It was my first step in developing an understanding of the concept of work ethic. I learned never to quit until the job was finished---never give in to mere fatigue or even say I was tired---always acquit oneself as "a good hand", and never ever slack on the job---always deliver more than expected, and don't whine or complain.

School children are admonished to "always do your best", but many adults fail to remember this lesson in fundamentals. It was a lesson in the basics of living which, I think and hope has served me well in many jobs with many different employers.

DEATH AND BURIAL

Death in Flomot involved ritual brought from the old country. The deceased was kept in an open casket at home, with friends of the family "sitting up" all night with family and the body until the burial. Caskets were open, and viewing of the body was expected at the end of church service before removal to the cemetery a half mile North of town. W. B. Gilbert was a young marine pilot killed early in World War two. My parents took turns, along with others, in "sitting up" with the Gilbert family until the funeral. Young Dale (Junior) Meese was killed in a light plane crash in Mexico, and his unrecognizable body was returned and viewed openly.

In my memory, no one was cremated, and no family chose to forego a religious ceremony. Cremation and a later memorial service or no service at all, standard today in much of the country and the world, would have been an indication of a flawed individual who the family did not wish to expose publicly. Embalming was standard.

The same funeral practices are still in place today, and, in fairness, many other parts of the country, although cremation and grave side or memorial services are creeping in. Many from other countries consider our burial rituals bizarre, but most were imported from ancestral European countries. Each culture and ethnicity has its own unique religious and non-religious internment observances, many of them strange to us.

The Flomot Memorial cemetery holds the remains of my grandfather and grandmother Morris, many aunts and uncle and cousins, and almost all the names mentioned above who lived their lives there. I walked the cemetery in 2010 and recognized almost all their names, and remembered some association with most.

DECLINE

World War Two took young men off the farm, many of them never to return. It also attracted many families to defense plants in Dallas and other big cities, and to ship building factories in California. The Morris and Garrett families were no exceptions. My Dad was exempted from the draft by age and the responsibilities of a large family, but many uncles and cousins joined the war effort, in uniform or in factories supplying the military. The war was life changing for the entire country, and the death knell for small farm communities dependent on the labor of next generations.

Flomot began its long decline as the war ended. Those who had left hardly ever returned to the hardscrabble life they had known. Transportation permitted living in larger towns with amenities such as indoor running water, better jobs in factories or businesses, with better schools, newspapers, and telephones. Many GI's took advantage of the GI bill to get college educations, after which they were better qualified for better paying jobs in cities. Technical obsolescence is the industrial name for a process or machine no longer needed. Just as surely, Flomot became sociologically obsolete. Modernity simply skipped over it.

The Flomot school system finally consolidated with the Turkey/ Quitaque system, and closed its own school building forever. Only the post office remained, as it does to this day, an indictment of government oversight of the U.S. postal system. All other businesses gradually closed down, and the town disappeared as an entity, although a sign on its outskirts still proclaims its existence. It had survived the great depression and the dust bowl intact, but finally bowed to the disruptions of the world war and its aftermath.

With modern farming techniques and sophisticated equipment capable of covering large acreages, small subsistence farms became non-

viable and were combined into larger and larger farms, without the traditional family farm houses or outbuildings. Pivot irrigation sprinkler systems
allowed watering of the uneven land, and fertilizers, herbicides, and biotech
seeds made the land more productive and valuable. Cotton, corn, and maize
are still the mainstays, but with yields higher than dry land farmers could have
ever imagined. And the farmers live in Quitaque or Turkey, away from the
land, with skeleton crews of hired workers, often Hispanic, operating the planting, irrigating, and harvesting equipment. The transition is complete. The family farm is gone forever, as is Flomot.

BOOK TWO
From These Genes

FRANK

Frank William Garrett was the first of the male Garrett line since Revolutionary times to make much of his living as a merchant and realtor. The clan had been plowing and planting the land since making the trip to the colonies from the British Isles, at least a quarter century before the war for independence. Sharecropping for a number of years after his marriage to Dillie Dean Morris, he and Dillie were hired to manage the Flomot Mercantile store, "on the halves", in the little settlement of Flomot. He never returned to the farm, but

Photo 6. Frank Garrett at Age 20 in 1926

continued to depend on farmers as his customers. Frank's ancestor Henry Garrett, born six generations earlier in Fairfax, Virginia on March 18, 1754, grew to adulthood at a time when the population of the thirteen colonies was 1.2 million, including 260,000 slaves. By 1790, the population had grown to 4.0 million, 700,000 slaves included.

Henry died at age 91, in 1845, and is buried in the First District of Williamson County, in Franklin, Tennessee, near Nashville, having outlived his wife, Sally. Williamson county archives show his estate was settled Oct. 4, 1847, with a value of $73.99, after payment of obligations.

Henry was drafted and served one year in the army of General George Washington at Valley Forge, PA, having been marched there as a replacement "on account of death" of regular army troops. He volunteered for a second tour of duty, this one six months in Fairfax county, VA, and served in Capt. William Mason's company.

He applied for and was granted a soldier's pension on Oct. 4, 1832, in Tennessee, at age 78. After the war, he moved his residence to North Carolina for 21 years, then Kentucky for 17 years, and finally to Williamson county, Tennessee. The migratory route followed by

Photo 7. *William Frank Garrett, and Candacy Barrett Garrett, living in Tennessee, with their six children. Top left is my grandfather, William Dickson Garrett, about age 10. Upper right is Robert, the oldest child, who later lived in Amarillo, and spawned his own large family.*

Henry was followed by thousands of families as they pressed relentlessly westward with government encouragement.

In Tennessee, he bought 262 acres of land from an original King's land grant, situated " on a ridge between South Harpeth & Turnbull, bound by Pigot"as recorded in the survey and entry book of Williamson County for 1824-1902. The land was surveyed May 16, 1827, by G. L. Nolen, S.W.C.. Later,this land was inherited by Matthew Garrett, Henry's grandson, from his father, Smith Garrett. Matthew Wesley Garrett and Melinda White were married June 20, 1844, in Franklin, TN., and raised six children, all shown living at home in the 1870 U.S. census. They were William, Nancy, Lucinda, Francis, James, and Sarah. Francis, the fifth child, age 13 in 1870, was William Frank Garrett, Frank William's grandfather, born 1857, in Maury county, TN.

Photo 8. *Newlyweds Dora Elizabeth Savage Garrett and William Dickson Garrett, parents of Frank William, 1903, Oklahoma. Dora is my grandmother, buried at Boswell, Oklahoma. W.D. is buried at Plainview, Texas*

At age 20, William Frank Garrett and Candacy Barrett married on July 1, 1877 in Williamson county, and raised 10 children, four of them born after the family moved to Grayson county, Texas , southwest of Austin. Why William Frank moved his family from Tennessee to Texas is unclear, but farming is what he knew and Texas was encouraging settlement. Reconstruction was underway in the South after the civil war, and Texas promised a fresh start. He and his family settled in Dripping Springs, where my Father, Frank William was born in 1906 to W.D. Garrett and his wife Dora Elizabeth Savage Garrett.

Around 1907, William Dickson, now married with two children of his own, moved north to the Durant/Boswell, Oklahoma area. All his siblings stayed in the Texas area not far from Dallas, and each had sizable families of their own. [2]

Always called W.D. or Dick, he was tall at 6 ft. 3 inches, around 200 pounds, and shown by pictures to be quite handsome as a young man. He was a touch eccentric, always dressed in bib overalls and high-topped shoes. He talked loud and fast, and his words were clipped short. My grandfather was not known to be religious, but he had a reputation for reliability and honesty. He never smoked or drank, and never swore. Neither did his sons or daughters.

In the 1930's, while part of bridge building crew on the WPA, (government employment program named Works Progress Administration) he was almost smothered when an abutment hole being dug by hand caved in on him. He was crippled in one leg by the weight of the dirt and walked with a limp that day forward.

W.D. was to become a "bottom" farmer in Oklahoma, choosing patches of mesquite and stump covered land difficult to access, always at the end of the road. The plots were interrupted by streams and hills, making the land difficult to farm efficiently. But efficiency was never the goal.

His sons, Frank, Eldridge Dee, and Ross Othel, became the primary labor in clearing the land with pick, shovel, and ax, before planting behind horse drawn plows.

In 1897, at 17, W.D. had married Dora Elizabeth Savage, age 16. They had five children, the oldest a girl, Pearl, followed by Frank William, Lila Mae, Eldridge Dee, and Ross Othel, in that order. Dora's Father, Zack Savage and his wife, name unknown, with their seven children, had come to Texas from Kentucky about the same time as the Garrett's, very likely

2. More detail about the Tennessee and Texas/Oklahoma Garrett's is included in the Garrett/Morris Family heritage reunion book, by Joe Garrett, published in limited numbers July 2004.

with the same desire to start fresh after the civil war. Zack had served in the Confederate army, while his brother Frank served on the Union side.

Dora was attractive, dark-haired, dark-eyed and a loving wife and Mother, as remembered by my Dad, who thought his Mother was some percentage Choctaw Indian, but did not know specifics. Dora and W.D. established their own base in Oklahoma to accommodate their growing family. Dora died suddenly at age 37, on January 26, 1917, during the worldwide influenza epidemic, which killed millions around the world. Her oldest child, Pearl, 13, had died the day before from this twentieth century plague, and both are buried in the cemetery at Boswell, OK., alongside William Frank, my great grandfather. My Dad, Frank, was only 11 years old,

Photo 9. William Dickson and Dora Garrett, with their four of their five children, 1912. Frank William, age 6, my Father, is center front. Lila Mae is on her father's lap. Eldridge Dee is on his mother's lap. Pearl, the oldest, died of influenza at age 13. One day after, her mother Dora died from flu during the worldwide pandemic of 1917. Ross Othel was not yet born.

and too ill from the flu to attend either of their funerals.

Losing his Mother at such a young age had to be traumatic for him and his siblings, but he never seemed disturbed when talking about her. He was now the oldest child, and, consistent with practice of the time, had to become the leader of the younger kids. This role extended to pulling an adult load in the fields, grubbing and burning stumps, and plowing, planting, and harvesting behind a single horse, while hauling and cutting wood for warmth and cooking, feeding the livestock, milking the cows, and helping out with those too young to do these tasks.

He hunted and ate squirrel, quail, and other game, and fished the nearby Blue and Bogchita and Muddy Boggy rivers where bass and catfish were plentiful. He was too busy and too much was needed and expected from him to permit extended mourning for his Mother.

First things first meant schooling took a back seat. This most likely was not seen as a problem by W.D., who himself was barely literate. Neighbor children and cousins his age were in much the same boat, focused on subsistence living, becoming hardened to the reality of death and epidemic disease taking its toll in almost every house. Families had to adjust and move on, and Frank's was no exception. Like it or not, common sense and no-nonsense maturity were character traits essential for survival.

He grew up quickly, utilizing farming methods and technologies little changed since Henry Garrett first sewed and harvested crops in Virginia more than 130 years earlier. Besides, his Father held a firm notion that the best way to do a job was also the hardest way.

Corn had to be picked, shucked, and shelled. Potatoes and onions were dug and stored under slide-back floorboards of the porch, or sold at farmer's markets nearby. Bees had to be swarmed in order the harvest their honey, fruits and vegetables had to be canned and stored. Pigs and chickens had to be slaughtered. Someone had to do the cooking and clean and mend the clothes. Frank's younger sister, Lila, age 8, was expected to shoulder some of this load. Eldridge and Othel were too young to be of much help.

It became apparent that this home had to have a working mother, and W.D. simply went to town and arranged a marriage with a young woman, named Viola, last name unknown. She was brought home and introduced as the children's new Mother. But her immaturity and inability to fill the role soon became apparent, whereupon W.D. did the obvious and returned her to her family. Seven years after the deaths of his wife and daughter, W.D. decided to move on. With his children and third wife, a young widow named Sally Mae Davis Seismore, he left the Oklahoma farm in 1924 and headed to the promised land of West Texas, a wagon ride of some 300 miles. The wagon was crammed full of household goods and utensils and farm implements. He made the trip with his brother in law, Walter Phillips, who drove his own team and loaded wagon.

We all knew Sally as our loving Granny Garrett. The fact that she was our step-grandmother was never talked about. W.D. and Sally had two children, Theo Olen, and Oletha Madge.

Frank was 18 at the time, and drove a flat bed Model T truck carrying more belongings, as well as his stepmother and three siblings. It was an earlier "Grapes of Wrath" migration, before the dust bowl or depression, with "Okies" going west in search of fresh land and opportunity.

Walter Phillips settled on the Plains, near Lockney, Texas,

Photo 10. William Dickson and Sally Sizemore Garrett, his third wife, in later life, Plainview, TX

but W.D. liked the rolling hills and grasslands around Flomot, below the Caprock, or "brakes", as they were called, about 30 miles east Lockney. The appeal of Flomot was dry land cotton farming, a money crop for which the Oklahoma soil and climate were not well suited. When the depression hit, W.D. and Sallie returned to OK. in search of a living, but Frank and Lila and their families, now responsible for themselves, stayed in West Texas and persevered.

During world war two, W.D. and Sallie moved to California to work in the shipyards, and later at Treasure Island, a small military installation beneath the Oakland Bay bridge. The war over, they tried farming once again in Oklahoma, but gave up after three years. Their last stop was Plainview, where Sallie died in 1952. My grandfather did not like living alone, and married three more times, outliving

Photo 11. Frank, leading sister Oletha, brother Theo, niece Janice Pyron, son Cal, and brother Eldridge in a noise making parade to swarm bees for their honey. Left front is me, bare-footed and in overalls, the standard for our visits to Oklahoma.

two of them, before his own death in late 1955, at age 75. He and Sallie are buried side by side in the Plainview cemetery.

Flomot was to be Frank's home for the next 21 years, beginning as a farm hand and concrete finisher and sharecropper, and then, with my Mother, an in-town merchant of some respectability.

This little country town brought Frank William Garrett and Dillie Dean Morris together, and they married in 1927 on Christmas Eve, while sitting in the back seat of a Model T Ford sedan, in Whiteflat, Texas, near

Matador. Their witnesses were Uncle Austin and Aunt Lillie Tanner, Mom's sister, in the front seat. All four remained in the car as the Minister came out, put his foot on the running board and recited the marriage vows. They returned to work the day after Christmas, never expecting the luxury of a honeymoon.

The offer from A.J. Hudson to take a partner in his mercantile store came as a surprise to Frank and Dillie, who had trouble believing their good fortune. Mr. Hudson had dealt with them as customers, knew them to be honest and hard-working, and saw in both of them the character, personality traits, and native intelligence needed for dealing with customers. They were straight shooters who also enjoyed a good story and laughed easily.

They soon moved into town and into a three room white frame house he built for them on property near the store, where they were to live rent free, while investing their labor, reaping half the profit earned. It was a generous arrangement. Mr. Hudson served as sort of a gentle grandfatherly coach, spending some part of each day in the store. He was a widower, alone, and up in years. They came to regard him as family, and treated him with the greatest respect, and he returned their kindness and respect.

Dad and Mom learned the basics of dealing with suppliers, managing inventory, keeping happy customers, and maintaining a solid business. They ran the store without help, except for brief period each harvest season when temporary Mexican labor was provided by contractors. Mom measured and cut cloth from bolts, sold patterns, sewing supplies, and some finished yarns, while Dad dealt with food staples and kept the shelves stocked.

As noted, self-service grocery shopping did not exist, although it would have been possible. It was thought that customers required special individual service, and need only ask for the items desired, and the customer was thusly treated. This meant that they could serve only one or two customers at a time, and that they, not the customer, did all the tiresome legwork. They built a satisfied and loyal customer base, many blood related, and nurtured relationships with suppliers. In a sudden turn of events to follow, the loyalty of both customers and suppliers was soon to reward them.

Unexpectedly, Mr. Hudson died of natural causes in 1940, and, lacking any binding contractual agreement with Frank and Dillie, his heirs decided to take over and operate the store themselves. While disappointed, my folks simply moved across the street and rented the ground floor of a three story stucco building and installed their own mercantile store in competition with the Hudson heirs, Ralph and Amy Merritt, a couple they knew well. Amy Bynum Merritt was the sister of my aunt Naomi Bynum Morris, so the competition was always cordial if not coordinated.

They were extended start up credit by their usual suppliers for stock and fixtures for the store, hung out the "Garrett Grocery" shingle, and were successful from the beginning in bringing their customers with them. Day to day operations were much as they had been in Mr. Hudson's store.

There were few surprises. They bought cream and eggs from farmers, and sold them at a profit in nearby towns, delivered there by a Mr. Ernest Fletcher, who delivered mail from Turkey to the Flomot post office, then loaded the cream and eggs in his Ford carry-all truck for the trip on to Matador and the return to Turkey. They bought ice by the pickup load from the ice house in Matador and sold it in 25 lb blocks to local farmers for their ice boxes. They sold flower and seeds in colorfully patterned sacks which were quickly transformed into homemade shirts.

The store was a new perspective. It opened the door to new hope and new direction, and the vision of a better future than they could ever have dreamed if they had stayed on the farm. It was a new life together, a renewed partnership in marriage, and ultimately propelled them on to the Great Plains and a different but more rewarding set of challenges with a growing family.

DILLIE

DILLIE's lineage also reached back to colonial America, when her branch of the English Morris clan chose Pennsylvania farmland to settle, following the wave of earlier Morris immigrants to the new world. There, William Morris was born in 1765, but orphaned at an early age, and adopted by his extended family.

At war's end, in about 1783, the Morris family moved South to the Charlotte, North Carolina area near the town of Huntersville, in what was later named Mecklenburg county. Here, William Morris married Elizabeth Ford in 1786. She was the daughter of John Ford, one of the founders of the county.

Photo 12. Dillie Dean Morris Garrett, age 51, in 1957, Plainview, Texas.

Their Youngest son, Zebulon, was born April 23, 1789, and died May 1 1872, according to an extract from the history of Mecklenburg county written in 1902 by J.B. Alexander, and handed down by my uncle, Robert Morris, Dillie's brother.

Zeb became a law enforcement officer in the county, with the title of Colonel. In turn, he was the father of James Morris, born about 1835. James served in the Confederate army, and suffered a crippling leg wound. He married a daughter of Kearns and Elizabeth Robinson Henderson who were settlers from Lancaster county Pennsylvania. One of James' sons was

Alexander Shakespeare Morris, Dillie's Father and my maternal grandfather.

Alexander, called "Shake" by friends and family, was born in 1859 on the family farm one mile east of Huntersville, a farm which remained in the Morris family for the next 150 years. His two sisters were Dill (Dillie) and Sarah, and two brothers were Charles and John. Alexander was two years old when the civil war began and six when it ended, with 20 battles of the war having been fought in North Carolina. Sherman's march to the sea had overrun Georgia and North and South Carolina. The area around Charlotte was left poor and with a long recovery period during Reconstruction. So at 17, "Shake" saddled his horse and left home, never to return.

Photo 13. *Lillie Grimes Morris and Alexander Shakespeare Morris, my maternal grandparents, about 1900, on a farm near Flomot. They had eleven children, the 6th of whom was my mother, Dillie. The eleven had 41 children.*

Lillie Mae Grimes, Dillie's Mother, was the daughter of Hiram and Elmina Kennedy Grimes. The Grimes family had come to Nebraska from Pennsylvania, as had the Kennedy clan, after immigration from Ireland. Hiram was born June 9, 1838, in Nebraska and died in January, 1901. Elmina, the daughter of a Robert Kennedy and Elizabeth Spry, was born February 24, 1840 in Knox county, Ohio, and died June 12, 1936. Both are buried in the New Harp cemetery, near Bowie, Texas.

Hiram and Elmina married February 3, 1860, and came to Texas by covered wagon in the late 1860's, after the Civil war. In Montague county, the Grimes raised a family of nine, including four boys and five girls, one of whom was Dillie's Mother, Lillie. Elmina was remembered by my Aunt Lillie Tanner as a "fixie little woman" who wore a dust cap with elastic and ruffles which stood out around her face.

The Grimes family farm house still stands in New Harp, having been acquired and remodeled by a Dallas attorney as a weekend retreat. The large Sledge family, sons and daughters of Lillie's sister Bert Grimes, still make their home in the area.

In this setting, A.S. Morris met and married Lillie Mae Grimes in 1886, at age 37. He had worked his way from Charlotte westward through Tennessee and Arkansas as a ranch hand and cowboy, a cotton gin manager, a bookkeeper, and cable ferry operator ferrying teams of horses and wagons across the Red river. Texas had achieved statehood only 30 years earlier, and was more of a risky frontier than the old South. He knew no one in the West, and his motivation for leaving North Carolina seemed to be a sense of adventure and a desire to build his own identity on his own land.

In later years, he would tell stories about encountering Indians and horse thieves along the way. We don't know how long the journey took, but do know that almost 20 years elapsed before he settled down with Lillie. Only later, through his oldest son Robert (Bob), did he establish contact with his family back home. Until then, they assumed he had died.

Shake and Lillie proceeded to raise eleven children, the sixth and middle child being Dillie Dean Morris, born July 15, 1906. Her older siblings were Robert (Bob), Pinkney Henderson (Bud), Bertie, Audric, Annie, and her younger ones William(Bill), Lillie(twins), John, Zula, and Boyd. Dillie was the last survivor of the eleven, and passed away in 2005, at age 99. In late 1906, when Dillie was four months old, the couple began a new adventure, homesteading 160 acres of land at Elida, New Mexico territory, not far from Portales. The family boarded a train in Alvord, Texas on October 28, 1906, with all their goods, and began the two day trip to their new home. The place was open prarie grassland, part of the Llano Estacado, short of rain and subject to howling dry winds.

They dug a 12' by 22', by 4' deep hole, called a dugout, covered with rough framing and a tarp, and called it home for at least six months of each of the next five years. Eight children and the parents survived in the one room structure with an outhouse, and, incredibly, had warm memories of the time spent there. Five half years living on the claim were required to "prove up" ownership, and get title and deed. The remaining six months of each year, the family went by covered wagon 125 miles east, down the caprock, to Flomot, where they worked the cotton harvest , cleared grassland of mesquite, and did day farm jobs to survive.

They fulfilled these homesteading requirements in 1911, six months before New Mexico became the 47th state, and owned the land until 1951, when my grandfather died, at age 92, in Flomot. But the family never lived there again.

This land was the first that Alexander and Lillie Mae owned. Not many were tough enough to endure the harsh conditions. Many gave up and left their dugouts empty shells. There were infestations of fleas, Grandma's inflammatory rheumatism during pregnancy with twins Bill and Lillie, who were born in the dugout, wagon trips back and forth to Texas for work during cotton harvest season and over the winters, and the extreme isolation and bone tough existence on a new frontier with living conditions almost unbearable. But they passed the tests and tolerated the life in order to claim land of their own. They lived the example of never give up, never give in, never quit until the job is done.

The family now moved to friendlier surroundings, and rented increasingly larger acreages around Flomot. They eventually owned their own farm, with a four room house, one of which was a separate structure which housed the kitchen with wood fired stove. It was about a mile west of town, where all eleven siblings worked and grew to be adults, and married and began their own families. The Flomot area became the hub of the greater family, which saw 41 grandchildren grow up in the immediate area. The huge clan assembled often on Sundays at my grandparent's farm house, eating freshly killed fried chicken or home grown beef or pork, and vegetables from their garden, and apples from their orchard.

Dillie was the middle child in the pack of eleven, and loved her crowded and never lonely childhood, and parents and all her siblings and their children. She considered herself more fortunate than most on the frontier, raised by kind parents who set good examples always. She grew up working in the fields by day and at home by lamplight at night, cooking, sewing, canning, cleaning, attending farm animals and chickens along with her sisters. They were her best friends all her life, and she theirs. In her long life of 99 years, she was never known to have an unkind word for any member of her family. She bore and raised seven children, with Frank, over a generation, without complaint, while showing special love to each of them. She lived to age 99, until 2005, and is buried in the Plainview, Texas cemetery. To date, Frank and Dillie's lineage includes seven children, 15 grandchildren, 28 great-grandchildren, and five great-great-grandchildren.

FRANK AND DILLIE

Frank and Dillie were strong and determined, their genomes filtered through millennia of working class northern white European ancestors. Through history, their bloodlines evolved from Romans, Mongols, Huns, Goths, and Vikings. Their stock descended from warrior barbarians, conquerors, and sea-faring explorers. They had no roots in privilege, no titles, no rights to King's grants. Their genes were practiced in doing, not leading or intellectualizing. Frank was 5' 10", weighed about 190, supple and very strong. He was a good athlete when young, and felt he might have been a contender for professional baseball under different circumstances. He batted left, had a good

Photo 14. *Frank William Garrett and Dillie Dean Morris Garrett, as newlyweds, December 1928, Flomot.*

eye, and good stuff on the mound as a right-hander. Aside from early sandlot sports and golf later in life, he never exercised. Work was exercise enough, in his view. He had several holes-in-one at Plainview's municipal course, and always walked the tract pulling a cart.

He wore glasses without rims and with six sided lenses and thin wire frames. Later in life, both he and Dillie wore dentures, and had cataracts removed. He loved his younger brothers, Eldridge, Othel, and Theo, and his sisters Lila Mae and Oletha, and was always concerned with their well-being. The early death of their Mother bonded them for life.

Theo and Oletha were his half brother and sister, but full to him.

He had a big nose, an American Indian profile, and lots of hair. He shaved with a straight razor, and his favorite games were dominoes and something called 42, a sort of bridge played with dominoes. I never saw him in a pair of blue jeans, but did see a picture of him in bib overalls and no shirt, seining for fish on the Blue River in Oklahoma. His usual dress was khaki pants and shirt, with tie, or a suit coat and tie. He wore a two-inch wide black belt and a medium brimmed western felt hat. He never wore boots.

For a number of years during the war, we went to my grandfather's farm in Oklahoma for short vacations, driving there in a 1936 red and yellow Ford pickup with a tarp covering the bed. My brothers and I rode in the back, sitting on benches, and often would get sick from the engine exhaust. We stopped for Mom's baloney and liverloaf sandwiches at roadside picnic tables, never in restaurants. On the farm near Durant, OK., we shot squirrel with 22 caliber riffles, and ate them. We also assisted the grown-ups in catching fish by stretching a net across a narrow section of river. The technique was probably questionable legally, but we had huge fish fries at night. We beat pots and pans and plowshares to swarm bees, and wore nets over our heads and gloves to avoid stings, then harvested lots of honey. We milked cows in the evening after removing ticks from their udders, and ourselves. Frank liked these trips back home where he had grown up.

Roaming over the Oklahoma farm, there were several native American burial sites, often marked by fences around them. It was also common to see Indians in traditional dress in the towns of Durant or Boswell. Oklahoma still has the largest Indian population of any state, a result of their forced removal to reservations there.

Once, during the war, we went through Dallas where an aunt and uncle lived and worked in a defense plant. We went to a professional wrestling match in some arena, and saw cowboy star Gene Autry ringside, wearing his army uniform, and got his autograph. This was a very big deal.

Frank chewed gum constantly, and smacked when chewing or eating. He liked bowling and was good at it, to the chagrin of Dillie, who thought he should have been at home. Frank did not smoke until world war two when cigarettes were rationed, and, for unknown reason, he took up the habit. In his 70's he started smoking ivory tipped cigarillios, and they stank badly.

In the real estate business in Plainview, in 1946, he made more money in one year, around $20 thousand dollars, than he had ever seen or imagined. For the rest of his life, he stayed in the real estate business, working with his friend Dave Standifer, in partnership with B.B. Howle, or together with my middle brother, Raby. They did very well, and were their own bosses.

He liked music, played some chords on guitar, and sang songs to us like "Little Brown Jug", and "Old Strawberry Rhone", which we like a lot. He and Dillie liked a country folk singer named Jimmy Rogers. If asked in church to lead a prayer, his stock answer was, "excuse me." I have always admired him for refusing hypocrisy.

He was politically conservative, and held traditional views on disciplining his sons, in keeping with expectations of fathers at the time. He did not spare the rod if persuasion failed to bring us into line. He was the enforcer to Dillie's more lenient approach. When the girls came along beginning in 1941, his thinking was revised, but even they were careful to show respect.

Frank believed totally in the life lessons young people could learn from working hard and responsibly. His sons heard this message often, and therefore knew to get and hold after school, weekend, and full time summer employment. We never asked for or received spending money from him. But we kept what money we earned.

Dillie was fine featured with expressive eyes, tall at 5' 9" and 140-

150 lbs, and a workhorse. She kept up with her older siblings in the fields, and was tireless at home with the usual frontier chores. Her upbringing in the big, warm Morris family anchored her all her life. The sibling stayed close after marriage, enjoyed each other's company, and laughed constantly over communal chores, and treats of pie, cake, and coffee. Their closeness in growing up together led them to know each other better than anyone else who entered their lives.

Unlike Frank, who learned disciplinary rules from his Dad, she was guided gently by her loving Mother and Father and older siblings. As a consequence, she could never discipline her own children harshly, and she could never bear to see children or animals mistreated or neglected. But if diplomacy failed with us, she lived up to her promise to turn the issue over to Frank. We quickly calculated that it was far better for us to resolve things with her.

Her life was always inside her home, which she kept clean and decorated carefully. Her children were also scrubbed and wore clean, ironed clothes. She had none of the usual outside women's activities or clubs, and never desired them. There was clearly no time to waste on such frivolity. She never had baby sitters, even though her seven offspring were spread over 22 years. Her husband and children and home were her total devotion. In the Flomot store, she worked long hours alongside Frank while we were in school. Much later, she ran a sort of day care in her home for her grandchildren and children of friends, while their parents worked.

Frank and Dillie were sober, responsible parents, careful always to set good behavioral standards for themselves and us. They did not use profanity or alcohol, were spiritual but did not practice any denominational dogma, encouraged but did not insist that we go to church. They treated everyone the same and fairly, and lived by the morality and ethics taught them by their parents and their community.

Theirs was a union of matching farm cultures and large extended families who expected to earn whatever they gained; of similar value systems and parallel aspirations. They were literate but not literary. They had not read history or philosophy or biographies. They did not know art. They had no "must read" list. There was no time for reading novels for pleasure. There were no daily newspapers or magazines delivered to their door. Their backdrop was working and doing, not reading about doing. They did not attend seminars or workshops. Working the fields and home chores took all their daylight hours. Oil lamps lit a room or two at night, but were inadequate for close reading or study. I recall no books at home except the Bible.

Yet this experience with survival on the land produced solid common sense and reasoning which guided them.

They understood each other, understood the rules for survival, knew how to raise their children, spoke the same language, made their own fun, showed respect for all in the community, and never avoided their duty.

ON TO THE PLAINS

In early 1945, the Frank Garrett family trekked up the 800 ft geological elevation known as the Caprock, with its 65 million years of layered sediment holding fossilized remains of large fish, crocodiles, rhinos, and long-necked camels, to the flat, windblown and featureless but irrigated plains. What beckoned was the bustling farm town of Plainview, 50 miles west, with 10,000 people, basic amenities, reasonably good schools, and a wider scope of opportunities to make a decent living.

The irrigated plains seemed to hold great promise for dry land farmers. The vast Ogallala aquifer had been tapped at 100 ft. depths with pumps powered by an adaptation of the automobile engine, and the water

flowed without limits onto the flat land.[3] A recovering economy at the
end of the war, together with rising land and crop prices, refused to be
dampened by the reality that decline was in sight from the beginning.

What hydrologists and agricultural experts seemed not to have fully
recognized was that the aquifer was and is a fossil lake, cut off from the
eastern slope of the Rocky mountains which replenished it before erosion
created the Pecos and Canadian rivers. The finite aquifer, really a large
bathtub, was renewed only by sparse 8 to 15 inches annual rainfall, and it
began to be drawn down rapidly with unchecked irrigation. Four decades
after Frank and Dillie moved West, the water deposit was 200 feet or more
deep, and had made irrigated farming uneconomical on a good part of the
Plains.

Some farms reverted to dry land, while many others were put to
non-agricultural use such as dairy or shoulder-to-shoulder cattle feedlots.
New conservation technologies such as pivot sprinkler irrigation and new
high yielding biotech seed varieties requiring less water have offered new
hope for sustainability, but the long-term prognosis for adequate irrigation
water is still negative.

Now away from the comfort of family and friends, in a much larger
community of strangers, they began anew.   All the years farming and
operating the Flomot store netted them a five thousand dollar nest egg.
Frank chose to invest some of it in a site 5 miles Northeast of town, outside
the city limits in an area known as Seth Ward, named after a Babtist
minister who first settled there.

Seth Ward was a poor area, definitely on "the wrong side of the
tracks", but we did not know or think of it that way. Relative to where
we had been, it looked on the surface like a vast improvement. My high
school friend Sarah Mickey Hudson also remembers her family's time

3 Caprock Canyonlands, by Dan Flores, 20th anniversary edition, Texas A&M
Press, traces the geological and recent history of the Caprock, the Ogallala acquifer, and
the Llano Estacado Plains.

living in Seth Ward with warmth, but recognizes poverty in retrospect. With a stable and caring family, we didn't recognize poverty at the time, even when we were in it. This is a realization often heard expressed by adults who were fortunate enough to be born into a family with warm and responsible parents. Only much later in life did they understand their economic circumstances were deficient when compared to the more affluent.

My Mother had rarely even been to Plainview, and had never seen the three room frame house with a barn and small fenced acreage, where Frank now moved her and her five children. The house was on the northern most road of the sub-division, with open land beyond. There was electricity, refrigeration, cold water plumbed to the kitchen sink, a first for us, and a bathtub with no plumbing, but we had the usual outhouse. I was 11 years old, Raby was 14, Cal was 16, and the two girls, Shirley and Norma, were 4 and 2.

Frank found a job right away at the Montgomery Ward store in town, and soon was made manager of the men's clothing department, at a salary of $37.50 per week. It was somehow stretched into a living wage, supplemented by fresh milk from our cow, and strawberries and onions, radishes, and cucumbers grown on the little plot. The boys were enrolled in schools a month before the school year ended. I went to the Ash street junior high, while Raby and Cal went to the the high school on Galveston street.

We all had some trouble adapting to the new system, which had specialized teachers in different rooms for each period of the day.. The confusing logistics, together with a curriculum requiring a greater depth of learning and homework in each subject, was a particular challenge to me. As earlier noted, Flomot's seventh grade courses were in reality sixth grade courses in Plainview, a fact quickly recognized and acted upon. I started my actual seventh grade in the Fall of 1946, and thereafter stayed on track through high school graduation in 1951. Unschooled as my parents were, they understood that this was exactly why they had chosen to move away from Flomot to a relatively advanced system with far better instruction and facilities. Neither they nor their children ever regretted the move. Dad drove into town early, six days a week, in his used Chrysler. If we were ready to go, we could ride with him to a central drop-off point. If we missed the ride, it was walk or hitch-hike the five miles, rain or shine. We soon found after school and weekend jobs at grocery stores, stocking shelves, sacking groceries, uncrating produce, or sweeping out, which kept us busy until, maybe, catching a ride home with Dad. During the day, Mom and the girls were alone, and without a telephone or car. Dad brought home whatever groceries were bought.

The Ruth Dean family lived directly across the street from us in Seth Ward. Ruth and her two sons, Jimmy and Don, had been abandoned by her husband a few years earlier, and she made ends meet by cutting hair in her living room, collecting whatever anyone wanted to pay her. Jimmy Dean was about 16 at the time, and finishing a stint in the Merchant Marines. He played piano and accordion and sang, and I often sang along with him. He later became rich and famous as a recording artist, song writer, TV personality, and sausage producer.

Don was 15, hardworking at a variety of grocery and milk delivery jobs, and devoted to this Mother. Unlike Jimmy, he stayed close to home in Plainview, and became a close friend to my brothers and me and a favorite of our parents. He became manager of a local Piggly Wiggly supermarket, highly successful because he was smart and had a winning personality. Later, he married Nell, a local girl, and partnered with his brother in the sausage business in Plainview, known as "The Jimmy Dean Sausage Company". In this capacity, he later moved to Dallas, where he lived, still smoking, until his death of lung cancer.

Jimmy Dean was an irascible character, unable to trust anyone, not even his brother, and the two eventually had a bitter parting and lasting quarrel which was never resolved. He and my older brother, Cal, remained friends throughout the remainder of their lives, with Cal dying first two weeks before his 80th birthday, and Jimmy a year later. He is buried on his estate near Richmond, Virginia. (More about Jimmy later)

The move to Plainview was the first time Mom had ever been too far away to see and interact with her brothers and sisters and their families on a regular basis. They exchanged letters and occasional visits, but the isolation on the outskirts of a new town, knowing no one, left a void she could not easily adjust to. She became severely depressed for a period in 1945 and underwent electro-shock therapy, a fact which was mostly kept from her children. She then became pregnant with Dora, her sixth child and third daughter, born April 24, 1946.

With Dora's birth, and the move in mid-1946 to a larger in-town house costing five thousand dollars, with a bathroom, hot water, and telephone , her circle of friends began to grow. The move to Plainview now looked better, with a number of siblings also choosing to move to the Plains. Their visits together became more frequent, and a bit of her old way of life was restored, as were her spirits.

Her brothers Bob, John, Bill, and Audric and her sister Lillie and their families now had moved to the plains to take up irrigated farming. With her family back together, her children adjusted, and Frank earning much more money in a new job with John Shropshire Real Estate selling farms and ranches, her outlook brightened. She could now have an electric washing machine with hot water, but no dryer, in a house almost big enough to allow two-to-a bed sleeping. She could walk to the grocery store if need be, and we could easily walk or ride bikes to school. It was time for another child, and Sharon Ann was born April 10, 1950, the seventh and last of Dillie's and Frank's large family.

ABOUT PLAINVIEW: JOBS, MENTORS, & GROWTH:

Archeologists have documented that prehistoric humans roamed the flat Texas Plains seven thousand years before Christ, and hunted and killed giant bison by herding them off cliffs at Plainview Point, near Running Water draw, just Southeast of the present town. In the early 16th century, Spanish explorers Coronado and Cortez rode North from present day Mexico across the vast plains, labeled them the "Llano Estacado", or staked plains, and claimed them for Spain.

Existing occupants had other ideas! Hostile nomadic Indians, the Comanche, defended their homelands and hunting grounds to the death, and went on to defeat and destroy intrusions by Spanish and Mexican settlers, and the armed soldiers who came with them. Other Indian tribes, including Kiowa and Apache, also played roles, but the fearsome and cruel Comanche, referred to by Professor Dan Flores as " An anarchistic mob of Hell's Angels on Horseback", were skilled and dominant fighters. Their brand of terrorism came mounted on Mustang ponies first introduced to the region by Spanish Calvary.

After Texas statehood in 1845, the Mexican/America war of 1845-46, and the American Civil war, frontiersmen were again eager to move west and claim the rest of the North American continent for the United States. The Comanche continued to resist, and managed a series of victories over U.S. military forces spread over many years. But the main tribe was finally defeated in 1874 at the battle of Palo Duro Canyon. General Ranald McKenzie captured and systematically killed 1400 Indian horses, and the remnants of the band were marched to Fort Sill, Oklahoma and the reservation.

Legendary chief of the Comanches was Quanah Parker, son of Cynthia Ann Parker, a white girl kidnapped at age 9, and later married to Quanah's Indian father. She chose to remain with the Indians in spite of several opportunities to be returned to her people. On the reservation, Quanah became a self-promoting celebrity, but also lobbied for improvements in the treatment of many tribes similarly confined.

With the Indian threat gone and renewed interest in new grasslands for cattle, the Plains beckoned again, and cattle companies soon moved into the Plainview area. In 1876, the state legislature created Hale County, named after John Hale, a hero of the battle of San Jacinto. In1884, the town site of Plainview was selected near historic Running Water Draw, and a tent-covered grocery store opened.

First homesteaders came in 1886, claiming 160 acres each, and building standard dugout structures. In 1888, Plainview was legally named the county seat. Prosperity was evident when a school opened in 1889, a bank in 1890, and Doctors started to arrive. The town was laid out on a grid, with numbered streets running east and west, and named streets running North and South. Seth Ward, to the Northeast of town, had its own grid system and street names. There is hardly a crooked or curved street to be found in either place. The town is on a featureless flat plain with no natural identifying landmarks. From a few miles away, it is undetectable except from the air.

Wagon and horseback were, until that time, the modes of transport to the new town, but two memorable events were about to alter the little settlement forever. First, in 1907, was the arrival of the North/South line of the Santa Fe railroad, soon after followed by the East/West line of the Ft. Worth and Denver railroad. Second was the technology to access the giant Ogallala aquifer just under the surface, waiting to be tapped.

The railroads and their terminals made Plainview accessible from all over the country, creating eastern markets for Plains cattle. Abundant irrigation water meant high yielding crops with far less risk compared to reliance on the Plains ten inches of annual rainfall and volatile, dry winds. Irrigation water also quelled the dust storms.

In 1910, a pumping system using car engines was devised, and the first well, 130 feet deep, pumping 1700 gallons of water per minute, was demonstrated. Irrigation grew rapidly, and Plainview's surrounding land was touted by promoters as an irrigation paradise.

But it was the end of world war two when the largest irrigation boom began, and land prices shot up from $60. Dollars an acre to many hundreds of dollars in a few short years. [4] The optimistic view was that the water would last forever. Optimism also trumped conservation and fueled denial, which continues today to some extent.

It was to this growing agricultural mesa that my Dad chose to move his family. Oil and gas were later discovered 100 miles North, and oil 50 miles South, but Plainview remained almost completely dependent on agriculture, served by a range of businesses meeting the farmer's needs. Increased farm wealth from irrigated crops added to the positive outlook for town businesses after long years of war, and jobs were available for young and old who were willing to work. In keeping with family practice, my brothers, and I, were expected to each hold one of them.

"MAKE A GOOD HAND"

Between May 1945, at age 11, and September, 1951, age 18, I held the following sequence of after school and summer jobs.

1. Bryan's Grocery, May 45 to September 45.
2. Mangum's Garage, September 45 to January 46.
3. The Fashion Shop, January 46 to June 46.
4. Cloverlake Dairy Farm, June 46 to September, 46
5. Plainview Bowling Alley, September 46 to January 47.
6. Southwestern Public Service, January 47 to May 47.
7. Plainview Herald, May 47 to June 48.
8. Wolfington Farm Hand, June 48 to September 48.

[4] There are many histories of this period to be found in the Panhandle Plains Historical Museum, Canyon Texas, and in the Llano Estacado museum in Plainview.

9. The Cook Company, Fall 48 to May 51.

10.Texaco Company, Seismograph crew, May 51 to September 51.

I learned from each of them during these formative years, but the last four stand out in my mind as key in terms of life lessons and lasting friendships.

BRYAN'S MARKET

Raby and I landed a job in May 1945, with Bryan's grocery on the North side of the courthouse square. We did everything that needed being done, including unpacking and cleaning produce, stocking shelves, sacking groceries, and delivering groceries to customer's cars or trucks. We also swept out at the end of the day. Mr. Bryan's was the first self-service market we had ever seen. Our experience at the grocery store in Flomot store enabled us to get up to speed quickly. Mr. and Mrs. Bryan were themselves hard working, and good employers. We probably earned fifty cents an hour.

MANGUM'S GARAGE:

I worked cleaning disassembled engine parts with gasoline, getting them ready to be reinstalled. Mr. R.C. Mangum lived next door to us on Ash street, and his garage was about 15 feet directly behind our house and his. I used rubber gloves about half the time, and grease and gasoline stains took a lot of scrubbing to remove from raw, cracked, and bloody hands.

Next came the Fashion Shop, at 8th and Broadway, where I washed the store windows, and packed ladies mail order clothes for shipping. My cousin Juanell Ingram managed the store, and, while my memory is hazy,

She, I am sure, is how I got the job.

CLOVERLAKE DAIRY FARM

In the Summer of 1946, Raby and I got our first taste of baling alfalfa hay on the Cloverlake Creamery farm North of town. It was owned and operated by the Garrett brothers, H.W. and Albert, who were quail hunting friends of Dad's, but not related. Cloverlake milked its own Holstein cows and supplied bottled milk and cream daily to residents in town, delivered to front porches very early each morning.   The milk was pasteurized, a new word to us.

I drove the J.I Case tractor pulling a hay baler as it scooped up the rows of mown and raked hay, while Raby either "tied out" or "blocked" the bales as the rotating plunger packed them in tight rectangles weighing 60 to 70 lbs per bale. The bales were then pushed on through the baling chamber and stacked by hand onto a trailer attached to the back of the baler. Finally the bales were "doffed" in stacks of 12, for easy pick up and transport to the barn and cattle feeding troughs. Usually, H.W. worked with us, stacking bales by hand as he got ready to dump them with a pull of a lever.

One day, we noticed a jackrabbit running parallel to the baler in the same direction, about 20 feet away. H.W. had a hay hook in his hand which he used to wrestle the bales into position. Without taking aim, he threw the foot long metal hook at the rabbit and scored a direct hit. The point went completely through the rabbit and out the other side. I stopped the tractor and we shut down baling for a minute to marvel at this marksmanship. H.W. was as amazed as anyone. Both Garrett brothers were good men with fine reputations, and we remained friends with them all their remaining lives. I have no memory of what we earned on this job.

JOBS BETWEEN JOBS:

After the haybaling experience, I held interim jobs at The Plainview Bowling Lanes, and Southwestern Public Service. At the bowling alley, I did night shift work setting pins, beginning at 5 PM. The pins and bowling balls had to be picked up by hand after each ball thrown, placed in an overhead rack, then the rack lowered by hand after each second ball, to place the pins in their correct setting awaiting the next bowler. The ball was picked up, also by hand, and returned each time on a waist-high rolling track much like automated ball returns of today. We earned twenty cents per game (line) for this exhausting work. The shift didn't end until the last bowler went home, often as late as 10 PM.

Southwestern Public Service needed a janitor, who was me, and I cleaned the place stem to stern each night, alone in the big office building. It was dimly lit at night, and I was a little anxious, looking around each corner and behind each door to make sure I was alone. I also washed their windows. Mostly, I worked alone, and learned principally that working in isolation is not much fun. Secondly, I learned that working alone at night with limited light can lead a 12 year old to imagine things in the dark, akin to the haunted house syndrome. I had to reason with myself a number of times to overcome a concern I thought had been conquered at age 6.

THE PLAINVIEW HERALD

In the Summer of 1947, I turned 13. I decided to ask for a paper route at the Plainview Evening Herald, the town daily. I used the direct approach and went to the front office and asked for work. I was told that no paper routes were available at that time, but that they had in mind another job for me. Without knowing any details, I was hired and started immediately.

Every day thereafter, immediately after school, I hightailed it to the Herald, where I cleaned the custom hand fed presses with naptha, gathered the lead type from disassembled pages just used on the big letterpress to print the evening edition, and trucked the lead back to the remelting area. I shoveled it into the melting pot, melted it, then ladled it into coated molds. I next moved the molten lead by rolling the cart to the side of each linotype machines, where it was dipped from the molds into the reservoir of each machine.

The linotype operators, black with soot, typed away on news copy placed in front of them, and the machine spit out lead type in columns, which was later made up and blocked into pages for the next press run. Handling molten lead was dangerous and dirty work for anybody. Lead fumes floated throughout the melting area and the composing room. Oily, flammable rags containing toxic cleaning fluids needed to clean ink from the presses, were constantly handled with bare hands.

After the daily press run of the full newspaper, my job became janitorial, emptying trash and sweeping the floors of both the front office copy and editorial and advertising offices, and the composing and press room. There was lots of paper everywhere; there were no electronic screens; everything was trial and error on manual typewriters. Rewrites meant lots of trash to be disposed of.

I also crawled into the grease pit under the big press, sometimes while the big rollers ran back and forth over the lead type pages locked into the press, mopped up all the oil droppings, of which there were many, then removed the layers of waste newsprint deposited there when the rollers clogged and had to be cleaned. I loaded all this into large trash buggies and rolled them to the central trash dumpster. Often, the job was not finished until after 8 PM. After the walk home to Ash street, and something to eat, there was little time to consider homework.

The press room housed the old technology main press, the flat bed of which had to be loaded with blocked lead type pages before each run. Gutenberg had invented letterpress printing in the 15 century, and the newer and less expensive offset technology wasn't widely adopted by newspapers until the 1940's. The press was a large, noisy, complicated, and expensive contraption. It measured about 12 feet wide by 20 feet long and 6 feet high.

When running, its traversing rollers literally pressed the newsprint onto ink coated type. The 8 ft wide paper stock was pulled into place from large rolls which were lifted into place by hand after being brought to the press on dollies. The pressman, George Frye, would sound an all clear before pushing the start button. Everybody knew to step a safe distance away and watch this dinosaur roar into action. It was noisier than a locomotive. George kept an oil can handy and squirted oil liberally when any part of the press made a suspicious sound.

After each sheet of stock was printed, the take-up roller would quickly pull it from the press and into the folding area, just in time for the next width of stock to be laid over the type bed. Fascinating to watch, treacherous to be near, and ear plugs essential to avoid deafness.

On Saturdays' we worked until midnight and later printing the big Sunday morning paper, which had advertisement supplements inserted by hand into each paper. We wore rubber tips on our fingers and became expert at slapping a flap of the paper with the left hand, raising it just high enough to quickly throw in the extra ad section, then moving that complete paper to the left and repeat the three step process on the next paper in the stack. We did this while the huge letterpress was running full speed right next to us. Old timers at the Herald all had a printer's ink pallor, and suffered significant hearing loss. Communication was possible only by shouting.

I did well and made decent spending money, working long hours as an eighth grader. The work was interesting, except the clean-up part, and a couple of people took a real interest in me, seemingly impressed that I worked this hard at such a young age. Tom Vaughn, a typesetter and page make-up man, was a special friend. He and his wife had no children after several years of marriage. They took me under their wing, with Tom showing me the ropes, teaching me something about page blocking, reading type upside down and backwards, and generally looking out for me. His personality reminded me of my favorite uncle Dick Washington, and Tom and I remained friends throughout my college years, although I did not see him much after leaving the Herald.

My reason for leaving after almost two years came as a surprise to me and to Mr. Miller, the paper's editor. The Texas legislature passed a new child labor law prohibiting children under 16 years of age from working around open, dangerous machinery. Mr. Miller called me in and broke the news to me, apologized, thanked me, then told me I could no longer do the work I had been doing. The law was most likely a good one, but was also most likely a result of lobbying by unions.

He also told me that he had arranged for me to become a partner in a delivery service which specialized in out of town papers, including the Lubbock Avalanche Journal and the Amarillo Daily News and Globe Times. We would be paid based on the number of papers delivered.

My partner had a jeep, which he drove around the route. We first folded the papers and piled them into the back of the jeep. I would toss the papers to customer's driveways, as he drove up and down streets and alleys making sharp turns. We did well with this routing for two weeks, splitting the profits, but a major problem soon developed.

I got serious motion sickness! The route took two hours, but my stomach and head could hold out for only thirty minutes. We would have to stop while I threw up and recovered, then resume the job, only to throw up again. It didn't work out well, after repeated tries and even some motion sickness aids. I chose not to get sick every day, and began looking for another line of work.

The Herald job was the first that taught me the value of mentors. Tom Vaughn and George Frye in the composing room; Mr. Miller, the Editor, Mr. E.Q. Perry, who owned the paper, all gave me many words of encouragement and a sense of pride in the small job I was doing. Working shoulder to shoulder with these good men, seeing the finished newspaper as product, enduring long hours through Saturday nights into early Sunday mornings, pulling a load we both felt was equal to theirs, developing an understanding of newspapering from ad sales to news copy, to typesetting and composing, to printing and delivery, was experience which left an indelible and positive impression, and which I have always remembered proudly.

WOLFINGTON FARM HAND

The first time I was actually hired as an adult, or at least fully expected to perform as such, was as a live-in farm hand on the James Wolfington farm, five miles North of Plainview. I was almost 14. The Wolfington family farm was next to the farm of my uncle Bob Morris, and it was through uncle Bob that I heard about the job.

I went to see Mr. Wolfington, and he hired me right away. He told me to call him Jim, and asked me to start the following Monday. And "by the way",he told me,"the job pays five dollars a day, plus room and board." He said that I would live with the family during the week and go to town on Saturday and come back to the farm Sunday evenings. It was adult employment, and I went for it.!

Mr. and Mrs. Wolfington had two young sons, James, 9, and Garland, 7, both too young to be much help. The boys became like little brothers to me, and they thought of me as their big brother. After long days in the fields, we played games at night and worked jigsaw puzzles. I ate all meals with the family. Mrs. Wolfington was a good cook.

The daily routine was this: Up at about 6 AM, feed the animals and milk the cows. There were several cows, and a milking machine was used. The milk was sold in town. We then cleaned the milking stalls and the milking machine and hosed down the barn floor. Then back to the house, wash up and a big country breakfast before wearing away a lot of calories in tough physical labor.

Jim Wolfington and I would then either work together scooping wheat and maize into storage bins or stacking bales of hay in the barn, or I would be taken a few miles away to irrigate his large tract of alfalfa hay. He would drop me there and leave. The irrigation well pumped water from an 8 inch diameter pipe into a holding pond, from which water was released down dirt irrigation ditches running across the top of the field from one side to the other.

My job was to monitor the flow of water, and, when appropriate,"change the set", meaning to move the stop tarp farther along in the irrigation ditch once the previous set had saturated the ground all the way through the field . Once a new tarp was set, I dug out holes in the side of the ditch, with a shovel, which would allow the water to rush from the ditch into a new patch of alfalfa. It was exactly like breaching a river dam, on a micro-scale.

When the new "set' was ready, the old stop tarp had to be removed, and the water released down the ditch to the next tarp. The no longer needed ditch cut-outs then had to be filled in by hand shoveling. The ditch, in effect, had to be repaired. I walked the length of the hayfield several times each day, following the progress of the water, and timed the need for the next set-up. I was alone all day, except when picked up mid-day to go back to house for lunch, after which it was back to the field and the same repetitive pattern for the afternoon. The well continued pumping overnight during watering season to refill the holding tank. Hay requires huge amounts of water.

Other days, I would drive a big Farmall tractor pulling a wide harrow. The purpose of this plow was to level the soil, pulling down whatever residue remained from previous crops, preparing the ground for listing and planting. Clouds of dust surrounded the harrow and enveloped the plow, the tractor, and, of course, the driver. I wore a large straw hat but no dust mask. Often, the West Texas wind would blow most of the dust away from the tractor, but if wind and tractor were moving in the same direction at about the same speed, the dust was suffocating.

These were long, lonely days, both on the tractor, and irrigating alfalfa, during which I was completely alone with no means of communication, several miles away from help if it had been needed. Needing help was not part of advanced planning on the farm, at least not that I remember. The unspoken rule was "look out for yourself". I kept a sharp eye out for snakes, as well as taking great care operating the tractor or making any adjustments to the irrigation motor and pump.

Evenings, animals had to be cared for again, then came clean up in a galvanized tub or cattle watering tank, and some clean clothes getting ready for Mrs. Wolfington's good dinner. She was a relatively young woman, which I did not recognize at the time. She did all our laundry and always had clean sheets on our beds, all dried in the sun on a wire clothesline. She also took care of chickens and eggs, and did other chores, with a little help from the boys. The boys slept in one room, while I had a twin bed in a small room. The house had three bedrooms. Again, there was an outhouse, but water was plumbed to the kitchen sink.

Jim Wolfington was also young, in his early 40's, but appeared old to me. He was wafer thin, and quiet, hardly uttering a word during meals or while working. My uncle Bob regarded him as a good farmer, and a man of his word. He was fair and even with me in every way, but taciturn to the point of making me uncomfortable. He was dark, small in stature, chain smoked, and didn't appear healthy.

Saturday evenings, he would pay me $30 dollars and give me a ride the five miles into town, where I was glad to see my family. They were interested in every detail of the work. I would sleep in on Sunday mornings. Sunday afternoons it was back to the farm, often driven there by Dad or one of my brothers.

I had just completed my freshman year in high school, and had never been away from family and on my own. I found that about Thursday of each week, I would start to feel homesick, an emotion I had experienced before, but not so intensely. I began to look at my Mother and Father differently, and remember thinking how hard my Dad must have worked during all those years when he was also a hired farm hand, or farming on the halves, trying desperately to make ends meet.

During the week, there was no news of them or my siblings, but from the fields I could see the outline in town of the Harvest Queen Mills, a large flour milling and grain storage silo complex that was perhaps 8 stories high.

And I thought of how hard my Mother worked for years without any of the conveniences later to become standard. Every time I left home to start a new job, regardless of what it was, my Mom would also say, "Make a good hand". And I remembered her words and they always meant something to me, and I always tried to do exactly that.

Three months of hard six-day weeks as a farm hand left me with a new appreciation of the back-breaking, unending work of farming in the late 1940's. Some automation was creeping in, but much of the drudgery was still handwork. We baled hay at night when dew held down the dust and gave the bales more moisture content. I rode the "tie-out" seat on the baler, threading two strands of baling wire around each bale, twisting the wires back on themselves, by hand, to make the tie secure before the bale pressure was released.

Today, hay baling is labor free start to finish, including loading the big bales out of the fields. We lifted them by hand onto flat bed trucks. The bales weighed up to 70 pounds, depending on moisture content.

We baled up rabbits and snakes and skunks sometimes. It was eerie seeing these dead creatures heads or legs sticking out of the bales as they came through the chamber, having been crushed to death by the plunger as it packed the straw together.

I sat on the side of the baler under a spot light, on a metal seat with holes in it to allow air circulation. Sores developed on my butt where flesh poked through the holes. I also developed chills and fever and wheezing several nights after inhaling all the "fly" from night baling, even though we tried to wear masks and goggles. These devices, especially the goggles, interfered with my vision and ability to tie the bales, so I often took off both the mask and the goggles. Invincible youth does not understand the concept of long term consequences of such things to health. Cause and immediate effect will register, but delayed effects from any activity will not easily be comprehended by the young.

The Wolfington boys, James and Garland, came to high school long after I had graduated, but I would see them occasionally in town. They grew to be handsome and tall, much larger than their Father, and with more of their Mother's personality. They always remembered my summer with them, and, I think, continued to view me as a sort of big brother.

At the end of the summer, Mrs. Wolfington gave me a big hug and thanked me for being a friend to her sons. Jim Wolfington shook my hand and paid me the ultimate compliment. He told me "You made a good hand".

During the three months, I would often walk the short distance North to the farm of Uncle Bob and Aunt Minnie Morris. Aunt Minnie always had delicious dinners, and Uncle Bob offered very long blessings before we could dig in. They were very kind to me that summer, and, I felt, were always looking out for my well being. Aunt Minnie came to my rescue more than once in the middle of the night when I had chills and fever and she heard me wheezing loudly. She treated me like her own son.

THE COOK COMPANY

J.C. Cook had come to Plainview from Shawnee, Oklahoma, intent on starting a new business. He surveyed the market, and decided that the area needed Venetian blinds, and sheet rubber and asphalt tile floor coverings. No existing business offered blinds, but there were a couple of carpet stores who also installed hard surface flooring. Mr. Cook reasoned that he could offer both, plus special order carpet, and offer a more appealing selection of choices to the growing residential market. His market research turned out to be mostly accurate.

He opened an attractive showroom with floor to ceiling windows on two sides, in a rented building on the corner of Broadway and 5th street. The showroom displayed examples of all products offered, and itself was a showcase of special "scribed" flooring installation techniques using a variety of colors. An imbedded multi-colored compass rose stood out in the middle of the showroom. The showroom also housed an attractive office area, so there was always someone in attendance when a customer wandered in.

The back of the building was partitioned off from the front, and housed a roomy venetian blind manufacturing space, plus storage for raw materials, rolls of sheet rubber and linoleum, as well as boxes of floor tiles, and a fan vented spray painting enclosure. Several machines were also housed there for cutting wood or aluminum blind slats, drilling wooden "headers and footers", routing holes for rolling pulleys for pull cords, as well as a hanging circular rack for holding the blinds for stringing and final assembly. It was piecework, not an assembly line, but a new order of blinds could quickly be built and on their way to the customer.

Coming off the farm job and starting my sophomore year in high school in the Fall of 1948, I decided I might get a job in this new store. It was conveniently just two blocks from our house. The brash, direct approach worked again. I asked for Mr. Cook, and he soon appeared, wearing coke bottle thick glasses which magnified his eyes and made him seem menacing, but he spoke to me in a friendly tone. I explained my mission, and he apparently liked my pitch. I started the next day, September 1, at an hourly rate which could not have mattered much because I don't remember it.

This job proved to be stable and interesting, in spite of the fact that Cook company cash flow was always on the edge of being negative. I worked there until graduating school, a tenure of 33 months, and learned to apply math I was studying, something about carpentry, how to install a variety of soft floor coverings including cove base, about how to meet a deadline, and for the first time, about dealing with customers and satisfying them.

John Roy Shackleford and his wife, Dell, had come West with J.C. Cook to start the business, but had no ownership. "Shack" was the head floor coverings guy and functioned also as the shop foreman. He bird-dogged the orders as they came in and made certain the quality was right and that the job was completed by the time promised. He was a craftsman, good with his hands, and knew his trade. He could cut perfect seams in inlaid sheet goods, and with a blow torch and linoleum knife, make sheet rubber conform to any contour. Cutting outside corner seams required experience and art, and he could do them well. He was also a good teacher and mentor on the job.

From Shack, I learned to measure customer's windows for blinds and calculate clearance tolerances needed for installation. I learned to help customers match décor with our aluminum color palette, or to choose custom colors for wood blinds. I learned to set up the machines and cut aluminum slats from rolls to correct lengths. I learned to calculate prices and quote totals to customers, to collect when the order was installed.

Spray painting headers and slats with fast drying primer and glossy custom colors was also to be mastered, as was measuring and cutting the proper lengths of "tape" for each blind and inserting the slats and threading cord through the slats. I learned every phase of the Venetian blind business, from getting an order, producing it, installing it, and bringing home the check. If need be, I could still make completed blinds with my eyes closed, more than 60 years later.

I became pretty skilled at installing, on my own, of all types of flooring, some with decorative and intricate patterns. As my ability to do these things alone grew, I naturally became a more valuable employee for Cook Company, and, as I remember, my hourly wage gradually increased all the time I was there.

But Mr. Cook always seemed to be on the edge, operating hand to mouth, having to pay his suppliers on cash terms, quickly convert raw materials, and collecting immediately when jobs were finished. He was clearly under pressure a lot of the time, and was quick tempered and irritable at times because of it.

In summers, after I got a driver's license, I drove the company carry-all truck to Amarillo at least twice a week to pick up a roll or two of aluminum, cotton cord for stringing the blinds, and wood stock and other supplies, always taking a signed blank check with me for payment. These supplies were quickly depleted, customers dunned for payment, then the next trip to Amarillo would ensue.

There were many weeks when the payroll couldn't be met on Saturday, and Mr. Cook would sheepishly ask me to wait until the following week for payment. I always agreed, as if there were an alternative. My belief was that the men and women with families had to be paid first, and there was not enough money in the till to also pay a young kid on time. I was pretty good at saving a few dollars, and was in better position to wait than the others. The shop employed six full time adults, and me.

Hours of work were immediately after school, as soon as I could get there, ending no earlier than 7 PM. Often, I would be asked to come back after supper and work until around 11 PM to rush an order to completion so it could be installed the next morning and collected for.

If there was a slack period, I cleaned, waxed, and power polished the showroom floor, and swept out the shop and tidied up all around. I also washed the showroom windows, which was no small job. As always, my rule for myself was to always be busy. The guy leaning on his broom would surely be the first to go. The work ethic, as taught by my Dad, was always in the back of my mind.

This is the job that transitioned me through puberty, and no doubt kept me out of mischief during my high school years. I was still flying model airplanes and building crystal set radios when J.C. Cook hired me. By the time I left after almost three years of defacto apprenticeship, boys my age were looking into all manner of heretofore adult interests, and so was I, at four inches taller and thirty pounds heavier. But the work imperative allowed little time for hanging with the teenage testosterone herd that was usually around. I went so far as to drink a little beer with Shack and Dell in their home, and, of course, smoking was a teen right of passage then, but we were never tempted with narcotics.

We were also shielded by never being ethnically or culturally divided into competing tribal gangs so prevalent today in cities. We did not speak different languages or come from radically different economic means. There were conflicts between boys over turf or girlfriends, some bullying as always, and drag racing of cars on country roads that did not always end well, but being very busy has its plusses, and I had that advantage.

Humans for all time have been unable to resist dividing themselves into bands, cliques, clubs, and tribes, the sociological instinct fulfilling the need to belong....the need for security in sameness. Being fully occupied with work after school hours perhaps allowed me to build my identity a different way, away from the need to belong to this group or that, away from the attention that accrues to the popular. Or so I thought. High school was to teach me that I was as narcissistic and vulnerable as anyone else in wanting and seeking recognition.

NAVIGATING HIGH SCHOOL.

The ethnic and cultural bubble we grew up in was an unreality. It was a form of innocent depravation. We knew about the segregated black school on the north side "flats", and even scrimmaged their football team in pre-season games, but the notion that there was anything wrong didn't penetrate our consciousness. We had social studies and history and civics classes in which we reviewed the injustice of slavery, but none which explored or debated the apartheid within a mile of our high school. That awareness would come somewhat later.

Sandwiched in with the preoccupation of being employed was the almost as important priority of schoolwork. Junior high, or middle school, had been a breeze once I got adjusted and on track. Particularly memorable teachers in seventh grade were Mrs. Joe Sharp, teaching Texas history, who liked me a lot. Therefore, I liked her a lot. Her daughter, Pernicia Lou, was in my same history class, and became a friend, I think at the behest of her mother.

Mrs. Fletcher, my eighth grade math teacher, also helped me a lot, and laid a good foundation for higher math in high school. Mrs. Fletcher lived across the street from us on Ash, and sometimes gave me a ride to school. She was a strong disciplinarian and showed me no favors. I also have good memories of Mr. D.C. Arthur, the principal, who believed in students towing the line, and we did. "Mrs. Zeigler, a home room and English teacher who practiced loud and abusive discipline as her instruction technique, earned our well deserved enmity by calling us "unnecessaries."

High school was a seismic shift, in a big building with an annex on the west side of town on Galveston street. It was a mile from our house, but an easy walk or jog, close enough to come home for lunch if I hurried. My oldest brother, Cal, had graduated in 1946, and was off to college at West Texas State. Raby was in his senior year. Neither had been eligible for sports in Plainview due to the rules governing eligibility of transfer students. Texas high school football was and is a very big deal, and strict rules prevented bringing in hot-shot ringers from other districts to beef up local teams.

The class curriculum was fixed for incoming freshmen. English grammer and composition, biology, world and American history, Civics, Algebra and PE were required, along with a study period. Foreign languages were not offered, but there was a Latin club which met after school. Four years of English were required, although we all spoke only English. There were no Hispanics, Asians, Blacks, or foreign speakers.

Those students who chose it could sign up for "Diversified

Education", which meant being released an hour early each day to go to their work, but farm boys who rode the bus home on a schedule were not eligible. An elective might be typing or choir, both of which I chose.

First year algebra was a disaster under Henry Loder, coach of the B football team and part time teacher. Big mistake. He was lousy as a teacher, intolerant of questions, threatening, and a turn-off, especially to me but to many others as well. The "round peg in square hole" metaphor was particularly applicable to Henry; a perfect example of over utilization of narrow talent. I turned off and flunked the course, with resentment. My "F" was self inflicted from spite, and I finally realized spite only hurt me, not Henry Loder. A good lesson for later life.

I took the course again under Bessie Howell, one of the best qualified and most patient and kinder teachers I ever met. This time I made an A, with a plus sign. Freshman algebra was the only course I ever flunked at any level in school.

Running a close second to Henry Loder in terms of temperament was Wayne Coleman, a returning shell-shocked and probably gay veteran of the war. However, he was a good teacher of English grammar, sentence structure, and literature. He demanded good compositions, and I responded well to this demand, turning in a number of papers which he praised to the class. As a consequence, I have believed ever since, perhaps incorrectly, that I could write well.

He had his class favorites, usually boys, who sat near him in the front row. His temper was unruly, with sudden outbursts typical of bi-polarity, and he kept a paddle handy and used it with gusto in front of the class. He would be arrested and jailed today, but teachers then had great discretion and authority in choosing their methods of discipline and ways to administer them. The class did not challenge him, and such a challenge would have been to no avail. R. W. Davidson, the school principal, never failed to side with his teachers and back them fully.

World history under Ida Mae Dunn consisted of the following: Mrs. Dunn would read from the text or from her prepared notes, and students took down her spoken words. Tests called for regurgitating these same words in the same order. What could and should have been fascinating and compelling was mundane and boring, all due to a teacher with 30 plus years of tenure who had never learned the first thing about effective teaching.

Typing under Carolyn Hancock was perhaps the most functionally useful course in my high school curriculum. We had old fashioned Underwood brand mechanical typewriters which had to be returned by hand, used lots of carbon paper, and learned touch typing the old fashioned way. Repetitive exercises and speed tests every class paid off. Girls most often became secretaries after graduation and were the best typists.

Lipperts Business College, with its court reporting school, was prominent in town, and a great many girls chose this route to employment. It was lucrative and a skill in great demand all over the state. My typing speed became acceptable, for which I thank Mrs. Hancock. I think of her often when I see the hunt and peck system used by many technology sophisticates who thought a rote typing class a waste of their time. The ability to type rapidly has served me well.

Elizabeth Cope was the choir director, and ran a tight ship. She knew her Bach, Brahms, and Beethoven, and we sang acappella classics, giving concerts around town, in school assemblies, and in schools in surrounding towns. I sang bass and liked it, and made good friends in the choir, male and female. Miss Cope chose me to sing bass in the barbershop quartet. Our repertoire consisted of six or seven old fashioned and well known songs which harmonized well. We clowned around some during the songs. Weldon Hayes sang baritone, Kenneth Rogers sang lead, and Charles Stennett, tenor.

One of our choir and quartet concerts was attended by the West

Texas A&M Music Director, Dr. Houston Bright, who called to offer me a music scholarship at the college and a place in his choir and quartet, much to my amazement. I accepted, but more about that later.

An extra-curricular activity during our final year was the senior play, "Junior Miss", for which I was selected to play the romantic lead. It was staged in the city auditorium on Broadway, and we played to a full house of parents and fellow students. I had quite a few lines to remember, which I managed to deliver on cue, but the most memorable moment was when the script called for me to kiss Peggy Joyce Hughes, one of the best lookers in school. My pals had dared me to go off script and make a big scene out of this, but I played it straight and closed mouth. She had half expected me to upstage her, and I think was a little surprised when I didn't. My pal Philip Thompson took a liking to Peggy Joyce, but it seems she was spoken for even then. Phil and I recently remembered her fondly.

Lester Hickman was a young and capable chemistry teacher. He was articulate and made chemistry relevant and interesting. Many years later we exchanged letters, after I had spent a career in the chemical industry with Monsanto Company. I had been asked to summarize my career for notes to be distributed at a class reunion. I concluded mine by saying that Lester Hickman would have a fit if he knew that I had made my living in the chemical industry. The class notes found their way to Mr. Hickman, of course, and he wrote to congratulate me. He revealed that at the time he taught high school chemistry, he was only three years older than we were, which we had not recognized . He had gone on to a teaching career in Dallas, and later joined a chemical industry trade association.

SPORTS

Organized sports had always taken a back seat to work, but in my junior year, I decided to try and blend the two. I tried out for the track team and was accepted as a discus thrower, but not a very accomplished one. We competed in our conference with teams such as Amarillo High and Lubbock High, but my technique and training never brought home medals. In hurdles and relays, and the 220 and 440, our team did well. Weldon Hayes and Roy Pogue were standouts in track, and remain good friends today, both still living in Texas.

I joined spring training football in 1950, preparatory to the Fall season. We had hard practices in Spring and Fall, and an eight game schedule against Amarillo, Lubbock, Borger, Pampa, and others, with a winning season. I played right tackle on offense and defense, but played behind big Jimmy Jameson, who, at 220 agile pounds, got most of the playing time. I weighed 170 and had grown to almost six feet, was strong but not fast. I lettered and had a good experience overall.

Coach W.C. Dub Harris naturally gave most of the playing time to kids who had been in his program for several years, and I understood and accepted that unwritten rule. Fair was fair, and they deserved it. Still, I made friends who I enjoy to this day, and have never forgotten the hard physical training and tough scrimmages we had to get ready for games. Line coach Buck Mundy knew his stuff and made sure we knew the assignments.

During practices, we used leather helmets with no face guards. Plastic helmets with face guards were reserved for game nights only.

While making an effort in sports, I continued to work a full schedule, going to Cook Company after practices and fitting into a later set of hours. I just did not want to give it up, and neither did my Dad, who always valued work more highly than sports as a means of learning anything. He felt football was a good way to get hurt, sometimes for life, and did not see much sense in it. I, on the other hand, saw it as a route to acceptance and popularity with the girls. It seemed to me that most of the prettier ones gravitated to football players, and I wasn't about to be left out. So much for remaining obscure!

It school assemblies on Friday's, the football players sat on the edge of the stage, wearing their letter jackets, while the band played fight songs and the cheer leaders and student body whistled and clapped. Coach Harris would introduce the players and give a motivational talk explaining how we were going to destroy that night's opponent, whipping everybody into a frenzy of school spirit. Who could resist that? I did not even try!!!

THE SOCIAL SCENE

My older brothers had joined the Navy in 1950 as the Korean war was heating up. They charged me with taking care of their new red hatchback Plymouth during my senior year. The mobility made dating feasible, while sports gave me some visibility, and I entered the fray with some fairly innocent enthusiasm. Don Dean, Jimmy's younger brother, also had some snappy wheels, so we often double-dated in his car or mine. Don usually dated Margie Cornelius, a good friend of mine.

Bob Hollars and I were also pals and doubled a lot, he with his steady, Audrey Bryant, and me with a variety of gals from all high school grades. My dates were with Alice Yates, Reika Robinson, Kay Hannah, Iris Roland, and others, none of them steady. Bob's Dad was a district judge, and his older brother Bill was later the county tax collector. My brother

Raby worked for Bill as tax assessor for a few years.

We went to the Granada theatre on North Broadway, which was the hot spot to be seen on Saturday night. The Granada was lavishly decorated with figurines and special lighting, floor to ceiling red velvet drapes, and a large mezzanine level which allowed smoking. We saw Cary Grant, Humphrey Bogart, John Wayne, Gene Kelley first run flicks, sometimes in color, shown from a cranky 16 mm projector in a balcony booth.

Projectors were not yet push button, and had to be threaded and re-threaded by hand when the film broke or slipped off a roller sprocket. There were often unplanned and disruptive breaks, bringing jeers and groans from the audience. The main feature was always preceded by a Woody Woodpecker or Bugs Bunny/ Elmer Fudd cartoon, perhaps a commentary on the mentality of those in attendance.

The Fair theatre, just down the street, featured western serials, but occasionally had an offering which caught our attention, but it was definitely not cool to take a date there. In earlier years, we had gone there on Saturday afternoons to see Hoot Gibson and Johnny Mack Brown serials and Three Stooges shorts, all for a nickel. We smoked in the balcony seats.

Inset in the sidewalk at the entrance to the Fair theatre today, is a star in tribute to Jimmy Dean, who , as noted was later to become a national celebrity and Plainview's best known citizen. Growing up there, he and Don and their Mother Ruth were the poorest of the poor and there were no such accolades then.

Another choice was the drive-in movie west of town, which was good for courting, but not to be seen, which was, after all, mostly the point. After the movies, we might go to Eddie's for Cokes, about our only choice in a dry town, but some more risk-takers made contact with local bootleggers. Plainview had a skeleton police force under Chief Hoyt Curry, but unless caught in the act of making an illicit purchase, very few got busted. Bourbon in coke is a good disguise.

One last impression of high school has amazed me over the years. We knew something about nearby colleges, but almost nothing about educational institutions outside the state of Texas. Our high school "counselor", Mrs. Allan, also did not seem to know much. Only one person from our graduating class of 170 went to an Ivy League School. Kenneth Rogers was accepted at Yale Divinity School. Otherwise, the one third who went on to college seemed to go to Texas Tech, West Texas State, Abilene Christian, McMurray, North Texas State, or maybe Texas Christian.

Why this was so had to do with missing guidance. There were many very good students in our school who could have been accepted at large Universities in the Middle West, East, and West, but Mrs. Allan worked alone, with guidance toward higher education an adjunct to her main job of teaching home economics. Home Economics was how she was graded. I doubt that she spent two hours a week on attempting any college placements or seeking scholarship opportunities, or meeting with worthy students discussing their capabilities and possible goals.

The image our school system had of itself and its responsibilities to students simply did not extend beyond preparing students for jobs after high school on family farms, or for secretarial jobs, or study at the nearby teacher's college to take up teaching roles. The higher education concerns of school boards and administrators in larger urban settings were not the concerns of the Plainview school board, made up as it was of lightly educated farmers and local small businessmen. Our lack of student and teacher diversity did not make apparent the greater needs of society, or the educational guidance needed to meet those needs. Our industries to be served were right in front of us, not far away.

The college guidance and placement "office" in the Plainview school system commanded no resources or commitment, and had no apparent leader to champion and sell its purpose. Consequently, graduates were oblivious to it, and unknowingly penalized in its absence. We had a lot of smart people performing in a closed society.

JUG HUSTLER

The most physically demanding job I ever had was as a "jug hustler" on a Texaco seismograph crew, the summer before starting college.   A chimpanzee could have been trained in a day or two to do the work, but the pay was good, so I chose it over continuing to work for the Cook Company.

Boiled down, the job meant going at a trot 7.5 miles each day, carrying a metal basket weighing 16 pounds, and bending down at each 20 ft interval to attach a 2 pound "jug" to metal clips on a quarter mile long, 1 inch diameter umbilical cable. The line was connected to a seismograph truck which records fissures and pockets in the earth when a dynamite charge is detonated 100 to 150 feet below the surface and creates in effect a small earthquake. The point is to find chambers in the geology which might contain oil.

Oil companies have seismograph crews exploring all the time, all over the world, on land and water, hoping to locate promising areas to drill. In our case, on the high Plains around Plainview, we shot as many as 15 holes each day, while the detector "jugs" we had clipped in place fed data to graph recording paper in the specially equipped truck. The recording equipment was housed in a chamber mounted behind the cab, and manned, behind closed doors, by a trained geologist.

Wound up on a huge spool behind this chamber was the half mile of one inch diameter line.   As the truck moved forward, the line, or cable, was rolled out ¼ mile on each side of each drill site, laid flat on the ground as the "hustlers , hanging off the back of the vehicle, dropped off the jug baskets each 40 feet. When fully laid out on each side of the "shot" hole, two teams of two men each would run in opposite directions for the length of the cable, attaching the jugs to the plenary line.

When finished, the explosive handlers in hard hats would screw together eight inch long, four inch diameter cans of dynamite to a length of about six feet, affix the dynamite caps, and feed the explosives down the hole by rope. Then came the all clear warning through the bull-horn. The signal to 'blow" actually came from the truck. The loud explosion sent a gusher of water and debris out of the hole and some 50-75 feet in the air.

Before each shot, a two man surveying crew had selected and staked the drill sites, laying out enough sites to stay well ahead of the drillers and the seismograph truck crews. The surveyor and his "rodman" assistant worked as a team, precisely measuring distances between holes, recording lat/lon coordinates and elevations. Sites were chosen in ditches along unpaved public farm to market roads, never on private property.

Following the surveyor was the drilling truck. The drilling tower would be winched into place over the marked stake, the truck leveled on pads, and the water- assisted drill completed its work in an hour or less, with rod sections added as the hole depth increased.

Our crew averaged about 15 "shots" each day, running the quarter mile each time, attaching detectors to the cable. After the shot, we ran the same quarter mile picking up the jugs, placing them back in their baskets. The truck then reeled the cable back onto its spool, while we picked up the jug baskets, and the crew moved on to the next hole to repeat the process.

We were picked up each morning at 7 AM at the Quick Lunch café in town and driven to the job site in the company van. It had no markings, in fact, none of the equipment carried the Texaco name. Clearly, Texaco did not want to bring attention to their exploration activity. We arrived at the job site by 8 and began the day's slog.

We took our lunch and snacks in paper bags, but cold drinks and water were provided during the day. Dehydration was a real danger. We worked in shorts and without shirts, sweating profusely in the hot, desert-like plains sun. Sun Screen products were not yet invented, but we did use tanning oils and wore big straw hats. Work gloves were a necessity, resulting in white hands at the end of very tanned arms. The oils only magnified the sun and attracted the ubiquitous dust, covering us with a sort of protective coating of soil.

The summer days offered plenty of daylight, and we worked the routine with only a 30 minute lunch break, until 6 PM, when van would take us back to the drop-off point in town. We worked Saturdays until noon, which was the standard work week. Saturday noon we were paid by check, too late to deposit at the bank. I remember an hourly rate of $1.50-$2. Per hour, a fine wage for the time.

As August came, the surveyor, a one-armed Texas A&M engineering graduate named Chuck, needed a rodman assistant, and, for reasons unknown to me, I was picked to become Chuck's partner on the surveying team. It was a great break and an incredible relief to get this "promotion", and off the drudgery of hustling jugs. And, I got a bump in pay of .25 per hour. At mid-day, I waved goodbye to my fellow crew members and followed Chuck to the survey truck, where I was to discover, to my delight, a new and much more agreeable routine.

Chuck had lost his right arm in a car accident years ago, and sometimes wore a shoulder-fitted prosthesis complete with glove covered hand. But on the job, he took the device off and left it in the truck because it interfered with his work. He had been right-handed, but trained himself as a lefty, and was very dexterous. He was single and popular with the women, loved a good story and also loved a few beers, which we sometimes shared from his private stock on the truck at the end of the day.

The survey crew started an hour later each morning, but logged in at the same time for pay purposes. Chuck would pick me up at home, and we would drive to a town not far from the sites to be surveyed, and have a leisurely breakfast at a local café, which Chuck bought with his meal allowance. Actual surveying began about 9:30 AM, and, working quickly, we laid out about 10 holes by noon. Then Chuck would either head back to town for lunch, or select a nice shady spot where we sat on the ground and had a picnic, followed by a brief nap. After a suitable rest, we laid out another five or six holes and called it a day. We were back in town by 5 PM, and with enough time and energy in the evening to perhaps go out on the town, as it were.

Surveying each hole, Chuck would set up his tripod and mount his equipment, while I drove the truck a quarter or half mile ahead and unfolded a 12 ft long, 6 inch width "rod" with elevation markings painted on it. He would have me move back and forth, left and right, then have me hold steady while he took the fix and had me place the stake. We had two way hand held radios for all this, and it worked very smoothly. After the fix, I folded the rod and drove back to retrieve Chuck, and we moved forward to the next area to be surveyed.

The survey job lasted just one month, after which I began college, and the entire Texaco seismograph operation moved to Brady, in central Texas. I was offered to chance to go with Chuck as his rodman, but was committed at that point to begin higher education, for better or for worse. I never saw Chuck again, or heard anything more about oil exploration around the Plainview area. There was some speculation about whether Texaco might have found good prospective drilling sights, but the geologist/engineer, Bob, never leaked a word about the structure of the earth there, or what his findings were.

Two months of jug hustling and one month on surveying had worked me into great physical condition. I went to my freshmen year at West Texas A&M, then called West Texas State, 15 pounds lighter than when the summer began, and with as great a tan as a sunburned red-head can retain.

REFLECTIONS AT 17

About to enter college, I wondered now what I had absorbed from my years of work and school and exposure to the people and culture of which I was a part. I had learned the value of hard work, which some might call the Protestant work ethic. I prefer to think of it as tenacity and endurance and taking pride in completing in good fashion whatever job or task is undertaken. These principles I had learned entirely from working closely alongside adults, a testament to the many advantages of apprenticeship in transitioning the young into real-world society and building respect for elders. More about this later.

Working on farms before automation gave me respect for these back-breaking laborers, as well as a lasting interest in ag economics and evolving technologies. I follow the markets for corn, cotton, wheat and soybeans just as I do the stock tables. I have family and friends who still earn their livings from the soil.

Various jobs opened my eyes to a spectrum of non-farm businesses, including food retailing, the fundamentals and economics of newspapering, small-scale manufacturing and customer service issues, and the technology of oil exploration. Getting these jobs on my own gave me confidence with adult business people. I learned there was nothing to fear in asking directly for a job.

Getting fired is another valuable experience. One Friday afternoon, I became irritated at J.C. Cook for some reason I cannot remember. For the first and only time, I called him J.C. instead of Mr. Cook, unforgivable for a 15 year old kid. His eyes got big and his face turned red, and her said, "You are fired", while writing out my last check. I left the store and went immediately home two blocks away, still angry but a little scared also. The party line into our house was ringing when I walked in the door. It was Mr. Cook, and he said this. " I think I made a mistake and I want you to forget what I said and come back to work". I also apologized and told him I regretted what I had done. The incident was never mentioned again, and I never again referred to him as anything other than Mr. Cook.

Wherever I worked, I have been most fortunate in having people take interest in me, volunteer their help and good advice. They have always thought well of my potential and encouraged me, perhaps seeing me as more capable than I saw myself.

This pattern was to continue throughout my working life. I had unforgettable and caring mentors like my older brothers, Cal and Raby, my uncle Dick Washington, Tom Vaughn and Mr. Miller at the Plainview Herald, John Shackleford at the Cook Company, Jim Wolflngton on his farm, Chuck the one-armed Texaco surveyor, and many others who were to come after. They were hands-on and outstanding teachers, more relevant in my young life than classroom teachers.

In the school/work equation, work had easily been my focus and the source of my most memorable lessons thus far. The values of formal education had been impressed upon me by very determined parents. Classroom instruction was to be honored and had its priority, but was as yet somewhat esoteric. World history, algebraic equations, english literature, biology and chemistry were all completed and filed distantly away for future use, unquestioned but compulsory intrusions on a schedule tilted toward learning by doing. Schooling in classrooms was to be respected greatly, but the immediate and winning example before us was of the work we had seen all our lives from our parents, and which we had heard emphasized very often at our family dinner table.

Conspicuously absent from either classroom or work were the perspectives of other cultures, other ethnicities, other religions, other languages, and the divergent ideas which naturally arise from the meshing of these social forces. I had witnessed but not subscribed to protestant evangelism. I had read enough of the old and new testaments to have serious and persistent questions about the concepts of monotheism or any theism. But these and other large issues were not for debate in this setting.

Warm friendships, both male and female, had become a conscious treasure. Bob Hollars, Bob Evans, John Long, Weldon Hayes, Don Dean were all good friends during these critical years. Participation in track and football satisfied the subconscious need to belong to and bond with a team, a tribe, a group of like-minded men. Similiarly, singing in the choir and quartet was also teamwork, and recognition there helped shape my self-identity and confidence. So did having a key part in our senior play.

At 17, perhaps greatest void was the sense of not having experienced what we knew about the world outside of Texas. World War two had created an awareness, but we did not live in such a mix, nor did our advisors and teachers come from such places. We knew about key battles in Europe and the Pacific, we knew to hate the "Japs", which really meant all Asians. We knew about combat deaths and returning bodies. We knew about the depths of human cruelty. We knew about sacrifice at home due to rationing of many products needed in the war effort.

At 17, a reasonable platform had been constructed, but building the real structure of life was to be a future and on-going project. As the idealistic young, we might have railed against the iniquity of racism at hand, but not even thinking of doing so is evidence of what humanity will accept as "normal" and "the way things are." As we now know, our acquiescence to ignorance and prejudice and human cruelty was not the exception but is endemic in youth the world over, and especially so if they have been indoctrinated into fervent political or religious causes by despotic propaganda.

BOOK THREE
College & Media Years

HIGHER EDUCATION AND A LIFE CHANGER

In early May 1951, a few weeks before high school graduation, I got the call out of the blue from Dr. Houston Bright, head of the music department at West Texas State University, and director of their coral program. I presume Dr. Bright had checked out my less than outstanding transcript with the school office, but he did not allude to it.

He called to offer me a four-year music scholarship to WT, covering tuition and books, but not living costs. I would be entitled to free voice and music lessons from Dr. Bright, who was a composer of some note. My obligation would be to sing in his choir and barbershop quartet, and tour with the group as it performed concerts at various school venues and functions in the West Texas area.

West Texas State had been founded forty years earlier primarily as a college to train teachers. Georgia O'Keefe, the artist, had been on the faculty there in 1917 and 1918, before becoming famous. A complete high school was located in the middle of the campus where education majors, men and women, did "practice" supervised teaching to specially selected students. The high school was a teaching laboratory.

West Texas was state subsidized and the tuition cost artificially low, meaning that my scholarship had little monetary but some prestige value. The school had earlier been known as West Texas Normal Teacher's college, but later broadened its undergrad and graduate curricula to achieve University status. Still, perhaps a third of students intended to teach after graduation. The school had an enrollment of just under two-thousand in 1951, and just over seven-thousand in 2010. In 1990, it merged with and became part of the sprawling and wealthy Texas A&M system.

Still uncertain about whether to go to college or where, and how to afford it, I accepted Doctor Bright's offer as the only inducement at hand. As I remember, I told my parents, but did not consult them beforehand. They were thrilled, of course. Neither they nor I understood enough about the nature of the scholarship to ask any critical questions. As it turned out, there really was no downside.

The college was just 60 miles North of Plainview, in the small city of Canyon, a few miles west of the iconic Palo Duro Canyon of Comanche Indian fame. The canyon is known as Little Grand Canyon, and remains a big tourist attraction, at least for Texans. I had no car, but could hitch a ride there with other students, or take the bus if need be. I had saved enough money from "jug hustling" to pay first semester room and board at Terrill Hall, an all male strip-motel type dorm in the middle of campus. I reported there after Labor Day, checked in at "Old Main", the central administration building, chose my courses, paid the dorm and meal ticket charges by check, and learned the names of my assigned dorm mates. Then it was on to the bookstore for the required texts.

The courses were required first year, but staggered Monday/ Wednesday/Friday, and Tuesday/Thursday/Saturday, each course meeting three days a week, with two labs, math and science, scheduled on Tuesday and Thursday afternoons. By choosing mostly morning courses, beginning at 8 AM, I had the afternoons free to work or study. Choir practice was twice weekly, with elective voice or music lessons scheduled privately with Dr. Bright.

My freshman year roommates at Terrill were two returning WW2 veterans on the GI bill. Jim Wright was 27 and a combat veteran of the European theatre. G.G. Gatten was 26 and had served in the Pacific. Jim was serious and studied a lot. G.G. was smart, but in the throes of a wartime hangover known as alcoholism. We managed to get along just fine, but rarely saw Gatten, who seemed never to sleep in the dorm in spite of the threat of bed check and a strict ban on alcohol anywhere on college grounds.

Amarillo, 17 miles to the North, was wet and full of bars, which G.G. frequented. G.G. also kept cold beer hidden in the toilet reservoir. Jim Wright was later to be elected Most Likely to Succeed, while his sister was elected most beautiful. G.G. Gatten dropped out at some point.

I developed friendships the first semester with Dan Haygood, who's family owned a department store in Floydada, Texas, and Bill Epps, who hailed from Pampa, Texas. They also lived in Terrill Hall and we shared some of the same classes, ate together in the cafeteria, and dated girls in Cousins hall who were friends. The three of us decided to become second semester roommates in Terrill, and made the switch in January.

The first semester had gone well and my grades were good. The academic experience was, for me, an extension of the high school format, focused on basic instruction with little give and take or debate. Socially, the scene was mostly student mixers and stag dances, on campus, free of alcohol, and monitored by dorm mothers and security.

My Plainview friend, John Long, was a third year student at WT, and invited me to join his fraternity, the Tri Taus, which I pledged during the fall semester. John was at the time entertaining a handsome young woman named Annette Wright, also from Plainview, who had chosen Southern Methodist University for college. Annette later transferred to West Texas, and she and John were married in the campus chapel. I was honored to be their best man. We have maintained a treasured, albeit long distance friendship all the years since. Annette's family, also with seven siblings, lived just up the street from mine in Plainview.

The Taus later became a chapter of Alpha Tau Omega national Greek letter fraternity. The pledge season was grueling and filled with hazing, which I tolerated in the name of "acceptance" into a tribe or herd. The members were campus leaders and good associations for me. Dan Haygood, my roommate, also pledged.

I chose a speech course under Professor Dr. Jack Walker, as one of my electives. At age 18, I could write well and had developed a deep voice. Dr. Walker took a special interest in my speaking and writing ability, and encouraged me to further develop them. We gave impromptu speeches on many subjects, and wrote and delivered critiques of various magazine or newspaper articles. The course was my first of its type, and, according to Dr. Walker, I excelled at it. To my surprise, this speech 101 course was to open a door in an entirely new direction not anticipated, and one which would be dominant in my life for the decade to follow.

I was nominated for and elected to the student senate during second semester, with my term to be served during sophomore year. Proving the value of organization, I had been proposed for the senate by my fraternity. This was to lead to a run for student body President during my second year, with a narrow loss to Martha Montgomery, a senior from Shamrock, Texas. After that brief contest, I was too busy working to continue an interest in student politics.

Work during the first semester finally took a back seat to study, and the results showed. Second semester, a group of us worked on farms in the area shocking feed, hauling hay, and doing odd jobs. We were paid by the hour.

KPAN, HEREFORD

At the end of the school year, Dr. Walker asked me to come by for a chat. He was complimentary, and told me of a job opening as an announcer at KPAN, a 250 watt daytime only radio station located in Hereford, Texas, a farm community of around 10,000 people some thirty miles west of Canyon. The station owners, Clint and Marshall Formby, had contacted Dr. Walker asking for candidates. Dr. Walker wanted me to go there and audition, and I immediately agreed. It was my first job prospect for the summer, and interested me. As I recall, another good friend and frat brother, Jerry Jones, was also auditioning at the same time.

I borrowed Dad's car and made the trip and met Clint Formby at the small frame structure on the edge of town, next to the tall transmission tower. The one-level building was cheaply built, and held just three small rooms. The office was also the entry hall, next to the control room with its console full of switches and knobs and large turntables and a suspended gold microphone. Through a large glass window was a studio with microphone on a stand, used when there were guests to be interviewed, or when Clint did his daily local news roundup.

Clint was a Texas Tech graduate only about 5 years older than I, and auditioned for him by cold reading United Press teletype news copy just in off the wire. I also read some commercials. He asked me to ad-lib some comments between records which were cued on the turntables. All this took place after sundown when the station was required to sign off the air.

Clint hired me and I reported to work the following Monday, this time driving my brother's red Plymouth, borrowed for the job. I rented a furnished room with a separate entrance on Sunday from a widow lady who's home was about a mile from the station, bought an alarm clock, and showed up at sunrise Monday morning. The announcer at the console was very busy as he read commercials, played music, and read news from the teletype when the schedule indicated.

As training, I sat in the control room with the announcer on shift, and observed how to control the turntables, turn on mikes, turn various knobs, or"pots", as they were called, to control audio volumes by keeping a close eye on the console volume needle to make sure it stayed within an acceptable range. I learned how to pull and organize and edit news copy, where and how to pull 30 inch records from the large Thesaurus Library, juggling one activity after another while a three minute music piece was in progress.

Finally, I was introduced to the daily sequential log, in looseleaf notebook form, placed in front of the announcer. The log book contained instructions on what was to happen minute to minute, held all the commercials to be read, indicated the time of each event and its name of each program. The log was the daily bible of the station. Each page was initialed as it was completed. The log was used as a record for billing advertisers. It was also kept as a record for the Federal Communications Commission. FCC rules prohibited any profanity or vulgarity, or any political commentary not paid for and identified as such.

Everything was totally live. There was no tape, no push-button access to cassettes, no recorded commercials, no cut-ins which gave relief to the shift announcer. Once daily, Clint would sit in the adjacent studio and read local Hereford news, primarily from the newspaper, and ad-lib about local events upcoming or perhaps charity fund-raisers or obituaries.

That day, at noon, I sat down at the console, relieved the morning shift announcer, and became the voice of KPAN for the next six hours. Six hands would not have been enough to manage my first day equivalent of a fire drill. If the log called for country music, it was up to me to select it from the library, chose the sequence, introduce it and play it. The patter was all mine, with very little coaching.

If the log called for news, I read it cold after ripping it from the teletype, then separating each story with the help of a ruler while trying to edit the mess into some logical order. The weather forecast was lifted verbatim from the local Hereford Brand newspaper. If the log called for jazz music or Big Band music, I picked it and programmed it. It was trial by fire the first day and each day thereafter, with not many questions asked or criticisms offered. Commercials were in the log notebook in sequence, and were read between records or news breaks, then initialed.

Marshall Formby was a lawyer in Plainview and former Texas Highway Commissioner. He was politically connected, had made a run for Governor and lost narrowly, with nephew Clint as his campaign manager. Marshall visited the station often, and we became well acquainted. It was a friendship which was to last until he died.

Through the hot summer, both Clint and Marshall encouraged me and made constructive suggestions. Clint often took me on calls when he went to visit advertisers to update their commercial copy. Soon, I was doing this job with clients during my off hours, and finding it helpful in understanding what advertisers wanted. It was hands-on and as close to the heart of small business as one can get.

Clint and his wife, Margaret, and Marshall and wife, Charlene, sometimes invited me in their homes for meals. Marshall introduced himself to my Dad in Plainview, and, according to Dad, always had good things to say about me.

After hours, I found four walls confining, and often went to the local restaurant evenings. The owner and waitress came to recognize me knew I was with KPAN, and treated me with special meals. I developed several friends locally, among them Randy Thomas, who's family owned the local drug store, and Sue Smith, a young friend of the Thomas family, who I dated from time to time. There were also students from WT that I knew who lived in Hereford, and I heard from a number of them over the summer. Some 30 years later, my oldest brother, Cal, became the golf professional at the Hereford municipal golf course, and met several people in the town who had known me when I spent the summer there.

Dr. Jack Walker also came to visit over the summer and got reports on how I was doing. Later, when I went on to work for larger stations in the area, including the local NBC television and radio affiliate in Amarillo, he invited me down to speak to his classes about the reality of TV and radio, and gave me much more credit than I deserved. Still later, after I had graduated, Dr. Walker offered me the use of his rustic cabin in the Colorado ski country, where I took my parents for a week of summertime camping and fishing.

The Hereford months and the grounding in small radio served me extremely well as I moved on to larger stations. I found out that radio was something I could do well; that I could work with my brain as well as my hands; that I could multitask. I could look back on my entire work history, and credit all of it with enabling me to wade into a new and strange work environment without hesitation, simply doing the best I could, and never stopping to think negatively about my capability to do the work.

Clint Formby died of cancer in the Summer of 2010, still owner of KPAN, almost 60 years since I worked for him that summer, but we stayed in touch periodically, and I visited him in his office in the Fall of 2008, where we remembered details of that time long ago. Margaret Formby had died years earlier, and Clint had already been battling cancer for several years. His son, Chip, is now in charge of the station.

Interesting to me is that I cannot recall what salary or hourly wage I earned on this or most of my jobs. I have to believe that the pay was therefore less important than the fact of having and holding the job. That was the thing to be proud of. "Make a Good Hand" first and foremost, and the pay will follow, as my dear Mother said often to her sons as they went out the door.

You might like to know that my friend Jerry Jones, who didn't get the job, enjoyed a very successful career as a Dallas attorney, having finished high in his class at the University of Texas Law School. Jerry and wife Billye, remain good friends today.

THIS IS KVOP, PLAINVIEW

Back in school for my sophomore year at WT, I elected to move a mile west of campus to the Hangar House, an informal frat house dominated by a number of my ATO brothers. We were two to a room, and my roomy was Garland Parks, a senior from Wheeler, Texas. There were four bedrooms and two baths upstairs, where we lived, while Mr. and Mrs. Hangar occupied the first floor. John Long, Jerry Jones, Hallie Earthman, Bill Karnes were all seniors, and had quietly taken many liberties with Mrs. Hangar's rules of no drinking or carousing. We were not subject to campus rules of inspection, but Mrs. Hangar posted her own list of behaviors she expected. There were no women allowed, no loud noise, no group parties. The no loud noise rule was observed much of the time. Rent was due every Friday.

Of the aforementioned, only Karnes and I worked regularly. He barbered his way through college in a shop on the edge of the campus. Some study took place in the house, but there was also ample time for the usual preoccupations of college men.

I worked weekends, having secured a job at KVOP in Plainview as the Saturday and Sunday announcer at the 250 watt Mutual network affiliate. The station signed on at 6 AM and off at 11 PM, and had three announcing shifts to cover the longer hours. I got the job by approaching

Kermit Ashby, the manager, and touting my KPAN resume. He knew my Dad, who by this time was an advertiser on KVOP, selling his real estate listings for farms and ranches. Dad had thirty minutes five days at week at 7:30 AM, and read and talked about his listed properties in a folksy voice. I suspect his ad dollars swayed Mr. Ashby's decision.

I drove the red Plymouth home on weekends to work at the station and stayed with my folks. Again, the shift announcer did what the daily station log told him. At Christmas season, one of my jobs was to read "letters to Santa", with me pretending to be Santa in my phoniest "Ho Ho Ho voice." I did this between Christmas music by Gene Autry or Bing Crosby or the Andrews sisters, and readings of Christmas poems. The letters were authentic and plentiful, and the feedback to my hopelessly silly act was mostly positive. Of course, commercials for local merchants selling toys and other Christmas wares were sandwiched into the show.

KVOP was owned by a gentleman named Bill Harpole, who came around only occasionally, but was never "on air." As I grew up in Plainview during junior high and high school years, I had listened to and mimicked various station announcer's melodious voices, including one named Keith, and another named Doug Sewell. Doug still worked at KVOP in late 52. On the network, Gabriel Heater gave and analyzed the national and international news.

In J.B. Oberthier's hobby shop , I had learned in 8th grade how to build and fly fairly complex free flight and U controlled model airplanes. I also learned to build crystal set radios from a spool of copper wire wrapped around an empty tennis ball canister, and solder the wire ends to the base of a quarter-sized crystal, purchased from the hobby shop. Also attached to the crystal was a lead wire connected to a headset, and an antenna line with safety pin on the end which hooked onto a metal window screen next to the head of my bed. The screen served to amplify and strengthen the KVOP signal.

With my brothers in the Navy, I now slept alone in a bed for the first time in my life. I could lie in bed with lights out, hook the radio up, and listen to KVOP until sign-off at 11. It was a form of magic, and required no electric power. In the days before television, this entertainment late at night was transforming. While the announcers played music and made comments, imagining them in the studio in front of a microphone, surrounded by hundreds of records, transmitting their voices across thousands of radio sets, was to be magically transported to a world beyond Plainview. As circumstances unfolded, I had now become one of those magic radio voices.

During my sophomore year, when the Taus nominated me to run for student body president, the campaign was basically a popularity contest, with neither Martha Montgomery or me running on a platform with identified issues. Sandwiched in to my work schedule, I met with two or three groups asking for their vote, but gave them no particular reason to vote for me. There were no debates between us, no banners, no campaign managers or staff. There were no assembly speeches, no rallies, not much of anything except a vote after perhaps a three week campaign. Both our efforts were not distinguished.

The loss taught me something about the value of organization. If ever I had a chance to repeat such an experience, I would devise and execute a plan, ask for help, work a strategy. I learned that I could not sit back and wait for something magical and good to happen. I had to take the lead and make it happen.

It also turned out that Martha Montgomery did a good job as student body president, and in her senior year. I suspect that I would not have had the time to devote to the job that she did, so things turned out best for the school.

The job at KVOP became full time the Summer after my second college year, and I found myself in my parent's home once again. I signed on the station at 6 every morning, and finished my shift around noon. The other announcers and I rotated shifts after each week or two, so I had a turn at afternoon and evening as well.

A professional minor league baseball team had started in Plainview, and KVOP agreed to broadcast their home games live from a local park, and broadcast their away games by "recreating" the play by play. This was accomplished by reenacting each play as it was transmitted to the studio by teletype from the out of town game site. I was selected to do both the live play by play from a remote booth at the local field, and to recreate the away games using the technique described above. It was my first foray into live sports broadcasting.

I had never played organized baseball, but knew the rudiments. The team had a 30 game schedule, half of them away. The teams pieced together ex college players and some who had light experience with major league farm teams, but the talent was pretty weak overall. At the same time, local games were well attended by families, and there were the usual hot dogs and soft drinks, and some events which showcased kids and the community. Again, television hadn't yet crowded out all other evening attractions, and interest in the team was high. Plainview had never had a professional team of any kind before. Town fathers thought pro baseball would help to put Plainview on a bigger map and become more attractive as a place to live.

The live broadcast routine called for me to be in the broadcast booth at the field an hour before game time. This prep time was needed to get updated rosters, talk to coaches and managers, and organize commercials to be read. I also got pitching and batting stats from each team, and tried to give some thought to attendance on hand, and local color which might be worked in.

After the recorded national anthem was played, play by play ensued, with me following and describing each pitch , each hit, each walk, each run, plays in the field, and each innings results. Commercials were read after each half inning.

In baseball tradition, each defensive player was numbered, and each had his own chart of what happened when fielding. If the batter hit a ground ball to the pitcher, and the pitcher threw him out at first, the out would be recorded as 1 to 3. If the batter lined a ground ball to the second baseman, it was recorded as 4 to 3. The right fielder was number 9, center fielder number 8, left fielder 7, short stop 6, and third base 5. When the order began rotating again, it was easy to glance at the graph and see what the batter had done his previous at bats.

I worked through nine innings this way, calling plays and reading commercials, offering comments about the weather or incidents in the stands, or the form of the pitchers, or action in the bullpen, or antics of the managers, or batting stats. It was a one man balancing act and a trial by fire, but surprisingly easy, with the numbering and graphing system, to keep track of action on the field. If there were rain delays or rain-outs, I sent it back to the studio to the announcer on duty, who played music until the situation was resolved.

Away games were called play by play from the studio, with crowd noise on a record playing in the background. I had first inning results in hand before beginning the broadcast, and, using the same graphing technique, called each play as if I were at the field, whacking a pencil on the table to simulate the crack of a bat, describing each play from information contained in the numbering system for each player. The broadcast was obviously fake, but listeners had the feeling of being at the game and seeing it unfold. My job was to make it as realistic as possible, bringing alive the data on a piece of paper.

I became adept at re-creating games, leaning hard on powers of description and imagination which, frankly, were inventions of the moment.. Farther on in life, I learned that Ronald Reagan had used the same game recreation technique, working for a small station in Illinois.

Later, the technique came in handy when I was asked to audition for Armed Forces Radio by re-creating a baseball inning. Little did they know I had done this for most of an entire season of West Texas/ New Mexico minor league baseball. I got the job, about which there will be more later.

A GLANCE AT ACADEMIA

Beginning third year college, and on the verge of starting a new full time job at KAMQ radio in Amarillo, I chose a major of Business management, thinking it to be perhaps the least demanding and time consuming option available. My college goal had become one of getting the bachelor's degree as soon as possible, with as little fuss as possible. I scheduled all morning courses, starting at 8 AM, leaving afternoons and evenings open for work.

Second year accounting and Statistics were two courses which took considerable time with hand-written practice sets and punch-key calculators, creating spread sheets by physically rotating a wheel to the next column requiring numbers. Modern accounting software automatically posts from T accounts and tabulates and verifies totals in double entry systems, and programs like Excel and others can extend data into useful computer models of almost any statistical thesis. In one generation, these "green eye shade" back office professions have been liberated from the deadly boring and inefficient data entry requirements of old.

I was to learn later that basic courses in strategy, finance, market research, and personnel management utilized the same texts and covered the same ground as undergrad courses at larger institutions such as Indiana University and the University of Texas. Professors at these sorts of prestige schools were better known, and often authored some texts, but the undergraduate grounding at West Texas was solid for those students applying themselves.

With my interests clearly fixed toward broadcasting, together with the need to pay college expenses, I thanked Dr. Bright for his help and ended my music scholarship. He was not surprised. I had sung base in his choir for two years, as well as in his barbershop quartet. It had been a difficult schedule to manage, often requiring swapping shifts with other announcers, or catching up on course assignments when the choir toured. Good friends were the dividend from my association with the music department, including Joe Coleman, tenor, Troy Thermond, baritone, Bill Epps, lead, all members of my quartet. The choir and quartet were good recruiting and public relations tools for WT with regional high school seniors. But, as a non-music major, my time commitment had to be elsewhere.

THIS IS KAMQ, AMARILLO

After the summer of baseball in Plainview, Dr. Jack Walker, my friend and mentor, again had a suggestion. He knew the owner of KAMQ, in Amarillo, a Mr. Robert Houck, who he met through Claude Fuller, chief announcer at KAMQ, and a former speech student. Dr. Walker had learned that KAMQ needed a staff announcer, and sent me to interview. KAMQ was a 1000 watt full time station with some live programming of music groups, mostly country and western. There I met Webb Smith, the station manager, who hired me that day. The job was only 20-30 minutes from campus, and well within my experience base at KPAN and KVOP. I became the afternoon and/or evening shift man.

My brother's red Plymouth had been shipped off to my oldest brother, Cal, stationed in Japan, where he sold it for three times its U.S.

value. Post war Japan needed American cars, and the Navy allowed servicemen to bring their personal cars over, freight free. Now without a car, I hitched a ride to the job at noon after completing morning classes, most often with fellow speech student Zell Sorrell, a beautiful older lady who's husband owned a Ford dealership in Amarillo. Easy to get to work, but hitch-hiking back to campus late at night was a challenge.

The station was also a Mutual affiliate, but much more upscale than the two earlier radio jobs. The two large studios on each side of the control room were outfitted with a variety of microphones for multiple guests or live music groups. It had a full-time news director, an ego driven narcissist named Bill Johns, a fastidious and aloof eccentric who insisted on being introduced as if he were a Hollywood celebrity. Johns wore a bushy but carefully trimmed mustache, and elevated heels. He felt this persona and his deep voice and Paul Harvey mimicked delivery would surely land him in the big time. I have no idea if he succeeded, but note that most personalities of his type do not.

KAMQ also had a two-man sales staff who brought in advertising dollars on an obviously larger scale than I had seen before. The station was full time and 1000 watts, with a significantly larger geographic coverage and better audience demographics. Amarillo was a city of about 150,000, of which an important component was Amarillo air force Base, housing several thousand airmen and officers and their families. One announcer/ disk jockey on staff was in fact an airman from New York stationed at the base.

Local businesses catered to base personnel. The hottest nightclub in town, the Aviatrix, slanted its entire pitch to drinking age airmen and their wives and girlfriends. It had large capacity and could afford big bands like Tommy Dorsey, Stan Kenton, and Billy May. These bands and their vocalists were the rage with students in the early 50's, and Saturday night at the Aviatrix dancing to big bands while mixing bring-your-own whiskey and Coca Cola, was the in thing.

My shift at KAMQ alternated between afternoons, 1 to 6 PM, and evenings, 6 to midnight. Signing off at midnight, then thumbing my way back to Canyon involved walking a mile to reach the three lane 17 mile highway connecting the two towns, and hoping a friendly trucker would have mercy on me. It worked most of the time, but meant I didn't get to bed until well after 1 in the morning. And its good to remember that there were no cell phones in the event something went awry. 7 AM was wake-up for the 8 o'clock class. Study time was nil.

I happened to mention to my folks what I was doing, and the phone went quiet. The next day produced one of the biggest surprises of my college life. My folks showed up in Canyon with a 1949 gray four-door Plymouth sedan, handed me the keys, and insisted I stop hitch hiking. It was totally unexpected, but welcomed, and I readily agreed to their terms.

Jess Richardson was KAMQ's play by play guy for football, and Jess asked me to do color and commercials for him. He knew I had done some play by play baseball and had played football. It was a pretty good fit for regional high school games. My Friday night shift schedule often had to be swapped with another staffer, and I was paid something extra for the sports broadcast. We did an entire Fall schedule of the Amarillo Sandies football team, home and away, no studio re-creations.

Several nights per week, I did a soft jazz program called "Joe's junction", from 10 to 11 PM. I chose soft and easy vocalists like Sinatra, Jo Stafford, Patti Page, Rosemary Clooney, Ella Mae Morse, Ella Fitzgerald, Sarah Vaughn, Keeley Smith, and Eartha Kitt. Anita O'Day was also a favorite. I boned up on their biographies and perhaps the history of the songwriter, and spoke limited words in soothing tones. The program had a nice following back on campus, during an important study hour, and before TV killed nighttime radio.

As before, close friends came out of the experience. Ralph Wayne, a fellow student, joined the announcing team, and I socialized a lot with he and his wife, Sue. Ralph later became an elected State Representative to the Capital in Austin, and, after that, a full time lobbyist there. Claude Fuller, Webb Smith, and Bob Hauck remained friends, as did a local country/disk jockey and his wife who called themselves "Smoky Joe and Dixie", and were good entertainers. I often stopped by to visit them long after I had left the station. The station had a strong country following, and Little Jimmy Dickens and other "Opry" stars would perform live in the studio when in town for a gig.

IN THE INTERLUDE BEFORE TV: ON WEALTH CREATION

Focusing on work and the work ethic, I have come to believe, is in direct conflict with achieving wealth. The emphasis on acquiring and keeping jobs is a manifestation of avoiding debt; of adequate cash flow weekly or monthly to pay the mortgage, educate children, secure food and transportation, and save some remainder. It is the obsession of those with little, and those trained in early life to meeting obligations with head held high, never having to admit defeat by debt, and regarding debt as immoral and shameful. Even the Bible says "the borrower is servant to the lender." George Washington, Ben Franklin, Thomas Jefferson all warned against debt, as did Shakespeare. Benjamin Disraeli said, "debt is a prolific mother of folly and of crime."

Agrarian mentality falls in this category. Living off the land has always meant sacrificing, and hoping that this year, the risk will pay off large enough to carry a family through the inevitable hard times ahead. Much of urban mentality is the same. Dependency on employment by others, of counting pennies carefully and allocating them wisely, of insisting children earn their keep, and of never daring to splurge on frivolity, of relying on extended family or union bosses for help if needed, of worrying always about illnesses destroying savings.

Agreed, personal household and installment debt should be minimized and paid on time. But debt to finance a business dream is another matter entirely.

Wealth creation people strive for debt. They think as business owners; as entrepreneurs. They look over the top for an idea to build on. Hedge funds, investment bankers, private equity funds, are all designed and built utilizing debt. Their energy is invested not in earning an hourly wage, except for short learning periods. They embrace and seek debt and partnerships to build out their dream, whether a restaurant, a bicycle shop, a software concept, or a retail chain.

The billionaires in this world are not comfortable working for others; of working to make ends meet. Their goals are always on wealth creation, not near term obligations. They understand the corporate structure, of ways to build and present a plan, and search out sources of investment capital. For the most part, they prepare themselves with educational credentials needed to open the doors to capital. But many are not academically trained, particularly in finance. Richard Branson, Barry Diller, and Carlos Slim are examples. Many began poor and still grasped concepts and ideas worthy of growth and wealth creation.

The Warren Buffetts of the world are people who's purposes were always for themselves, not working for others. They wanted from the beginning to create wealth, and knew that large-scale debt was the only way to do so. They know that not every idea will work out, and are not afraid of failure and loss of capital. They often simply start over. Debt is an essential means to the end. And capital will follow them to the next venture.

My own concentration on work has been distracting. Instead of working on the farm, my thoughts might have focused on owning the farm.

Rather than work in a factory for an hourly wage, why not think of taking the knowledge and owning the factory. Announcing or sportscasting on broadcast stations owned by others should have been a wake-up call to think of and plan for ownership of a chain of stations. I had the knowledge, but had pegged myself as an employee, not an owner.

Having worked in a newspaper and learned something of its functions and economics, why did I not dream of owning that newspaper or starting a rival newspaper or magazine. Fundamentally, the reasons for not doing any of these things were that I was trained as a worker, to think of making a good hand; a good and honorable employee, and to avoid debt. I was therefore restricted by my own mentality, or perhaps lack of mentoring at an early age.

How is a young person to avoid trapping himself or herself mentally. Three thoughts. First, become an entrepreneur early, whether a lemonade stand, a lawn service, or selling used toys. Second, enlarge every idea with other people's money until the idea has reached its optimum level of development. Don't ever be afraid to borrow money in support of a good business idea that you can articulate to parents, banks, friends, or hedge funds. Third, study corporate and personal debt financing as early as you can comprehend it. Learn to understand and set up a corporate structure. Learn to read and understand a balance sheet and income statements, which, in the final analysis, is all stock and bond analysts do for a living.

Do not think of commercial debt as a moral question or issue. Debt is a societal need, and, along with equity financing, is the only way to experience large-scale success in our capitalist system. Use debt, think ownership, train yourself this way, and your odds of becoming wealthy will be far greater than the certainty of not becoming wealthy, thinking conventionally.

THIS IS KGNC TV, AMARILLO

In early Spring of 1954, while working my shift at KAMQ, Larry Filkins, chief announcer at KGNC TV and Radio, called to offer me a staff announcer's job there. The TV station had gone on the air with a test signal in March of 53, the first in the Panhandle of Texas, and their existing staff needed some additional manpower. Filkins said he had been listening to me on the air for awhile, and liked what he heard. He asked me to come over for a talk after work. The call was a complete surprise!

KGNC Radio was the 10,000 watt voice that blanketed the Plains in all directions, East to well into Oklahoma, South to well past Plainview, 75 miles away, North past Clayton, New Mexico, and West almost to Tucumcari, New Mexico. KGNC had long had the biggest signal footprint, the best demographics, and the most respected image among all broadcast media in the Panhandle/Plains. Part of this was because of its affiliation with the Amarillo Daily News and Globe Times, the twice-daily newspaper and big gorilla of print media. The newspaper had a large reporting and editing staff, the most complete publishing operation west of Dallas, and, like KGNC radio and TV, was owned by the large and oil and gas rich Whittenburg dynasty.

KGNC Radio and TV, in turn, gave a longer reach to the newspaper's news gathering talents. KGNC had a broadcast studio directly in the middle of the newspaper editorial room, from which the broadcast staff could pick up and report fresh copy before the print edition hit the streets. The operations were overlapping and highly complimentary, commanding higher advertising rates from local and regional businesses, and also attracting combination national advertisers who bought their media through big city agents. KGNC Radio and TV were represented nationally by the Katz Agency, in New York City, who funneled significant ad volumes from national brands to the Texas Panhandle.

The Whittenburg's also owned broadcast and newspaper media in Lubbock, 125 miles to the South. Together, their properties were the "must buy" for clients with products to sell in that part of the world.

KGNC Radio and TV had full time staff of over 100, and the latest equipment. Staff announcers did not operate broadcast consoles. Engineers took care of that. The station had a large copy department, an extensive art department, separate and large sales staffs for Radio and TV, and a cadre of Directors calling the shots on every program. Creative programming talent, charged with coming up with new programming, was on staff. The station also had a variety of independent talent signed up to do various daily or weekly shows.

The news department was headed by Bob Izzard, a decorated P-47 pilot with 150 missions and several Oak Leaf Clusters attached to his Distinguished Air Medal. His Father, Wesley Izzard, came to Texas from Illinois to accept the job as Publisher of the papers. Wes Izzard had a daily front-page column, A to Izzard, and was widely regarded in hard news circles and as a businessman.

A key programming and music talent was Weldon Bright, brother of Dr. Houston Bright of the West Texas State music department. Another musician/announcer on staff was Gordon Suits, who called himself "Red Robbin" on the air. KGNC radio employed its own meteorologist, Dan True, as well as a PHD agronomist named Cotton John Smith, who gave news early each morning about agricultural developments and commodity market prices. There were other personalities, "Uncle Jay" among them, who came in several times weekly to perform.

Filkins introduced me to a number of staff, made the formal offer, and we agreed on a start date which allowed two weeks notice to Mr. Hauck at KAMQ. He understood that I was a college junior and scheduling would have to work around that fact. We shook hands on it, and that was that! In West Texas, this was the pinnacle.

The new job and driving to and from campus convinced me that I should rent an apartment in Amarillo, and I quickly did so with a couple of students I knew. I could close out the night shift at midnight, and be in my apartment in 15 minutes, but had the reverse commute to campus for early class the next morning.

What neither Filkins nor I knew when he hired me was that appearing on TV, doing commercials for local jewelers, clothiers, and banks, would quickly become part of my assignment, all for extra money per ad. All TV commercials were done live, so I had to go to the studio at off hours whenever the commercial happened to be scheduled by the station's traffic department. I sometimes made two or three extra round trips to do TV commercials, before my regular 6 hour shift began. So it was important that I live close. We had no videotape in those years.

Later, I would play the role of roving news reporter, taping and filming local news from newspaper copy leads, and reporting full 30 minute newscasts live on TV during weekends.

But it started on the radio side, in a broadcast booth, being cued by a Director, aided by an engineer in the control room. Many commercials were pre-recorded, or read by a second announcer always on duty. There were also frequent news breaks from NBC, and the all important evening news with H.V. Kaltenborn, one of NBC's best known wartime news analysts and correspondents. Announcers at KGNC did not read the news. The atmosphere was worlds away from the isolated work-alone environment of the other stations in my experience.

I attended training sessions given by Dr. Wallace Clark, an on-call expert on pronunciations of difficult proper names and foreign places. We were expected to emote clearly and correctly at all times. It was Dr. Clark who was sent to coach the naive country boy out of me when, on the air, I read Sir Laurence Olivier's name as Sir Laurence Oliver. Bob Watson, the station's professional manager and broadcast veteran, was a perfectionist, and one wrong word such as this meant a call to the broadcast booth from "Pappy" Watson, for an unambiguous and often heated correction. He seemed always to be listening and taking notes.

Trained on the stage, "Pappy" had come to Amarillo in 1935 as manager of the Interstate Theatre on Polk Street , which staged dramas and dance revues. His wife, known professionally as Dixie Dice, taught dance and drama to young women students. When AM radio began in Amarillo, Pappy was part of the original cast, and he stuck with broadcast the remainder of his life.

But as before, it was follow the log exactly, initial the log, no off color remarks, ever. The cardinal sin, of which I was never guilty, was to be late for your shift. The broadcast air did not wait.   That training has kept me on time all my life, and taught me that never being late is a mark of respect for those you are meeting or working with. I have low tolerance to this day for tardiness, no matter what the excuse.

I began my first shift in the radio broadcast booth with Gordon Suits as my team announcer on duty. The room was about 8 X 10 feet, with two microphones affixed to each side of a chest high cabinet, looking toward the engineer through the glass. Announcers had to stand upright and flip a waist-high switch to turn on each microphone, and read the copy from a book placed between the microphones on top of the cabinet. I would read one commercial or promo, then Gordon would do a station break and read another message of some type before going back to the program in progress. There were still some network drama and comedy shows on night radio then, so the announcers on duty functioned like caretakers of the log, keeping everything on track until sign off at midnight.

Fiber Magee and Molly, Lamont Cranston and the Shadow, Amos

and Andy, Red Skelton, Jack Benny, George and Gracie Burns, and Bob Hope, were highly rated by Nielson. Families still gathered around their radios at night.

This night shift pattern continued five nights a week, with me doing some homework in the booth between breaks. There was no other time. Filkins thought he was doing me a favor by sticking me on the night shift, and, I was a new hire, single, and available nights. I finally insisted on having some afternoon shifts so that I could maintain a reasonable college routine.

I got acquainted with Margaret Abrams, a talented writer on staff, who was writing and producing a new classical music program called "Music Modal and Modern". She asked me to be the narrator, and I agreed. The audiotaped show ran one hour from 2 to 3 each Sunday afternoon. Radio was still the dominant broadcast medium. Football on Sunday TV was in the distant future. People actually listened to radio, and became fans of the show. I learned a great deal about classical music from Margaret, having the opportunity weekly to listen to great music and learn about the great composers and orchestras. Names like Dvorak, Tchaikovsky, Mussorgsky, Mahler, Debussy, Wagner, Rachmaninoff, Weill, and more modern composers like Bernstein, became familiar to me.

Summer came and with it a more flexible schedule and more free time. I was now crossing over frequently from the radio side, across the building to the TV studios, doing more on-air commercials. As commercial "talent", I was asked by the sales department to visit clients who's commercials I appeared on, to get acquainted with their management and their business. These were useful visits, with helpful suggestions from them. I felt knowing something about the nature of their business gave me a better perspective to represent them. The visits with clients were time consuming, but good public relations.

Grady Hazlewood, former State representative and owner of

Hazlewood Dairy, invited me to look over his operation and then ad-lib his commercials on TV. Hazlewood bottled and sold milk in the Amarillo metropolitan area.

I became a spokesman for Hub Clothiers, the largest men's clothing retailer on downtown Polk street. I wore their suits and sports-jackets on the air, and helped write their commercials.

I did commercials for the First National Bank, 8th and Tyler, in Amarillo. FNB was the largest Amarillo bank. I got to know their CEO, Gene Edwards, and VP Frank Arnold, as well as their ad agency principals, Don Curphy and Bob Mills. The commercials were all about bank trust and confidence, and were on-camera, which meant I had to memorize them. If I screwed up a word or phrase, I had to ad-lib my way out of it. The Director in the control booth understood that glitches do happen when everything is live. There were no teleprompters.

I also did commercials for Midas Muffler, Butler commercial buildings, a hardware store, and a chain of lumber yards. I was 20 years old and the youngest of the staff, and was honored to be chosen by clients to speak for them. The experience of appearing live on television was one I could never have imagined, ever, and I am still amazed that the station and their customers placed that much trust in a young college student with my background. The freedom and scope that station management gave me astonishes to this day.

Television in 1954 was immediate and unforgiving. The "talent" either had to memorize every word in the commercial, if he was on screen the whole time, or prepare a large cheat sheet to read from, which could be taped to a leg of the camera or held by a technician. The commercial might be a break in a newscast, or a break in a network soap or drama or musical show. Talent had to be on standby the entire time period and ready.

Some sponsors bought entire shows or episodes which came to the station on film, and the talent would have beginning, middle and ending wrap-up commercials. Becoming a spokesman for a local advertiser took a lot of preparation, and the few extra dollars earned was more than justified.

Television was still black and white, and part time. There were simply not enough network-fed shows to stay on the air full time. Test signals appeared until 2 or 3 in the afternoon. Many daytime shows were created on the spot by local talent, intended for kids at home. Captain Kangaroo was just getting underway, and was very popular. Dave Garroway did the Today show on NBC, but then there was a network void until late afternoon.

Some Soap operas were beginning to creep into the schedule, but remained as radio serials for the most part. For filler, we had something called kinescopes, which depicted leading vocalists of the day singing one or more of their hits. These came to the station as short 16 mm films, and often were scratchy and poor quality. Later, with the advent of excellent quality video tape, entire programs were built around these taped performances, and the best know artists embraced the format

HERE WITH THE NEWS

In January 1955, mid-way through my senior year, Bob Izzard, the news Director, approached me about joining him in the news department and learning the basics of man-on-the-street remote reporting. Bob had checked this out with station management. News had always interested me, and I knew the basics of journalism from college classes. I also knew I could write pretty well, and, by this time, ad-lib reasonably. I accepted immediately, although it meant giving up the extra bucks I had been enjoying by doing commercials.

I had come to know and like Bob and his wife Kay. After his evening newscast, in which I did commercials, we would often go to the local watering hole and socialize, while he told legitimate and hilarious war stores. The news professional photographer, Bill Rheu, was usually with us.

Quickly, with a battery box over my shoulder and a mike and 16 mm wind-up camera in hand, I was driving to fender benders, chasing fire trucks and ambulances, interviewing people on the street, and doing feature stories about dogs and horses. The radio interview came first. Once it was securely on tape, I took film of the incident or interview, without narration. Then it was a rush to the film lab with two or three clips and a half-hour wait to get the film developed, then back to the station to write a narrative for the film for Izzard to deliver.

Next was a rush to the radio side and editing the tape in time for Izzard's radio news preceding the NBC evening news. I often introduced the radio story, cued the taped interview, then followed up with closing remarks, much in the mode of modern radio and TV reporters.

When Secretary of Agriculture Ezra Taft Benson came to town, Izzard paid me the ultimate compliment by assigning me to interview him. In this case, Bill Rhew shot the film and recorded the entire 10 minutes for both broadcast media, while a Globe Times reporter sat in an captured his own take for the afternoon edition of the paper. I naturally had a list of questions for Secretary Benson concerning agriculture policies of the Eisenhower administration and how they might impact the most important industry in West Texas. Izzard no doubt helped me construct the list, but I do no remember him doing so.

The secretary had a couple of aids with him, but there was no pretentious motorcade or grand security detail. Apparently no one thought it necessary to protect a mere cabinet officer with such attention-grabbing ostentation. Mr. Benson had been a leader in the Mormon church and a leading supporter of Mr. Eisenhower's candidacy. In hindsight, the cabinet post was his reward, a fact of patronage I did not understand at the time.

In any event, the Secretary was patient and gracious, and, I think, a little surprised to be interviewed by a young kid rather than our most senior newsman. I did not retain a list of the questions asked, but presume a kinescope of the event remains in the station archives.

After graduation in late May, 1955, my news assignment became full time and more varied. I covered early morning and late day events as a remote reporter, occasionally doing a live on-the-spot report on radio, depending on the newsworthiness of the event, and how much time we had to set up for it.

A band of Gypsies visited Amarillo and set up camp on the edge of town. I did a remote broadcast with them, and managed to get comments from a few. They were perceived by local law enforcement to be a thieving and criminally inclined group, encouraged to leave the area very soon. As I recall, my story focused on artifacts and jewelry included in their burial caskets. Definite human interest, with a need for everyone to know!!

I was on hand live for the opening of a new shopping center, newsworthy in that it represented new advertising potential. A burning warehouse on the South side of town warranted Sunday morning live coverage. Extreme weather, a part of the history and lore of West Texas, was always a good topic, and especially if measurable rain fell in this normally drought-stricken region. Cotton John Smith, the station's colorful ag expert, had to be consulted and quoted after rain or snow or damaging winds.

I did a live remote from Cal Farley's Boys Ranch, some 30 miles west of town, and interviewed Roy Rogers backstage after his performance in a fund-raiser. Boy's Ranch took in young homeless and delinquent boys, gave them a home and taught them the value of work, provided them on-sight with a high school education, and placed many of them in colleges. Mr. Farley, a radio personality in his own right, set up the charity, donated the ranch land, and launched the effort with tireless fund-raising. He had great success with hundreds of boys over the years, and was strongly supported by all media in the area as well as family foundations and trusts.

I began doing newscasts in Bob Izzard's slot early mornings and on weekends and some mid-day reports, on both AM and TV. The experience of selecting my own stories, editing my film and audio and texts, writing and delivering the news start-to-finish, was invaluable and quite rare, which I recognized. Would be TV/radio journalists rarely have such a range of opportunity on which to hone their skills. This was the period Dr. Walker chose to invite me to speak to his classes, and the journalism department under Bill Lee, also asked me to meet with his students. I was complimented to be asked, but still a little anxious about what to say. I remember talking about the competition between broadcast and print media for ad dollars, and a little about news prep. Many in my audiences were older than I.

At the AM studio inside the newspaper, I gave daytime and evening radio news from a mix of Associated Press wire, and local newspaper reporter's efforts. I would walk through the editorial offices, picking up carbons of local stories just written, and edit the package into fifteen or 30 minute newscasts, which I learned to time correctly. To this day, my sense of the passage of time or of the time of day, without referring to a clock, is still close to being accurate. I attribute this to my years of work in radio and TV, and in timing newscasts, particularly.

While on duty at the newspaper broadcast booth, preparing for an evening newscast, the Associated Press bulletin declaring that President Eisenhower had just suffered a severe coronary attack. I tore the news off the teletype machine just in time to meet the 6 PM news start time. It was my lead story, of course. Problem was, I was not familiar with the word "coronary", and pronounced it "cronary". This misstep did not produce an immediate call from Pappy Watson, so I assumed it to be correct, until a reporter out in the editorial offices corrected me after the broadcast. No apparent permanent harm done, and thereafter, the correct pronunciation was used.

Reflecting on two years at KGNC radio and TV, having had a range of exposures I never anticipated, earning the confidence and trust of station management to the point that they were willing to let me make mistakes and even embarrass them and the station, made me grateful for their attitude and their helpfulness and friendship. My fellow announcers, the sales department, traffic department, art department, Directors, Writers, Producers, outside talent, the accounting department, and management had all believed in me.

I felt warmth and support in that setting, as I have in most jobs. held. And I also realized that, once again, work took precedence over study; that doing was my major source of learning; that apprenticeship trumped textbooks; that peer approval was far more important to me that academic approval. It was an unconscious leaning that I would later learn should be more evenly balanced.

BOOT CAMP AND KOREA

Civilian radio and TV in a hands-on, for-profit business, was soon to be my ticket into Armed Forces Radio. During college, draft deferments followed a passing transcript, while immediate active duty through the selective service draft followed failure to maintain decent grade point averages. With the Korean War in the fighting and dying phase through most of 1953, the incentive to stay in school required little explaining to a student of average intelligence. With graduation, deferments automatically ended, and it was only a matter of time until my draft number would float to the top of my draft board's list.

Reality struck in November 1955, when I was ordered to report for a physical in preparation for being drafted into the United Sates Army. I had considered enlisting in the Navy like my older brothers, but the four-year Navy commitment was unattractive versus two years as a draftee in the Army. At one point, I flew to Albuquerque and tested for regular Navy Officer's candidate school. I was advised that quotas for regular OCS were filled, but qualified for fighter pilot training school as a route to a commission. I had visions of carrier landings, and said no again.

J.B. Linn, known on the air as Uncle Jay, a World war two pilot and KGNC staff celebrity with strong political connections suggested that he could get me an appointment to the first class of the newly chartered Air Force Academy, in Colorado Springs. Pursuing this made no sense to me, having just tolerated four years of college, and having a degree in hand.

In college, I had two mandatory years of R.O.T.C., and, had I continued it, would have been commissioned as a second lieutenant on graduation, with three years additional to serve. I didn't like the regimentation of R.O.T.C., or the three year requirement, and said no. I decided to take the draft option.

My new 1954 Ford coupe was left with my parents in Plainview. I passed the physical and reported to Amarillo in late November, with train tickets to Monterrey, California and Fort Ord, for basic army training of eight weeks. The usual induction routine followed, and the standard eight weeks of mostly physical training progressed uneventfully. Formations, marching, vaccinations, rifle training and target practice, spit and polish, discipline, bivouacs, inspections, chow lines, and fatigue followed.

It was my first real experience with interracial living. There were soft white guys who had never worked who had a tough time with the physical demands. There were African/Americans who performed well, and some from urban settings who rebelled at imposed discipline. There were Jewish boys from New York who understood the rules would have to be followed, and navigated basic with humor and tolerance. But the toughest guys in basic were farm boys, followed by the hard knock kids from Puerto Rico and Hispanic neighborhoods of New York, Chicago, and Los Angeles. They were accustomed to much worse than this regimen.

Most of our training cadre were WWII vets who stayed in the army to get their 20-year retirement benefits, and most were African/ Americans. They had no time for whiners, regardless of race. Many were combat hardened. Some had just returned from Korea after hostilities ceased there. They knew survival training and were determined that we be prepared for combat.

Early on, I was appointed a squad leader, perhaps because I was 22 by now and older than many. I was never gung-ho military, but figured to make the best of the situation. We had competition between squads and platoons, on the range, in the barracks, and best in inspections. Some thought of it as fun; others resented it.

It was easy to see the need for cohesion in the ranks, but building an obedient team from such a disparate group of boys and men was both the army's goal and its biggest challenge. A few were deemed psychologically unable to serve, unable to bend to demands of authority or the physicality required. Others were held back to finish with a later group. Disease knocked out a couple. And a couple went to the stockade for fighting.

One was actually shot with a stray bullet as we fulfilled the requirement of crawling under a blanket of machine gun fire over a specified distance. As a squad leader, the guys I saw eye to eye with most were a couple of Hispanic ex boxers, two smart and funny Scandinavian college grads from Washington state, named Vernon Schaat and Menton Sveen, and an Oklahoma University grad named Ray Stevens.

At the end of basic, several of us were again offered a chance to go to Officer's Candidate school in Fort Benning, Georgia, with a three-year obligation after graduation.

No thanks was the answer, and off I went to Fort Chaffee, Arkansas, for second eight weeks of basic as an artillery fire direction control specialist. This meant sitting in a control room back from the firing line, taking artillery shot pattern feedback from a forward observer, usually a short-lived second lieutenant, and calculating the degrees of elevation or lateral correction needed to hit the target. The crew manning the 105 mm Howitzer would then input the corrections manually on the gun, fire again, and get a final correction from the FO.

Fort Chaffee in January can be cold and wet, just as the Monterrey peninsula was in December. We had stacked bunk-beds in the barracks, and a coal-fed stove in the center of the Quonset. Rotating details brought raw coal periodically to feed the monster. Coal dust covered everything on Fort Chaffee, just as printer's ink blankets everything in a newspaper composing room.

Basic discipline assumed, the nonsense was dispensed with, and days were devoted to math in the classroom, and field trips to the artillery range. On range days, we were transported for an hour in two and one-half ton open-bed trucks. Starved for sleep, I learned it is possible to sleep soundly on a flat metal truck bed, with only a fatigue jacket for a pillow. To aim the big gun, one had to know how to load it and pull the lanyard, was the army's reasoning.

The math was challenging, but I had an advantage. Sleeping above me was Al Freeman, an MIT graduate, who tutored me through the whole course. He finished #1 in class, and I was #2, thanks to Al. We also became pals off duty, and had a little more freedom than in Ord. But, typical army, we had to police cigarette butts off the ground after reveille each morning, and still had rotating KP duty. I spent an entire day on KP peeling smelly onions, while eating a lot of them with soda crackers. I had grown up on onions and loved them.

We were issued combat helmets and large back-packs which contained bed rolls and cooking/eating utensils, as well as ponchos for protection from rain and snow. These had to be kept handy at all times, as part of our preparedness training.

During this phase of basic, my folks, and my uncle Dick and aunt Annie Washington came down to Fort Chaffee to visit me. We had Saturday afternoon and most of Sunday together before I had to report back. At that point, I was not allowed to wear civilian clothes. Later, Al and I got a weekend pass, with civvies, and drove up to McAllister, Oklahoma to date a couple of girls Al had somehow heard about. We never saw them again, but did enjoy their company, he practicing his best New England brogue, and I putting on my best Texas drawl, smoking and drinking a little beer all the while.

During the entire eight weeks there, I do not recall ever going into the town of Fort Smith. The motel where my folks stayed was adjacent to the base, and we ate nearby. I have no idea what the town is like, or exactly how it benefitted from all these army guys who never spent a nickel there.

On graduation in early March, 1956, we still had no idea where we would be assigned for duty. We packed our duffels and were transported to the local airport for a military charter to Ft. Lewis, Washington, and a replacement depot there. That was at least a clue that the Pacific theatre might be in our futures.

We settled in our bucket seats on the small C-47 sized plane and headed west into the roughest airplane flight I have ever taken, before or since. The two gasoline engines and technology of the time could achieve limited altitudes, so the weather had to be faced head-on. In this case, strong clouds and head-winds slowed our progress and bounced us around to the point that every man on the plane was throwing up and hoping for an emergency landing. Stresses on the plane were huge. Rivets in the fuselage were literally spinning. And smoking was not allowed.

We stopped twice for refueling over the nine hour run to the Northwest. Each leg seemed rougher than the last. By the time we arrived

Fort Lewis, dehydration was a real issue, as was out-and-out exhaustion from anxiety and stress. It was a memorable flight from hell. We stumbled into bunks at the replacement center and slept for most of the three or four days while awaiting specific orders.

Finally, the news was posted that Korea was our destination, as replacements for seventh infantry division regulars who had completed their tours of duty. Scuttlebutt went around that the 7th was stationed north of Seoul, near the 38th parallel, and was engaged primarily in army training exercises and on full alert at all times to the possibility of a second invasion from the North. Of all the possible venues, this was probably the least welcome.

Airplane avoidance was our mantra after the flight from Ft. Chaffee, so, of course, we were to fly to Korea on a C-97 cargo troop carrier, a large gasoline driven version of the twin-engine rattletrap which had just discharged us. First stop was to be Hawaii, followed by Japan, and then to Inchon, Korea, to the replacement depot there. We got our gear together, were marched to the plane, and departed. This time, the flight was very smooth, perhaps because we were over the Pacific. The flight took most of nine hours, averaging less than 200 miles per hour.

Landing in Hawaii, we were advised that we were being bumped due to a military priority in Latin America, and would be billeted at Schofield barracks until a replacement aircraft was available. The well known barracks were on the beach near the Royal Hawaiian hotel, one of the best known beaches in the world. We had days and nights totally free to surf and swim, but had to check in twice a day for new information.

A couple of buddies and I took to the beach and salt water, which we had hardly ever seen before, and frolicked and partied wildly for two days. When we came to our senses, we were severely sunburned, with blisters, to the point that we had real trouble wearing clothes on our backs or legs.

In obvious distress, the three of us met a kindly Mother/daughter duo who took pity on us and rubbed us with soothing creams and cold packs in their nearby apartment. It sounds awkward, but it was a perfectly innocent act of mercy and friendship offered by two citizens of a territory not yet a part of the United States. Their medications helped us board a continuing flight on the third day, and continue on to Japan.

Severe sunburn to the point of lost duty time was an article 13 infraction in the army, and we narrowly avoided that penalty, while sitting upright for the nine hour leg to Wake Island, where we stopped for refueling. The island was little more than a narrow landing strip, captured from the Japanese during the war at great cost of life. Tokyo was still nine hours away. Altogether, 27 hours of flight time was required to reach Tokyo from the United States West coast. On modern aircraft, flight time is 8 or 9 hours tops.

A GAME CHANGING DAY IN JAPAN: THIS IS AFKN, SEOUL

We landed at Tachikawa military field near Camp Drake, not far from downtown Tokyo, and had a two-day layover. In the barracks at Drake, I heard a broadcast of Far East Network, part of Armed Forces Radio serving troops of Army Forces Far East and the Eighth U.S. Army, all under command of General I.D. White. I decided to take a bus to FEN headquarters and explore the possibility of getting my orders changed to an FEN assignment in Japan. There was zero excitement in my current orders to report to the hills above Seoul and the life of an infantry soldier guarding the 38th parallel and the DMZ.

In proper uniform, I asked to see the civilian station manager, who soon appeared. I explained my circumstances, and my extensive experience in radio and TV, and asked for a job. Be direct was what my experience told me. But he introduced me to the military head of the network, Colonel John Obermeier, who took the time to hear my story. The Colonel told me he was powerless to change my orders on short notice, but explained that Major Joseph Gigandet, his counterpart and head of the Korea Armed Forces Radio Network, was at FEN on a visit from Seoul at the moment, and offered to introduce me.

The meeting with Major Gigandet was another crossroads moment, which altered my life dramatically for the 16 months to follow. We talked for about 30 minutes, and he listened carefully to my experiences in civilian life, then wrote down the name and phone number in Seoul of his First Sergeant, named Al Miller. He instructed me to call Master Sergeant Miller as soon as my plane landed in Inchon.

Early in the Korean war, the port of Inchon outside Seoul was the site of General McArthur's surprise landing at high tide with a force adequate to recapture Seoul from the North Koreans. In their initial invasion push, the North had pushed the South Korean and American armies all the way to Pusan by the sea, at the Southern tip of the country.

It was thought that the short high tide at Inchon would not allow enough time to bring in enough men and arms, and the North Koreans had not bothered defending it. It was an early turning point in the war, and split the invading force in half, making reinforcements to their Southern forces impossible. McArthur's strategy of surprise and divide was considered brilliant.

Meanwhile, Gigandet had talked with Miller, and when I called, Miller knew about me. He said he would arrange with replacement depot friends for me to board a bus for Seoul, where I would audition for a slot with the Korean Armed Forces Network. I arrived there with all my belongings in one duffle bag, dismayed at seeing a totally destroyed Seoul city, with only a couple of buildings standing after four fierce battles for control of the city.

Radio Vagabond, as the station was code named, was located high on a Seoul hilltop, in a low barracks structure, with a mobile broadcast equipped truck unit parked outback in case of enemy attack. Thus, the name Vagabond. The Quonset hut for staff quarters was located halfway down the hill, and the head and showers were in between the two structures.

Sergeant Miller found out I was from Texas, and we bonded like favorite relatives. He hailed from Alabama, had been in the army for 30 years, knew where all the bodies were buried, gave and collected favors, kept careful records, and effectively ran AFKN in Major Gigandet's absence, which was often. Even with the Major present, the master sergeant directed most things, being careful to cater to the Major but not to junior officers.

Major Gigandet had a king-sized alcohol and womanizing problem, and a strange quirk of following every sentence with the words, "On there". It was the verbal equivalent of Captain Queeg's ball bearings in Mutiny On The Bounty. Miller covered for him, and the Major in turn protected his very competent Master sergeant. Sergeant Miller effectively told the Major what was going on, and what to do. The Major complied! Then he was gone again on some trip, or hiding with his mistresses.

My audition, as mentioned earlier, was the re-creation of an inning of baseball from teletyped instructions, over recorded crowd noise. I went into the mobile broadcast unit to do the audition, while Miller and and two draftees, Pfc. John Stirewalt and Pfc. Chuck Wassel, listened on the other side of the glass. When I came out, it was to handshakes, and an assignment in the barracks. I trudged down to my bunk and locker, and sergeant Miller did the work of officially changing my orders. I never went back to the Inchon replacement depot.

Thus began the "good life" in war torn but friendly and crowded Seoul, far preferable to the life of my pals playing war games with rifles up and down the cold and rainy mountains up north.

Seoul City might as well have been Hiroshima, judging by the extent of its destruction. From 1950 until the armistice of 1953, the city had changed hands four times after intense fighting. A city of 2 million people had been leveled by artillery and aircraft, to the point that only the central train station depot and the Chosun hotel were identifiable. Always a poor city, even the shanty-towns had been leveled. Hundreds of thousands of civilians had been killed or evacuated to the countryside.

Korea, known as the Hermit kingdom, had always been agrarian poor and peasant. Its homogeneous population descended from tribes of Mongols in central Asia who migrated to the tiny peninsula some five thousand years BC. They farmed rice, vegetables, and huge crops of cabbage. Cabbage and peppers, fish parts, and spices, fermented in large earthenware pots, made varieties of kimchi, the national dish. Without refrigeration, farmers buried the pots at varying depths to control the temperature and rate of maturation (rot) or fermentation. Controlling temperatures with this method assured food supplies through the bitterly cold winters. It was the Korean technique of canning and preserving food. Together with rice, their diet was healthy in today's terms, relatively meatless and centered on high fiber.

Korea had been annexed by Japan in 1905, and, until liberated in 1945, had been brutally occupied for 40 years by the Imperial Japanese army. Koreans were effectively slaves. Japanese culture and language studies were strictly required in all schools. Korean grown rice was confiscated when harvested, and shipped off to Japan, as was any other resource of value. Most Koreans existed on potatoes and kimchi, which the Japanese did not want.

Japan installed its own military government with absolute authority. Firing squads met any who resisted. Korean men were conscripted into the Japanese army or forced labor in Japan. They were allowed no weapons, and all Korean businesses paid confiscatory taxes to Japan. Koreans could not legally travel outside the country. Many fled North to Chinese Manchuria, and hundreds of thousands remain there today, having assumed Chinese citizenship.

Japan ruled its colonial territory with blunt force, more unjust and demanding than the usual master/colonial relationship. Japan limited infrastructure development, and Seoul in the mid-fifties had limited bridge crossings of the huge Han river intersecting the city, few passable roads during monsoon season, and no reliable sewer system or electric grid. Sewage was still hauled from city to countryside in "honey buckets" atop A-frames carried on men's backs like oversized back packs.

The human waste was spread on crops as fertilizer. Consequently, in the 1945-60 period, all locally grown food was officially banned from consumption by American forces stationed there.

Unlike sea bound and earthquake vulnerable Japan, Korea's mentality was never that of an island culture, and its soil reached stable bedrock. Korea is part of the Asian land-mass, and served as a strategic entry point for the Japanese military in their march on Manchuria to the Northeast. Korea has always allied itself more closely with China, and, while it has its own language and alphabet, Koreans read Chinese characters and therefore understand much of the written Chinese language.

In rebuilding itself into an industrial economy after the war, Korea formed large trading conglomerates, called Chaebol, patterned after the large Japanese Trading companies. Their job was to secure technology and industrial raw materials and investment to put the educated Korean labor forces to work. Koreans prize education, specifically science, math, and English, and historically have down-played sports as part of schooling. South Korea was the first country in the world to supply all students grades 1 through 12 with computers and internet access.

With post war investment and aid from the developed world, and America in particular, Korea became one of the most successful industrial economies. Seoul in 2010 is crowded with almost 12 million of the country's 50 million population. Its skyline is dotted with New York City style skyscrapers housing an efficient stock market and headquarters of world leaders like Hyundai and Samsung. After years of military rule, it is now a fully functioning democracy. The peninsula remains divided at the 38th parallel, with communist North Korea among the poorest nations on earth, while free-enterprise South Korea boasts the world's 8th largest economy with an excellent standard of living.

In spite of very large trading volumes with Japan, Koreans have not forgotten history, and privately hold bitter contempt for the "barbaric" Japanese Islanders, bad memories softened somewhat by the passage of the generations most oppressed.

With all its faults at the time, Seoul was still a prized assignment in post-armistice Korea. Seoul's refugees from the war were returning to the city, and a number of universities were again open for students. The beginnings of industrialization attracted rural young people to the city. Shops and restaurants were opening, but the latter were off-limits to GI's.

As headquarters of the U.S. 8th Army, Seoul had the largest concentration of Allied and ROK military personnel, and their logistical support. Museums and art galleries were popping up, and catered to soldiers with money. Large scale infrastructure and rebuilding efforts were getting underway. The streets were safe. Crime was low. Products and services were cheap. We had young Korean houseboys, Tommy and Johnny, who came to the barracks daily to take care of our laundry, shine our shoes, polish brass, change our beds weekly, all for a weekly carton of American cigarettes. These they sold on the black market for enough money to help take care of their families.

Civilian clothes were not allowed off or on base, but were allowed during R & R (rest and relaxation) weeks in Japan, which were granted twice annually at so-called 'Peace' hotels, run exclusively for American troops.

It was against this backdrop that I started working the standard control room shifts at Radio Vagabond (AFKN) in the Spring of 1956. Initially, I was assigned the morning 6 to 11 shift, and did DJ shows featuring country music for an hour, followed by an hour of jazz, progressive and Dixieland. Both shows had lots of called in requests. The movie, Good Morning Vietnam, with Robin Williams, depicted the routine perfectly, but Williams was truly funny and less reverential. Sergeant Miller made guest appearances on the country show. He loved country and hamming it up with "cousin Jody" as he called me. We built a strong friendship, which I later used to help out a friend.

The jazz show featured music by Art Tatum, Thelonius Monk, Miles Davis, as well as Duke Ellington, Dizzie Gillespie, Billie Holiday, Ella Fitzgerald, and, of course, Louis Armstrong. This music was a hit with staff at the large 8th army medical center, while the country sound was more popular with troops in the field and cooks and wait staffs in the mess halls. I got good feedback from both.

Elvis Presley was just becoming the rage in the States, and a lot his recordings were played on the station. Presley's peak popularity in the U.S. came at the very time of my military service, and the teenage mania surrounding him was a stateside phenomenon which was lost on many overseas servicemen.

A local act of note at the NCO club down the hill was the Kim Sisters, three very talented and pretty Korean sisters who sang hits patterned after the Andrews Sisters. We carried some of their performances live. The Kim Sisters went on to become big recording and concert stars in the States during the late 50's and 60's.

At scheduled station breaks, I read advisories to the troops warning against white lightning alcohol, locally grown foods, base regulations, schedules of various events at Osan or Taegu, or Pusan, where AFKN had auxiliary stations, and movie and sports line-ups. Of course, there was no television, but there were plans to bring in TV in coming years. Hourly network news feeds came in from FEN Tokyo, which had a more or less professional staff of newsmen.

My fellow staff included Stan Dale, a big-time disc-jockey at WGN Chicago before being immediately drafted when he divorced. He left a big money career in Chicago which he was never able to reclaim after returning to civilian life. Stan worked the night shift at the time, playing pop music and taking calls for requests from the field, but could not air the calls or their location because of security. GI's on night duty called in from all over Korea, while Stan had a one sided conversation with them on the air. Stan was a true pro. Much later, Joan and I visited Stan and his new wife, Helen, at their home in Chicago. In civilian life, Stan and Helen turned out to be liberal minded in the extreme, campaigning against monogamy in marriage, touting multiple sexual liaisons with others. They detailed this philosophy in a book which became a sensation at the time. Googling Stan revealed that he died in San Francisco in 2007, leaving his third wife. His obit detailed his leadership of the open marriage movement, and various humanitarian awards he had received.

Stan and Mike DiAngelo, a writer from Pittsburgh, were selected as the team to put together and produce a show for the Commanding General, I.D. White, known as "Salute To You", paying tribute each week to a different unit under the General's command. It had to be assembled in Japan, at the Far East Network, because AFKN did not have the editing and taping equipment needed to do the job. Stan and Mike went on extended temporary duty (TDY) to FEN at camp Drake, and we were all envious of this plum assignment. They returned to Seoul only once each month. Tokyo had been rebuilt, had a fixed exchange rate of 360 to the dollar, cheap and delicious sushi and soba noodle restaurants, and a good transportation system, mostly public buses, to move around the various sections of the city. Civilian clothes were allowed off base at any time.

The rest of the staff filled in behind Stan and Mike. On air guys, like me, were John Stirewalt from Indianapolis, Ed Pribula from Scranton, PA. ,Joe Henderson from a small town in Oklahoma, George Beres from Chicago, Bill Bishop from Kansas City, and the aforementioned Chuck Wassil, a good looking would-be actor from New York with singing talent who aspired to leading man roles in Broadway musicals. Man of LaMancha was his favorite song in the showers.

Behind the scenes supporting cast included Artie Goldberg, Bob McGonagle, Chuck Goodwin, Bob Wasaluski, and Lt. Ben Okulski, an ROTC officer who correctly learned never to cross Sgt. Miller, but cater to him instead. Okulski survived AFKN, and later became a time salesman for WABC, New York.

About 30 of us bunked in a Quonset hut heated at each end by oil burning stoves. Many of the base buildings and much of the city were heated with coal, and a coal haze hung over everything in Winter, just as it had in Ft. Smith, Arkansas. The heads and showers were about 50 yards from the barracks, so the most practical relief in the middle of cold winter nights was about 10 feet outside the doors at either end of the hut.

Don Collins, from Columbia, MO., had become a friend in the second leg of basic in Fort Smith, and Don went with the unit to the 7th infantry up North. He came down to visit me for a weekend, and I was able to use my friendship with Master Sgt. Miller to get Don a job as company clerk for AFKN. Miller arranged to get him transferred the next day, and Don was forever grateful. He later became an agricultural lobbyist in Washington, D.C.. There were many others serving as engineering techs and file clerks, but there were no bad jobs at AFKN.

Otis Ratliff, an old high school classmate, heard me on the radio and came down from division to spend the weekend with me. We toured Seoul and remembered good times in high school. I did not see Otis again. In

2008, a friend wrote me that Otis had died of alzheimers, in Abilene,Texas.

The large military base had a huge, full service Post Exchange, or PX, selling everything from jewelry to food, to haircuts and shaves. The PX had a bank, sold insurance, hardware, blankets, panchos, pillows, tours, all at zero markup. It was cheaper then Walmart is today, but nobody had much extra money on military pay. Mine was in the neighborhood of $100 per month, but went up a few dollars when I got a promotion to Specialist first class, the rough equivalent to sergeant.

As a voice on the air speaking English, I found myself in demand as an English teacher, and was soon meeting with a group of 8 Korean women college students, at one of their homes, singing songs in English and allowing them to practice their English conversation skills. I was paid 40,000 won per month, which translated to about $25. I was driven to the home by Chauncey, the station's Korean driver, in a 2 and ½ ton truck, and picked up there after two hours.

These students were from well-to-do Korean families who had managed to profit, one way or another, from the war. One of them, Miss Kim, invited me, with her brother as chaperone, to a celebration at Seoul Women's University, at which hundreds of students wore traditional Korean gowns and carried identical blue umbrellas. There were stage performers singing traditional songs and doing traditional dances, an impressive and elaborate ceremony. For refreshment, we had flavored ice, much like American snow cones.

I lucked into some additional money by doing English narration for Korean government films, about 30 minutes each, which I learned later were essentially propaganda films for Syngman Rhee, then President of South Korea. These films were distributed to South Korean embassies around the world. For these jobs, I went to the Information Ministry building, where the English script was handed me. I read the script as the film was shown, and was immediately paid in Korean Won. I narrated perhaps a dozen such films before being sent to Japan on temporary duty.

Inter-service league baseball began in July, and AFKN broadcast some of the weekend games. George Beres and I did on-sight remotes, alternating play by play and color duties. It had turned out that I was the only staff with sports broadcasting experience. Beres was a statistics nut and very articulate, but had no broadcast experience. He was a very serious minded straight-laced Greek from Chicago, with a sense of humor he managed to keep hidden most of the time.

Top college players, even those with professional potential, were drafted along with everybody else, so the quality of baseball was very high. Their units exempted them from regular duties once they were accepted as players. In effect, they trained and were coached like professionals, and competed very seriously.

When fall football season came, we followed the same format, broadcasting games between the 24th Calvary division, and the 7th Infantry division, for example. Beres and I took the day of the games to set up at the remote sight, sometimes near the 38th parallel, talk to players and coaches, and do play by play. All games were day games. Again, quality of play was at least at large collegiate level, and many players went to the pros in later civilian life, citing their military football experience. In 1956, professional football was below the big college quality of today. The NFL had yet to be formed, the stadiums were yet to be built, and live TV coverage with instant replays, which brought fantastic wealth to the owners and players, was a dream in the distant future.

The nine months at AFKN, Korea instilled in me a respect and admiration for the Korean people which has stayed with me all these years. I found almost all Koreans to be very appreciative of the American role in saving their country, and in taking major responsibility for rebuilding their country. The Korean culture and common language give it cohesion and common purpose. Koreans are ethical and honest with each other, although there are some regional "tribal" differences, and equally forthright and honorable with foreigners. They will bargain aggressively, but live up to the letter of agreements when made.

They smile and laugh easily and often, work very hard without complaint, compete fiercely, but are warm and hospitable. There is crime in Korea, but it is very small relative to almost all other countries, especially those with multi-cultural and ethnically diverse populations. Seoul is one of the most densely populated cities on earth, yet people there live together with sensitivity and grace and lack of conflict. Americans can walk anywhere in this huge city without fear, and with smiling assurance from vendors and average citizens on the street.

I have seen and lived among Koreans at their poorest in the post war, post occupation period, and I have worked closely with them in their rich, modern industrial state. They were proud then and are proud now, but never arrogant, with the same tenacity, the same willingness, and the same trusting character. In all of Asia, Koreans have my vote as the warmest, most amenable, most thoughtful of people.

JAPAN AND SALUTE TO YOU

In December, Stan Dale and Mike D'Angelo came back to Korea to choose their successors, pack their bags, and rotate back to the States. Salute to You, the General's program, had gained favor with officers all over the Far East, and was required listening for all command officers every Tuesday night at 7. General White decided he wanted the program to continue, with a focus on his Korea command.

Ed Pribula was chosen to replace Dale as the announcer for the show, and I was chosen to replace D'Angelo as writer, editor and producer. We were in Camp Drake at FEN in time for Christmas, working on the next show. We were assigned to billet near FEN, but were free to live off-base if we chose and could afford it. We couldn't. Captain John Tuckerman was to review our scripts, and was the liason with General White's office at Camp Zama, some 40 miles away.

We got the list of units to be saluted from Capt. Tuckerman, and went to work. I researched the unit's history, called the unit to identify officers and men to be interviewed, wrote and timed the script. On Monday of each week, we took either a staff car or helicopter to Zama to record the Army Forces Far East marching band, under the Direction of Chief Warrant Officer Dawson McAfee. We recorded an hour of the band's music, packed up and went back to Camp Drake, timed in each music piece, and left room for two interviews, plus a message of salute from the General.

I then boarded a plane for Korea, usually a C-47, for a night flight from Tachikawa to Inchon, where I was picked up by Chauncey and transported to the unit being saluted. There I interviewed one officer and one enlisted man about the unit's current mission and its history during combat in Korea or World War Two.

With tapes in hand, Chauncey took me back to the airport for the trip back to Japan on the next available transport, sometimes a C-124 cargo and troop carrier, or a C-119, normally used for parachuting men and cargo over enemy territory. Both planes were old, with bucket cloth seats along the sides of the fuselage. The C-124 had a vertical ladder which troops had to climb. Personnel seating was up top with no escape doors, while large cargo such as jeeps, trucks, and tanks were pilled in on the first level. On C-47's and C-119's, we were issued parachutes and told how to use them in the event of engine failure. On night trips, I used my parachute as a pillow and stretched out on the deck.

Back in Japan after a three hour flight, I edited and timed the tapes using FEN's Ampex machines, which were state of the art at the time. We then recorded Pribula, and pieced the whole thing together, splicing audiotape with Scotch tape and a razor blade, to make a master copy of 29 minutes and 30 seconds. It was a very tight and nerve wracking deadline, but we somehow always made it.

The production engineers at FEN would then make 20 copies of the tape, which were quickly sent by courier to each of the Armed Forces radio stations throughout the Far East. We worked just one week ahead, so any glitch had to be caught and corrected without delay. At air time, we were already working on the next week's program.

Around FEN at all hours, I met a creative writer named Walt Sheldon, who was working on a new western series patterned after Gunsmoke, the highly successful U.S. TV program. It was called Boots and Saddles, and the lead character was Sgt. Dan Donavan, Trooper, U.S. Calvary. Sheldon showed me the script and asked if I would like to read for the part of Donavan. I thought it would be fun and jumped at the chance.

I got the part. Boots and Saddles was a weekly 30 minute show with self-contained episodes, with Donavan leading his platoon through some dangerous situation each week, usually encountering hostile Indians. Walt liked my Texas way of depicting Donavan, and gave me a sidekick much like Festus as comic relief. We completed about 20 shows before I rotated out, the tapes of which I still have but have never listened to.

Sheldon had a Japanese wife and they had a son. The son sent me an email in the 2005 period telling me that his Father had died, still in Japan.

Pribula and I worked the Salute To You schedule for six months, until early June, 1957, when we both were due to rotate home. This time, successors were chosen by the powers at FEN, not AFKN. I was offered the job to stay, as a civilian, at Captain's pay, and continue writing and producing the show. I figured that Captain's pay, a civilian GS 12 job rating, totaled about $12-15 thousand a year, huge for the time, but not enough to entice me to stay in Japan. I wanted to get home and resume my life.

Throughout the six months, there was very little time to explore Japan as I had hoped, but one day a week, Sunday, did allow getting acquainted with Tokyo. I learned to love Japanese food in all its forms, especially a big platter of sushi and a large beer for $1 dollar total, and a dish called Go-mak-soba, which had five ingredients in a tasty soup. Soba buckwheat noodles also became a favorite, and are to this day.

One Saturday, a friend and I took a train out of Tokyo, hiked through the snow for five hours, and ended the day in a small seaside village in a small Ryokan, where the hot baths and tasty sushi dinners were memorable. The staff there spoke no English and wore traditional Kimonos with geta wooden shoes. It was my introduction to Japanese style hotels, and they have since been my favorites.

Early on, Dale and D'Angelo had toured us around Tokyo a bit. We hit Shenjuku, Shibuya, Rippongi, and Takatanababa. In Shibuya, we went to an ornately decorated ceremonial hotel named Haku-en-Kaku, where Japanese go to honor their deceased ancestors. Each room had a different and elaborate façade. We met the manager, who invited us to stay overnight when possible. Insofar as we knew, we were the only Americans extended this privilege. Pribula and I went there three overnights, enjoying a soaking hot tub, lots of hot sake, and complete dinner served in our room. Geisha came and played music on samisen guitar type instruments as we ate, and left afterward. We slept on futons laid out on the floor, with a rice pillow. The cost was around $20 U.S. dollars.

On another occasion, Dale and D'Angelo allowed us to tag along to a party at the Overseas Press Club in the Ginza area of downtown Tokyo. There, I met and talked at length with Shell Silverstein, then a cartoonist with Stars and Stripes, the military newspaper. Silverstein later became world famous through his cartoons and illustrated books for children.

Later, when I travelled to Japan regularly on business, my first stop at the Okura Hotel in Tokyo, after a hot bath on arrival, was at the great sushi bar at the hotel or, alternately, a small café down the street serving go-mac-soba.

Twelve years after the war, and five years after the U.S. occupation had ended , Japan in 1957 was still relatively poor, but its recovery had been accelerated greatly by its having served as the main supply point for the Korean war.   General McArthur's recovery plan established a new representative system of government, a new constitution, and universal suffrage.

Emperor Hirohito was forced to disclaim divinity, and lost all political and military power. The large trading companies , known as Zaibatsu, who fed Japan's war machine and controlled the economy, were broken up, and a new Ministry of Trade and Industry formed. The banking system was reconstituted, and free enterprise capitalism introduced. War criminals were put on trial. Some 500 military officers committed suicide after the surrender. The old guard disappeared over time. McArthur was Supreme Commander and became the law during the occupation.

The automotive industry was in its infancy, with cheap and poor quality a hallmark. Cars in the city were mostly taxis, tiny Datsuns careening through Tokyo at breathtaking speed, with few red lights or stop signs. Toyota motors had not yet begun to export or manufacture abroad. Inexpensive and largely unreliable exports were mostly toys and trinkets, but with an exchange rate of 360 and plenty of available labor, Japan was the export model much like China or India today.

Computers and other chip based high-tech consumer goods did not exist. Flat screen TV's and the internet were unheard of. Cheap transistor radios were Japan's main electronic export. MITI had not yet settled on the national strategy of focusing on highest quality autos or consumer electronics as a means of wealth generation for the country. At home, housing was extremely cramped and personal and household consumption ignored in favor of exporting to a wealthier world of buyers not decimated by the war. Average per capita income in Japan in dollar terms was 1/10th that of per capita income in the U.S.

Even with old style air travel to and from Japan, tourism was growing rapidly due to the artificially low exchange rate, but American style hotels were few. Consequently, many Americans and Europeans discovered the pleasures of Japanese style hotels, known as Ryokans, where visitors could get steaming hot baths, beds on the floor, called Futon, with hard rice filled pillows, and traditional Japanese dinners served in their rooms. For many, going native, wearing kimono and geta (wooden sandals) became the much preferred way to visit Japan.

Leaving Japan in June 1957, I had no idea when, or if, I would ever come back again. It turned out to be a generation, 27 years, before I would see modern Tokyo, stay in the finest American hotels, take the bullet train to Kyoto and Osaka, visit rebuilt Hiroshima and Nagasaki, and again go native in the most famous Ryokan in Kyoto, now costing $400. Per night.

BACK TO CIVILIAN LIFE AND TV: BUT IN BUSINESS

The troop ship home from Korea was 17 days of dread, alternating between mild seasickness and nausea from too much grape juice. Troops were stacked three deep in cloth, hammock style bunks in the hold of the ship. They ate buffet style, off metal trays, standing at chest high long narrow tables. Ventilation was poor in the bottom of the ship. There were no windows, and no horizon, just a rhythmic rolling and pitching and yawing guaranteed to release most of whatever meal had just been ingested.

On embarking, volunteers were requested to work in the ship's hospital tending Asian flu patients. Asian flu was epidemic in the military at the time, and, if so diagnosed, GI's went to the hospital instead of the hold. Naturally, the infirmary was filled.

I saw a way out and volunteered, took my duffle and reported to the hospital on the main deck, already a vast improvement with a view and circulating air. Luckily, volunteers were assigned bunks in the hospital and ate hospital food, also huge advantages. So for 17 days, I served grape juice and light food to bed ridden patients during the day, but slept on a thick mattress in a bed with springs. Relative to life in the hold of the ship, it was Plaza five star quality. I also consumed large quantities of grape juice myself. It was the only beverage available, other than suspect water purified by the ship's own system. Whatever its effect, I remained healthy, and credit grape juice, which I have carefully avoided since.

The Pacific ocean played its part and remained mostly pacified. But the big engines turning the large propellers created their own bow pitch, so that the ship became something of a bucking horse, even in a calm sea. When seasickness was felt coming on, I repaired immediately to my bunk and laid flat on my back. This position was the only one which seemed to prevent nausea, so I resorted to it often. There was Dramamine available in the hospital, which we all took, but found out that too much of a good thing had its own ill side-effect of sleepiness and lethargy.

June was the shoulder season between Spring and monsoon season, so heavy rains accompanied us for at least a week during the trip. I do not recall seeing another ship during the entire 17 days.

The port of Oakland was a welcomed sight, and we were soon docked and disembarking. Final paperwork took most of a day before we were officially released from the Army, in uniform, with all belongings in one duffle bag. I left the processing center and greeted my parents at the base gate. They and my four young sisters had driven from Texas to meet me, and also visit my Dad's brothers and their families who lived in the area. The army had told me while on ship that they would be there.

We visited relatives for a couple of days, and toured San Francisco.

A cousin thought I should visit Finokios, the well-known transvestite night spot, so we did and saw their stage show. I borrowed some civilian clothes for the outing.

On the third day back in the U.S., we headed East toward Texas, driving Dad's big Chrysler four door sedan across the desert to Las Vegas, with after-market air conditioning and a container of water in case of a flat tire or engine break-down. The car had no seat belts and no center island in the front, so three could sit up front and my Mom and three girls sat in the back seat.

We made Las Vegas about dusk and checked into a strip motel which was actually on the strip. We had two rooms. Dad and I shared a room, while Mom and the four girls shared another. Las Vegas had almost no high-rise or fancy hotels at the time. The Desert Inn was perhaps the high-end casino, with rooms all at ground level. Rooms at our little motel cost no more than $20. Each. We ate at a diner nearby. Dad would have liked to visit a casino, but Mom discouraged it.

Next morning we were on the road again and made Plainview late that night without event. Mom and the girls had never been to California before, so spending most of a week there and seeing nieces and nephews and cousins from both the Garrett and Morris families was a treat for them. Usually, the visits were from California to their house in Plainview, as many as 7 or 8 at a time, annually, as the families who had moved west during the war made visits back to their homesteads in Texas or Oklahoma. My parent's home was always open.

BACK TO WORK

I reclaimed my 54 Ford, and, after three days home, and it was back to work. Back in Korea, I had exchanged letters with Pappy Watson at KGNC, explaining that I wanted to go into the business side of television. He wrote to tell me they would see what could be done, and to come to the station when I was ready. I did so around the first of July. Pappy had assembled the executive team for the occasion, including himself, Bill Clarke, the TV sales manager, Aubrey Jackson, head of radio, and Jack Liston, a member by marriage of the Whittenburg family. Jack was stationed on-sight to ride herd on the family interests. This reception was a pleasant surprise.

After talking about my Armed forces radio experience, Bill Clarke volunteered that the group had discussed my reentry and he would like to welcome me into the television time sales department. It was exactly what I wanted, and I could not have been more pleased. No details were discussed, but that seemed not to matter. The group took me to a welcome home lunch at a downtown buffet frequented by business types. I had gone to the station in slacks and sports coat, sans tie, not expecting to see anyone but Pappy Watson. They were all in suits and ties, so I felt a little out of place.

I was to show for work the following Monday, which gave me that afternoon to find living quarters. Don Reynolds, a staffer in radio, heard of my plight and invited me to temporarily share his apartment in the west part of town. It was one bedroom with twin beds, but a good start, and I moved in on Sunday, having bought some basic civilian clothes.

William A. Clarke, Jr., Sales manager of KGNC TV was a natural leader and excellent coach. He led by example, with high energy and good organizing and time management skills. He was firm, fair and honest with his sales people. They liked and trusted him. He was a patient and natural mentor. He was the younger brother of Robert Clarke, the well-known Hollywood actor who appeared in dozens of sci-fi films in the 50's,60's, and 70's, and in a wide range of television shows as late as the 1990's.

Bill had grown up in Oklahoma City, and attended Oklahoma State University, where he formed a friendship with T. Boone Pickens. In 1957, Pickens headquarters was in Amarillo as CEO of Mesa Petroleum Co., a young oil and gas exploration and development company, which he owned. Pickens was known in the area as an up and comer, but was still a long way from multi-billionaire status which came later.

In introducing me to his business connections in Amarillo, Bill sometimes took me by Boone Pickens office for coffee and conversation. Boone was very cordial and interested, and wished me the best. It was my brief encounter with super wealth. Later, after I had left Amarillo, Pickens induced Bill Clarke to come to work with him at Mesa. I heard that it was a lasting association.

Joe Collins, John Clinton, Lou Harris and I worked for Bill. Each of them was experienced and had longtime client lists. I began my sales job with no clients, and was expected to win advertisers away from competing radio stations and the newspaper. Many businesses had been exclusive print buyers up to that point. Bill Clarke held my hand during these early cold calls, making sure I had convincing ideas, cost per thousand data , and a story to tell about the value of diversifying media.

In some cases, I asked the art department to invest with me, and showed potential clients graphics and suggested ad copy. With Bill's coaching, I learned to be specific about ad schedules within highly rated programs and newscasts. Many leads were developed from scouring the daily papers, and transposing the message to a TV format.

I carried a briefcase with all my reference data, as well as contracts for run of schedule, which was basically a discount plan under which the ads could run at any time slot available. I had plans for program sponsors, although many regular programs were sponsored by national advertisers. If time slots were not filled by network shows, we could import syndicated game or comedy shows and project audience size, showing mock-up commercials.

Bill spent more time with me than he did with his seasoned salesmen, to get me going. Mine was the swing sales job, and whatever business I generated was new revenue and fell mostly to the bottom line. I had pretty good early success signing up people who had not tried TV before. A racetrack in Raton, New Mexico wanted to pull gamblers from Texas. A small chain of dry cleaners had never advertised beyond the yellow pages, but now bought a small schedule directed to daytime shows appealing to women, with good results. A restaurant bought spots and built traffic for their dinner specials. A movie theatre tried TV in addition to newspaper listings, and liked the result.

I opened a large floor coverings and decorating store as an advertiser, and the owner, Jess Tucker, became a good friend of mine. This friendship would later be very beneficial in a surprising way.

After three months, the boss felt I was ready for a couple of larger accounts. He worked a house account with his longtime friend and college classmate, Gene Edwards, President of the First National Bank. I had done commercials for the bank before, but now was assigned to service the account, working with Frank Arnold, Vice President, who I had come to know. This account helped my book a great deal, and again put me in contact with the two most prominent ad agencies in Amarillo, Monte Rosenwald Associates, and Don Curphy/Bob Mills. These relationships led to servicing other accounts which they handled.

The Hollywood Dress Shop, an upscale women's fashion retailer, owned by Clarence Solnick, signed up with me. I brought Mr. Solnick a secretary from the station to act as his exclusive spokesman, which he liked. She visited him weekly, and together, we wrote his copy, which she read off camera while various fashion ensembles were shown on screen.

Happier than anyone with this new business were Pappy Watson and Jack Liston, who monitored all incoming orders like hawks. I heard from them often, in positive terms. I was welcomed to join in their daily luncheons, when time permitted.

Within a few months, I was back on air again with First National Bank's commercials, and gradually assumed an expanded on-air work-load, strictly limited to commercials. The Daily routine of calls and service to clients allowed me to get to know the principals and some of their concerns, and about the nature of their particular businesses. I knew accounting terms and had a sense of how to calculate the bottom line, so it was useful to be able to talk top line, gross margins, and bottom line with some. I helped them establish appropriately sized ad budgets in some cases, and won a lot of trust by working in their best interests.

By September, I had leased my own apartment on Hayden street, with two bedrooms, living room, kitchen, and carport. The converted garage was owned by a gracious widow lady who lived in the main house next door. I think I paid $25. Per week, including utilities. She invited me often for homemade ice cream.

I traded in the 54 Ford for a new 57 Chevy Impala with long tail fins and ornamental lights on each front fender. The car had no seat belts, safety headrests, or turn indicators, and a straight across front seat with no center console. The engine was gas guzzling V-8 which required frequent tune-ups. It was built of thick steel which added weight needlessly. Suspension was layered metal springs typical of American car making technology at the time. Frequent oil changes and grease jobs were required maintenance. After a year, the car was gone. In its place was a new Volkswagen Beetle, at a cost of $1400. The Beetle could be lifted and bounced sideways to fit into tight parking slots.

The Chevy is a collector's item today, valuable because of its representation of the gaudy styling, least energy efficient, and lowest quality era of American car making.

That October, college friend Garland Parks and I drove the Chevy to Las Vegas for a rowdy weekend at the Desert Sands hotel and casino. We saw Patti Page the first night. The next night, we saw Nat King Cole, one of the most impressive shows I have seen before or since. Shows were then considered an aside to the main attraction of gambling. We paid $5. for tickets, including filet mignon dinner. I tipped the usher five silver dollars, in return for which we were seated next to the stage. Drinks were free. Rooms were cheap, and we had the sun and the pool to recover if we celebrated a little too much.

Garland connected with some lady, and I met a hat buyer from Milwaukee. We danced the night away and recovered poolside.

Lounge entertainment was free at all times. Drinks in the lounges were .50-.75 cents each. Some of the highest caliber jazz and blues shows performed there around the clock. Las Vegas did not yet charge big money for their biggest shows, but that would soon be remedied.

Social life in Amarillo's young community was active. I dated a number of women, without serious involvement. Parties were mostly tame and often in someone's apartment, with no illegal substances. Driving under the influence was rarely enforced in those days, but should have been. We had drive-in's and conventional movie theatres, night clubs on the Northeast 8th strip such as the Aviatrix, which featured big name bands to dance to, and the Avalon, showcasing some of the biggest names in Country music.

The Amarillo hotel featured dancing to Snozz Dunn's jazz and pop band. My older brother Cal was later the featured vocalist with the group. During the day, Snozz sold radio time on KGNC. There were also a number of trendy private drinking clubs which could be joined for a dollar, discovered and frequented by media types. One of these was owned by, of all people, a young Mormon woman, Jan Olson, who I dated for a time.

Color Television was now fed from the network for selected shows, but color TV sets were very expensive, heavy, and space consuming. Perhaps 2 % of homes were able to receive color. With black and white still dominant and program choices slim, evenings at home watching TV were far down the list of attractions. Dating still involved "going out" to movies and restaurants, or perhaps listening to music or dramas on the car radio.

Restaurants came in several ethnic varieties. A late-night favorite was Lomax's, where enchiladas laced with fresh garlic could stop romance in its tracks. Another popular choice for dates and singles was a Mrs. Whizzenant's boarding-house, a family style restaurant in a private home setting. She had a half-dozen big round tables and continuous servings of foods in large bowls. Diners spooned out their preferred quantity. There was one fixed price and no menu and no reservations. Customers seated themselves as seats became available, and served themselves. Each diner ate on his own schedule.

West Texas in the late 50's was filled with young people who came from smaller area towns, with college graduates seeking a beginning, with war veterans resuming or beginning careers, with air force pilots and their families, and with young engineers headed for jobs with Pantex, the U.S. Government super-secret installation in Amarillo that defuses and stores atomic and hydrogen weapons.

Amarillo had teachers, ranchers, farmers, oil wildcatters, building contractors, banks and brokers, artists, television trainees from the East with internships in TV directing, camera operations, and writing. It had University professors, museums, distribution centers, the full range of retailers, a thriving motel and hotel industry, and a booming nightlife, and a respected public and private school sytem, excellent medical facilities, and good newspapers. Before Walmart, Sam's Club, Costco, Best Buy, and today's ubiquitous chains, Amarillo had critical mass which made it a desirable place to live and raise a family. It was at the crossroads between the crowded East and the sparsely settled West, and a beacon for young professionals.

Two years back in Amarillo, and with some understanding of the business of radio and television, I was confronted with another life changing decision which I knew immediately I would not refuse. For the first nine months of 1959, as I prepared to leave Amarillo for good, my TV time sales effort paid off big…...a total of $9,000 before taxes. $1000. monthly at that time was respectable. In addition, I had been allowed $15. Dollars a week to offset gasoline expenses and the use of my own car.

BOOK FOUR
New York Years: Joan, Scott & Jon

TO THE BIG APPLE

Jack Liston was interested in FM radio. To this point, FM, or Frequency Modulation, had been licensed to the same licensees as AM, Amplitude Modulation, but very few station owners programmed FM separately. There were few receivers capable of receiving FM signals. Separate programming would have been costly, with little advertiser appeal, so it was not done.

FM signals travelled over a narrow geographic range and relatively even terrain, but with greater fidelity and clarity and less static than AM signals. But AM had the advantage of reach, and the ability to travel over widely varying terrain. Owners did "simulcasting" on FM, meaning they simply carried AM programming at the same time. For advertisers, any audience was a bonus.

Exceptions were in major cities with great population density, where large audiences could be reached with special programs. Classical music, for example, could be broadcast with greater tonal range and clarity on FM frequencies, a fact much appreciated by urban dwellers. In these markets, like New York, Boston, Philadelphia, and Chicago, FM had unique value, and was programmed and sold separately from AM stations. WQXR, the New York Times owned station in New York, played classical music full time, and captured a large number of listeners.

In the Spring of 59, Jack had asked me to accompany him to an FM conference in Chicago to find out more. We flew there on a TWA Constellation, and spent two days listening to various presenters extol the merits and bright future forecast for FM Radio. Back inAmarillo, Jack hatched a plan.

Working with Musak, the company that feeds bland music into elevators and office buildings and medical facilities the world over, Jack proposed to apply to the Federal Communications Commission for FM station licenses in 6 major cities. The cities were Boston, New Orleans, Philadelphia, Indianapolis, Chicago, and Atlanta. His plan was to tie the stations together into a network utilizing Musak automated programming technology. The stations would broadcast the same classical music simultaneously, with standardized local breaks for news, weather and commercials. In effect, the format would be an extension of the WQXR format, but with a fraction of the overhead.

The plan included only large cities to appeal to national brand advertisers, especially prestige high-end brands who liked the association with classical music. The network "buy" would package all six cities and deliver a sizeable aggregate audience with the demographics sought by fashion and jewelry and elite automotive brands like Mercedes and Bentley.

Musak had devised centralized tape banks which could feed an entire day's programs to the network, with a minimum of personnel and "on-air" talent. Perhaps two dozen employees could run the entire network, including central programming.

Revenue projections looked appealing, gross margins were very large, and bottom line estimates were off the charts. The Whittenburg family agreed to finance the venture, with Musak taking a minority interest, the business plan was in place, and now action was needed in New York City to drum up support among advertisers.

That job fell to me.!!

Jack offered me the job as Manager of FM Associates, as the network was to be named. I would move to New York, open a small sales office in the Musak building at 18th and Park Avenue, and lay out our plans in detail to the key ad agencies, laying the groundwork for sponsors to come in as soon as the stations were licensed and on the air. I was ready to move within two weeks of the offer.

I had never been to New York, but the concept excited. My friend Don Reynolds was now a copywriter for J. Walter Thompson, the largest New York agency, and he found the environment stimulating, even thrilling. It was the big time, after all, and we had frequently talked about New York as the ultimate destination if we were to continue in media.

I sold the Volkswagen for the same $1400. I had paid a year earlier, to a good-looking lady corporate pilot from Denver who, judging from two days and nights with her, liked partying more than flying. I packed a single suitcase, said goodbye to my family in Plainview, and boarded my first jet flight, with Jack Liston, to New York's Idlewild airport. The date was October 1, 1959. The plane was a Boeing 707, new at the time. Flight time from Dallas was little more than three hours, at altitudes above the mass of weather which propeller planes often had to encounter.

From Long Island, the skyscraper lights of the city across the East river were impressive, unforgettable to a 26 year-old first time visitor. Exiting the midtown tunnel into Manhattan, gawking at the crowded sights as we made our way south on Park Avenue, my feelings were mixed. I knew only one human in the city, with whom I had agreed to share an apartment. I had two suits, a sports coat, two pairs of shoes and some underwear and a toothbrush, as my earthly belongings. Other than Don

Reynolds, I knew only one other person within a thousand miles. He was Jimmy Dean, by now a star of his own CBS TV show and a true celebrity. I had some reservations about contacting him as a friend from long ago Plainview.

We stayed at the Gramercy Park hotel, at 20th street and Irving Place, facing east with a view over the Park. Next morning, we walked to the Musak building around the corner, listened to their bland product in the elevator on the way up, and met John Ralls, senior VP and the Musak representative to our new joint venture. John showed me to a small interior office, and introduced me to Dotty, my new secretary, and a number of other Musak personnel. We talked briefly with John about the station applications. Everything seemed on track.

New York City at the time was at its economic zenith relative to other large cities in the world. Europe's major centers were growing rapidly but, as a priority, recovering from the destruction of war. Tokyo was the rising superpower in Asia, but lagged America in almost every category. Latin America remained poor and splintered by small nation-states, many of whom were dictatorships. Africa had not even begun to be a factor on the world stage, and was still in the throes of apartheid.

By contrast, New York City during the Eisenhower administration was and remains today the financial and communications capitol of the world. Manhattan's 33 square miles housed 1.5 million people, with a density of close to 70,000 per sq. mile. Daily commuters into Manhattan from the four other borroughs and New Jersey and Connecticut brought the daytime population to around 5 million. Total population of the larger city was over 8 million.

Manhattan had Wall Street, all the major broadcast networks, Broadway and its theatres, Times Square, and the mile-square Central Park, the grand design of English architect Frederick Law Olmstead. Manhattan also boasted the Metropolitan and many other famous museums, and the massive Rockefeller center. More importantly, it was the headquarters of more major corporations than the rest of the country combined. It was home to the United Nations, the Statue of Liberty, Grant's tomb, and a rich history reaching back to the beginning of the country. Perhaps most important, it infrastructure was intact and functioning, unlike war torn Europe and Asia.

The twin World Trade Center towers were under construction, and New York State, under Governor Nelson Rockefeller, had just committed to lease 40 full floors in one of the towers. New York was a boom town, and a symbol to the world of free enterprise and capitalism.

Jack Liston stayed the weekend and departed for Amarillo, leaving me to make my own schedule. We agreed on regular telephone updates. He expected to visit New York once a quarter. He was married to the former Bonnie Whittenburg, and there had been quiet rumors around that the marriage may be in jeopardy.

With a couple of drinks together that weekend, Jack talked a little about their relationship, and the rumors were confirmed. Obviously, the family's allegiance would be with Bonnie in case of a split, which concerned me a little since FM Associates was Jack's baby,... financed by the Whittenburg family. If he left the family, what would be the future of the venture? The answer would come within a few months.

A SHORT JIMMY DEAN STORY

After Jack left town, I took a chance and called Jimmy Dean's home number in Tenafly, New Jersey. Dean answered, and, from all appearances was glad to hear from me. He insisted I take a bus to Tenafly that evening. He would meet me at the Tenafly terminal. I found the Port Authority bus terminal on the city's west side, and did some sightseeing as we went uptown passed Grant's tomb and on to the George Washington bridge across the Hudson river.

Jimmy met me on schedule, and it was old home week. He and Sue were gracious hosts, and listened while I told the story of FM radio and what I would be doing. We reminisced about Seth Ward and his Mom's barbering, about how poor his family had been, and how his life had changed.

His children were still young. Gary, the oldest , was perhaps 14, Connie, 12, and Robert no more than 7 or 8. We played gin rummy while Sue cooked. Their house was spacious but non-pretentious. The large family room was decorated with his memorabilia, gold records, concert posters, and scenes from his network television series, still live weekly on CBS.

Singer Jerry Vale and his wife lived a couple of doors down. Vale sang pop backed by big bands, and was high on the charts at the time. Later, at Jimmy's TV show, I would meet Carol Burnett and Roger Miller. Still later, Howard Keele and his wife would be guests of the Deans in Tenafly, joined by Joan and me.

I remained close friends with the Dean's after Joan and I were married, (more on that later). And we vacationed with them on their large yacht at Block Island and Martha's Vineyard, and at the Ocean Reef Club in Key Largo, Florida. Jimmy named his yacht Big Bad John after his mega-hit of the same name. They also visited our home in Connecticut many times. The close friendship lasted until the early 90's. In his later years, Jimmy became reclusive and distrusting of almost everyone. I suspect he did not enjoy his wealth or his family, but hope I am wrong on both counts. His children, Gary, Robert and Connie, all had families of their own, and also had much of Jimmy's winning personality.

Our friendship ended when Jimmy and Sue divorced, and Joan and I chose to remain friendly with Sue, which Jimmy resented deeply. But Joan and

I told him that we saw no reason to turn our backs on her, and that was that.

A PLACE TO LIVE IN NEW YORK

Don Reynolds and I found a studio apartment at 20 Gramercy Park South, at the corner of 20th st. and 3rd Avenue. It was on the 17th floor with a small balcony which permitted an oblique Northwest view of a slice of the park. We bought and moved in twin beds, some kitchen utensils, a couple of folding chairs, and a small kitchen table. Next door were three young women who had moved into the city from Queens, the borough directly across the East river. One of them worked as a secretary to the Johnny Carson show. They befriended us with the occasional invitation to come over for dinner and drinks.

Don by this time was a non-drinker, which I welcomed because I had known him back in Amarillo when he was still imbibing and sometimes out of control. Don later took me to a couple of "open" meetings of AA. At one of these meetings, the speaker was Charles Jackson, famous author of "The Lost Weekend", an international best seller made into a popular movie starring Ray Milland, one of the best Hollywood actors of the day.

Jackson told a harrowing story of his own alcoholism and near death from alcohol poisoning, his road to sobriety as told in the book, becoming wealthy, then relapsing deeper into alcoholism. He was a compelling speaker, and his message made a lasting impression.

WORK

Time to go to work on Monday, and I compiled a list of advertising agencies and their media buyers to make appointments to tell the FM conceptual story. Conceptual was the operative word because at least six months would be required to get the six stations up running with personnel, leased broadcast lines, and office and small studio space. Musak was to do most of the programming, and leg work in the markets, where they had established offices. My job was to bring in national advertisers at the time the stations began broadcasting.

Before Power Point computer presentations, there were old fashioned flip charts, hand lettered, to tell a marketing story. I put my flip chart together explaining who we were, what we were going to offer, the unique appeal to prestige brands, and estimated air dates for the stations. I made appointments with J. Walter Thompson, the largest agency, McCann Erickson, The Grey Agency, Ogilvy and Mather, Young and Rubicam, Doyle Dane Bernbach, and the New York office of Leo Burnett, the Chicago based agency.

I had never even sat in on a presentation to an agency media buyer, and had no idea what to expect. I dove in, in spite of not being a complete extrovert. The first few were the most difficult, but the more times I told the story, the easier it became to answer questions I knew would be asked.

The feedback was polite intrigue. Yes, they would be interested in the concept and could see the benefits, and come back and see them when stations were ready to air and we had a better idea of rates in each market. It was cut and dried, and clear immediately that these folks bought by the numbers. It also became clear that meaningful commitments to ad schedules could not be expected until after cost per thousand and listener demographic data had been developed. In other words, to sell at this level would require at least some history, some market research, some ratings feedback, and a reliable audience profile.

I dutifully wrote reports for Jack Liston and Musak and updated Jack by phone. Everyone understood the challenges. It was a chicken or egg issue. Selling the concept was simple and easy. Repeat calls were really pointless until firm progress had been made in generating the required statistics. I continued to make calls on smaller agencies in New York and Philiadelphia, with the same feedback.

About this time, I learned of a meeting of New York FM stations to conference about the future of the medium. The media buyers I had met told the group about FM Associates, and I was invited to attend the meeting. Attendees included the sales director of WQXR FM, the Times owned station, and we developed a telephone relationship. The conference itself focused on the quality story behind FM radio, the growth in separate programming of FM frequencies, and the rapid growth in dedicated FM radio receivers being sold across the country. Clearly, FM radio was in ascendancy and an inexpensive investment for most AM stations who already owned their FM frequencies. I began to attend regular meetings of the group, and reported on them to Liston and Musak.

In February, 1960, word came that our applications to the Federal Communications commission were being held up as a result of cross filings by other interested parties in the same frequencies. Granting our applications, if at all, would come after hearings before the F.C.C. regarding uses to be made of the channels, financial health of the applicants, knowledge of markets in the selected cities, and other information as requested. This meant the expense of high-powered law firms in Washington, D.C., as well as others in the individual locations.

The whole process seemed to be a surprise to the Whittenburg family and Jack Liston. Their payoff would be diminished or even disappear if litigation dragged out. They were big dogs in Amarillo, but small potatoes in Washington D.C., and the prospects of success with the venture now seemed remote.

Additionally, Jack Liston, during his last visit, told me that he and his wife had agreed to divorce. I felt almost certain that the expense of extended litigation plus the Liston family breakup would lead to abandoning FM Associates, or at least postponing it to some future date.

Old friend Bill Clarke was frequently in New York to see the Katz Agency, who represented KGNC TV to national advertisers. Bill was not connected with FM Associates, but knew the score back home, and had alerted me to the attitude of the family, as well as Jack Liston's sudden departure from his office at KGNC, for reasons unannounced but well understood. He was caught having an affair with one of the secretaries, who happened to be the wife of the head of the accounting department.

Shortly, in April, I received the confirming call from Mr. S.B. Whittenburg himself, who explained the situation I already knew, and asked me to come back to Amarillo, to KGNC TV, until a final decision could be made about FM Associates. I thought of this as a step in the wrong direction, and told Mr. Whittenburg that I had thought it over and would elect to stay in New York and seek other employment.

The call was brief, with few details, and no mention of severance. It was my decision to stay, and, presumably, that choice made me ineligible for any sort of subsidy. I had no argument with it, and strangely, had never anticipated any payment, which says something about my mindset at the time. I was single and had few obligations, and believed I could get by just fine with meager savings. Pride kept me from bringing the subject up.

In retrospect, I speculated that the Whittenburg family agreed to limited financing of the FM idea as a concession to Jack Liston's enthusiasm and a token attempt to salvage his marriage to Bonnie, without a thorough understanding of risk and potential problems. A cursory analysis might have suggested that other applicants would show interest in having FM outlets in these major markets, especially since FCC rules required publication of the applications. Or that the ad agency concept presentations might have been done by rep firms like Katz without opening an office and moving personnel to New York prematurely.

I had been eager to move to New York, and frankly did not have the knowledge or critical thinking skills to ask these basic questions myself. I still believed in the wisdom of experienced elders and was youthfully gullible in assuming someone would look out for my best interests. Lesson learned as part of maturing!! Think critically, challenge conventional wisdom, and when money is involved, beware of assuming the benevolence of others.

SOCIAL LIFE

A word about social life and the surrounding area. Working alone, I had met only a few Musak employees. Among these was a psychiatrist's daughter, Paulann Azorin, who educated me to some degree about the Jewish community and took me to a couple of Jewish singles mixers. Another was a young Italian married couple who invited me to their apartment in the Bronx to meet her single sister. The three girls next door were Irish and native New Yorkers, and were as intrigued with my Texas accent, which I exaggerated, as I was with theirs.

At some point, a social circle developed around an older couple, both professional writers, who lived across the park. Ken and Lee, invited many young people to their regular neighborhood mixers. They were wine and classical and Broadway musical lovers, and their large apartment was always filled with loud music. Male and female singles were regulars. Among these were a young woman from San Antonio, and a widowed Italian mother of five, two gay male artists, and a jingle writer from upstate New York.

With an address on beautiful Gramercy Park, we each got a key to enter its locked gate. Dog owners were the big users, and it showed. On the southern side of the Park was The Players Club, a gathering place and semi-retirement home for old timers from the Broadway stage. On Irving place, to the west, was the former home of Theodore Roosevelt, restored but not open to the public. One block east was 3rd avenue, with its small hardware, grocery, and antique stores, and a couple of really good fish restaurants.

On Park Avenue south, previously known as 4th avenue, Horn and Hordart, the automated cafeteria, was still big. Put your change in a slot, and a small glass door opens allowing access to the food item selected. Ala Carte only, the food was cheap so long as you chose only one or two items. Homeless and near homeless were regulars. The fast food revolution quickly put H&H out of business.

Further south, at 14 st., was Herald Square, made famous by the song "Give my regards to Broadway". West of Herald Square was the artsy Chelsea District, and south below 10th street was eclectic Greenwich Village, notable for some lovely residential streets, hippies, writers, nightlife, gays, clubs, and eccentrics. New York University, one of the country's most respected, was just south of the Village. Washington Square Park was the entrance to NYU, always filled with druggies, homeless hippies, musicians, and students, and the potential for some violence.

CITY FOR WALKING

Manhattan, I believe, is the most fascinating city on earth for walking. The Frick , Metropolitan, Whitney, and Guggenheim museums uptown, the Modern Art museum midtown, the New York Public Library at 42nd and 5th, the private Morgan library at 36th and Lexington, are world-class attractions. The classiest shopping in the Americas is on Fifth and Madison Avenues, and the most attractive antique salons are on 3rd, 2nd, and 1st avenues. Rockefeller center and Radio City music hall are internationally recognized, as are all the famous Broadway and off-Broadway theatres. The absolute best and most famous and expensive restaurants are in Manhattan, as are inexpensive bistros and neighborhood high quality eateries.

And everything is in easy walking distance. Every Manhattan dweller, me included, has invested dozens of days walking the streets, visiting Chinatown, Little Italy, sampling ethnic foods, stopping in at pubs, art gallery hopping, all for very little outlays of cash. The Metropolitan museum alone can consume a week or more. Walking is a big part of the social life and culture, and the proximity of all these things in New York is unique in the world.

But better than all the museums, galleries, monuments, and restaurants are the whole of humanity seen on every avenue and cross street. People of every race, of every age, of every persuasion, some wearing native or ethnic costumes, speaking on street corners, playing music, demonstrating for or against anything, are crowding every sidewalk during daytime and much of night. Tourists and natives and commuters and bums and panhandlers mingle side by side. People watching is easily the greatest New York sport, and its most educational past time.

In 1960, the hard drug criminal culture in the city was not yet pervasive, but soon would be. The stats for serious crime began to rise concurrent with usage of cocaine and heroin, and with the rock-and-roll, beat and hippie culture leading to Woodstock. Drug cartels were competing for control with a variety of ethnic and segregated neighborhoods, against the larger Italian mafia. Violence became endemic as a means of resolving territorial disputes, much as Mexican drug cartels war with each other today.

Prohibition of such drugs fed an underworld which continues to thrive, and gave rise to a bloated and corrupt law enforcement cadre charged with stopping the unstoppable. Society fails this test over and over again. Legalization and taxation is the only long term answer, but is entirely too rationale and reasonable, and too many entrenched interests have too much to lose by admitting the stupidity of our current law enforcement effort to stop drug distribution.

By Spring, 1960, Don Reynolds had quit Thompson and enrolled at Columbia University in upper Manhattan, studying museum management. I decided to move to a 3rd floor brownstone walkup studio at 127 E. 36th, between Lexington and Third Avenues, at $125 dollars a month. It would be my home for the next two years. A job search now became my first priority. For the first time in 8 years, I was about to be out of the media business.

EXPERIENCING NON-PROFITS: MAKING CHOICES

L aying the groundwork for a job hunt involved two immediate steps. First, sign up with an employment agency, give them your best resume, and wait. Second, call someone who has a job in your field of interest to see if their connections might produce something.

I called my WQXR Sales Manager acquaintance and explained my situation, after checking in with an agency. WQXR friend asked me to come up and see him. I did and he speculated that they might be expanding their sales force, but needed approval from higher-ups, and it might take awhile. He officed in the New York Times building, a prestigious address. The New York Times was the world's leading and most influential newspaper in 1960, and was respected for its balanced depth reporting and analysis, as well as for its financial pages. I left encouraged, but with no timetable to decision.

The employment agency contact assigned to me saw a chance to place me in some aspect of media, but this too involved uncertain timing. I had three meetings with him and he seemed about to send me on a round of interviews for jobs in the production side of TV, where I was not sure I wanted to be.

Don Sbarra, who had worked at KGNC AM as a time salesman, had moved on to Wichita, Kansas as Manager of a TV station there. That station also had an equity interest in a TV station in Fargo, North Dakota. On one of his trips to New York, I met with Sbarra and he offered me the job of Sales Manager for the Fargo station. I looked into it briefly but quickly decided against it. It seemed too isolated and cold for me.

Here was another crossroads, which, had I taken it, would have changed the rest of my life. Like the civilian job I turned down at FEN in Tokyo, either choice would have channeled me onto different paths, where I would never have met Joan, never had Scott and Jon, never been the grandfather of Jack and Audrey. I cannot now imagine these outcomes, but these were real life choices of the type that change lives forever.

Over the course of six months in New York, I had been in touch by telephone with my old Amarillo friend Jess Tucker, owner of the Flooring and Fashions business there. Jess was a national retail award winner of the American Carpet Institute, and had recently been to Chicago to accept his award in an elaborate ceremony honoring him and other outstanding retailers for their accomplishments over the years. The award was presented at an industry dinner by Paul W. Jones, President of the Institute. Jess and I talked occasionally, and of course I explained my plight.

Jess was eager to help, and called Paul Jones about me. Jones told Jess that the Institute was expanding staff to make a big push into the architectural and building materials market, and, on Jess Tucker's recommendation, would like to talk with me. Before two days had passed, I was sitting in Paul Jones office on the 29th floor of the Empire State Building, listening to him talk about building a marketing force to blanket the country with a new story educating various commercial markets about soft floor coverings as structural building materials with measured acoustical, safety, and noise control virtues.

I took along a resume which he hardly glanced at. He simply asked me if I might be interested in joining the Institute as Merchandising Director and being a part of the planning and execution of the strategy. Jess Tucker had made a strong pitch, I was sure, and Paul Jones was willing to go with his vote. Paul had been head of the National Cotton Council in Memphis before coming to the ACI. He knew trade associations, was a good politician, and had experience selecting people. He knew, he later told me, that I would fit into the culture of his membership.

The American Carpet Institute was made up of about 35 manufacturers of carpet. Their dues were based on a percentage of sales, with special projects funded separately. Most members were in the Northeast, and made commercial and residential broadloom carpets using technology brought to this country from England and Scotland. Wilton, Velvet, Axminister, were the designations of the woven looms, each loom type chosen based on the design and pattern requirements of the finished goods.

The velvet loom was used for lightly patterned fabrics. Wilton looms were used for moderately intricate designs. Axminister looms were chosen for the production of the most elaborately patterned and most colorful floral fabrics. Each used pre-dyed fibers, either batch or "stock" dyed as raw fiber, and "skein" dyed as yarn. More economical piece dyeing had not yet been adopted as part of woven carpet making technology.

Many of the families involved in carpet manufacture had ties to the industry in Europe. The Shuttleworth family owned Mohasco Industries, which included Mohawk, Alexander Smith, and Firth brands. Magee Carpets of Bloomburg, Pennsylvania made mostly woven velvets and wiltons, as did names like Philadelphia Carpet Company, Roxbury,

Bigelow, Masland, and Hightstown. All were prominent in producing the types of materials to be merchandised to selected commercial markets, and all members were eager to open new end uses.

Most mills were privately held, and most CEO's and owners served on the Board of Directors of the American Carpet Institute. The Institute operated on a committee structure. The technical committee set minimum recommended quality standards for a variety of end uses, as well as standardization of terminology. Such standards were necessary for use in competitive bidding, the standard means of purchase for commercial buyers. A research group directed independent contracts with acoustical, safety, and medical experts to document the specific contributions of soft flooring in settings such as schools, hospitals, nursing homes, and high-rise office and apartment buildings.

Government Affairs effectively directed the Institute's lobbyist in Washington. Charles Jones, (no relation), who had formerly been chief of staff for Mississippi Senator John Stennis, headed the Washington office. The publications/PR committee directed development of educational literature for various end uses, as well as consumer education on judging and buying home carpet. A great deal of effort also went into training literature and retail floor training sessions, giving salesmen the basics on how to lead customers through quality, decorating, and price decisions.

Then there was the statistics committee which gathered and aggregated all production data, inventory data of raw materials and finished goods, sales per residential household, average wholesale prices, percentage of production intended for the non-residential market. They produced the quarterly Bible against which every manufacturer measured his own performance and determined his market share.

The Institute's activities encompassed most all the generic educational and informational needs of the industry and its distribution chain, but carefully avoided any references to particular brands or individual company pricing or marketing practices. Minutes were kept of each committee meeting agenda and discussions, and a lawyer present kept each group focused on the agenda if discussion began to stray.

I would receive a starting salary of $9200. per year, plus expense account for travel and entertaining. Entertainment could include a wide range of retailers, architects, building owners and managers, and marketing/merchandising personnel of member companies. Absent profit sharing or stock options or bonuses, expense accounts were liberalized.

I accepted the offer with a start date of June 1, 1960, which gave me a couple of weeks to make a trip back to see my family. As I was preparing to leave New York, I got a call from my friend at WQXR telling me that he had worked out something and felt he could now talk to me about going to work there. With very mixed feelings, I thanked him and explained that I had just accepted a job and considered it a commitment, so could not consider his offer.

At about the same time, the employment agency called to say they had an interview lined up at CBS for the position of Unit manager of a network television series. As before, I told him that it was too late, and I would not be going on the interviews.

It was a transitional moment when a choice made leads one forever in a different direction than that previously chosen, a seminal and life-changing time when, if I had elected to backtrack and consider either interview, my life that moment forward might have been forever changed. But my rather naive sense of obligation and ethics led me to honor my word and go into an entirely new field.

A more sensible approach, clear in hindsight, would have been to explore both options before making any decision. If either had proven to be more advantageous and attractive from the standpoint of making better use of my experience and talents and enhancing my career prospects, a reasonable course of action would have been to go back to Mr. Jones and refuse the job. This may have disappointed him and my friend Jess Tucker, but would not have been unethical or immoral or unusual or selfish. It would simply have been intelligent.

But I chose to stick to my word, and, in so doing, made a decision which affected the rest of my working life, albeit in good and rewarding ways I could never have perceived at the time. It would be the path to meeting Joan , to a career in the chemical industry, to two wonderful sons, to living in Connecticut and unexpected new cities, to travelling the world over, and ultimately to starting my own business. I would never know what taking the other roads might have brought.

The notion that leaving behind eight years of valuable experience in all phases of media might be analogous to abandoning the equivalent time needed to become a Neurosurgeon or a University Professor or a PHD research scientist, was one that never registered in my consciousness. I needed a job, and left-brained pragmatism recognized a bird in the hand. Waiting around for the media to open its arms to me was an unaffordable luxury.

AT THE INSTITUTE

The first day at work at the Institute, I met Eugene V. Connett IV, a Princeton graduate like his Father and Grandfather before him. Gene's family had come to Long Island with a King's land grant. Unlike the Garretts' and Morris', they stayed in New York, where Gene's colonial family had opened a successful hat factory. The Connett family continued the business until well into the 20th century, when Gene's Father, the 3rd, sold it to concentrate on writing and publishing art magazines on fly fishing and fox hunting. It was known as the DerryDale Press, and continues today under other ownership.

Gene had grown up in privilege and decorum, as part of the yacht and hunt club set, in a spacious beach home on "The Island", as native New Yorkers knew it. He had graduated Princeton early to join the Air Force during WWII, and had served in Intelligence in England.

Gene was Marketing Director of the American Carpet Institute, a position for which he had been recruited from the David Ogilvy advertising agency. We became immediate and unlikely lifelong friends. Pairing a patrician blood-line and elite Princeton education with a dust bowl frontier Texan from an obscure college, would not seem the obvious basis for friendship, but we managed without effort to like each other as we worked side by side for the next six years.

Gene was something of an expert at dissecting consumer research. He took raw data from National Family Opinion surveys, and drew conclusions on how the industry could better market its products to housewives and commercial buyers alike. Gene wrote or co-wrote much of the literature aimed at architects and developers of commercial property. He also prioritized the decision sequence of women when purchasing carpet for the home, arguing that color, texture, performance, and price, in that order, should be the rule for retail salesmen to follow when dealing with an uncertain consumer making an infrequent big-ticket purchase. This sequence became the basis for store displays and advertising all over the country.

So began travels to every major city in the country to hold seminars for architects, educational foundations, hospital administrators, Universities, Building owners and managers. We were equipped with slide shows and hand-out books. We hosted luncheons and dinners for interested groups and told them our story. We flew to Boston, Cleveland, Dallas, Houston, Indianapolis, Denver, Chicago, San Francisco, Los Angeles, Pheonix, Miami, Charlotte, Seattle, Detroit, and San Diego, among others. These were cities new to me, and the trips revealed an urban world outside New York I had only read about.

Curiously, I discovered that many native New Yorkers had also never been to other major cities. They were at least as parochial and myopic as this most cloistered West Texan. Many I talked with seemed actually oblivious to life west of the Hudson river. Living an entire life in Long Island, the Bronx, Queens, Brooklyn, Manhattan, and Staten Island seemed to be enough. New York is of course a hub for travelers, but it seemed to me that only a small percentage of New Yorkers had ranged more broadly than a fifty mile radius from their birthplace.

Gene and I and fellow staffer Ian Graham would leave New York on Monday morning, hold meetings in the afternoon, and often have dinner meetings with groups of local retailers in the evening. We used the Kepner-Tregoe method of training, dividing the group into round tables of 8 or 10, asking them to appoint a chairman whose job was to make sure everybody at the table got a chance to speak.

We then explained that the procedure would be in three phases. Phase 1 was problem analysis; phase 2 decision analysis; phase 3 potential problem analysis. We then asked the following question: What is the most important problem facing the industry today? Each table deliberated, collected and prioritized their issues, and each took turns at the podium reporting to the entire group.

After problems were listed and agreed upon, the same format was used in the decision phase. What are the best solutions to the problems we have identified? Another round of discussion and reporting followed.

Finally, phase 3 kicked in to identify potential problems with the solutions proposed. With Kepner Tregoe, everyone in the room had his voice heard, and there was always a remarkable degree of agreement on the substance of all three phases.

Kepner Tregoe as a training format was taught at Hillsdale College in Michigan, where we spent a week on how to run the technique and hosting meetings for best results. Gene and I also attended a two-week executive course in Retailing, taught at the graduate Business school at Indiana University. Professor Bert McCammon assembled an excellent group of professors to teach the course, lecturing on key issues in retailing, and also using specific cases developed around the flooring industry. It was an intensive crash course, taught on campus. We lived in campus housing, and ate our meals in cafeterias there.

In the office, we prepared for the next round of seminars and followed up the last round with letters and booklets to those who had attended. We also reported internally to various committees on what we were seeing on the road in terms of architectural acceptance of our themes, and the state of retail training. Local manufacturer's reps often attended our retail meetings, and their own reports back to their parent company supplemented ours.

THE DOWNSIDE OF NON-PROFITS

The schedule was a tough grind, and I knew after the first few months that this job could not be a long-term interest, both because of the extensive travel and the repetitive nature of the work. I also learned a lot about the functioning of non-profit organizations. In the beginning, I had not thought much about the role of financial incentives and the profit motive in driving job satisfaction. With no opportunity to earn bonuses for outstanding performance, and with no stock grants or stock options, and incremental automatic salary increases, I began to disassociate and loose energy and drive toward doing excellent work. This happened insidiously, and I came to recognize it only over time.

People are clearly motivated by ambition, altruism, greed, and a variety of other conscious and unconscious needs. While the ACI did many worthwhile things for the industry, the fundamental weakness of the non-profit concept, which was by definition the void of profits, kept creeping back into my awareness. Profits, in my view, are the lifeblood and great motivator of businesses. Profits reinvested bring growth and employment and opportunity for individual advancement and financial gain. Profits enable incentive bonuses, stock grants, stock options, and extraordinary monetary recognition. Profits drive stock values and stimulate interest.

Non profits, on the other hand, are inevitably lethargic over time. All the ingredients of excitement at work can be present, but if profits are not part of the equation and the ultimate goal, disinterest leads to half or sporadic effort, and the sense of career ending boredom takes over in spite of best management efforts.

Politicians and government employees are precise examples of half is good enough philosophy, and even they often expect to profit handsomely once out of office or on government pensions and free to take on work elsewhere. Corrupt law enforcement personnel are another example of extracurricular profit taking. Those choosing military careers get psychic or retirement rewards tantamount to profit. Large charitable groups such as Red Cross or foundation employees may be altruistic initially, but loose motivation over time and risk sinking into graft.

Teachers are probably the most admired employees of non-profits, but their unions enrich themselves while achieving little for teachers on the line and regimenting the delivery of education to the point that innovation is stifled. Public employee unions wield great power in electing politicians, then get payoffs in the form of higher wages and benefits from those same, now beholden politicians. This corrupt and destructive cycle is now beginning to unravel as the taxpaying public comes to understand that they are the losers in this game of mutual back-scratching between office holders and public employee unions.

Experiencing a non-profit run of 6 years led me to the conviction that they are useful as a training ground, but deadly and disheartening as a career. Never work for non-profits given a choice, and if you must, make sure it is for your own foundation, set up to give away the great wealth accumulated while owning and running a for-profit enterprise.

My associations with Paul Jones, William Rockwell, William Reynolds, Ruth Holman, Len Moser and other staffers were all rewarding. The friendship with Gene Connett and his wife, Effie, continued until the end of their lives. On one occasion, I invited Gene to be my guest at the annual Christmas luncheon of the Sales Executives Club of New York, which I had recently joined. We bought tickets for the door prize of a new Nash Rambler station wagon, winner to be drawn during lunch. Of course, the bar was open, and when the drawing came, we were ready to cheer for somebody......anybody.

When Gene's name was drawn as the winner, he did a celebratory athletic back flip at the table. He and Effie had three daughters and new twin boys, and needed a larger family vehicle to transport the clan.

Bill Rockwell, the staff attorney, and his wife, Liz, invited me for a weekend at their home in Pound Ridge, New York, in Westchester County. So did Bill Reynolds and his wife Nancy, who lived in Armonk, New York. Ruth Holman, a former teacher of English at North Texas State Teacher's college, in Denton, Texas, owned and car and often invited me to use it on weekends. Len Moser and his wife Betty, residents of the upper East side, became fairly regular dinner companions.

JOAN ARDITH HENDERSON

I was still single at 28, but that would change soon enough. In the Fall of 1961, a young woman named Cessie Blennerhasset, who worked in the Empire State building for the Dupont Company, called to invite me to a party at her apartment. The party was in honor of her sorority sister at San Jose State in California. I had met Cessie in the course of Institute business, since Dupont was a large producer nylon and polyester carpet fibers.

The sorority sister was at that time a flight attendant with Pan American World Airways, and was based in San Francisco, but returning from a vacation in Europe. She would be passing through New York, so Cessie decided on a party.

Her name was Joan Ardith Henderson, and Cessie's party was the catalyst for a relationship which has now lasted 48 years and counting. It was probably not romantic love at first sight. We had not met before, and were both old enough to think things through, but she was very attractive and I liked her personality. It was a memorable meeting, and I did not forget her. I was not sure what her impressions of me were, but she held

Joan Henderson
PRESIDENT
1953

Photo 15. Joan Ardith Henderson as President of The Madrones, a girls club at Oakland High devoted to community service.

onto my phone number. She went back to work flying the Pacific route out of the San Francisco base. We had little contact.

A year later, she transferred her Pan AM job to New York and began flying the European route. The Federal government had tight, almost socialistic controls over routes and fares at the time, and Pan AM was never granted domestic routes. As usual, government intervention in what should have been free market decisions all but assured the ultimate demise of Pan Am, as emerging countries financed their own national airlines as both status symbols and as sources of foreign exchange.

But at the moment, Pan Am was the premier airline, and Joan had travelled the world for over five years, serving on both propeller driven Stratacruisers and transitioning to Boeing 707 jets when jet technology replaced props.

THE NEW LOOK   The uniform suit and topcoat modeled above by Miss Joan Henderson has been selected by Pan American System. The complete uniform was designed and will be made by Don Loper, internationally famous designer of women's clothes. It is anticipated that PAD will have all our Flight Service girls in the new uniform by February, 1960.

Early in her experience*Photo 16. Joan in uniform suit and topcoat* as   a   flight attendant, Joan worked a flight from San Francisco to Hawaii aboard a Boeing Stratacruiser. The flight was long, and passengers actually put on pajamas and slept for a good part of it. The starboard outboard gasoline engine caught fire about an hour from destination, and the captain put the plane into an accelerated dive to extinguish the fire. He leveled out at about 200 feet above the ocean surface, fire out, but with some uncertainty about getting the rest of the way to Hawaii. Coast Guard aircraft came out and escorted the plane the rest of the way, prepared to salvage what they could in case ditching became necessary.

Exiting the plane, passengers and crew saw that the engine was completely gone, with only a small part of the cowling remaining. The incident was her only close call in six years of regular international long hauls

Joan was selected on several occasions as crew onto prestigious charters for heads of state. Sukarno of Indonesia hand-picked his Pan Am cabin crews, and Joan was always among them, accompanying President Sukarno to State dinners with Tito of Yugoslavia, among others, and aboard Tito's private luxury yacht. The crew was rewarded with luxury vacations in Bali, and gifts from the President.

On moving to New York, Joan called me, saying I was the one person she knew in New York, (her humor) and we arranged to get together. From that day on, when she wasn't on duty, we were together much of the time, sometimes with "day" dates, while I disentangled from another relationship. Joan claims I didn't have the money for dinners, and she was partly right.

Over the next year, we juggled travel schedules and dated when we were both in town, and in 1962, we began talking about marriage. We decided on the following January 14th, and chose the chapel at the Fifth Avenue Presbyterian church at 10th street and fifth avenue as the sight of the wedding. Meanwhile, Joan and I made one trip to California to meet her family, Alice and Edwin Henderson, and to announce our engagement, the notice of which appeared in the Oakland Tribune, Ed's employer for 46 years. None of my family met Joan prior to our marriage.

On the appointed day, 10 inches of snow had fallen on the city. Joan's Dad's flight landed in Philadelphia and he came to the city by train, barely in time for the ceremony. Alice had come a couple of days earlier. Joan and I had located a rent controlled two bedroom apartment, 8 A, at 15 Park Avenue, and had taken a lease at $145. Per month.

Rent controlled apartments were prized, and their availability was not often advertised. I found the apartment by slipping the doorman, Russell, a few dollars to keep me informed. There were no signs indicating an apartment was available, but the tip to Russell paid off . We moved her furniture and what little furniture I had into the apartment a few days before the wedding.

Betty Lou Ruble, Joan's apartment mate in New York and fellow Pan Am flight attendant, was to be her bridesmaid. John Roughan, who worked for Chemstrand, owned by Monsanto, and who also officed in the Empire State Building, was my best man. A couple of years later, I was to be best man for him and Harriet.

I had met John several times in the course of discussing carpet fibers , which Chemstrand produced, and liked him very much. He had grown up in Lowell, Massachusetts and attended Lowell Textile college, graduating as a chemist. He attend the Wharton Business school at the University of Pennsylvania, then went to work as a chemist for American Viscose, a producer of rayon fiber. Later, American Viscose and Monsanto joint ventured to form Chemstrand, a producer of acrylic and nylon fibers and yarns. Chemstrand headquartered in the Empire State Building and had large market shares of the carpet and apparel end uses. John's marketing effort was focused on the same commercial applications of carpet as I was, so we had a lot in common.

He lived in the building next door at 10 Park Avenue. We got into our tuxedos, put on rubber boots, and trudged two cross town blocks in deep snow to Fifth Avenue to catch the downtown bus to the church. We arrived just in time.

The limo I arranged did manage to get Joan, Betty Lou, and Alice and Ed to the church, but the weather made the ride downtown difficult. There was no time for him to come back for John and me. Joan said her Dad, Ed, was concerned I wouldn't show.

Quite a few friends filled the chapel, both mine and Joan's. A few of her Pan Am pals, but mostly people I had met since coming to New York, and who lived in or near my Murray Hill neighborhood. Some were staffers at carpet companies, others with fiber companies, and still others were a group of National Airlines stewardesses and their boyfriends or husbands. Ruth Holman and her boyfriend Roel Wolfson were there, as were Len Moser and Betty. Palmer (Ron) Ronholm, a TWA Captain, was there with his wife Noreen, a stu with National. Peggy and Bob Moran, and friends Nick and Anita were present.

The ceremony went as planned, and we soon adjourned to Joan's old apartment at 51st and second avenue for the champagne reception and cheers and toasts. It was crowded and happy. At some suitable but late hour, Joan and I departed for the Plaza hotel, where I had arranged a small suite for two nights. The next day, Joan had a dental appointment for a root canal, my first spousal bill, and that night had an elegant dinner at Seito's Japanese restaurant, one of the two or three Japanese restaurants in the entire city at the time. We checked out of the Plaza on the third day, took our belongings to our new apartment, where a new mattress had just been delivered, and slept there for the first time.

Next night, January 17, we went to Idlewild Airport and took an overnight free Pan Am flight to Rio de Janero, Brazil, for a week of honeymoon at the Continental Plaza hotel overlooking Ipanema beach.

The free tickets had been a parting gift for Joan. Airline rules at the time discouraged married women from continuing to work.

It was summertime Brazil, before the revolution there, and our suite was $10. Per day. Brazil was still a poor country then the dollar/cruzero exchange rate was highly favorable for us. We ate in excellent Portugese restaurants every night and beach walked or shopped or went to the pool during the day. On March 31 following our January visit there, a revolution would engulf Brazil and the military would take over and run the country as a dictatorship until 1985.

Photo 17. Joan and me on our honeymoon in Rio. My favorite picture of us together.

Leaving Rio, we flew to San Francisco to see Joan's parents, but had a surprise stop in Panama, where the Pan AM 707 was commandeered because of some military emergency, and we were bumped. Another flight picked us up about 12 hours later, and we continued on to California. Altogether, the trip from Rio to San Francisco had taken more than 24 hours, and we were beat.

In Oakland, at Joan's parents staged a reception and introduction to their many friends. Two days later, we flew to Texas so Joan could meet my family for the first time. Frank and Dillie loved Joan instantly and always, as did many siblings, aunts, uncles, and cousins. My uncle John Morris burst into the front bedroom where we were sleeping and demanded to meet this newest member of the family. There were lots of relatives around during our visit there, and, when we left after two days, Joan had been through the trauma of meeting the stares an entire clan, most of who's names she could not remember.

Back in New York after two weeks, it was back to work for me, while Joan decorated and furnished the apartment with the basics. I was still with the Institute in spite of some misgivings about the long term.

In the short term, it was secure employment, so I decided to stick with it but keep an eye out for something more favorable. It would be another two years before that something came along.

Photo 18. Joan as a beautiful wife, Mother, and Grandmother.

Joan and I were married somewhat later than most, at age 30 and 28. We both had experienced other relationships, but were fortunate to have waited and found each other. We were both out of college and had maturity and work experiences. Joan came from sturdy Swedish and English stock, and has been a loyal and loving companion from a stable family environment . She endured my corporate transfers and extended travels without complaining, working hard as a wife and Mother to help make each move successful. When the boys were high school age, she went to work in her dream job, that of interior designer, and continues her artistic pursuits even today, helping friends with interior design issues, making jewelry as gifts, decorating her own home with great taste, enriching our friendships with her warmth and personality.

Meeting Joan was providential. Marrying Joan was an act of will; a path chosen which I have never regretted; a path leading to Scott and Jon, and Terry and Jack and Audrey, who make life worthwhile.

STARTING A FAMILY

Scott Edwin Garrett was born Sunday, August 30, 1964. His imminent presence gave Joan enough time to pack a small bag and head to Mt. Sinai hospital in upper Manhattan. He wasn't expected just then, and I had no money in the house, but, over the past few months, had begun to deposit change in "Scott's" Piggy Bank. I emptied it and took the change for cab fare, which was around $10.

Dr. Shapiro had been called and was waiting. He told me it would be awhile, so I took a walk around the corner trying to find a coffee shop. Instead, I located a small gift shop and purchased a tiny cannon commemorating the occasion. It wasn't long before all 7 pounds 13 ounces of him appeared, and in good health. At the time, Fathers were discouraged from being in the birth room, so I waited outside.

Scott was ruddy and wrinkled for a time, but we were both thrilled to see that he had all his fingers and toes, and a healthy voice. The emotions I felt were the usual ones for new fathers, I am sure. New responsibility, new commitment, resolve to be a good father, pride, happiness for his good health and Joan's good health, some thinking about an education, and, after awhile, a home out of the city.

Joan's Mother Alice arrived from California while they were still in Mt. Sinai hospital. Alice stayed a week or longer to help Joan get back on her feet and into a routine. She was a wonderful help, and knew just what to do.

Joan and Scott were home within three days. Joan had invested time in decorating his room. A special crib with canopy, a changing table, a supply of diapers, and some toys. We were well equipped and comfortable, waiting. We lived around the corner from Gristede's market, where formula, diapers, and other supplies were at hand.

Mrs. Rex Stark, a widow and former social editor of Better Homes and Gardens magazine, lived across the hall, and paid a welcome home visit with a gift. Everyone in the building welcomed them home. Several gifts arrived from friends at the Institute, and from many friends with whom we socialized over the months. And gifts and notes from family in Texas and California, and Joan's old friends at Pan AM. Scott was off to a good start.

I went back to my office on Monday with the news, and resumed work, but avoided travel for the next couple of weeks. Paul Jones and Gene Connett invited me to lunch at the Empire State Club, and we celebrated with martinis, a daily routine for Paul, and often, Gene as well. Those were the halcion days of Madison Avenue and images of men in grey flannel suits drinking heavily at lunchtime with impunity, then slinking away in the afternoon while waiting for the commuter train.

The Institute had an open bar before lunch, with lunch prepared and served from our own kitchen by a lady chef and server. Drinking was expected then, but is much less of a corporate ritual today. In any event, after a couple of martinis and an extended lunch, I walked the two block back to the apartment to check in on my new son and Joan and Alice. We literally lived that close, and on rainy days, I could walk through Altman's department store on Madison Avenue and come out on Fifth across the street from the Empire State, with hardly a drop on me. Office hours began at 9 AM in New York, so sleeping until 8 was feasible. Commuters would have to start their day at least two hours earlier. I could also be home three minutes after leaving the office.

Time passed, Scott grew, work continued, and we became accustomed to having another human live with us. At three months, he was very alert and active, with great curiosity he exhibits to this day as an attorney.

In New York, we had been to Broadway shows, the best restaurants, usually on expense account, and all the galleries and museums. Joan regularly took Scott on the Madison Avenue bus uptown to central park, with stroller, and spent much of the day. They had lunch in the park, strolled down Fifth Avenue, and shopped our own neighborhood of Murray Hill almost daily. Local merchants knew Scott, and often gave him samples of food and candy, or a special toy. The neighborhood could not have been more like a friendly small town.

At three years old, Scott, curious always, could let himself out our front door and call the elevator. Fortunately, it had not yet been automated. Joan was terrified he might disappear and kept the front door chain locked after missing him one day and finding him in the basement laundry room. Russell and Tommy, the night doorman, knew where he was.

Mrs. Stark became a good friend and invited us over often for drinks and snacks, and Scott was free to browse and touch everything. Before his arrival, we had carpeted the entire apartment with an attractive shade of green. The carpet had been lightly used in our Chicago Merchandise Mart showroom. I paid to have the carpet shipped to us in New York, and an installer to lay it. Joan made matching drapes with her sewing machine I had "thoughtfully" and "romantically" given her for Valentine's day.

The place looked great, with soft surfaces throughout the place when Scott began to crawl. We had a wood burning fireplace, high ceilings, front windows overlooking Park Avenue, and a view on the east side of the building looking toward the East river. A Pullman sized kitchen was adequate, and opened on a small dining area seating six. Best of all, under the archaic rules of rent control held over from the World War Two housing shortage, our rent could never be raised.

We lived there happily until Summer of 1967, three and one-half years, before moving to a home in Connecticut, next door to Gene and Effie.

Photo 19. Joan, age 2, with older brother Bob, in 1937, Oakland, California.

Photo 20. Joan, with her family, brother Bob, Mom Alice, and Dad Edwin Henderson, 1943, Oakland, California.

Photo 21. My favorite picture of "our boys", Jonathan (Jon), and Scott Edwin, as adults.

Photo 22.   Scott as a Dad, with his son Jack, age 11 in this picture.

Photo 23.   Scott's wife Terry and daughter Audrey, age 10.

Photo 24. Jon and Scott together, about ages 6 and 9.

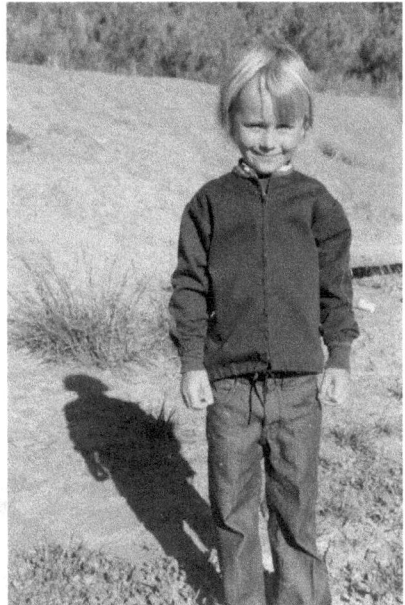

Photo 25.   Jon, age 6, taken in Atlanta.

Photo 26. Jonathan, # 507, finishing the second leg of a triathlon, Ventura, CA, 1997

Photo 27. Jonathan, in formal, on his way to his high school prom, St. Louis.

Photo 28. Edwin and Alice Henderson, Joan's parents, as young marrieds, with son Bob, 1934, Oakland.

Photo 29. Alice, Joan's mother, with grandson Scott, at our home in Connecticut, 1968

THOUGHTS ON RESPONSIBILITY

This narrative will now be delayed by a brief essay on self-responsibility. The gradual aging process, the transitioning from early life to maturity, the experience gained through a variety of work environments and the association with many individuals with differing degrees of intelligence and talent, have made clear the necessity of self regulation in all areas of living.

I have observed that individuals of each generation rarely learn from or accept the wisdom of previous generations. The young have and will always test the limits of accepted societal ethics, morals, laws, parental rules, religious dictates, and any such handed-down sagacity. For a period of years, they will not accept that established codes of conduct and behavior actually are applicable to them as individuals.

They will and must learn for themselves that certain boundaries and limits are desirable and essential in order for useful life to follow; that the rules imposed on themselves, by themselves, will define their life course of success or failure; that freedom is not license; that self-discipline always wins over self-indulgence.

As soon as this enlightenment is attained, each thinking person can devise his own standards defining clear and realistic limits for each facet of his or her life. These disciplines can include ethical and moral codes the individual will not breach. These particular aspects of the code need not be religiously based, since ethics and morals evolved from tribal and community interactions over thousands of years, and not from pious religious edicts.

The limits of indulgence in foods, addictive substances and those with the potential for mental impairment, can be prominent in the code.

So can health maintenance, weight management, financial boundaries, humanitarian/charitable interests, commitment to academic or work habits, resolutions related to attitudes and disposition, and limits on adventures with potentially lethal outcomes. Actions and reactions to mates and offspring, siblings or parents, bosses and subordinates, can be calculated and implemented according to the life philosophy, which is the summation of the rules.

The purpose of a consciously derived code is to place the brain, the head, in charge, rather than emotional and compulsive urges. Recognizing and anointing the brain as the central control room for the body means that the brain has the power of altering what the genome may crave, of keeping the body on course, of keeping the ship airborne, or the sails full, and keeping the self prepared, sober, and ready. My own parents, Frank and Dillie, were circumspect models of self-restraint. They curbed their appetites. They were never self-indulgent. Their lives were sober and balanced, never personally weakened by addiction. They lived lives of self-denial in order to provide best for their family. Never perfect, but never losing sight of the need for living responsibly.

Much of the destructive behavior individuals visit upon themselves can be corrected or even avoided through awareness of inevitable pitfalls, and constant reference to the rules for living which have been self-developed.

We read often of those who climb mountains known to be dangerous, yet expect to be rescued when trouble erupts. Skiing off marked trails is treacherous, but many want to be saved when their lives are threatened. Hiking alone in deserts cannot be seen as intelligent, yet dozens are stranded each year and their lives threatened or ended by careless, unthinking adventure. Yet these are mere metaphors for everyday risky actions such as driving drunk, ingesting narcotics, over medicating with prescription drugs, over-eating to the point of dangerous and unbecoming weight gain, or perhaps breaching our moral and ethical codes by skating on the edge of honesty with our employer or spouse or children.

Responsibility for self, growing from an understanding of the needs of self, and a corresponding unique code of conduct developed and implemented by the user-self, is, in my opinion, the most important life document. It is the document to which self will commit, and the positive thought process to assure guilt free satisfaction, and make realization of life's goals most likely.

It is not the invocation of religion. It is the antithesis of guilt-based bromides. It is proactive forward planning. Like planning for achievement in any area of career or life, the act of setting goals, of thinking through and writing parameters as guideposts, is the most critical planning step in reaching those goals.

Former President Harry Truman was quoted as saying, "In reading the lives of great men, I found that the first victory they won was over themselves...self-discipline with all of them came first."

Buddha said, "It is better to conquer yourself than to win a thousand battles. Then the victory is yours. It cannot be taken from you, not by angels or by demons, heaven or hell."

ANOTHER CROSSROADS: TRANSITION TO CHEMICALS

T he Institute routine put me increasingly in the company of fiber producers like Dupont, Chemstrand, American Cyanamid, and Beaunit, who were orienting their marketing and merchandising campaigns toward displacing traditional wool fiber in the carpet industry. Synthetic fibers could claim significant processing economies and performance characteristics over wool. As an example, they were non-allergenic. They could be piece dyed with differential dye uptakes, creating multi-colored colors with acid and disperse dyes in a single dye bath.

Nylon, the longest wearing, could be purchased in continuous yarn form, skipping the costly yarn spinning step. Carpets could then be dyed to customer order from greige-undyed inventory, a huge cost advantage. Nylon, acrylics, and polyester fibers were produced in the United States, while coarse wool had to be imported from Scotland and New Zealand. Wool was cumbersome and costly to store and process. Plastic fibers could be engineered to process and perform in superior ways. Raw materials inventory costs were reduced drastically. It was an easy choice for newer carpet mills.

Tufting technology was also gaining a foothold as the technology of the future, gradually displacing woven technology as the industry standard. With tufting, a prefabricated backing was fed through a wide bank of sewing needles which literally sewed the face yarns into the backing. The technology was cheap and fast, a fraction of the capital and operating cost of woven equipment. Soon, a new industry had taken root in Dalton, Georgia, with the full range of support infrastructure such as commission dye houses, commission yarn spinners, warehousing and truck terminals.

The southern tufters formed their own trade group, named The Tufted Textile Manufacturers Association, and membership encompassed broadloom tufters as well as throw rug and bath mat producers, and a full range of associate members like fiber producers, and any and all suppliers of goods and services to the industry. The TTMA began to compete with the ACI, who still had mainly old-line woven manufacturers as members.

Carpet mills in the South could be profitable and prosperous with half the costs of New England mills. A large pool of eager non-union labor was at hand. Southern Universities like Georgia Tech, North Carolina State, the University of Alabama, and the University of Georgia created Textile engineering schools to accommodate the technical needs of the industry. Fiber Producers plants were sited in the South, with local monetary incentives such as tax holidays, excellent transportation by truck, rail, and barge, and plentiful labor.

Monsanto' acrylic plant was located on the huge Tennessee river. The river gave barge access to the Gulf of Mexico, where raw materials like Acrilonitrile could be shipped in from Monsanto's large chemical Intermediates plant in Texas City, near Galveston.

High profit margins enabled large advertising and marketing efforts toward building new brands. Traditional woven mills could see the signs clearly. Their residential markets would fall to the tufters, and their choice was to fight them or join them. Many moved their most important operations to the South and out of New England, consistent with the wholesale transfer of most all other textile operations to lower cost non-union labor in the now industrialized tech-savvy South.

The commercial, non-residential market was a different story. Woven technology could produce higher quality, tightly woven and dense face weights required for heavily trafficked uses like school, office buildings, and hospitals. Most bid specifications contained construction and density terminology favoring woven bidders. Tufting still could not compete well in this arena, a market of priority interest to Chemstrand and the Institute.

By early 1966, Monsanto was the sole owner of Chemstrand, and the respected joint venture Managing Director, Robert Smith, had decided to move on. He joined Beaunit Company, charged with building its nylon franchise in the growing and profitable fiber business. Smith began putting together a marketing team, taking a couple of Monsanto people with him to the new assignment. One of them was Frank Loughran, a marketer I had known and worked with in running joint Monsanto/ACI workshops for architects.

I received a surprise phone call from Bob Smith, who I knew. He told me of his plans at Beaunit, mentioned Loughran's name, and asked me to come over and talk to him about joining Beaunit. A couple of conversations later, I had an offer substantially above my present ACI income, and went in to discuss the matter with Paul Jones. Paul listened with interest, and asked me to hold off making a final decision until he made some phone calls.

An hour later, I got a call from Frank Hartmann, Marketing Director of the Monsanto/Chemstrand carpet fibers effort, who said, "I hear you are in play." I was flattered by all this new attention. As it happened, a week before, I had done a joint meeting with Hartmann with a large group of retailers in Syracuse, New York. He had seen my presentations at a number of similar meetings. He asked me to come down to the 17th floor and meet with him and Bruce Kenworthy, his acrylic guy.

I did so, and came away with an offer to join Chemstrand as Manager, New Markets, at a salary I could only dream about a week earlier. I bee-lined back to Paul Jones' office with the news, and he was wearing a big smile. He had been the set-up man with Hartmann. I resigned my job at the Institute, wrapped up my work in progress over the next couple of days, and took a week off.

Joan got the news first, and I am pretty sure we had a toast or two. This would allow us to consider buying a home in the suburbs and providing a more desirable setting for Scott and perhaps a family addition. Monsanto had the best marketing reputation of the fiber companies, even though Dupont was larger. Monsanto was a broad based full line chemical company with resources and depth of products, staff, and management, and I felt relieved and honored to be asked to join them.

Hartmann was a huge man with a commanding presence, a Harvard Business school graduate, and a superb golfer. He had grown up in Huntington, Long Island, where his family owned Hartmann's department store, and he and Margo now lived in Roslyn, Long Island, with their four daughters. Frank, together with Bob Smith and Bob Borne, was the principal architect behind the marketing strategy driving Monsanto nylon and acrylic fibers into the carpet industry. They were strong brand advocates, and Acrilan Acrylic and Cumuloft Nylon were heavily promoted in consumer shelter magazines and in trade publications. Monsanto also did cooperative advertisng with both mills and retailers, essentialliy paying half of the ad costs showcasing the manufacturer/retailer and Monsanto brands.

Monsanto initiated a heavy and continuous schedule of training seminars for mill reps, wholesalers, and retail floor salesmen, as well as architects, building owners, hospital administrators, and others, outlining the plusses of its fibers and how to present these virtues to consumers and bidders alike. The marketing program was high dollar and extensive across the country. A sizeable staff of merchandising and design specialists were fanned out to various regions at all times, holding hundreds of meetings each year. Monsanto turned over every stone in its sales program, far more thoroughly than any other fiber company.

Bruce Kenworthy was a Dartmouth man and war veteran who had

been recalled to active duty during the Korean War. He and Hartmann were old friends, and had collaborated to some extent on details of the marketing plan. Bruce supervised the Acrilan merchandising programs, while George McGrath, another Chemstrand veteran, rode herd on the Cumuloft nylon team.

The man thought to be a merchandising genius inside the Monsanto fibers business was Robert Borne, who devised the "Wear Dated" program to market fibers into apparel and home furnishings end uses. The "Wear Dated" tag guaranteed consumer satisfaction for one year, or a full refund of the purchase price, no questions asked. The guarantee had been used primarily in knit garments such as sweaters, socks, scarves, and children's wear, and had been highly successful in setting Monsanto (still using the name Chemstrand) apart from the pack. Borne was fast thinking and fast talking, and slightly intimidating.

After visiting with Frank and Bruce and accepting the job, I was led down to Borne's office for a cursory introduction. He lived up to his reputation, asking me penetrating questions about myself and my marketing views. Mainly he talked about progress Chemstrand had made from a standing start, in spite of some commodity chemical mentality at Monsanto headquarters in St. Louis.

Monsanto had been founded in 1901 in St. Louis by John Queeny, a moonlighting wholesale chemical salesman, who discovered a huge demand for saccharin, the artificial sweetener, and found a European supplier to fill the demand. Still employed by a wholesaler, or jobber, Queeny named the company after his wife's maiden name, Olga Monsanto, and the name remained.

In the late 1960's, Monsanto's chairman and CEO was Edgar Queeny, son of the founder. Monsanto grew through two world wars producing and supplying basic and industrial chemicals to the war effort, and to corporations using chemical ingredients in consumer branded products like toothpaste, foods, and plastics, tires, and a wide range of consumer and industrial products. At one point, the company was the largest producer of aspirin, and produced and marketed its own washday detergent, named ALL. Later, Monsanto acquired G.D. Searle pharmaceuticals.

The joint venture with American Viscose was Monsanto's first move into synthetic fibers. It had been successful and highly profitable. It was the only division with headquarters separate from the St. Louis campus. The management team for the Chemstrand joint venture had remained largely intact and operated with great latitude, free of the regimented hierarchy in St. Louis. This was beginning to change, however, and the departure of Robert Smith was one important signal.

Monsanto had sent T.K. Smith, a corporate Senior Vice-President and member of the Boatman's Bank founding family, to oversee Chemstrand, which would hereafter be the Monsanto Fibers Division. Ed Frey, a Chemstrand staff lawyer, had been assigned much of Bob Smith's responsibility, reporting to T.K. Smith, who basically knew little about fibers or the textile industry.

My first assignment, working under John Roughan, was to invent a marketing/merchandising strategy for Monsanto's pigmented acrylic fiber in the Indoor/Outdoor growth market. The fiber was injected with light fast pigments while still in the molten state, had excellent resistance to fading, and was impervious to ultraviolet degradation. In a synthetic prefabricated backing, or woven into contract grade carpets, it performed very well outdoors or in, and would withstand repeated cleanings without color loss.

Roughan had valuable experience with pigmented fibers, having been a key member of the Astroturf synthetic grass development team, and, in conjunction with the owner of the Houston Astros baseball team, had given "Astroturf" its name. John had drafted the original business plan for Astroturf, and it was off to a good start.

Our product, dubbed solution dyed Acrilan, had a lot of good marketing handles. We worked with Doyle Dane Bernbach, our ad agency, on several themes, finally settling on the name A-Acrilan Plus, A+, as our brand. We introduced the theme and graphics to our mill customers with good reception, and they immediately introduced new residential and commercial grades carrying the new performance story. We went to the International Home Furnishings Market, at the mammoth Merchandise Mart in Chicago for the January show, heralding the new grades in literature and trade ads.

Some fifty new broadloom carpets from 15 manufacturers were shown and well received. Additionally, General Felt Industries, a padding producer, introduced its non-woven needlepunched indoor/outdoor of A+ Acrylan Plus. Needlepunched technology provided a product to satisfy the low priced end of the market, and it was a big seller. The Horwich family owned General Felt, and they had many friends and contacts in the industry.

A close friend and supporter in bringing these new product grades to market was H. Bruce English, our Director of Field Sales, and his team, who succeeded in introducing A+ to mill purchasing agents and technicians, and conducting many successful technical trials under supervision of Mickey Finn's large technical service department. Bruce, from Thomaston, Georgia, was a Georgia Tech Textile engineering grad who longed to get back to the Atlanta area, but for the moment was based in the New York office and living in New Jersey with Barbara, a true Southern Bell. Bruce and Barbara and Joan and I formed a lasting friendship, and Bruce was an important influence in my career moves to come. Bruce remained a very close friend until his sudden death from a heart attack in the summer of 2007.

Bruce had long argued that the carpet business group should be moved out of New York to Atlanta, closer to mill customers. This argument had been resisted by the marketers/merchandisers, who insisted that advertising and field marketing were the dominant arms of strategy, and that these functions were better served in New York. Bruce was an up and comer in Monsanto, but his point of view on this issue was seen as self-serving. However, office space in Atlanta was much less expensive, and there were longer term advantages in having the entire carpet fibers group under one roof. Down the road, Bruce's argument would prove persuasive.

For now, the "pull through" marketing program was the compelling clincher for mill management. They saw substantial ad dollars behind the new product launch, and also saw a chance to enter new markets with net additions to sales, with exciting new products.

Chemstrand had high visibility in sponsoring network television specials like the Barbra Striesand and Perry Como hours, around which lavish customer parties were staged at the Plaza hotel. The stars themselves graced these parties, and were a big draw for mill principals and large chain retailers and department store buyers. The largest single buyer of carpets in the country was Sears. Clem Stein, head of their buying group, was courted extensively and lavishly on such occasions..

Markets in Chicago were held in January and June, attended by furniture, drapery, upholstery, and carpet retailers and wholesalers from all over the United States. Chicago became the industry wide watering hole for one of the largest and most far reaching industries in the country. Every significant mill had large and attractive permanent showrooms in the Mart.

During market week, their national sales forces would be in Chicago with customers, showing the lines and entertaining key customers. Chicago restaurants and hotels were overflowing with furniture and floor covering sellers, buyers, and lookers. Monsanto's entire fibers marketing force was there also, holding educational meetings, taking the pulse of the market, entertaining the floor coverings industry with a lavish ballroom party at the Drake hotel.

Media devoted to decorating and design, newspaper home fashion editors, House and Garden magazine, Better Homes and Gardens, House Beautiful, Home Furnishings Daily, Floor Covering Weekly, and many other media reps were covering every event in detail and trying to uncover new style trends and innovation. Excitement was high, comparable to national electronics or automobile shows. It was where business was done, new products placed, where dates were made and contracts signed. Decisions made here impacted virtually every home and commercial building in the United States. Home furnishings, in total, represented the largest piece of the U.S. economic pie

GETTING TO KNOW CHEMICALS

A brief primer on chemical fibers is in order here as a platform for understanding career assignments upcoming. I admit to resorting to esoterica in this section, so bear with me. I am completely mesmerized by the complexity, capital cost, and incredible range of talent required to duplicate or replace basic "natural" products like cotton and wool. Visit a modern chemical plant if you get the chance, and see the genius basic to conceptualizing, designing and erecting these behemoths. They are an integral part of the evolution of economies, rivaling the automobile, personal computers, or the internet in terms of their impact on our lives. And, in all their variations, they will become more and more important to society over time.

Everyone understands that everything in our world is traceable directly to the periodic table. Yet environmental extremists relish in naming chemicals as evil, in plastics, in our water, and in our foods. Obviously, chemical elements can be combined and arranged to produce any effect, including hydrogen bombs. But their arrangement can also produce miracle cures, adequate food supplies, plentiful energy, safe transportation, and warm clothing. Chemistry is the only long-term hope for environmental sustainability, versus the political nonsense of cap and trade, and artificial regulation of carbon dioxide, ala Al Gore and company.

In this spectrum, modern synthetic fibers plants are chemical and industrial engineering marvels. In the early days at Chemstrand/ Monsanto, I visited our acrylic and nylon plants, starting with acrylics in Decatur, Alabama, to get something of a starter education. It was an introduction into the processes required to convert chemical intermediate products into fibers suitable for the full range of home furnishings and clothing and industrial products previously made from cotton, wool, and cellulosic Rayon.

Chemical engineers determine the formulas and processes. Industrial engineers must convert these instructions into production lines capable of withstanding the temperatures and pressures specified to convert monomers into polymers and transform raw chemicals into plastics in forms which can be knit, woven, tufted, or molded.

Acrylic continuous polymerization fiber production lines require several acres of space. The fibers are extruded from devices known as spinnerettes, which look like grouped shower heads. Thousands of these shower head-type outlets are affixed to the ends of long production chambers, in which acrylonitrile, the key raw material monomer, is polymerized, then forced through the spinnerettes in molten state at constant speeds and temperatures.

Acrylonitrile is barged up the Tennessee River from the Gulf of Mexico after having been produced in Texas City, Texas, near Houston, as a pale, colorless, yet volatile and potentially explosive liquid. There, in a huge Monsanto raw materials production complex, AN is made by reacting propylene, ammonia, and air with a catalyst. The monomer has a wide variety of end uses, including ABS (AN, butadiene, styrene) plastics, paints, resins, adhesives, dyes, and pharmaceuticals. Its by-products included HCN, hydrogen cyanide, a highly poisonous liquid used in making pharmaceuticals, carbon fibers, and the poisonous vapors used in gas chambers. Together with its nearby sister plant, Chocolate Bayou, the locations produce a wide variety of raw materials for a number of Monsanto chemical divisions.

Texas City first claimed notoriety on April 16, 1947 when two barges loaded with ammonium nitrate fertilizer exploded, creating the largest man-made disaster in the country's history to that point. Almost a quarter of Texas City's small population was killed or injured, almost half of the houses were condemned afterward. Metal shards from the blast killed hundreds in the immediate vicinity. The explosion was heard 150 miles away, and huge metal chunks of the ships fell as far as 20 miles away. People on the streets of Galveston, 50 miles away, were knocked off their feet by percussion from the blast.

The environmental calamity and loss of life and property and the national and international news coverage would likely be the ruin of a major corporation in 2010. The disaster would probably have been considered more consequential than the British Petroleum Gulf of Mexico oil spill. But 1947, there was no organized environmental political movement, and the community and the company and its insurers simply buried the dead, rebuilt the town, and started over with new plants, which were the town's largest employers. It was soon after the big war, and Texans wanted to get back to work rather than join a political fight over environmentalism.

A few more esoteric details about acrylic fiber production. After extrusion, acrylic fibers are bundled into a rope-like continuous strand known as "tow", then "quenched" or solidified in a mild solvent bath before being fed into a mechanical stuffer or "crimper" which adds kink or zig-zag shape to the fibers. The crimp has the effect in yarn of adding volume or bulkiness, much like curly hair occupies more space than straight hair. The long ropes of tow are then fed into a series of open buggies which are wheeled manually into sealed autoclaves, which "heat set" and make permanent the crimp, and extract moisture from the tow.

Next, the ropes of tows are fed to the cutters, which chop the tow into whatever length specified. Larger diameter, more coarse 15 deniers go to carpets uses, finer 1, 2, and 3 deniers went to knitting, for fleece and sweaters, or to woven garments. Denier is defined as the weight in grams of 9000 meters of a fiber or yarn.

After cutting, the fiber goes to baling, much as cotton is baled, then shipped to customers by truck or rail. The multiple fiber production steps are under tight quality control, with samples constantly tested for uniformity, dyeability, abrasion resistance, and other parameters .

Once at the customer, many other more traditional processing steps are required, including stock or bulk dyeing, carding, pin drafting, spinning onto bobbins. Bobbins can go directly to knitting or tufting, but beaming is required for weaving. Beams feed hundreds of yarn ends into the loom, which combines woof and warp yarns into one integral fabric. Edges are trimmed before the fabric is packaged into rolls around cardboard cylinders, then warehoused ready for shipment.

The need for pre-dyeing the raw fiber adds substantially to the inventory cost burden versus piece or yarn dyeable fibers. Independent dye houses and independent spinners often are middlemen in the production chain, and absorb some of these steps at a cost less than the mill maintaining these stocks in-house.

In carpet production, independent or mill owned wholesalers speed deliveries and ease the cost of finished goods inventories by buying and stocking roll goods for fast cut-order service to nearby retailers. Some fully integrated mills prefer to own their own regional service centers to provide faster deliveries to retailers, who normally can afford to stock only a fraction of the grades they show and sell.

In solution dyed or pigmented acrylic fiber, the cost and inconvenience to the mill of dyeing raw fiber is eliminated, but the color inventory burden now rests with the fiber producer, who must maintain a palette of colors at all times to satisfy multiple mill customer needs. The pigmented fiber performance properties and on demand delivery of colors permit charging a significant price premium over undyed fiber. Pigmented fibers are also a perfect color match batch to batch, whereas stock dyeing in the mill produces some shade and color variability which has to be blended out.

The plant's technical center rides herd on quality, trains plant employees in QC, hosts customer visits and training seminars, and does all physical testing and color matching using special equipment. The location also maintains a staffed guesthouse for visiting management and customer groups. Customer managements are often transported to Decatur by private Monsanto aircraft, updated on the latest innovations by Tech center personnel, and treated to dinners. It is a favorite outing of customers, sometimes including quail hunting on a nearby lease, or late night poker playing. The name of the game is customer bonding.

NYLON SURROUNDS US: GET TO KNOW IT

Nylon 66 staple and continuous filament fibers and yarns are produced in plants in Pensacola, Florida, and Greenwood, South Carolina.   Greenwood produces shorter runs of carpet filament yarns through batch "extruders", the hoppers of which are top-loaded with polymer chips. These chips are produced by reacting adipic acid with hexamethalene diamine to make nylon 66. Adipic acid and bagged polymers are also sold in the merchant market, principally to nylon producers. The Greenwood plant produces most nylon products used in industrial markets such as high performance engineered plastics for gear parts for autos, planes, and machinery, and industrial filtration and fish and camouflage netting.

Monsanto's Pensacola complex makes a full line of nylon products using continuous polymerization technology, meaning the nylon polymers are made and extruded in one continuous operation, a far more cost efficient method compared to batch processing, but with less flexibility. Nylon carpet deniers produced here can go the staple processing route, in which filament tows are cut into 4 to 6 inch staple lengths and sold in bale form. The customer must then assemble them into yarn on his staple spinning frames.

Continuous filament is spun, drawn, twisted, and air textured in one operation, wound on bobbins ready to ship to customers for tufting, weaving, and piece dyeing. Independent middlemen processors known as "throwsters" also purchase nylon filament and customize the drawing, twisting, and texturing to customer order.

Staple spun yarns can be used in subtle residential styling and coloring effects, as well as plush, cut pile carpets. Filament yarns in cut pile constructions have less styling flexibility, but are better suited to commercial installations where high performance is needed in low, level loop textures. As the carpet industry transitioned increasingly to tufting technology, filament nylon became heavily favored for its efficiency in production and piece dye-ability in multi-colors suitable for most applications.

In the middle and late 60's, the Fibers division was the largest profit producer in Monsanto, with the greatest degree of autonomy. The division also had the highest advertising and publicity profile, leading to some resentment from old timers in the more commodity oriented organic, inorganic, agricultural, and specialty chemicals divisions. One concern was that Monsanto was becoming too closely identified with fibers, and that fibers needed to be reined in.

Over time, the branded fiber franchise would itself sink to near commodity and lower margin status, partly a result of restraints imposed by corporate, but more the effect of inability to develop constant technical innovations required to sustain the branded approach. Lower prices on an aging product line were predictable, particularly so as competition increased, and mill customers consolidated and aspired to build their own brand identities.

But until the late 70's, fibers carried the profit flag for Monsanto, and ad and merchandising budgets remained substantial.

A SUDDEN CAREER MOVE UP

L eonard Cohn, a chemical engineer from the University of Iowa, was named Business Group Director of Carpet fibers in mid-1969, and set about making organizational adjustments. His obvious intent was to streamline the marketing structure while imposing tighter controls on ad and merchandising budgets.

In December of that year, after having conducted a late dinner meeting with retailers the night before, I was called to Frank Hartmann's office for an unannounced meeting with him and Len Cohen. Frank explained that he and Len had reached a decision on the new organization, and that I was to become the new Director Of Merchandising, reporting to Hartmann. In this role, I was to have responsibility for developing and overseeing advertising themes and have some liaison with Doyle Dane Bernbach, our agency. More challenging was the supervision of all merchandising personnel and their expense budgets. This meant that those I had been reporting to would now report to me.

As background, I had recently written a long essay, on Hartmann's assignment, analyzing current marketing structure and programs, and recommending ways to go forward with multiple brands with multiple constituencies, including mills, wholesalers, and retailers. The branded approach was embraced, supplemented with a "branded light" label for products no longer considered protected or proprietary. This essay had been circulated by Hartmann. Len Cohn had read it, as had Louis Fernandez, the VP, General Manager of the Fibers Division, based in St. Louis. Unknown to me, this document became the springboard for the promotion.

The situation was delicate and uncomfortable in the beginning. Egos had been damaged. I had to walk a fine line with George McGrath and Bruce Kenworthy and Dick Thompson, among others. They had key positions and seniority and had been reporting to Hartmann since formation of the team. Now, they reported to me, a relative newcomer. John Roughan, our old and dear friend, had been transferred to St. Louis in 1967 to join the Astroturf group, but a year later came back to New York as Director of Advertising. He had John Bunbury reporting to him, and the two were instrumental in developing the concept of a special feature section in House and Garden Magazine, to be discussed later.

We had a series of staff meetings on our new assignments, but it was clear that I would need stronger personnel management skills to succeed with the group. January Home Furnishings markets gave me another chance for team building, and I gave a talk to staff there about working together as a team with mutual respect. It helped to some extent.

My biggest reaction to the sudden new assignment was shock and complete surprise. I never saw it coming. There was no "heads-up" from anyone, even though I knew my relationship with Frank Hartmann was good, and that I considered him my "Rabbi". My contacts with Len Cohn had been minimal, with no hint. I have no recollection of what my reaction was at the time. I left the room with instructions to devise an organizational chart I wanted for my new reports, which I did prior to a follow up meeting that afternoon to review the structure with Hartmann and Cohn. They approved.

LIFE IN CONNECTICUT

The promotion had important monetary significance because Joan and I had just bought our first home in Connecticut in mid-1967, next door to dear friends Gene and Effie Connett. Effie found the house for us. We paid $42 thousand for the three-bedroom center hall colonial on an oversized lot at 219 Riverside Ave., Riverside, CT. We barely met the 20% down payment requirement, but made the commitment. Jimmy Dean was interested in the news, and insisted that I accept a $5 thousand loan to help furnish and decorate the place. I reluctantly accepted, and repaid him within the next couple of years.

ALONG CAME JONATHAN

More importantly, our second son, Jonathan Dean Garrett, had been born October 21, 1967, at Greenwich hospital, a welcome addition and the impetus for our move out of the city. Jon was healthy and handsome, like his older brother Scott, and both had very high energy levels. I will always think of Jon in a picture I took of him as a two year old, wearing his blue winter cap, sitting on a wooden chair in our living room, smiling. He looks the same to me today, at age 43, still, in my mind's eye, the little boy who dearly loved our dog Chumley, who ran after his big brother, and who later became a talented athlete. He was just four when we moved to Atlanta, but more about that later.

The little home was perfect for our growing family. The

neighborhood was child friendly, and St. Paul's Episcopal Church was just a block away. St. Paul's had the best nursery and preschool in town, and Scott was soon enrolled.

We moved into the house in August, after three weeks of hard, sweaty cleaning, stripping, and painting to get it in livable shape. The previous owners, Brack Nagle and his wife, were known to be active alcoholics, and had neglected and abused the house in every apparent way. Every room had to be stripped of wallpaper, sanded, and painted. We installed carpet to cover damaged hardwood, repaired the bathroom fixtures, scrubbed the kitchen and its appliances, carpeted the kitchen floor to cover worn out linoleum, washed and caulked windows. I took two weeks off and did all the work alone, while staying at the Connett's at night.

Effie kindly insisted that I have lunch and dinner with them. Joan was 7 months pregnant and came out on the train for part of the time, but mostly the work went on all day, every day, to meet our moving deadline. When the moving truck arrived from Manhattan, the house was in decent condition. It was modest but comfortable, and a first home invested with a lot of love and hard work. It was the home which was always our favorite, with our most lasting memories of our boys first years there. The following year, I sanded and painted the exterior of the house and put on new shutters.

We plunged into Connecticut living with a vengeance. Greenwich had just under 50,000 people, and included the small villages of Old Greenwich, founded in 1640, and Riverside, Cos Cob, the central business district of Greenwich itself, and Byram. Connecticut had no state income tax, therefore, most of Wall street bankers, brokers, and investment bankers chose to live there. There were no hedge funds then, but Greenwich became and remains hedge fund headquarters for the New York metro area. New York City and State taxes still had to be paid on the days worked in the city, but corporate types who travelled out of state extensively could realize substantial tax savings.

Greenwich was a haven for sailors. The town had a beautiful deep water harbor on Long Island Sound, with its entire coast line sporting lovely beaches and unobstructed views of Long Island just 7 to 10 miles of protected salt water away. Sail boat racing competition between many private and public yacht clubs on the Sound, together with board sailing, kayaking, wind-surfing, power boating, fishing for blue fish and stripped bass, as well as lobstering, and beach-going were the primary recreational activities. Together with several large well maintained parks, including Tod's Point in Old Greenwich, the town boasted the highest living standard with the greatest amenities in New England, all just 30 miles and one hour on the New Haven railroad to Manhattan.

Golf was a secondary sport in Greenwich, although Greenwich Country Club, which we joined at company expense, was among the best and most reputable in the state. In early 1971, we were also admitted to the Riverside yacht club, near our house, after purchasing a Southcoast 23 ft. sloop. Owning a sailboat was essential for admission, as was several member sponsors, lots of support letters, and interviews with the admissions committee.

The club had first class junior sailing and swimming programs in Summer, and was a bike ride away. Club by-laws limited the number of members. There was a standing back-log of applicants. Sponsors and cosponsors had to be active in rounding up the needed votes for admission. Competition was intense.

Commuting to the city on the New Haven/Harlem line of the railroad involved one hour on the local train, which made all stops between Greenwich and Grand Central, and 50 minutes on the express train, which made no stops except Portchester, and Harlem, before Grand Central. At the time, there was no station platform in Riverside, where I caught the train. We had to climb stairs to board the train, and late-comers regularly chased and grabbed the stairs and pulled up just before the conductor retracted the stairs. The monthly train ticket was around $30.

Parking at the station was limited and required a permit. We had only one car, so parking was never an issue. I walked the 10 minutes to the station every morning, rain, snow, sleet, or shine. In winter, during daylight savings, out of bed at 6 AM, dressing in the dark, walking to the station for the 7 AM train, became the morning routine. On arrival at Grand Central, I faced another 10 block walk in weather to the Empire State building, getting to the office at 8:30 AM.

One dark morning, I followed the pattern of dressing in the dark so as not to awaken the family. At the Empire State building, I discovered I had on one brown shoe and one black shoe, but nobody else noticed, maybe because my socks matched.

On the return trip, leave the office at 5:30, take the 5.50 or 6.15 express to Greenwich, walk home, and arrive there 7:15 to 7:30 PM, in time for dinner. This schedule didn't allow much time during the week to be with our boys, who were often already in bed when I arrived.

Life aboard the train was quite different from the rules facing today's commuters. Smoking was allowed on every other car. Cell phones, laptops, iPad's and the like were not invented yet. The New York Times was sold at the train station, and was the primary time consumer on the way in to the city. Some worked from their briefcases after finishing the Times, which was my pattern. Train time, was a good time to write memos, prepare agenda, plan the day, go through mail backlogs, and enjoy a cup of coffee. Some read novels, others the standard weekly magazines of the day including Time, Newsweek, Fortune, and, of course, the Wall Street Journal. There were pay phones at the ends of every other car, but were not much used. Toilets were also to be found in alternating cars, but were often clogged.

The bar car usually jammed on the way home. Smoking was allowed. Here I met my soon-to-be longtime friend Verne Westerberg, then

Sales Director of House and Garden magazine, and later to be publisher of House and Garden, Gourmet, and Vogue. Verne lived on Lucas Point in Old Greenwich, on the water. He and his wife, Lee, both from Chicago, became close friends and remain so today. We sailed together, vacationed together, drank together, and relished meals together, before both retiring. More later on Verne and Lee.

Our house at 219 Riverside Ave was still on septic system when we bought it. In 1970, the town laid the sewer line down Riverside Avenue, and we connected at considerable expense, payable in higher taxes over many years. The gas furnace circulated hot water to old fashioned exposed radiators in each room. These were hazardous for young kids, and covers had to be built for them to prevent burns, but not before Jon had his arm severely burned by one of them.

The house was 50 years old. The separate one car garage was intended to house smaller cars from a different era. When our 67 Chevy wagon wouldn't fit, we knocked off the old doors for new ones, and pushed out the back of the garage to allow room for the front bumper.

In 2010, the remodeled house, with the Basham's as owners, is worth on the order of $2 million dollars or more. We sold it in 1972 to Bob and Marsha Wilson, for $69,000, a significant return on the $42,000 we paid five years earlier.

Virginia and Don Armstrong lived just East of us. Effie and Gene lived to the West. Don Armstrong was involved with Pond's face cream and told Joan that all face creams had the same active ingredient, and not to bother buying expensive ones. Don had also taught at college level, and tutored me when I wrote an internal essay at Monsanto on our marketing programs. He famously shot squirrels in the neighborhood, probably illegally. One of these poor squirrels landed dead on our back porch, frightening Joan and the boys who were sitting in the sunroom at the time and saw the squirrel fall. Don took the hint, and thereafter limited his shooting to his own property.

At the Connett's we often had impromptu spaghetti dinners with the family, after a serious helping of "berbs", as Gene called Old Crow. Their daughters, Stacey, Bevin, and Kate often baby-sat our boys while we went out to dinner with Gene and Effie. At this writing, in 2010, both Gene and Effie have gone, and their oldest daughter, Stacey, is battling serious cancer.

John and Harriet Roughan moved down the street from us in 1968, to 261 Riverside Avenue, where they still live today. We socalized often with them, as we have for almost 50 years since. Their son Howard is two years younger than Scott, but they became good and lasting friends. Howard is a well-known writer of novels, on his own, and in collaboration with James Patterson, one of the all-time best sellers in publishing. Their daughter Shari was very young, perhaps six, when they moved down the street from us. Shari now lives with her husband, Mark, and their two children, Jake and Shana, in Boca Raton, Florida.

Joan and I learned sailing and navigating, first with a small sunfish, and later with the 23 foot sloop, Scojo, which we sailed extensively up and down the Sound. We both took the standard Power Squadron courses on safety, rules of the road, chart reading, and how to handle emergencies, including man-overboard drills.

One of our favorite overnight harbors was Zeigler's Cove, near Norwalk, CT. We moored there and had lunch and swam, sometimes with our friends Bob and Marty Swats on their power boat, or Gene and Effie on their creaky, leaky sailboat, named Benevolent. Joan dove overboard at one point and came up without her gold wedding ring from Tiffany's. A search in the murky salt water produced nothing, and the ring had to be replaced the following week with another gold band from Tiffany's.

Joan and I took courses and tests to get our Realtor's licenses, which we did, but never used them. We must have had some idea of breaking out of the corporate mold, but never seriously followed up on the idea. Still, the courses were useful and topical. Real Estate values in Greenwich were rising rapidly.

Scott started 1st grade in 1970 at Riverside Elementary, a classic and traditional school 15 minutes walk from our house. The school had an old English façade, and a great reputation. Most young parents in town, regardless of means, sent their kids to public schools. Neither Joan or I remember having any qualms about sending Scott off to school on foot. Most kids walked to school in that little town, without fear of predators or horror stories so common today.

Scott and Jon were just old enough in 1969, to be rousted from sleep in time to see Neal Armstrong land on the Moon, watching the event on our small black and white TV in our little sunroom. Scott remembers it, but Jon was just too young.

I joined a small poker group which met weekly at Robbo Robbins house across the street. Among the players was Alfred Brittian, who I later learned was Chairman of Banker's Trust, as his Father had been before him. Frank Peard, Gene, Edgar Walz, all neighbors, also played. We also both became active in the yacht club, and there met Miles and Pat McDonald, who have remained friends and still live in Riverside, the Jim Vaughn's, the Baker's, the Lawson's, the Steve Swopes, and Jacques and Winnie Balterman, all neighbors and good sailors. We remain members of the Riverside Yacht Club after 40 years, many of them non-resident.

And Effie brought us "Chumley" a miniature black lab/half cocker spaniel. We loved Chumley for the next 17 years. We could never think of replacing her with another dog. Effie sold us Chumley after Kate brought her to their house, but the Connett's already had an Irish Setter, Heather, so Effie put her foot down. Effie told Joan, "Dearie, every family with two young boys must have a dog." And we did.

BACK AT WORK

Back in the office, I was beginning to get comfortable with the new job. In 1970, our group sponsored the largest color spread, 24 pages, in House and Garden's history, in their special Spring edition. The full color pages, with editorial comment, featured Frank and Margo Hartmann's home in Roslyn Harbor, New York. Our design consultant, Emily Malino, had selected Acrilan carpets for each room in the home, and accessorized and decorated the home as a showcase for Monsanto fibers.

The special section was reminiscent of an Architectural Digest feature, and was pre merchandised to the mills and retailers well in advance. Both had blow-ups of the feature as showroom and store displays, and we did co-op advertising with them to feature their own new introductions in trade papers and the same House and Garden issue. Further, we did our own Monsanto ads in trade journals like Home Furnishings Daily, and Floor Coverings Weekly.

We spread our merchandising staff to all regions to hold informational meetings, preparing retailers to do tie-ins with the H & G feature in their local newspaper advertising pages. At the June market, the feature was on prominent display in mill showrooms. The positive recognition factor for the Acrilan brand registered an all time high with carpet consumers, and trade informal feedback was almost uniformly complimentary. As a brand marketing event, we clearly had been correct in focusing our message in a single strong seasonal message which could be the platform for generating sales up and down the marketing chain. New carpet grade introductions with Acrilan fiber showed big increases, and actual sales of the fabrics appeared to be very strong.

In the Fall of 1971, Len Cohen, Bruce English and I made the trip to the North of England for the annual Harrogate Carpet show. The show's exhibitors attracted attendees from all over the world and was thought to represent the latest trends in design and construction. Monsanto's American customers were in attendance, as were all our manufacturing customers in England and on the continent. We followed this with a trip to London and meeting internally with our counterparts in the U.K. I then flew to Berlin to meet members of our New York agency, Doyle Dane, who had chosen Berlin to shoot our new TV and print ads for Spring.

Checkpoint Charlie still stood as the dividing line between East and West Berlin. A thorough search of our limo and our personal effects was required before admission to East Berlin, where we had lunch at the well-known German opera house not far from the Brandenburg gate. Returning to West Berlin in the afternoon, the same intrusive search was conducted before clearance to pass. We were relieved to be back on the West side of the Berlin wall. Back in London, where Bruce English had remained, we wrapped up our meetings and flew back home to New York

Inside the organization, Monsanto had by now retired the Chemstrand name completely. Monsanto human resource procedures and compensation scales were imposed on the division. Management by Objectives became the new corporate wide method of setting goals and evaluating the performance of individuals. Panel interviewing, based on a formula created by consultant Richard Fear, became the standard through which all prospective new hires must pass. Setting goals, reviewing quarterly individual performances, grading progress against goals, and preparing detailed results reviews at year-end became cumbersome, formulaic, and time consuming if not time wasting.

The Monsanto standardized way overlaid what had been an agile, fast moving, flexible, and sometimes free spirited money making machine. Monsanto was finally bringing the division to heel.

BOOK FIVE
Atlanta Years

THE MOVE SOUTH

T he years 1971 and early 1972 foretold changes to come. Bruce English succeeded in convincing Len Cohn to move the business group to Atlanta, in stages. Cohn in turn presented the program to the division management board in St. Louis. Largely on the strength of lower rents, proximity to mill customers, and cohesion under essentially one roof, approval was granted. English and Cohn moved in early 72, and all but a couple of field salesmen and a skeleton merchandising/advertising force were to move in 1972.

1971 was a slow year for the economy generally, but GDP growth was positive and unemployment low. The very unpopular Vietnam war was winding down amid anti-war protests all over the country. In Atlanta, Jimmy Carter was elected Governor of Georgia, a springboard to his Presidency in 1976. Atlanta was a city still in transition from the Civil Rights Movement, and, with 54% of Atlanta's population black, Maynard Jackson was elected Mayor, and Andrew Young as the first black congressman from the South since Reconstruction.

Atlanta was considered the capital city of the South, with a slogan of "too busy to hate." With laws on their side, Atlanta's black community, concentrated on the South side, still had not realized the equality promised by the Civil Rights movement. There was significant labor unrest beginning in 1972.

In the broader economy of the country, big-ticket purchases were affected, marketing programs were delayed, margins flattened as our branded franchise began to weaken from age. Some price erosion was a natural outcome of slowed product innovation.

For the first time, I had the disagreeable job of having to reduce staff, as Monsanto cut employees across all divisions in an attempt to salvage reasonable bottom line numbers. Dan Kressler, Bob Rogers, and Walt Getty were good men and long time merchandisers who had made important contributions to our marketing success. I had to tell them they were released due to forced headcount reductions. John Donahue in advertising was also terminated, as were a number of clerical staff. I learned that leadership is many faceted, and that supervising a range of people means dealing with the positives and the negatives of the job. It was my first experience in firing people.

I would also learn firsthand that a negative review of employee performance or potential can bring with it strong emotional reactions. Those who believe they have the qualifications to continue moving up the pyramid will not easily accept a negative judgment, no matter how positive current performance may be. In these cases, human resources and senior management were alerted to possible adverse reactions, and back-stopped the reviews by confirming and supporting the decision. But, review done, the experience is highly unpleasant and draining.

Bruce Kenworthy had by this time been transferred to San Francisco to open an office and showroom there to serve our growing West Coast mills and dealers. Gene Carter was sent from Atlanta Tech service to perform mill trials and give quality feedback. Mand, Holleytex, Burke Industries, and Walters carpet mills proved to be excellent customers for both our acrylic and nylon products. The office reported to me, and, naturally, I made the occasional trip to San Francisco, and on down to Pebble Beach for rounds of golf with mill principals. These outings also proved popular with East coast customers,, often with corporate aircraft.

Meanwhile, Frank Hartmann had made a decision to refuse the move to Atlanta for personal reasons, and had left to join Beaunit, with Bob Smith. John Roughan elected not to go due to Harriet having opened a successful antiques business in Greenwich, and he too joined his old boss at Beaunit. George McGrath in nylon merchandising felt he could not leave New Jersey, his longtime home.

Joe Tucker, a seasoned marketer, assumed Hartmann's duties for an interim period. Joe was a friend, who, with his wife Betty, lived not far from us in the community of Cos Cob, CT. They had 10 children. A chain with lock kept this brood out of the refrigerator. Only Betty had the key. Joe Tucker also decided that the Atlanta move was not for him and his family.

Joan and I chose to make the move to Atlanta in the Summer of 1972.

Monsanto practiced "cross training" for people rated high potential. The idea was to give these candidates broad exposure to a variety of disciplines and management circumstances to season and hone their skills for broader responsibility later. Moving to Atlanta, my "cross training" slot was to be Director of Commercial Development. The job boiled down to working with the R & D, technology, and manufacturing units to improve existing products or find totally new ones.

In this effort, I was to work with Ken McIntosh in Technology, Dr. David Bowen in R&D, Bert Snooks in Pensacola Manufacturing, and Dick Phelps in Greenwood Manufacturing. John Steen was also staff involved in this effort. We travelled frequently to plant locations to review ideas and products, with some modest success in nylons, but overall, the assignment was unexciting and not a very good match for my abilities, but the intent was to make it a learning and broadening experience and to gain perspective on these disciplines. I was exposed to and learned a great deal about our nylon technology.

Joan and I made a house-hunting trip to Atlanta, and quickly settled on a new Deerfield Colonial replica in the North Springs section of Fulton County. The three- story classic was just being finished by local builder Walton Smith. It was in a development known as Princeton Square. All the houses were new, and new residents were with IBM, Westinghouse, and similar large corporations. We paid $79,500 for the house, flush with down payment after just having sold our Connecticut house of $69,000.

Scott had just finished second grade, and Jon had completed St. Paul's pre-school year and was ready for kindergarten. Spaulding public elementary school was just a mile away, and had a good reputation. Jon was enrolled in a private kindergarten. We still treasure his graduation picture with white cap and gown.

The house had more than twice the space of our Connecticut house, with a two story, two car garage, with large playroom above it, four bedrooms, three baths, huge eat-in kitchen, large dining and living rooms, and a lovely and spacious family room with fireplace. It sat atop a hill, with steep lawn rolling down to the street, Large pine trees dotted the property. The neighborhood had a community pool and tennis courts, and was pristine and green. The house was ideal for guests and family visits.

We were at 7455 Old Main Trail, and were comfortably ensconced by July 1. The boys were young and the transition easy. Kids of their age populated the neighborhood, albeit with deep Southern accents, and the open woods behind our house invited exploration.

I resigned our Greenwich Country Club membership, a big mistake I would later learn, but we chose to keep our Riverside yacht club spot, becoming non-resident members. Little over a year later, I joined the Cherokee Town and Country Club, a perk, which featured strong junior golf and swimming programs.

This happened in mid 73, when Len Cohn went to a new assignment in St. Louis, English became the new Business Group Director, and I became the new Director of Marketing. Joe Tucker decided to leave the company. Bob Sparacino was in place as Field Sales Director, placed there as a "cross training" assignment on the suggestion of Dr. Louis Fernandez, who was soon to become Executive VP and Vice-Chairman of the Corporation. Lou had become Bob's "Rabbi" during their days in organic chemicals together.

Bob and I had formed a strong friendship. Unfortunately, he developed cancer and was soon on leave of absence, never to return. I visited him several times during his illness. He and Joan had two sons and a daughter, all young. He told me that for the rest of his life, he would not deny any request from his children. It was a poignant moment which has stayed with me. Sadly, he died soon afterward, and the entire office mourned his death.

Leonard James became my Field Sales Director, and Durwood (Mickey) Finn continued as Technical Service Director. The musical chairs program continued. The New York advertising/merchandising effort now reported to Atlanta, and Dick Thompson, Bob Docherty, and Don McBride moved down from New York to run commercial and retail merchandising programs out of Atlanta.

The corporation's data and billing center, housing large IBM mainframe computers behind glass walls, was located in Greenville, South Carolina. Every order was recorded and billed in Greenville. Customer historical data was stored there. Inventory data, shipping data, computer codes and tracking, routing of orders....all were activities centered in Greenville. International orders, letters of credit, banking documents, telephone inquiries, order status, product merge numbers (showing compatibility of one order with the next) were also handled by staff at Greenville.

In the 70's, personal computers on computer terminals in each office were only wishful ideas on the part of Information technology. Memos on paper were sent by interoffice mail. Requests from International customers were received by fax or telex, and answered the same way. Internet and Email communications which advanced office productivity from the horse and buggy to the jet age, were yet to come. In the 70's, every document first had to be hand written, then typed, then sent to Greenville, where it became part of the official company record. If it wasn't on Greenville's mainframes, the order or shipment didn't exist.

In the marketing role, I asked the organization to prepare a data base on all customers. We had bits and pieces of information, but nothing comprehensive. I wanted a profile of each customer's technology, capacities, existing product line, key personnel, purchasing history, our share of each customer's business, each competitors share, our goals with each for the next two years, and resources required to reach the goals. Technology, R&D, Maaufacturing, Tech service, Planning….all who would have a hand in achieving the goals were asked to input to the plan.

The book was an elaboration on a standard marketing plan format, intended as a reference for preparing individual and team goals, and evaluating performance. The outcome was a six-inch thick document circulated to staff, management, merchandising/advertising, and all departments affected. Today, the document would be assembled electronically on a computer spreadsheet, and distributed electronically to all concerned, in a fraction of the time we spent doing it.

We used the plan to prioritize our marketing efforts and allocate finite resources among our top 10, next 10 , and bottom half of customers, rated according to market share and growth potential with us. It was the most complete picture of our business base assembled up to that point.

There was no small amount of grumbling about the time required to build the profiles, but it was finally agreed that the effort was worthwhile.

The next year saw increased market shares with target customers. I spent a lot of time between Atlanta and the plants, sometimes helping to host customer visits there to do product reviews and preview marketing programs. The drive to Dalton, Georgia, where a lot of the tufting and support mills were concentrated, took about two hours, and I was often there with a salesman or sales manager to talk with key customers. Technical service kept our processing problems within a manageable range, and claims were small with mostly minor glitches. And trips to the New York office were frequent, all expected as part of the job.

We met or exceeded all key goals for the 74 performance year, and bonuses were at the high end of the range. During this year, matching IRA's were introduced for the first time. It was a no-brainer choice to participate, with guaranteed high return by company matching alone, yet, some chose not to participate. In talking to some of those who elected to pass on the program, it was clear that they either did not trust the program, or had expenses at or above their incomes and could not get by with any deductions from their gross pay. Transparently a good thing, participation initially was only about 50%.

During this period, Joan's Dad, Edwin Henderson, passed away in California after a lengthy illness and a stroke. We knew his health was failing, and had anticipated bad news, but the news of his death was still a shock. Ed and Alice had sold their home in Oakland after Ed retired from the Oakland Tribune after 46 years as head cashier. Ed was well liked, had been extremely active in Shriners, and was an officer of his Masonic Lodge. He had been born in Victoria, Canada. His Mother, Agnes, was Canadian, and his Father, George Henderson, was an American, about whom little is known.

After his Father died, Ed's Mother married Fred Verliger, an accountant. Agnes was a strict Christian Scientist and "reader" in the church, and Ed was raised in that faith. Ed had grown up in Oakland, and Alice, Joan's Mother, had grown up in nearby Danville. Alice was of Swedish heritage and daughter and granddaughter of immigrants. Alice was a jump center on her high school basketball team, secretary of her senior class, and had a key role in her senior play. Ed and Alice had met at work, and married early.

We decided that I should stay in Atlanta with the boys while Joan flew to California for the funeral and to be with her Mother and her brother, Bob. She was in California for a week, helping Alice and Bob sort out Ed's affairs. Alice was a smart woman with good financial skills, and was very capable and healthy at that point, so we knew she would be alright. Ed and Alice did not pursue the Christian Science faith, but Joan and Bob were introduced to it in some detail, mostly on the effort of their Grandmother Verliger. Ed was cremated, and with no religious ceremony, buried in the Chapel of The Chimes, in Oakland, later to be joined there by Alice, who died in 1988.

After two years as a widow, Alice married Robert Moore, an old high school boyfriend who's wife Alma had died years earlier. They enjoyed a very happy and eventful twelve years together, travelling extensively by freighter and sharing Bob's comfortable home in Lafayette, CA., and later, a golf course condo in Walnut Creek. Bob had retired from Pacific Gas and Electric as a plant manager, and was a humorous and well-read companion for Alice. They visited us in Atlanta, and several times in Connecticut after we moved back there in 1977.

In mid-1975, we had been in Atlanta three years. Scott was entering sixth grade and Jon second grade. Both seemed well adjusted to life and friends in Atlanta, as did Joan and I. We had visits from my family and Joan's Mom, Alice, and her step-father. We had an active social life, especially with Bruce and Barbara English and their children, Robert and

Patricia, who were about Scott and Jon's ages. We hob-nobbed some with Atlanta based customers and co-workers.

Halsey and Sharon Burke of Burke Industries, San Jose, CA., and a good customer, came to visit us as friends for a long weekend. John and Harriet Roughan and Lee and Verne Westerberg came down from Connecticut for visits. Frank and Dillie came from Plainview to visit. Some neighbors were also in the mix. Jim Everett, manager of International Sales, and his wife Helen, also ex Connecticut residents, were friends and fellow members of Cherokee Club. Dick and Angie Edwards were occasional dinner companions. Jim Corr, a customer, and wife Judy, were dinner dates.

Our neighborhood was filled with friends for the boys. Jim Schneider and his brother Bill, Richard and Marty Buckman, Donnie, Donna, and Christie Pinkney, all lived within a stone's throw. A neighbor up the street had a huge great Dane, Erik, who frightened the boys and us. Next door, Bob and Betty Zucker on one side, and Curt and Anne Steinmann on the other, were good and friendly neighbors.

Scott joined a soccer team named "Mad Dogs", and the boys under coach Kevin Grass won the 12 and under Georgia State championship. Scott and Kenny Miller were the standouts. Jon joined a junior Mad Dogs team with younger kids, and played at least one game with the senior Mad Dogs because he was so fast. Both boys had bikes with shock absorber front wheels and devised jumps for them on the street. Skateboarding was perhaps their favorite. They wore helmets and pads and did daredevil tricks like hand standing and skating over plywood-rigged jumps. Skinned knees and elbows resulted in spite of padding.

They hiked the forest preserve at the rear of our house, which led all the way to the Chatahoochee River a couple of miles away. The River was Atlanta's water source from Lake Lanier, the large reservoir 45 miles North. I went with the boys and couple of their friends on their hike to the River, and was terrified to find their "hideout" was a cave dugout high up the cliff side of the river bank, about 50 feet above the fast flowing water. One slip and they would have been carried away by the water with little hope of rescue. The hideout was off limits immediately.

In 1975, we bought a small condominium on the golf course in Pinehurst, North Carolina, and went there on weekends. The boys had good luck fishing in the lake behind the condo, as well as playing a little golf. Joan bought furniture in Atlanta for the condo, and had it shipped up. It was comfortable and fun and a true escape. We sold the property when we were transferred back to the New York office.

At age nine, in June, we put Scott on a Delta jet and sent him off to Plainview to spend the summer with his grandparents and uncles there. He had to change planes at the big Dallas airport, but Delta said they would see to it. In Plainview, he learned to shoot rifles and pistols, play golf, and chew tobacco and smoke, taught by my brothers Cal and Raby and my Dad. At one point, Cal flew off to Kansas with Scott in the back seat of a Piper Cub. We didn't find out about this until much later. When I went in August to pick Scott up, he had grown in every way and needed a haircut badly. The first barber didn't cut enough, so I took him to a second, with instructions to cut some more. He said I was "taking control of him".

At Cherokee Country club, Scott was introduced to golf as part of their Junior program. He has remained an avid golfer and today regularly shoots in the 70's at Blue Mound Country club in Milwaukee. He has thanked me many times for introducing him to the game. Jon also likes golf and is pretty good at it, although doesn't play often.

Atlanta was still antebellum South in many ways. The people I worked with were almost all graduates of good southern Universities, and sported rich southern accents. They were genuine, very bright, and positive in their work and attitudes. But parts of Atlanta had still not managed to break free of the old South. I sponsored Alfred Gussin and his wife for membership in the Cherokee club. Al was a good customer at Trend Mills, and lived near us in Atlanta. Al was also Jewish. After months on the waiting list, the chairman of the membership committee called me aside and told me "in confidence" that Al would never be admitted. He said that Jews had their Standard club, and that Cherokee will not admit Jews.

On another occasion, a young black woman I had hired as an intern from the University of Georgia Engineering school, came with my staff for an off-site meeting at the Cherokee Town club. We had a private room but intended to lunch in the main dining room. The club manager pulled me aside, and said, "Mr. Garrett, we have never had a black in our dining room." I was shocked, but to avoid embarrassment, had lunch served in the private meeting room. But I never felt the same about the Cherokee Club after that day.

Reflecting on this, I concluded that this overt discrimination against blacks and Jews was not much different from the subtle bias at private clubs everywhere. How many blacks or Jews were members of the Riverside Yacht Club or the Greenwich Country club or the New York yacht club? Tokens, at the most!! Tribalism and exclusion in all human activity is real and is as old as humanity. The Bible itself openly excludes and separates one tribe or group from another, creating human divides, choosing favorites, indiscriminately punishing innocents for being on the wrong side of a bloodline. Human beings have and will always choose to be with their kind, and no legislated edict will ever change this innate expression of security and comfort. There is also the superiority of being able to dispense rejection.

Should I have resigned from those clubs in protest? Should I protest the Standard Club for admitting only Jews? Should I indict a particular faith for its exclusionary beliefs? Should the NAACP....could the NAACP ever have a white counterpart organization? Should the congressional black caucus suggest a white caucus? Should Mecca exclude Christians? Fraternities and sororities secretly select or reject candidates based on totally arbitrary standards or no rules at all. Bias works in many ways in our society and in all societies. We can feel it and know it is there, and try our individual best to avoid practicing it, but we, as human beings, can never eliminate it. Choosing and discriminating is in our genes. We persist in categorizing people by race and religion, even in census taking and in passport and visa applications. The standard answer to any query about race should be "human" and nothing more.

A final word about Atlanta living. We could never fully acclimate to the weather. It was either too hot or too cold or too stormy. Winter brought snow and ice and slick roads without adequate clearing equipment. Spring brought severe, tornado-like storms with high winds snapping off the soft pines with cannon-like booms. Trees fell on power lines during ice or wind-storms, and, although our electric lines were buried, feeder lines went down and left us without heat or lights. We were without power or heat for three days during one winter spell, and, with hotels all full, slept on couches in the office. We ate all our meals in restaurants.

Atlanta had heavy annual rainfall and temperature extremes greater than we had experienced in New England. The airport was often under siege from the weather, and flights delayed. Humidity and heat during summer made for uncomfortable conditions.

In 1976, we bought Jimmy Dean's small power boat which he had used as a tender for his 90 ft. yacht, Big Bad John. The boat had the name "Little Bad John" across its transom, which we kept. We put it in a slip at Lake Lanier and went there on weekends to escape the Atlanta heat, and get the boys some water skiing time. It had 6 cylinder inboard gasoline power and could move fast. It was know affectionately as "The Big Orange".

July 4 weekend of 1973 we flew on a small wing-over turbo jet down to Sea Island, Georgia, where we met Sandy and Pam Jackson and Bob and Jerry Hipps, old friends from Connecticut. The Jackson's now lived in Atlanta. His uncle, Bill Jones, had founded and developed Sea Island,

and his cousin, Bill Jr., still runs it today. It was my 40th birthday, and the boys threw me in the pool to celebrate. We walked the beach and shelled, and played golf on both of the great Sea Island courses. In 2010, Sea Island filed chapter 11 bankruptcy and was taken over by a group of members and continues to operate. Sea Island had been one of the most successful developments of its type anywhere in the country, but the deep recession at the time took its toll on high-end resorts .

Scott and Jon have good memories of the years in Atlanta. Both boys became more involved in athletics, and both developed friendships which lasted for a long time. Joan and I had active social lives with a variety of friends. For me, it was a time of corporate advancement which I would never have had if I had refused the move. At this point, I was married to Monsanto, and my career and subsequent moves were entirely in their hands, which I guess I trusted. This was not a good position to be in, but it happened to work out well.

BREAKTHROUGH ASSIGNMENT

John Roughan told me once that the secret code to success in Monsanto was, LIDBTY. He had seen a Monsanto executive with this lettering on his tie-clasp. It means" look Irish, dress British, think Yiddish." I perhaps looked a little Irish, did dress Paul Stuart when I could afford it, but unless my grandfather, Alexander Shakespeare Morris ,was one of God's chosen people, I had no qualifications to think Yiddish. Still, through good fortune, I seemed to be getting ahead.

My next promotion was mid-1975, to Business Group Director. Bruce English had been made General Manager and moved to St. Louis, and, as in our previous jobs, I followed him up the ladder. Subtly, Bruce had become my sponsor and mentor and good friend. I now occupied the job that Len Cohn held back in 1969, and had profit and operational responsibility for the business.

Robert Burke was now the Managing Director in St. Louis for the Fibers Division. Bob had just come from Rubber Chemicals, but was a long timer at Monsanto, having joined after graduation from Holy Cross university. Dr. Fernandez was now Corporate Vice-Chairman under CEO and Chairman Jack Hanley, who had been recruited to Monsanto from Proctor and Gamble. Hanley was a brand idealogue. Commodities were in his strategic plan, but only as businesses to shed. He was a Harvard Business School grad of the post war class of 48, had risen to executive VP of P & G, and now was determined to make his mark in the CEO chair at Monsanto.

Up to that point in company history, differentiating products through branded advertising and merchandising had been largely the domain of the Fibers Division. Only the Monsanto Agricultural chemicals division was beginning to break out branded programs with Roundup brand herbicide, under an obscure product Manager by the name of Dick Mahoney, who later rose to Chairman and CEO of the company based on his success with Roundup.

Bob Burke was a part of Hanley's "cabinet" and got the message quickly. Branded was the way to progress within Monsanto. Commodities would be shown the door. Bob quickly got the Boston Consulting Group on the case. BCG set about doing studies and charting all products on their infamous growth rate/market share matrices. BCG staff converged on Atlanta and began doing research.

The apparel side of Fibers, still based in New York, was still heavily branded and promoted under the Wear Dated label, guaranteeing consumers a full year of satisfactory performance or a full refund, no questions asked. Bob was intrigued with the idea of applying the Wear Dated guarantee to carpets, and selling the concept through the distribution chain to retail customers. Mills had resisted the idea because the message seemed to place too much emphasis on functionality instead of differentiation through style and fashion. Inexpensive carpets meeting minimum standard would get the same warranty as higher-end carpets, and the retail shopper might be tempted to trade down instead of up. Higher quality luxury grades could be very big-ticket purchases and required a degree of salesmanship and romancing that purely functional floor coverings did not. Plus, the mills themselves stood behind quality.

There was also the obstacle of dollar liability to cover claims. Unlike low cost knit garments, claims for refunds on costly installed carpets, if they came, could take big dollars off the bottom line, while relieving the manufacturer of quality responsibility. Then there was the cost of Wear Dated testing of each grade to make certain its construction qualified for the label. In apparel, garments were regularly tested and meticulous records kept. A reserve was set up for claims. Rejected garments had to be catalogued and records kept for extended periods. And conceptually at least, carpets intended for commercial applications like office buildings or schools would not qualify for the warranty, yet were the very places where function was emphasized over style. So the case was not clear-cut.

Nevertheless, BCG began testing the premise, while at the same time holding meeting with plant, R&D, and Technology departments to review overall strategy of the business. All of this made complete sense to me as the head of the business. I was glad to have the attention and resources focused in my area. Change was in the air.

A good starting point for BCG was the customer data document that we had just assembled. It was a time-saver for them, and immediately allowed them to ask pertinent questions across the organization. Among their issues was the breakdown of staple fiber usage vs. filament nylon, and customer's abilities to process each. A larger issue was the competitive quality of our filament and staple products vs. other suppliers such as

Dupont. BCG spent a lot of time on this issue, and concluded after six months of studies and trials that Monsanto's strategic emphasis should be focused on staple nylon and staple acrylics rather than filament.

As explained earlier, we had high productivity and low cost using continuous polymerization lines (CP), but after extrusion, our drawing and downstream processing did not rate the equal of Dupont. Staple nylon, on the other hand, was dry extruded in tow form, then crimped, cut, and baled much like our acrylic staple. Mills then had flexibility to introduce a greater range of yarn and finished goods styling through blending and spinning, then piece dyeing. This styling latitude was considered critical for residential applications, which was the end use intended for the Wear Dated label.

Strategy meetings were held up and down the organization, and decision was made to focus more on nylon staple and acrylic staple, with a five year Wear Dated warranty as our marketing theme. Efforts were begun to construct the Wear Dated testing and record keeping programs and prepare the program for launch. This roll out took time and budgets and training and logistics. Before public banners, mills, spinners, dye houses, stylists, all had to have presentations on the workings of the program, and an allowance for their feedback to improve the launch.

Meanwhile, we had a business to run. Field Sales and Technical service was engaged as usual with existing programs. Bruce English and Bob Burke were in the Atlanta office frequently. Visiting executive like Lou Fernandez and Harold Bible, an executive VP, came down for a day-long briefing. Staff like Ken McIntosh, Dave Bowen, Len James, Jim Swink, Dick Edwards, Ralph Conwill, Len Millar, Hugh Wilson, Buck Tucker, and Nick Nicodemus made presentations about their areas and did impressive work. Mickey Finn kept Technical service on its toes. We made our targets and met our goals, in what was a transition year.

One useful business gathering was held each year in Point Clear,

Alabama, at the fancy Marriott resort there. Pensacola was nearby, and we bused everyone from the resort to the plant for technical presentations, then back to the resort for fishing in the Gulf and dinners of great seafood. Key customers and their wives were invited, key issues discussed. An economic prognosis was offered for the coming year by Frank Horn, our in-house expert. Golf was a central activity of the second and third days, while wives shopped in nearby Mobile.

The outing was a pay-off for good customers, and a chance to exchange ideas in a social setting. One year, we had professors from Indiana University Business school present research on communicating with young people coming into the home furnishings purchasing market for the first time. Understanding their language, their music, their mores, was critical in product styling and ad appeals

In early 77, Wear Dated Carpets were launched with a heavy trade ad schedule and in Shelter magazines such as House and Garden, House Beautiful, and Better Homes and Gardens. Wear Dated carpet testing was ramped up in the Decatur Technical center. Details of the warranty and customized labels were provided to mill customers. Service centers labeled cut orders with Wear Dated before shipping to retailers. The program was off to a smooth start. BCG kept a close eye on both the launch and the strategy acceptance.

With almost two years of running the business under my belt, with a lot of help from above and below, it was only natural that another change would be in order. This time, it would mean another relocation, to a surprising place.

BOOK SIX
New York, Connecticut, Harvard

ANOTHER BUSINESS GROUP IN N.Y.

F rank Dayton had been my counterpart in the New York office as head of the Apparel, drapery, crafts yarns, and industrial business group, within the Fibers Division. Bob Burke advised me that I was to take Frank's job, while Frank moved to St. Louis to a General Manager slot. Exposure to the other side of Fibers would give me a complete overview of the business, and move us back to the New York area, which, for us, meant Connecticut. We began to make preparations to move as soon as the school year was over. Joan and the boys were excited, as was I. Frankly, we preferred New England to Atlanta.

Frank Dayton was a Bucknell graduate, a year or so older than me, and another protégé of Lou Fernandez from Organic chemicals. Increasingly clear was need to have sponsors or mentors or Rabbi's at each stage of the career ladder. Frank Hartmann had been my booster and mentor. Len Cohn was Bruce English's Rabbi. Bruce, to some extent, sponsored me and helped groom me to succeed him as he moved on.

Like Major Joe Gigandet, of Korean Armed Forces radio network, with his "On there" affectation, Dayton also used a verbal crutch, a sort of dramatic interlude, as if he felt it was needed for you to catch up with his thought process. His was "in fact", or "as a matter of fact". These little dangling participles or phrases were sprinkled in to lend authenticity to an otherwise transparent point. As an example, he might say, "as a matter of fact, the plane leaves at eleven", or "in fact, today is the first day of the rest of your life". He was so accustomed to throwing in these types of superfluous fillers that he was completely unaware that they were distractions for the listener. It was natural to expect something profound after "as a matter of fact", but profundity rarely followed.

Yet, he was analytical to the point of absurdity. There was always a tablet of graph paper on his desk, and whatever issue was raised, he instinctively reached for paper and pencil to chart the question horizontally and vertically. "Looking at this problem in this dimension", he would say, " as a matter of fact, we might conclude thus and so, but "looking at on a vertical scale might lead us to another thus and so." Finally, he would decide on the basis of weighing the scales, and, once decided, he was a man of action, even if wrong. An admirable trait Frank had was to stand and fight for his position, even if Management above him thought him wrong.

While detached, Frank was a fair boss, and, outside the office, had a good sense of humor. He and his very smart and funny wife, Joanne, had spent a career with Monsanto in a variety of locations, and loved Manhattan living, but now moved to a condo not far from downtown St. Louis. They much preferred New York, but had been in St. Louis before and knew it well. Later, Joan and I would become friendly and socialized some with them in St. Louis. Within two years, Frank would be transferred to an assignment in Brussels, his "retirement" gig, which was his and Joanne's favorite.

I would report initially to Dayton, and later to his successor, Wiley Hogeman, who had a manufacturing background. The wide span of reporting relationships to me was a concern, with seasoned Monsanto career men in key jobs of marketing, technology, Key accounts management, Merchandising/advertising, Field Sales, and Wear Dated management. We had specialists managing the sweater market, the hand-knit market, and the Industrial nylon market. Matt Dalton had been a corporate regional Vice-President, but was now in charge of the Deering-Milliken account. Joe Buck was a sales director now handling the critical Burlington account. These two major customers dominated a good slice of the markets for filament polyester, and were crucial to our success in the polyester business. The Charlotte office, with it field sales and Tech service groups, also reported to me.

I began to think about how to streamline this as much as possible. I was the new guy dealing with the old pros Matt Dalton, Herb Rabinowitz, Yvette Neier, Wayne Harrison, Archie Wilbanks, Carlton Kennedy, Joe Buck, Sam Harwell, Jim Allison, and Art Dunham. This was much too wide a span and much too involved when setting goals and expense and sales budgets, reviewing performance, reviewing salaries, approving expenses, approving various business plans, checking financial results, and monitoring pricing. It became apparent that clerical duties would tie me to the office and prevent involvement in each business segment in the way I wanted to be. The pitfall was becoming a full time administrator rather than an activist ahead-of-the-curve manager.

The array of different markets under the Business Group was also daunting. Single knits, double knits, circular knits, wovens, sweaters, hand knits, craft yarns, sewing threads, upholstery, draperies, and industrial specialty yarns for belting, filtration, tenting, high performance polymers for engineered mechanical parts. All were different markets with different customers, distinctive technologies, different products and processing requirements, different distribution chains, and unique marketing plans.

In these applications, we sold acrylics, nylon filament, and, the newest horse in the stable, polyester filament, all in many permutations. Monsanto had recently purchased the polyester filament plant of Rhome and Haas Chemical Co., in Sand Mountain, Alabama, on the theory that polyester was the fastest growing fiber in double knits, and we had to have a supply position in it to hold position with our largest customers. Lou Fernandez held the Managing Director's job in Fibers when the decision was made to buy the polyester plant, but Lou had moved upstairs, and making the acquisition work technically, integrating it into our existing business, and making it profitable now fell to Bob Burke and his team. It was make or break time in the Fibers division, all revolving around filament polyester.

As if this was not enough complexity, Monsanto adopted a matrix management system, with product Directors for acrylics, nylon, and polyester taking responsibility for overall strategy and profitability of each of the three major product lines, with dual accountability with Business Groups who carried out the strategies on the ground. This introduced another element of approvals, and, frankly, political jockeying. The product guys were planners with good credentials but often with little if any line experience. There was no apprenticeship from which they might have learned reality. These guys were the metaphorical planners in the bowels of the Pentagon who end up second guessing the generals on the front. But matrix management was good Harvard Business School practice and remains so today, though flawed in many ways.

We were fortunate to have Alan Shenton, a Brit expat, as Product Director of Acrilan. Alan knew acrylics first hand from his stint marketing them in Britian. Bob Pennell had nylon and was also respected for his line experience in both the U.S. and Europe. Smart but less experienced or respected was Dr. Joe Privett, a former researcher, who had the polyester hot potato. We all had useful debates and disagreements from time to time about marketing and strategy, but managed to resolve them amicably.

Polyester filament technical issues persisted, however, and a swat team was formed to meet weekly in Pensacola to review and update programs intended to make the product competitive with Dupont, the market leader. These weekly meetings required inordinate travel and reporting time, another complication in transitioning smoothly into the new job.

My first month in the assignment was spent entirely on the road, following a rigid schedule of visits to key customers who included, spinners, throwsters, vertical powerhouses like Milliken and Burlington, hosiery makers, cutting and sewing operations, sweater knitters, double-knit producers, and craft yarn makers. Our Charlotte office briefed me on much of this, and itself was filled with great people I needed to get to know. We also had a small Los Angeles office headed by Bob Goldman, who worked with West coast retailers and cut and sew operations to set up merchandising programs. I was determined to get educated and properly grounded in the fundamentals before being immersed into the day-to-day tangle of events.

THE MOVE BACK TO CONNECTICUT:

First, get the family moved and ready for the new school year. Scott would be entering 8th grade, and Jon 4th grade. We knew the Greenwich area and wanted to be there. Old friend Verne Westerberg called to say that his neighbor down the street, Dr. Paul Yudkovsky, wanted to sell his house at 21 Cove Rd., on Lucas Point, and move to a bigger house. (Paul passed away in January 2011, in St. Petersburg, Florida.)

Joan and I took a look and decided to try to buy it. It was a two story picture-book colonial on a corner lot, one block from the Lucas Point private beach. Three bedrooms, two baths, one car garage, oil heat, and no air conditioning. But what we thought was a perfect location, with a homeowner's association. There was no realtor. Yudkofsky bought another house at the end of the street with a panoramic waterfront view stretching all the way to Manhattan, for $300,000. Today, with little improvement, its worth would be in the range of $10 million.

After some light dickering, we agreed on $163,000 and made a September closing date. This meant renting for two months before we could move in, which we arranged to do. Initially, we had to stay in the Marriott Stamford for two weeks before the Riverside rental was available. The hotel was right on top of I-95 Interstate and noisier than a jet aircraft on take-off. I commuted from the hotel during this time, with very little sleep.

Back in Atlanta, we had to sell a house, and did so in short order for $109,000, not a bad return for five years of ownership. The housing market was in "always-up" mode, and we believed it would continue.

By now we had two Chevy station wagons and a boat with trailer. We shipped the boat and trailor and one car, loaded our essentials and Chumley in the newer wagon, and drove North to still another new adventure. We visited Colonial Williamsburg and Jamestown on our way up. On arrival in Connecticut, the boys were able to immediately join the summer program at Riverside yacht club, and renew friendships. Joan and I also reconnected with old friends.

Lucas Point neighbors were welcoming and hospitable. The Westerbergs saw to our introductions all around. I resumed the wonderful commute to Manhattan, but this time lived too far away from the Old Greenwich station to walk. I drove the second car to the station. This required applying for a parking permit, for which there was a wait list. Waiting, I either hitched a ride or Joan drove me. Busses picked up the boys for school.

While we were in Atlanta, Monsanto had moved offices out of the

Empire State Building to brand new mid-town quarters, in the new Monsanto building at 42nd street and 6th avenue, so named because Monsanto was the major tenant, occupying four full floors. Since fibers used the most office space, I was in designated as being in charge of the office. The structure was 50 floors, contemporary, glass-sided, flaring outward at the bottom like a ski jump, much like the similarly designed Avon building at 58th and 6th. The building was new and more desirable than the 45 yr old Empire State bldg..

My 10th floor office was actually a two-room suite, with the large office opening onto a private conference room with sofa and easy chairs. Meetings of more than three people were moved in to the conference room. Both rooms overlooked 43rd street, with a wide view North to Rockefeller Center and beyond. Walking from Grand Central to the office was two blocks and five minutes at most, and could be done entirely underground in bad weather.

Mary Gendron, my secretary, sat just outside my office. She was a superb professional, took perfect dictation, and was efficient, fast, and tireless. She knew the organization and personalities I had inherited, and understood very well how to prioritize their requests. I had no machine for dictation, no voice mail device, no computer terminal. We were modern enough to have a buzzer intercom between us. Any memo or letter I sent was either hand written or dictated to Mary, who then presented it to me for proofing, after which it went to the mail outbox. The system was 1940's at best.

Next to me was Herb Rabinowitz, head of merchandising. Yvette Neier was next to Herb, and their people were arrayed along the North/ South axis in smaller offices or cubicles. East of my office, also overlooking 43rd street, were sales, advertising, Technical, and Wear Dated offices. Accounting and planning people were on the South side of the 10th floor. Assorted store rooms and other offices were located on the 9th floor, and other regional offices of the remaining Monsanto divisions were located on the 8th floor, having consolidated there from a number of locations in the city.

Back in Connecticut, Lucas Point association had 64 homes, lots of kids, its own dock on Greenwich Cove, perhaps the best gunk-hole on Long Island Sound, its own private beach with great views across the Sound, and plenty of neighborhood social events. Resident's boats, large and small, sail and power, were stored for Winter on the Lucas Point dock, lifted onto cradles by a large hired crane. Neighbors pitched in to sand and power wash barnacles off keels. "Taking Out" was followed by a big party to which everyone contributed.

"Launching" in the Spring was equally hard work but festive. Weeks of preparation preceded to actual lifting of the boats and putting them in the water. Boats had to be unwrapped, power washed, bottom painted with anti-fouling paints, auxiliary engines tested, hulls waxed, bright work varnished, and guide lines attached. Timing the large 10 ft. tidal swing had to be just right. The tide table determined the day and time. Low tide meant being stuck in the mud. The whole operation was at least as delicate and precise as the Inchon landing of MacArthur. Ray Haney was the unofficial "dock master", assisted by David Erb, Westerberg, me, and whoever else had boats they wanted to store there.

The rituals of launching boats in Spring and taking boats out in Fall required teamwork, with men working together side by side, cooperating in a mutual endeavor, metaphorically like old fashioned house raising in Colonial times, when everybody pitched in for a common good.

Immediately past Lucas Point was Greenwich Point, known to the locals as Tod's Point, after the Mr. Tod who used to own the land and its waterfront. He built his own mansion there, with golf course and stables. Tod partnered with George Lucas to bring landfill from the Third Avenue subway dig in Manhattan, and construct Lucas Point on the man-made peninsula that resulted. Lucas Point was an island of dirt and rock that had recently been a part of Manhattan.

Tod's Point had been acquired by the Town of Greenwich for a modest sum and turned into one of the most spectacular and unique public facilities anywhere on the East Coast. There were beautiful beaches, running trials, yacht moorings in the Cove, picnic tables and cooking facilities, and small boat storage racks at the small public yacht club. Fishing off the rocks for blues and strippers was good. Young and old alike loved the park. It was the favorite destination for residents, and passes were necessary to gain entry.

Scott and Jon were back in the excellent Greenwich public school system. That fall, Jon became the star running back in the Pop Warner football league, which fielded eight teams from area schools. Jon was an excellent athlete, very muscular and extremely agile and fast for a 10 yr old. Scott went to Eastern Jr. High, while Jon enrolled in Old Greenwich elementary school, about a mile from our house.

Old Greenwich adjoined Riverside, both villages at the Eastern end of the town of Greenwich. That winter, the whole family got into ice skating. Benny park pond, in central Old Greenwich, froze over quickly, and attracted many ice skaters from all over town. The scene was like a Christmas card snapshot, full of color and the beginning of the holiday season.

Meanwhile, Joan decided to take courses in Interior Design at Fairfield University a few miles east of Greenwich. She had talent going in, and earned excellent grades in all courses. Later, in St. Louis, she would work as a professional Interior Designer for 10 years, for Hal's Interiors, very successfully. Even later, she commuted to Manhattan to attend the Isabel O'Niell school of "The art of the painted finish", and created special designs and exotic finishes for art pieces for our home and sailboat.

Connecticut living during this three-year stint in the New York office is something of a haze because I was on the road so much. Almost weekly, there were committee meetings at St. Louis headquarters, or presentations to Bob Burke's Management Board. I might fly directly from there to one of the plants for more meetings, then from the plant to the Charlotte office for reviews of one type or another, and from there to a key meeting with Milliken and Company in Spartanburg, S.C. Then there was the Customer service center in Greenville, or a meeting with this texturizer or that spinner, or so and so knitter.

Meetings in the New York office with out of town visitors were very frequent. Everybody liked visiting New York, and our office was a must business stopover. The very important Burlington account was just up 6th avenue, and commanded lots of attention for luncheons and technical and price discussions. We had a two bedroom company apartment at 37th and Park, where I often stayed the night after a late dinner to be followed by an early breakfast. Joan and the boys were alone much of the time. We had weekends together, but very little time Monday through Friday.

Union Carbide was a sizable chemicals buyer from Monsanto and we from them. They invited three of us from the New York office aboard their Gulfstream jet for a special golf outing in Pennsylvania at Arnold Palmer's home course in La Trobe. We boarded at Westchester county airport in White Plains, flew 30 minutes to the course, spent two nights with two rounds of golf, dinners, drinks, prizes, then flew back to Westchester.

Starting in 1977, I began to be more aware of the need to get and stay healthy, and began jogging. The well known author Jim Fixx had jogged past our house a number of times, and I became intrigued. Jim wrote "The complete Book of Running", and started the running craze across the country. I began slowly and worked up at six miles a day in a short period of time. And it became something I had to do daily. Wherever I was at night, in St. Louis, Charlotte, Pensacola, or Connecticut, I would put on my running shoes and get in my quota. In 1979, I logged one thousand miles, and Scott and Jon ran the last three miles with me around Tod's point. Running became something of an addiction.

Conrad Tietell and I became running pals. We had previously played indoor tennis together when we lived in Connecticut before, but he now was a serious runner. We did the Westchester half-marathon together over a hilly course on a muggy fall day, 13.2 miles, and finishing was tough under the circumstances.

Jon and I entered a five mile run through Greenwich on one Saturday morning. He was 10 at the time. The idea was to choose a reasonable pace which could be sustained over the entire course. Jon had not run in this kind of "race" before, and his intention was to beat everyone, not just finish. At the starting gun, he took off running as fast as he could and never looked back. He said he ran the entire five miles at the same pace. He finished near the top of the field, which included some expert adult runners. When I caught up with him afterwards, he was bright red and dehydrated. He truly was a fast runner, and surprised many adults.

I continued to run regularly for the next 25 years. I credit running with keeping my stress level down while performing in a series of demanding jobs, beginning with the New York Business Group assignment. When I stopped running in 2002 due to knee concerns, I was so into the habit of regular exercise that I immediately switched to gym aerobics and weight lifting to stay on the health track. My smoking habit had been kicked in early 1964 when the Surgeon General first announced its ill effects. The combination of stopping smoking and beginning sustained serious exercise has, I am convinced, been the catalyst for maintaining good health and proper weight.

1978 and 1979 were extremely busy and went by quickly, but there was still no fix in sight for polyester filament in spite of large amounts of R&D and technology invested in trying to create product and package uniformity. Heat setters (throwsters) had problems running the product at high speeds and achieving competitive products in weaving, double knitting, and other applications. Dupont continued to turn out excellent product with increasing capacity, while we were penalized in pricing because of imperfections and seconds, slow throughput in customer fabrications, and lack of dye uniformity.

Pressure built quickly from D Building, where top corporate management resided, on Burke's management team. Dick Mahoney had ridden the herbicide business to top profitability in the company, and had earned the President's slot under Jack Hanley's Chairman and CEO slot. The other Managing Directors, Mahoney contemporaries, had lost out. Patience had grown thin. Mahoney was now the man demanding answers, and had tossed aside any pretence of political correctness. It was clear that if a pathway to success in polyester had not been clearly identified within one more year, changes would be made.

HARVARD BUSINESS SCHOOL

The summer of 1979 brought the most surprising and least expected turn of events. Notices were posted on bulleting boards in all worldwide locations that Jack Hanley had designated a group of high potential executives to attend extended Executive Management courses at top Business schools in the country. Among these were Stanford, Wharton, and Harvard Business Schools. These were the most coveted appointments in the company, and implied that those chosen would go on to higher executive positions in the near future. There was also high value in the psychology and recognition with existing top management. These dozen men and women were recognized as solid executives who could perform at high levels in the corporation.

Nominated by Dayton and seconded by Burke, I was honored to be selected to attend the Advanced Management Program at Harvard Business School, a 13 week full time program requiring complete separation from existing day-to-day duties. Harvard was Jack Hanley's school, and the most prestigious. The AMP program was taught by regular Harvard Business School faculty, themselves on three months sabbatical from their regular Chairs teaching the B school two year program. The professors were well known authors and consultants, and all served on Boards of Directors of leading Corporations.

164 attendees from throughout the world, representing major international names in all categories of products and services, converged on Harvard and lived in campus housing, attending classes and seminars five and one half days a week. Our 82nd AMP ran from September 15, 1979 to December 15. We lived in "can" groups of six, each with our own small bedroom but sharing a bath. Can members were comprised of different disciplines such as legal, banking, automobile manufacturing, electronics, energy, chemicals, and consulting. Some had been trained as attorneys and were now moving into other broader management areas.

There were insurance executives, retailers, airline execs, an ex astronaut, Bill Anders, head of G.E.'s aircraft engine division and later CEO of General Dynamics, and a small young Saudi, Naimi Ali, who would become the first non-Royal head of Arabian American Oil Company (Aramco), and the Saudi Oil Minister and head of the OPEC oil cartel.

Only four were women, in the sciences, in public relations, in strategic planning. One of my can mates was Sammy Sanyal, an eloquent Indian executive of a mid-sized company there. In the larger group, there were two or three medical doctors who had gone on to found or run healthcare companies

There was a bright young executive from IBM, and a Merrill Lynch exec who would become well known as Executive VP of that company. We were a completely diverse assortment of executives who would study and debate Harvard Business School cases, bringing to bear our various backgrounds and disciplines.

Preparing to leave the Monsanto business Group job to go to Harvard, lots of loose ends had to be looked after. Bob Burke instructed me to delegate everything and instruct staff not to call me except in emergency, which I did. Each of my reports was to follow plans already in place, and submit regular reports to Burke or Dayton. Attendance at the regular weekly polyester swat team meetings was also delegated to Joe Buck or Matt Dalton. Mary Gendron could call me if serious need arose, or if particular people were attempting contact.

The biggest issue had to do with my family. I had already been away from home too much, and now would be away another three months, with only rare Sundays at home. I drove a car from Connecticut to Boston, so I could sneak away on Sunday morning, have a few hours at home 4 hours drive away, then be back on campus that night. On one weekend, Scott came on the train to visit me and stayed over on Saturday night. We went to see the movie Breaking Away, about a young bicycle enthusiast, and he was inspired by it.

Later, taking his cue from the movie, Scott and his friend Nickie Mark, would ride their bicycles from Greenwich to Cape Cod and back in an incredible adventure which we permitted, without fully appreciating the risks, I am sure. But the boys camped out, made new friends, and survived a trip never to be forgotten.

Jon also visited on another weekend, riding the New Haven railroad up and back by himself. He told me he learned to shoot pool in the rec room of the Harvard dormitory where we stayed. We probably went jogging, although neither of us remembers. He had just turned twelve.

The final week of the program, Joan and all the other wives were invited to attend special lectures and seminars and study cases relating to adjustment after the Harvard experience. This special week, we moved off campus to the nearby Hyatt. It was a highlight of the three months.

Harvard was a life-changing experience for me in that I not only made many international friends, but I also began to think more globally as I listened to their stories. I jogged with Ali, the Saudi Oil executive, and with William Anders, who had orbited the moon aboard Apollo 11. He was, in 1979, head of General Electric's Aircraft engines division.

I met the President of Hyatt Hotels, Pat Foley, who presented me with a Green Courtesy card which has worked magic at Hyatt hotels around the world for the past thirty years. I became friendly with Mike Robertson, a Harvard grad, now a minister in Squantum, Mass. Steve Guittard, an attorney and can mate, has stayed in touch, and now lives on Manhattan's upper East side, while his wife Helen focuses on marketing high-rise condos.

I came to understand something about the worldwide chemical and oil and energy giants like BASF, BP, Imperial Chemicals (ICI), Rhone Poulanc, Montedison, Mitsubishi, Asahi Kasei, Sinopec, Sumitomo, Royal Dutch Shell, Rhodia, Akzo Nobel, and Pemex,. Most had attendees. GM and Ford also sent executives, who I remember telling us that Toyota would be a formidable competitor in automobiles throughout the world, because of their exacting quality standards taught them post-war by an American, Professor Deming, and their subsequent huge investments in technology. At the time, Toyota and Honda were little known outside Japan.

In a later assignment within Monsanto, this grounding would become relevant as I travelled around the world and dealt with many of the companies I came to know at Harvard.

Daily rigorous exercise continued as an important part of the routine at Harvard. I upped my daily jogging mileage and began intensive workouts in the gym, often at the close of the day or early before classes began. Perhaps stressing my system, I suffered several serious gout attacks, and had to resort to crutches for a two-week period. Sitting in class while suffering from gout in my ankles was very uncomfortable. I began taking medication for elevated uric acid, and, after awhile, the gout was brought under control, only to recur many times later before being stabilized by daily doses of Alopuranol, which I continue to this day. Still, jogging and working out while at Harvard became an important and relaxing ritual. Freedom from business travel, train commuting, and the demands of family permitted more time for exercise, and I perhaps overdid it.

BOSTON AND CAMBRIDGE

The Fall season in Cambridge and Boston is filled with with all the colors which attract tourists to New England. The Charles River basin separating Boston and Cambridge is active with sailing and rowing competition between Harvard and MIT and other area colleges such as Northeastern, U of Mass, Boston College. Runners dot both sides of the 19 mile shoreline. The Charles becomes the Fall inland playground for the Boston Metro area , while the Atlantic and Cape Cod and offshore Nantucket Island and its beaches are the larger Summer paradise.

Boston calls itself "The Athens of America" because of its reputation as the educational and historical cultural seat of the country. Boston proper has just over 650 thousand people, while the greater Metropolitan area counts close to 4.5 million. Its history parallels that of the American revolution. Ben Franklin and John Hancock, both from Boston, signed the Declaration of Independence. Eli Whitney, Alexander Graham Bell, Samuel F.B. Morse, Robert Frost, and George H.W. Bush are natives, as was John Fitzgerald Kennedy. The mass Irish immigration centered on Boston, as did the great American Industrial revolution. Boston is the center of Catholicism in America. One of these Irish immigrants was my friend John

Roughan's mother and father, who settled in nearby Lowell and became part of the labor force in textile mills there.

Harvard University was the first in America, founded in 1636 as a Methodist college by John Harvard. Today, it has 20 thousand students and a dozen graduate schools, all turning out leaders in their fields. The larger University is located across the Charles in Cambridge, a city of about 100 thousand, while the self-contained Business school is on the Boston side of the river, just a short walk from the central campus.

Among the most notable graduates of Harvard are Ben Bernanke, John Updike, T.S. Eliot, John Adams, Franklin Delano Roosevelt, Theodore Roosevelt, and Samuel Adams. Of those attending Harvard but not graduating, Bill Gates, Mark Zuckerberg, and Matt Damon are well known. Harvard Business School graduates who head American corporations are too numerous to list, and include those leading the largest companies in the United States.

Massachusetts Institute of Technology is the other institution of higher learning in Cambridge, a couple of miles down the river from Harvard. MIT is the most prestigious University in the country for math and science, and graduates international leaders and Noble laureates in these fields.

Living on the Harvard campus and being associated with the history of the institution and its graduates was, for me, an incredulous and humbling experience. I was aware every day of the contrast between my upbringing and modest schooling in the rural Southwest in a tiny farm community no longer in existence, and the sophistication and urbanity of Harvard University and its assemblage of the best minds and the most privileged students and faculty on earth. Some of the most important of world political leaders, statesmen, ambassadors, writers, scientists, economists, performing artists, mathematicians, medical researchers, consultants, inventors, and business entrepreneurs had their formal educations on this campus.

But I would also discover through discussion, debate, and exchange of ideas, that many students at Harvard, in all disciplines, came from modest non-elite backgrounds; that wealth and bloodlines do not breed intellectual superiority; that many in the AMP group and in Harvard undergraduate schools shared at least some of my small town, fringes of society attributes. In other words, I began to grasp that small beginnings do not constitute a disadvantage, and that any sense of not belonging or intimidation or inferiority is unwarranted.

It was a revelation which led to the insight that my unconscious self-image was one of a degree of inadequacy relative to my business peers. My selection to attend Harvard and the experience itself helped to balance and make more realistic my own self-perception. While I never regarded myself as superior, I never again looked at myself as "less than" anybody, or deficient in analytical or managerial ability.

POST HARVARD

On leaving Harvard after completing the 82nd AMP, it was clear that Monsanto's investment of more than $100 thousand dollars in developing me would lead to still another job assignment in the near future, but the timing was not at all clear. I had been careful not to speculate on the nature of anything new, and trusted Monsanto to act in their own and my best interests. A general assumption was that the assignment would be within the Fibers Division, perhaps in a General Manager position of broader authority. This feeling, and that is what it was, was naïve in the extreme.

The prevailing attitude in the 60's and 70's was that the corporate unwritten contract was a long-term mutually beneficial commitment of employee to company and vice versa; that outstanding performance would be rewarded; that both parties were in the relationship for the long term career. As the 80's began, it was clear that the mutual commitment concept was starting to fall apart, and that a rational plan for the individual would be to have a well developed "fail safe" or fall-back career plan if the corporation pushed him aside or abandoned him.

Turbulent times prevailed in Fibers due to the continued failure of filament polyester to become competitive in spite of big new capital invested in technology and process improvements, and large investments of managerial time and effort. Additionally, the Acrilan branded franchise faced increasing headwinds from offshore finished garment inroads, and domestic price erosion from cheaper cotton/polyester blends in knits, wovens, and industrials. The Fibers division went from major profit producer to breakeven to profit drag within a relatively short period.

I resumed my old post in the New York office in January 1980, recognizing that the long term future of Monsanto in Fibers was under the scrutiny of "D" building's microscope. This naturally meant that my own future was connected directly to the reputation of Fibers, which was no longer in "star" orbit. If any negotiation was to be involved in defining my next job, this Fibers springboard would not likely enhance my leverage. In corporate life, I had learned, the best place to be was on the crest of the wave, not the trough.

The news of a lateral and radically different assignment would come to me within five months, and it would mean another major challenge for me and another major upheaval for Joan, Scott, and Jonathan.

But before beginning a new job, a brief essay on a subject which has bothered me for a long time.

ON LEGALIZATION OF DRUGS

Ihave been baffled for several years by the question of who benefits from the continued prohibition of secondary intoxicants like marijuana. Clearly, the religious lobby does not want legalization, claiming that smoking the substance clouds judgment and leads young people the use more addictive drugs such as cocaine, heroin, and methamphetamines. This in turn, they say, leads to loose morality and a breakdown of family unity and structure, and ultimate denial of religion.

Law enforcement organizations campaign against legalization because, they say, marijuana is a gateway drug leading to criminal behavior and a weakening of the social order. Yet some 75% of police arrests and incarcerations across the country relate directly to marijuana possession, sale, and use. Prisons are populated by non-violent marijuana offenders, and officials request ever more and increasingly expensive prison facilities to house these "law-breakers." Legalizing marijuana would obviate that need and permanently reduce the need for a significant percentage of uniformed officers, squad cars, holding cells, and long term prison cells. The rolls of police unions would be decimated if marijuana and other presently illegal drugs were made legal.

Alcohol and tobacco producers do not want legalization because the substance can be grown, stored, and distributed inexpensively and would compete directly with nicotine and beer and hard liquor sales. This in spite of the documentation that cigarettes and alcohol impose far more health and accident costs, and overall societal damage. Nicotine and alcohol are clearly the most addictive gateway drugs leading to all sorts of antisocial behavior and deadly consequences. Legal weed would have a competitive cost advantage, especially over alcohol, which is costly to store and ship.

Teachers unions and many PTA groups and school boards oppose legalization of still another addictive substance invading their hallowed halls, remaining in denial of the ubiquity of marijuana in school book bags, lockers, student pockets, and from pushers on every corner of the school grounds. They suffer substantial costs employing security teams to search out marijuana and expel users, without making the slightest reduction of use. Like sex, or prescription legal drugs, any forbidden substance takes on added luster and desirability to young people in the stage of discovering their own boundaries and refusing received wisdom.

Medical societies oppose legalization on much the same grounds, while seeing its use increase astronomically within their own ranks. Interns, nurses, orderlies, security police, and yes, doctors, buy and smoke marijuana as avidly and often as high school teens, while publicly proclaiming opposition to the proscribed weed.

The public at large seems not to recognize the exact parallels between prohibition of alcohol and the rise of Al Capone like criminal syndicates, and the huge criminal drug cartels resulting directly from the criminalization of marijuana. Criminal drug cartels support police unions, pious religion, teachers in denial, and hypocritical medical societies, providing them with "moral" cause and real employment, while robbing state and local governments of potential taxes and channels of control which could put the cartels out of business.

Drug cartels feed police corruption by paying cash for protection. A police officer making maximum $75 K per year is hard pressed to turn down a doubling of his income, tax free. It means he can send his kids to college, take family vacations otherwise unthinkable, and enjoy a much better life style, providing he enjoys it discreetly.

All these elements of society, these institutions we trust as leaders of community and nation, persist in refusing to accept the reality that anyone, at any time, with only a polite phone call, can have marijuana and other drugs delivered to his door by a criminal underground much larger than Al Capone ever dreamed.

This same huge enterprise has billions of dollars at stake, and will not tolerate interference in its farming, harvesting, packaging, shipping, and retail delivery.   Marijuana grown in Colombia and several other Latin American countries is funneled through Mexico and trans-shipped to the United States by illegal immigrants crossing the Texas, Arizona, and California borders, blatantly and through elaborate tunnels. The U.S. consuming market is vast, and will be served legally or illegally. The sham of legal "medical" marijuana sidesteps the issue and makes a joke of the governing process, bringing further disrespect to legislatures and law enforcement.

Thus, the only real winners are the criminals, the police and their unions, and church leaders who can take the moral high ground and preach forever on the evils of marijuana . The clear losers are municipal and state governments, who lose taxes and control, yet have to bear the cost of tracking, arresting, imprisoning, and prosecuting offenders, and suffering the even higher cost of police corruption. The biggest single losers are young people whose reputations have been ruined, perhaps forever, by the stigma of felony criminal records which should never have been imposed.

The "will" of the people is not always right, as exemplified by the recent vote in California to deny legalization of marijuana. Logic and reason should, but do not prevail on this issue, often because community leaders and influential media are catering to their darker influences and constituencies who vote in blocks.

Just as legalization of the rights of gays should never have been subjected to a public vote, so the issue of legalization of marijuana or any other addictive substance should not be subjected to the traditional political process. Its criminalization was not subjected to popular vote, and neither should its legalization. There is still right and wrong, and criminalizing marijuana is one of those wrongs. Only the true criminals and pious hypocrites win, as was exactly the case during prohibition of alcohol.

BOOK SEVEN
Saint Louis Years,
International Business

KNOWING LATIN AMERICA

In June of 1980, Bob Burke called to advise me that I would be moving to St. Louis to become Area Director, Latin America and Caribbean, in what was to be my first exposure to Monsanto's International business. Consistent with the Monsanto practice at the time, I was not asked my opinion or preference. The company assumed the wisdom of this move would be apparent, and that I would accept their judgment. Obviously, I could have refused the assignment, but that would have upset the domino chain of personnel moves already planned and blessed by senior management. Refusal would indicate an intractable and uncooperative attitude, and raise red flags about the value of the investment the company had just made by sending me to Harvard.

I was to report to Bob Walter, a veteran of Monsanto's plastics business, and now with overall responsibility of Latin America and

Canada. Walter also happened to be a close personal friend of Bob Burke. My managerial scope would include the sales and marketing teams in each country where Monsanto had corporate entities, and managing agent relationships in non-entity countries. Each country entity was a separate legal Monsanto corporation with its own Board of Directors and officers. I was named as an officer of each entity, often President, and Chairman of its Board. These titles were official but with little practical meaning, since annual meetings were a formality consisting of paper documentation that the Board had met and approved the minutes as drafted by the secretary. The intent was legal and tax separation from the parent company, while meeting local in-country requirements for establishing business entities there.

Monsanto had joint venture operations in Mexico, Brazil, and Argentina, producing chemical, plastics, and agricultural products for local consumption. In these countries, I had duel responsibility with Dick Vance, Country Mgr., Mexico, George Clegg, Country Mgr., Brazil, and Rafael Gaviola, Country Mgr., Argentina. They looked after the joint venture relationships, while my sales and marketing team sold a wide range of products imported from the States. Monsanto's other entities included those in Colombia, Chile, Venezuela, Costa Rica, Gautamala , Puerto Rico, each headed by a country manager with staff. All other countries in the region were covered by independent agents under contract.

St. Louis staff included four regional Latin American specialist managers with logistical assistants who expedited shipments to their geographic areas of expertise, divided between North, South, and Central Latin America. These Managers worked closely with their counterparts in Monsanto's operating divisions on product availability, pricing, quality, and processing issues. Almost all exports were sold direct to customers on confirmed letters of credit, meaning that payment was guaranteed by the issuing banks. Exports included the full line of all Monsanto products, focused on detergents and phosphates, agricultural herbicides, rubber chemicals, polymers for plastics, and specialty chemicals. My job would be my first detailed and valuable exposure to broader Monsanto chemical products and to key product and general managers in each of the company's divisions. I would begin to see the total Monsanto picture for the first time.

I began working in "A" building, the International building on campus, in St. Louis, in July, commuting back to Connecticut on weekends. House hunting on my own had turned up a good prospect in Ladue, a St. Louis suburb two miles from the sprawling Monsanto campus. Ladue had a reputation for excellent public schools and was rated at the top of communities within St. Louis county, to the West of the city itself, which was situated on the western banks of the Mississippi river.

The house was at 7 Conway Lane, around the corner from both Ladue high school, known as Horton Watkins, and its middle school. Scott would enroll as a high school junior, while Jon would be a 7th grader in the middle school. The house was two story brick and frame with five bedrooms plus two family rooms and traditional living and dining rooms and a full basement opening to a separate garage. Over the years, additions to the house had added new levels, now totaling eleven, with lots of step-downs and step-ups. It was much larger than our Connecticut house, so new furniture would be needed.

We bought the house after Joan had only a cursory look. Dick and Julie Rogers, the owners, could not move to their new place until early November, so our family move to St. Louis was postponed until the week before Thanksgiving. Meanwhile, the boys attended schools in Connecticut, and I continued to commute at company expense. The family and Chumley finally occupied the home and started the boys in new schools just in time to see eleven inches of snowfall on Thanksgiving morning. It was our first real understanding of St. Louis weather and its extremes of cold in winter and heat in summer, with humidity high due to the city's location at the confluence of the Missouri, the Mississippi, and the Meramac rivers.

St. Louis had been founded by Frenchman Pierre Laclede in 1763 and named for the French Monarch. It became part of the United States through Thomas Jefferson's Louisiana purchase. The city was considered the gateway to the west, and was the starting point for the famed Lewis and Clark expedition, the first to explore the West all the way to the Pacific ocean.

As the principal river city in the middle of the country, St. Louis became important as a trading post and staging and supply point for settling the West. Trappers and traders sent their furs down the river to markets in the East, and steamships on the river brought back rifles, textiles, fine wines, machinery and food supplies from Europe and New York. Fresh water was plentiful, and bulk shipments of grain attracted German beer makers, who later made St. Louis the beer capital of the country. As the country grew westward, St. Louis also became a major industrial and distribution center, aided by its central location on major navigable rivers.

Arriving in St. Louis in late 1980, we found a friendly but somewhat insular social environment, with old family and social ties dominating. From its French beginnings, St. Louis overall had remained heavily Catholic, with a large Jewish concentration in Ladue where we chose to live. School adjustments were not at all easy for Scott and Jon, although by the time Scott entered his senior year and Jon entered 8th grade, friendships had developed and any trauma from the move was not evident.

As a senior, Scott made the school hockey team, and Jon joined little league football until entering high school, where he played freshman football. He remained the fastest man on his team, but weighed 95 lbs, too small at that point to compete with boys who already were as heavy as 150 lbs or more. Jon's major growth came late relative to many of his classmates. Scott continued to grow in height until age 21.

Next door to us at #5 Conway Lane were George and Mimi

Helmuth. George was the founder of Helmuth, Obata, Kassabaum, now the world's largest architectural firm. Two of their sons had also become known architects, and another son became a St. Louis attorney, while their only daughter became a medical doctor. They were an accomplished family with close ties to St. Louis society. They loved Joan and our boys and made us feel very welcome in the town.

We had decided to keep the Connecticut house at 21 Cove Rd. as rental property, with the intent of returning to it one day. This decision luckily turned out to be the best monetary decision we ever made. The house was rented profitably for the next ten years, while allowing us depreciation and maintenance and repairs as deductions from our taxable income.

Joan soon became interested in making the best use of her interior design certificate from Fairfield University, and found employment as a designer at Hal's Interiors, a high end boutique in Clayton, Mo., the neighboring community. Joan worked at Hal's for our remaining years in St. Louis, and made many friends of her clients and co-workers and suppliers. We also were able to furnish our St. Louis house at special prices through her purchasing connections.

VENEZUELA

My first task in the new job was a get acquainted tour of the Latin American's region. A three-week trip took me first to Venezuela and time with Bill Witter, Country Manager, and his staff. Bill was a 40 year veteran of Monsanto International, fluent in Spanish, and an excellent and resourceful manager. Some years later, Bill and his wife Phillis and their guests were tied up and robbed in their Caracas apartment during a dinner party, when armed thieves knocked on their door and threatened to kill them. They managed to free themselves after several hours, and soon afterward left Caracas and chose retirement in Northern California. Eugenio Maslowski became his successor, having been a successful Sales Manager under Witter.

Venezuela in the early 80's was a vibrant economy with liberal politics and lots of oil. The Venezuela of 2010 under socialist dictator Hugo Chavez is among the poorest countries in the region, with poverty levels exceeding those of the smaller "banana republics" in spite of its billions of oil and refining income. Venezuela has become the shame of Latin America. Its neighbors predict an armed revolution there in the not too distant future. Even Castro's Cuba, a tiny island economy, is admitting its socialist experiment has failed, while Chavez tries through his intransigence, nationalization of industry, and confiscation of private property to bring attention to himself and cover his failures.

BRAZIL

Then it was on to Sao Paulo, Brazil with George Clegg and his team. Brazil had been colonized by the Portuguese at about the same time Spain was claiming the balance of Latin America. Brazil was to become by far the largest and most important country for business in the region, noted for Petrobras, its oil company, and for mining and diversified agriculture. I had been in the country before, but only to Rio, while Sao Paulo was the center of finance, business, and government.

George Clegg and Cumming Paton, a Scotsman, reviewed our chemical sales and joint venture there, and introduced me to Brazil's national dish, called Feijoada, a stew made from pig snouts, ears, tails and feet, mixed with black beans and beef. It is a required staple of the Brazilian diet, so much so that a war was once fought with Bolivia for

Bolivia's hoarding black beans and withholding them from Brazil.

After lunch, Cumming Paton invited me to a round of golf at his club, where we played in a howling wind of about 40 miles per hour. Early in the round, my ball came to rest under the branch of a tree near the fairway. I was preparing for the shot when a limb separated from the tree and fell directly on my head, knocking me flat. I barely retained consciousness, received a little first aid from the caddy which entailed bathing my bloody face with a wet towel, and we proceeded to finish the round. That night the Feijoada kicked in and made for very little sleep.

ARGENTINA

Next was Argentina, with Gaviola and his staff and a tour of beautiful Buenos Aires, which I learned was dominated by Italians, followed by Spanish, and very few aboriginal Indians. When the Spanish colonized South America around the time the British colonized America, they were even less tolerant of the native Indian population than North Americans had been, and simply enslaved or killed them. Many survivors of the massacres died later of Spanish introduced diseases.

Today, Buenos Aires very much resembles Paris or Rome in its architecture, and the streets and shops feel European rather than Latin American. Shops in the elite tourist districts feature fine leather goods, a product of Argentina's cattle growing industry.

Like their old country ancestors, Argentines eat large and late, with restaurants opening for dinner around 10 PM. Beef with red wine is the popular dinner fare. Unlike the old country, regular office hours do not allow for siesta in the afternoons, as is common with farm families. At a fancy restaurant one evening, I entered a restroom market "M", only to discover that the designation means Mujeres, Spanish for women. A valuable lesson learned with only small embarrassment.

URUGUAY

After Argentina, a quick stop In Uruguay to meet agent Basilio Bernat, the German fat man and our agent for many years. Basilio lives in Montevideo and has a second home in Punta Del Este on the Coast, which we visited. Here, he insisted on taking me on his boat to fish the saltwater bay, with excellent results. Then it was back to Montevideo and a huge meal of filet mignon at his club, all the while talking about customers and his import business and where it was headed.

I learned from Basilio about the sinking of the German super battleship, the Graf Spay, in Punta Del Este harbor, and that early glaciers stripped Uruguay of all trees. Today's trees, mostly beautiful Eucalyptus, were imported and planted in rows by hand.

Basilio is a collector of fine art by Uruguayan artists, and owns the largest private collection of Uruguayan art in the country. He insisted on taking me to several galleries and also insisted that I buy two original oils from artists he respected as becoming more valuable. I bought them and they hang in Scott's house in Milwaukee today.

CHILE

Next was Santiago, Chile, and country Manager John Breit and his staff. John was a German immigrant, married to a Chilean native. I would learn that Chile is heavily German, with somewhat more evidence of native Indian blood compared to Argentina. With 16 million people, Chile adopted Milt Friedman free market capitalism early, with the blessing of its dictator Augusto Pinochet. Chile's social security system rests on completely privatized accounts controlled by the owner, and is the envy of the world. Chile has no social security issue.

Chile's principal exports are fish meal, fine wines, grapes and copper. One of Monsanto's important exports to Chile is the combination of bone ash(real powdered cattle bones) and mould coat, used to line brick-like molds when preparing the molten metal for shipment. Chile is the ski resort capital of South America, with the tallest mountains in the Andes chain to the Southeast of Santiago.

I reviewed the business and its prospects with John and his staff, and learned that he was among the most knowledgeable and thorough of our South American mangers.

PERU

Peru and Ecuador were represented by the Kuster family from Switzerland, who long ago came to Peru to make their fortune. Both Kuster sons had attended Harvard University and were now back home to run the family empire, which was extensive. The family had large manufacturing interests processing basic crops into foods and food ingredients and fertilizers, and imported, stocked, and resold many process chemicals from the U.S. and Europe. The family was fluent in both English and Spanish, which made business talk easy. They owned a large plantation North of Lima, to which I was invited for a weekend. The main compound had multiple houses, perhaps 20 full time staff, and many more workers taking care of planting and harvesting. The visit was a reach back into time, reminiscent of old Southern pre-civil war plantations of the South.

I stayed at a comfortable $80. Dollars per night Hyatt hotel in Lima, using the famous green courtesy card given me at Harvard by Pat Foley, President of Hyatt. Outside the Miraflores section where the Hyatt was located, was abject poverty, endemic in Lima, particularly the historic old central square, where young and old beggars lined the streets, and where I was advised not to go alone. 30 years later, in 2010, in California, I met a businessman from Peru who manufacturers flip-flop shoes there and exports them. He told me that Lima is extremely prosperous and expensive today, with hotels in Miraflores priced at $400. Per night.

COLOMBIA

In Colombia, Victor Zaretsky, Country Manager, took me on a tour of the city and the world famous gold museum, before lunching with his staff on perhaps the best seafood I had ever eaten. Chile, Peru, and Colombia are noted for their seafood varieties and freshness, and restaurants in both countries are skilled in preparing it.

We spent an afternoon and evening going over budgets, customers, forecasts, reporting issues, and reviewing goals. A couple of years later, Enrique Bolanos Jr. would succeed Zaretsky as Country manager. Enrique's father, Enrique Bolanos Sr., was elected President of Nicaragua, while his son managed Colombia for us.

As in Peru, I was advised not to leave the hotel alone, but to wait to be picked up by staff. Kidnapping and holding for ransom of visiting American executives had become a problem in parts of Latin America. Short of that, simple mugging and robbery of obvious gringos was also a problem. I took walks and jogs in Santiago, Mexico City, and Buenos Aires, but was cautious in other cities, forewarned by hotel staff in many cases.

In making this tour, I traveled on Pan American Airlines, still flying in Latin America, Brazil Air, the Argentine national airline, Lan Chile, and Avianca, the Colombian Airline. Whenever possible thereafter, I tried to stay on American carriers, but this was rarely possible.

MEXICO

Back in St. Louis, I scheduled a trip to Mexico City to meet with Dick Vance and his staff, and spent three days there in getting acquainted with staff and customers and reviewing budgets and goals. One challenge I recognized early was standardizing on goal and budget setting and review procedures. Our sales manager in Mexico was competent but accustomed to more casual and informal supervision. The difference was cultural for the most part. Managers preferred to be rated on overall accomplishments at year-end rather than interim progress points. They also preferred, naturally, that some goals be fluid and non-specific as to time and degree. We negotiated successfully on these points, but it took me a while to accept that not every culture embraces the fairly rigid goal tracking structure common in the U.S.

PUERTO RICO

Finally, a trip to San Juan, Puerto Rico and meeting with Haratio Navarette, an exiled Cuban who had been assigned to manage the Caribbean. Old San Juan is very historic and among the earliest stops of Christopher Colombus. The Island was ceded to the U.S. at the end of the Spanish American War, but remained independent in it governance. Puerto Rico was a big compounding and packaging center for American pharmaceutical companies, for tax and labor reasons, and Haratio's main effort was centered on these companies. We shipped large quantities of acetaminophen to McNeil who converted it to pill form, packaged and marketed it under the Tylonol Brand.

UNUNITED IN LATIN AMERICA

Latin America's total population of almost 400 million is concentrated in Mexico, with 105 million, Brazil, with 175 million, and Argentina, with 42 million. Basically, all but 70-80 million in all of Latin America live in these three countries. The remaining significant markets are Colombia with 49 million, Venezuela with 25, Chile with 16, and Peru with 27 million. El Salvador and Nicaragua were good markets for ag division products such as Roundup, especially useful in coffee growing. Costa Rica, perhaps the most democratic of Latin American states and one filled with natural beauty and blessed with good year-round climate, was also a good ag market. In Guatamala, it was possible to fish the Atlantic in the morning, and the Pacific in the afternoon, towing a boat across the narrow peninsula.

Simon Bolivar was the George Washington of Northern Latin America, leading and winning the revolution against Spain, establishing formal Independence between 1813 and 1824 for various countries. Bolivar is the principal hero of Northern Latin America, crediting with liberating Venezuela, Colombia, Ecuador, Bolivia, Peru, and Panama. He attempted to pull them together into one united block of states, but was unsuccessful because of many different ethnicities and interests.

The multiplicity of small states supporting their own national priorities with different political, cultural, and economic systems, some with dictators, have fragmented Latin America deeply and severely weakened its negotiating power when dealing with the U.S. and other large blocks. Resources and governing styles vary widely. Brazil, Venezuela, and Mexico are oil rich, while Argentina excels in farming and cattle and industry. Chile and Peru and Ecuador and Colombia are rich in mining metals and seafood, especially during El Nino when currents deliver huge fish harvests for export.

Brazil is a mixed bag of African, Asian, and European ethnicities. Northern Latin America is heavily Indian/Spanish mixed. Argentina and Chile identify themselves as primarily European. Blending them into a united block is unlikely. They have the Spanish language and the Catholic church in common, except in Brazil, where Portuguese is the national language. But, unlike Europe, where disparate states are cooperating on a common currency and building a unified trading union, Latin America is nowhere near that level of sophistication.

LEARNING SPANISH

Another quickly apparent need was to build some capability in the Spanish language. I began this by having Blanche Salinas, a matronly Ecuadorian woman and Spanish teacher, come to my office twice each week for an hour of one-on-one Spanish for three years. She did her best and I learned a great deal about the structure of the language, but also learned that becoming even partially fluent meant living in the culture and speaking the language full time, day and night. Full immersion is the answer to speaking and understanding any non-native language, no matter how much classroom instruction is available.

BACK IN ST. LOUIS

In "A" building, the International building, I spent a good deal of time working with executives and product managers from our member "supplier" divisions, projecting demand for each of their products, reviewing competitive conditions in Latin America, and setting revenue and profit targets. Budgeting for the year ahead involved detailed "road show" presentations from my group, acquainting division management with the characteristics of the Latin American and Caribbean markets, and carving out supply commitments from them to the various countries. This experience afforded a unique overview of total Monsanto which few managers had the chance to get.

Support staff in St. Louis included the aforementioned regional export specialists who came up from Latin America to fill these roles, and comptrollership, human resources, and legal, all of whom played important parts in putting plans together and trouble-shooting as we implemented.

Settling into the job as the family settled into St. Louis, a pattern of travel developed of three weeks in St. Louis or domestic travel, and one week per month in the Latin American region. Supplementing this were visits from the various country and sales managers to St. Louis to stage reviews, especially during budgeting season. On one occasion, Joan and I hosted the Country managers and wives, together with St. Louis support staff, in our home for a group dinner. On many other evenings, we entertained individuals who were visiting St. Louis on business.

The Latin American experience impressed on me the need for adaptability and flexibility in conducting business or social exchanges with other cultures, for whom English was a second language. It also opened an entire new sphere of understanding of a grouping of nations about which my assumptions and biases had been wrong in the sense that I had cast them as an extension of Mexico. I had travelled briefly in Europe, mainly

England and Germany, including Berlin, and had spent military time in Korea and Japan, but sustained managerial involvement in Latin America was completely different.

While the language barrier was real, the human interactions with peers and subordinates from radically different backgrounds and expectations meant a different starting point for building trust as a basis for effectively working together toward common goals. I had to become a better listener…..listening within the context of individuals within the region. Hopefully, I became a more conscious and caring listener in both business settings, and in my own family setting.

In this regard, I never became fluent in Spanish, but never stopped trying, a fact appreciated by those in the region I was working with. In 2011, I remain on the lookout for new Spanish verbs and their conjugations, and new phrases I can practice.

NEW COMPANY MOVES

In mid- 1983, Monsanto began a reorganization of its various divisions under the leadership of Dick Mahoney, CEO, and Jack Fitzgerald, President. The moves reflected the economic environment of the time and the expected cycle of adjusting the corporation to reflect new product lines and achieve efficiencies. The trend direction was toward consolidation of various chemical product lines into fewer divisions, and toward placing international responsibility within those divisions. The effect was to be one of merging the occupants of "A" building into and under the control of these various divisions and operating companies. This took time and planning to accomplish.

Bob Walter moved into retirement, and Thomas Gossage was named Managing Director of Monsanto International. Tom had been head of

Inorganics, now merged into other divisions. He was a chemical engineer from Georgia Tech, and had been a star football player there, and a magna cum laude graduate. Gossage moved to "A" and I began reporting to him directly. He had little exposure to Latin America, and was interested but increasingly occupied with Europe and Asia.

Word was that Gossage was unhappy at being passed over for the President slot now filled by Fitzgerald, an old associate of Mahoney. After each trip to the region, I wrote extensive trip reports and scheduled dates with Gossage to review what was going on, positive or negative. Vance, Clegg, and Gaviola did the same, but all of us together did not succeed in placing Latin America high on his priority list.

Within a few months, Gossage resigned to become CEO of Hercules Chemicals in Wilmington, Delaware, a big step up for him. Jack Fitzgerald, corporation President, assumed temporary control of International, and I began reporting to him. This lasted several months, to mixed reviews. Jack was obviously preoccupied with broader Monsanto, had spent several years in Europe, and knew it best. He seemed to have little time for much depth involvement in Latin America.

At my year-end review with Fitzgerald, our face-to-face included rating performance on each goal set a year earlier. As it happened, my group had met and exceeded profit goals by a significant margin, however, two days before the review, Brazil and Mexico had devalued their currencies substantially, forcing other trading partners in the region to adjust their currencies correspondingly.   This meant that profit goals exceeded the day before, had, by poor translation of devalued currencies back to dollars, come in well below our stated Dollar profit goals.

I explained to Fitzgerald that these devaluations by government fiat were totally unexpected and completely out of our control, and should not therefore be used as a basis for judging performance on goals or eligibility for bonuses. I got to know the real Fitz in a hurry when he leaned back in his chair, put his feet on his fancy "D" building desk, and said, "Why are you telling me your troubles?" He took a hard line and refused to budge, which I felt was unfair and completely outside the spirit of a reasonable performance review. The translated lower dollar number would be used to measure performance against goals. I must have reflected disappointment in some of my statements at the time, because the meeting was soon over, and I do not remember talking to him again.

Within a year, Fitzgerald was dead of a sudden massive heart attack. His death, in turn, brought in Bob Shapiro, Chief Legal officer of G.D. Searle pharmaceuticals, a Chicago based company wholly owned by Monsanto. Searle had been headed by Donald Rumsfeld at the time Monsanto bought the company. Searle made and marketed the Neutrasweet brand of artificial sweetener. Emphasis on branding was the firm direction of Hanley and Mahoney, and Shapiro had played an important part in the success of Searle and Neutrasweet. He was soon in the President's chair, and, together with Mahoney, now CEO, began a complete remake of Monsanto into the Agricultural Chemicals company it is today.

SOLUTIA IS BORN

Shapiro and Mahoney, with consultants, began organizing to shed any basic and commodity products from the company portfolio. This process would take time and the company was not actually split apart until the early 1990's, but the general direction had become very clear to all. Ultimately, only ag chemicals would survive with the Monsanto name, while traditional chemicals were spun off into a company to be known as Solutia. The substantial pension liabilities and high capital costs and associated debt of basic chemicals also were loaded onto the newly created company, so Solutia began life with a questionable balance sheet, with which it struggled for many years before ultimate Chapter 11 bankruptcy and reorganization.

This radical division and major new course for Monsanto became a final reality seven years after my next assignment.

Scott had graduated high school and was now enrolled in the University of Colorado, his choice after exploring several Universities. Jon was now in Horton Watkins high and attempting sports, but his relatively small size was an obstacle. Joan was still at Hal's Interiors and would be for several years to come. My family had been supportive and patient with the moves and disrupted friendships and travel time away, but, like all families, our lives were not perfect; the boys friends were not always the right ones, and hard earned experience brought good lessons.

The Latin American experience was personally broadening and enriching. I was busy and totally occupied in trying to make the job a success. Looking back, the boys and Joan seemed to see advantage in being forced to adapt to new circumstances and make new friends in new schools. But I have no illusions in thinking that three upheavals in 8 years did not take their toll on everyone's relationships, including those within our family.

WORLDWIDE FIBERS AND INTERMEDIATES:

It was no surprise when, in early 1984, Bob Burke asked me to come over to G Building and pay him a visit. There, he advised me that I was to become Director, International, Monsanto Fibers and Intermediates. This was, I recognized, a lateral move which probably could not be described as developmental, even though my responsibilities would now be worldwide for the first time. I accepted the job, said goodbye to my pals in A building and the region, and moved to the big gold, glass encased building on the west side of the campus.

In a real sense, the move was a homecoming. Products and people were familiar. Burke had been something of a mentor, but not always a dependable sponsor. He had his own issues, not the least was the albatross of filament polyester, which soon brought his forced retirement. Mahoney brought in Earl Brasfield, a chemical engineer graduate of the University of Texas, as Managing Director for Fibers and Intermediates Division.

Earl had been a process engineer and plant manager at the Chocolate Bayou and Texas City plants before moving into management, was very well liked and respected. Earl inherited Burke's polyester issue, and set about trying to get us out of the business. Unlike Burke, Earl also had the respect of Mahoney and D building, and a reputation as a straight-shooter, in contrast to Burke's smooth-talker image.

In hindsight, I recognized subtle hints that my decision not to use Dottie Burke, Bob's wife, as our real estate agent when we bought the St. Louis home, was not politically astute. I had felt it best to avoid any appearance of conflict which might have arisen had we used the boss's wife as our agent. But clear-cut Southwestern ethics clearly clashed with Northeastern pragmatism, and a mutual friend later shared with me that Dottie and Bob felt slighted. Career issues aside, the decision clearly did not endear us to the Burkes.

Under Earl Brasfield, a fellow Texan with whom I had a good rapport, an objective assessment of the future of Fibers/Intermediates indicated a daunting new challenge. This operating company had recently been the brand leader of the corporation, with Acrilan, Acrilan Plus, Wear Dated heavily advertised programs at the vanguard of our marketing effort.

But in mid-1984, it was evident that high capital and operating costs to produce these near-commodity products could not justify new expansion capital, and that brand maintenance costs were increasing as our technology franchise weakened relative to competitors. Our proprietary advantage was slipping away. The traditional apparel textile business had begun a massive move offshore, and consultants charted this trend as one continuing to erode our domestic brands.

Technical weaknesses in nylon filament and polyester filament forced branded emphasis toward residential carpet replacement with nylon staple fibers, while polyester filament was basically in a holding pattern awaiting disposal or dismantling.

The division had positive margins over variable costs and therefore very positive cash flow, but negative reported net income after depreciation and amortization of large fixed plant and equipment costs. These facts did not go down well on Wall Street, and the business became something of a pariah in the eyes of "D" building, and one to be milked for cash flow awaiting longer-term decisions.

With the new emphasis on pharma-like branding of life sciences and biotech patented and products, the fortunes of the Fibers/Intermediates company were clearly in decline. Cash thrown off from traditional chemicals and fibers was being used by Mahoney and Shapiro to fund research and products in the new arena.

In this environment, I met my new international team, most of whom were based in Atlanta. There was Jim Everett, the old Chemstrand pro who had been exporting fibers and polymers for more than 25 years and knew all the nuances of international business. John Tung, a Chinese immigrant who grew up in Beijing, and became an American citizen when he married Joan, his caucasian wife.

John was our resident China expert who spoke both Mandarin and Cantonese, and oversaw exports to Asia, working primarily through longtime agent Cheong-On company, based in Hong Kong. Through family on the mainland, John had excellent connections with Chinatex and Sinochem, two large government purchasing agencies.

Claudio Sopena, a young Spaniard now handling exports to Europe and the middle East, was working both with Monsanto Europe and agents in Africa and Egypt. Barbara Walsh, a logistics facilitator, from Greenville, S.C., now living in Atlanta, and Judy Highfill, her counterpart in St. Louis, rounded out the team.

Our direct group was supplemented by technical support for polymers out of Pensacola, and fibers tech service from Atlanta and Charlotte, as well as the Greenville, S.C. data center. And in-country entities in Japan, Korea, Taiwan, Hong Kong, Singapore, Jakarta, London, and Brussels, and a variety of independent agents also were key in developing and servicing orders. Incredibly, Monsanto had no entity in mainland China at the time. Hong Kong claimed responsibility for larger China.

Nylon polymers for plastics and fibers, Acrilonitrile for making fibers and ABS plastics, Hydrogen Cyanide for producing carbon fibers and pharmaceuticals, Acrylic fiber for the growing textile industry in China, and Adipic acid, were the most demanded items for export.

Japan bought mostly polymers and adipic acid, and some Acrilonitrile (AN), and some HCN. Korean customers bought very large tonnage of AN and acrylic fiber, and polymers for extrusion into nylon for tire cord and industrial materials.

Chinatex, and Sinochem imported acrylic fibers in large quantities, and some AN. Australia and South Africa and Egypt bought and converted nylon polymers into myriad products to serve their markets. Taiwan imported and converted AN to fiber, and nylon polymers into industrial and fine denier hosiery yarns. An Italian nylon producer used our polymers as raw material. Altogether, about 30% of dollar sales of the division went to International markets.

Monsanto also produced AN in Europe at Seal Sands, Northern England, and acrylic fibers at plants in Coleraine, Northern Ireland, and Lingen, Germany. Both these plants were sold to MontEdison, and the AN complex was sold to BASF, the big German chemical company. Nylon intermediates were retained for the moment and production shipped to the States to supplement domestic output of intermediates. Prior to the sale of the European facilities, AN sales from U.S. plants and Seal Sands were closely coordinated in terms of volume and pricing.

AROUND THE WORLD IN A MONTH: JAPAN

In the Spring of 84, Jim Everett, John Tung and I embarked on a trip around the globe to meet customers, agents, and entity staffs. It was to be a one month twenty city educational and get-acquainted tour primarily for my benefit.

For the first time since 1957, I would be back in Asia, but this time touching almost all of it except Vietnam. Laos, Cambodia, and the Philippines. Vaccinations were required, as well as visas to all destinations. Trip planning and preparation took considerable time. Pre cell phones and laptops, we expected to be out of touch many days. International communications were still primitive, and placing international phone calls through local hotel operators presented challenges at times.

First class seating on inter-country flights longer than four hours was allowed, and we took advantage of it. The hop to Japan from San Francisco took nine hours versus the twenty-seven hours required 28 years earlier. Tokyo was our first stop. We were met at Narita airport by Sam Fujiwara, second in command at Monsanto Japan behind George Clegg, who by now had made the move from Brazil. The limo to the Okura hotel took an hour and a half, during which I tried to take in the transformation of Tokyo from the city I remembered earlier. Most impressive was the labyrinth of stacked highways and bridges, and the array of modern Japanese cars, both absent in 1956 when Japan was still in recovery mode from the war.

Also immediately noticeable was the absence of traditional Japanese Kimono and wooden geta on neighborhood streets. Western dress was now standard during the day and evening, a contrast to the kimonos with colorful Obe sash, both common evening dress for men and women in the 50's. Taller office buildings and wider avenues and divided highways were a rarity in post-war Japan, but now a reflection of a rebuilt and wealthy nation.

Earthquake vulnerable Tokyo had obviously adopted construction methods allowing taller and safer structures. Most of these newer technology structures survived the recent quake and tsunami in Japan's Northeast, but older buildings were swept away by both the quake and the flood which followed.

A drive by today's Imperial Hotel revealed a modern high rise which could just as well be located in New York City, bearing no resemblance to Frank Lloyd Wright's rambling wooden one-story structure which stood on the same ground in 1956.

Okura was and is one of Tokyo's finest hotels, and, starting an arrival in country tradition, a very hot soaking tub was followed by dinner at the Okura sushi bar, and then early to bed to try to shake off the time change. Next morning early, I jogged the six miles around the Imperial Palace in a light rain, and prepared to go to the office for appointments.

After a brief greeting from George and a few introductions, we met with Fujita-san and Sakata-san, two sales managers who, along with Fujiwara-san, would guide the meetings with Toray, C Itoh, Mitsubishi Chemicals, Mitsui, Marubeni, and Mitsubishi Trading companies, and translate for us.

This series of meetings was about nylon polymers and adipic acid, the latter used by Toray in combination with diamine (HMD), to make nylon 66 for industrial applications including parachutes, climbing rope, brush bristles, tow ropes, tennis rackets, guitar strings, and tire cord. AN and HCN was used by Mitsubishi Rayon and other members of the Fiber makers cartel to make both acrylic fibers and carbon fibers.

In Japan's economy, general trading companies, known as Sogo-Sosha, play a unique role in purchasing and importing raw materials which local producers are not set up to do. Trading companies, as omnipresent middle men, then become conduits for exports for those same closely related customers. Ownership stakes in each other are also common. It is the trading companies who have offices around the world, staffed with experienced personnel, who efficiently facilitate imports to and exports from Japan. The United States has nothing comparable, for antitrust reasons, and is therefore not as efficient as Japan, which depends on international trade for survival. The Sogo Sosha are instruments of national trade, set up and encouraged by Japan's legislature, or Diet, as it is known. Japan's raw materials prices and finished goods prices are an open book as a consequence.

The next three days brought more informational meetings and discussions about the U.S. and Japanese economic outlooks, questions about our European operations and the intentions of the Italians and the Germans who had just purchased most of our fibers and intermediates capacities in England and on the continent. Of particular interest in Tokyo, and later in Osaka, was our take on raw materials propylene and ammonia which go into making AN, world demand for AN, capacity utilization in Europe and the U.S.

Mitsubishi Rayon is the leader of the acrylic fibers association in Japan as well as the largest producer. MRC acts as the negotiator and group buyer for the association when buying AN, and Mitsubishi trading company acts to make the price and volume agreement become a reality. Koga-san and Dan Yabuta-san were key men in the trading company, and always present monitoring the negotiations, often translating and asking questions.

EATING AND GIFT RITUALS

Lunches and dinners in Tokyo were elaborately hosted at the finest eateries, and gifts were exchanged at dinners. Dinners are often followed by routine visits to Karaoki bars, where everyone takes a turn singing after a few drinks. These outings, with their bar hostesses, are expected and respectable after-dinner relaxation and get-acquainted sessions. It is said that if a Japanese businessman comes back home too early, the wife starts to worry about his job security.

The homes or apartments of even well to do Japanese are very small compared to the average American home. Entertainment in homes there is very rare as a result. Visitors are almost never invited to a Japanese home. The spaces are just too cramped. One senior managing director of Toray told us of moving into his spacious new home of about 100 square meters, or about 1100 square feet.

The gift ritual is embedded in Japanese culture, and must be observed by all without fail. The cultural system of "On" is strictly observed in honoring obligations and gift etiquette. A gift received carries with it an understanding that it will be returned with one of like value, thus, gifts have to go both ways. Oddly, it is perfectly acceptable to pass a gift along to satisfy an obligation to a third party. The theory is that a lot of gifts of liquor or wine are usually not opened, but simply re-gifted.

The bullet train from Tokyo to Osaka is a technological marvel while delivering all the desired comforts and amenities. The three-hour exhilarating ride is much faster than planes between the two cities, and less expensive, without the security and weather hassles. Tokyo central and Osaka central are easily accessed terminals. Service on the train is consistent and polite and clean, with good food and a full menu of drinks.

High speed trains in the U.S. may be comparable in years to come, but in 2010 are still far behind in technology and comfort, and may never be economical on more than two or three routes. Only Japan and France have successfully operating bullet trains. Japan's mountainous topography forces great population density onto the small proportion of habitable land. Density favors train or bus travel over individual cars, and supports the popular rail system connecting major cities.

The U.S. large land mass has very little comparable density and has built infrastructure encouraging individual cars. This is unlikely to change. Most Japanese use their cars only on weekends, if they own a car at all. The Obama administration policy has allocated 65 billion dollars to states to develop high speed rail systems, but Wisconsin, Ohio, and Florida, have already rejected this federal government boondoggle on the grounds that the states would then be forever responsible for maintenance and operations costs of a flawed concept which could never be economical.

Only bankrupt California seems eager to go forward, with critics warning on huge state debt to subsidize and maintain the system. High speed rail in low density America is a blatant liberal attempt to impose central government control over still another large swath of the economy.

A side trip to Kyoto for one overnight brings a stay in the city's most famous ryokan, Hiiragiya, sleeping on futon after soaking in a steaming cypress Onsen wooden tub, followed by traditional 12 course Kaiseki feast served in room. Kyoto was spared Allied bombing during the war, and remains the artistic and historic capital of Old Japan.

The highlight of Kyoto included a day touring castles from the Edo Shogunate and Sumurai era. Sumurai, in history, were private warriors of powerful landowners, and, in the Tokugawa period, were the only people in Japan allowed to carry swords.

They lived by the strict "Bushido" code of self-discipline and fanatic loyalty to their owners, and, if defeated, committed Sepuuku or suicide, by disemboweling themselves with knives. This method of ritual suicide, known as hara kiri, still prevails in Japan today, with a suicide rate 2 and ½ times that of the U.S. and Europe. At the end of world war two, more than 500 Japanese military and government officials committed Sepuuku rather than face the shame and disgrace of surrender.

Among these was an Admiral Haruke, who's son was now a key executive in Itochu in Tokyo. I worked closely with Haruke-san in finalizing chemical contracts with Tory, represented by Itochu. On one occasion, Haruke-san and I met in Maui for negotiations and golf with Toray executives. This was a travel compromise we both enjoyed.

BACK TO KOREA:

The new Seoul, South Korea, impressed even more than Japan. Without fear of earthquakes, skyscrapers now dominated the skyline. Virtually every structure was new, interconnected with subterranean walkways which doubled as upscale shopping meccas and bomb-shelters, and by the new network of subways connecting the city and suburbs. Seoul boutique storefronts boasted designer names found in Hong Kong and Paris and New York.

Its Itaewon discount district appeals to foreigners and tourists looking for bargains, especially leather goods and textiles. For those in a hurry, custom suits can be measured, made, and fitted within 24 hours. And downtown retains a mixture of historic buildings and monuments such as wooden pagoda city gates dating to the settlement of the country. The downtown national historical museum is rated among the finest in the world.

As noted earlier, the Korean people are determined, smart, loyal, and gritty survivors. Starting from almost total destruction a little over 50 years ago, they have built an economy ranking in the world's top ten, with automotive and electronic technologies often excelling those of Japan, or the U.S. and Europe. After the war and liberation from the Japanese, Korea's economy experienced what is known as "compressed" industrialization, skipping over much of the low technology labor intensive phase to go directly into microchips and computers.

Korea's education system, from elementary through University, is recognized for the quality of its graduates in science, math, and in music, performing arts, and fine arts. Typical of their no-nonsense approach to education, most schools have no organized sports teams such as football or basketball, and have no stadiums or gymnasiums for this purpose. Students or communities may gather for team sports, but not under the auspices of school systems, where the intense focus in on serious academics. By all measures, Korea is an accomplished country with very high living standards, in spite of being under constant threat of attack from the North.

Its culinary standards are also quite high. Every type of international and ethnic restaurant can be found in Seoul, but Korea itself is the land of kimchi, the fermented cabbage, garlic, fish, and peppers national dish which, along with potatoes, sustained Koreans and prevented widespread starvation during the Japanese 40 year occupation.

Bulgogi beef with whole garlic cloves, barbecued in thin strips at restaurant tables, is another mainstay. Visitors who want to know Korea must dive into these garlic laced foods and become part of the "aroma" of Korea. These foods, supplemented by rice, are tied to the proud culture and survival of Koreans, both during the Japanese occupation and the Korean war. They are also addictive!! More than 50 years after my introduction to them, I have a craving for kimchi and bulgogi which must be satisfied.

Shingo pears are a treasured fruit of Korea. These are yellowish orange in color and larger than a softball, mild and fibrous and sweet and firm. Joan and I search for and buy them whenever and wherever we find them. On trips to Seoul, one of my first stops was the public market to buy half a dozen Shingo pears to enjoy in my hotel room over several days.

South Korean loyalty to the U.S., who they correctly regard as their liberator, is apparent everywhere. In virtually every business meeting in Seoul or other cities, Korean businessmen acknowledged their debt to America and their great appreciation. At the same time, their animosity and anger toward the Japanese colonialists and occupiers has not receded, except among those too young to remember. The image of Japan held by the average Korean is one of Island nation warlike and uncivilized barbarians, cruel and opportunistic plunderers with a violent history of aggression. Ironic that Korea would be among the first nations to pledge support to Japan after the recent huge quake and tsunami.

This same attitude of distrust and derision toward Japan is held by most Asian nations, tied to Japan for trade and technology because of proximity, but resenting any permanent Japanese influence on their cultures. China, Indonesia, the Philippines, and Singapore are particularly weary of the Japanese, and this distrust, as part of the history of these countries, may not go away for generations.

At the same time, the residue of Japanese influence all over Asia is firmly imbedded. Japanese tourists flood Korea and China, served by fine Japanese restaurants and hotels catering to them. Japanese trading companies are major tenants of Korean and Indonesian office buildings, and these trading companies handle a great deal of these country's imports and exports, particularly to and from Japan. Japanese technologies are licensed to Korean and Chinese and Indonesian companies, and vice-versa. Its art, literature, music and product billboards are displayed throughout Asia.

Japan lost the war, but its infrastructure reconstruction and economy recovered quicker than those in the rest of Asia, due both to its role as a supply base for the Korean war, and to the drag of communism on the Chinese mainland economy. Grudgingly, Asian nations have accepted Japan as their largest trading partner, but this is changing as China becomes the major exporter of consumer goods to the world, and Korea strengthens its position in high technology exports.

South Korea fears reunification with the North mainly because of the economic stress foreseen in dealing with a flood of refugees from the North. Unlike West and East Germany, South Korea already has extreme density of population who are well educated and enjoying a degree of labor supply/demand balance. The almost certain influx of job and welfare seekers from the very poor North would overwhelm the social structure and institutions of the South, resulting in increases in crime and violence, and national debt.

Educating the hard-core socialist indoctrinated Northern population in the ways of free market capitalism would take longer than a generation, and the South fears mass uncertainty and disruption. Reunification is not even much talked about within the South's business and political leadership, even though China makes some noises along these lines due to North Korea's dependency on China to keep its people from starvation.

Almost nothing was as I remembered it except the familiar Vagabond hill, now home to the new AFKN AM-TV building housing modern TV and radio studios. Young army and air force staff toured me through the facility, and were especially interested that I had worked at the station 27 years earlier when AFKN radio Vagabond broadcast from a shortened Quonset hut and mobile trailer.

We stayed at the huge Lotte hotel in the center of the city, located next to the now rebuilt landmark Chosen hotel. Lotte chewing gum built the Lotte center city complex, connected to the hotel, and housing a world famous food emporium rivaling Harrods in London or anything in Paris. Exotic and rare foods from the world over, as well as cars, furniture, and safaris can be bought at the Lotte market, which itself is only two or three blocks away from the crowded center city open-air market where shouting vendors in stalls sell clothing, carpets, furniture, electronics, hogs-heads, every fruit and vegetable imaginable, art, books, sculptures, kitchen appliances, eels, live fish, whale meat, pets, and knives, rice and noodles, just to give you an idea of the scope.

This market and others like it throughout the country are where Korean housewives do most of their shopping for the family. In Pusan, for example, beach vendors sell a similar variety of goods, including large cuts of whale blubber, and dried whale jerky. Fancy foreign brands in boutique storefronts are intended for tourists from Japan and the U.S. and Europe, not for local Koreans.

Korea in 1984 was well on the road to democratic government and capitalism, encouraged and subsidized by the U.S., but had proceeded haltingly through a series of relatively benign dictatorships under army strong men. General Park Chung Hee had seized power from Syngman Rhee, and had successfully fought the threat of communist takeover until his own assassination by a close aide in 1979. Chun Doo Hwan was President in 1984 and the civilians were once again in charge. Another General, Roh Tae Woo, militarized the government after Chun, but was later elected on a civilian democratic ticket and proved to be very popular. Finally, Kim Young Sam was elected President of a stabilized democracy, and Korea has had solid democracy since.

In this setting, trying to retrace familiar steps from the 1950's, I first met our agent representing our fiber products to Korea, Taiwan, and mainland China. John Tung and Jim Everett knew T.Y. Hung and his sons, Michael and Tony well and had worked with them for years, but this was my first encounter.

Named Cheong-On company, their offices were in Seoul, Taipei, and Hong Kong. T.Y., a dapper old gentleman who spoke no English but understood quite a bit, officed in Hong Kong with his son Tony. Michael headed the Taiwan office, while Kyun Choi managed the Seoul office. Tony had been educated in California and had become an American citizen, had married a Chinese/American woman. His wife and teenage son lived in Los Angeles, where Tony visited from time to time. Conveniently, he had taken an apparent second wife in Hong Kong, with whom he later had a child.

Michael's wife and children were Canadian citizens and lived in Vancouver, while Michael also appeared to have a second family in Taipei, to the consternation of no one. T.Y. also had a sister in Taipei, Jenny Hung, the widow of an official of the Chiang Kai Shek Nationalist regime which established a shadow government in Taipei after being pushed off the mainland by Mao's Communist revolution.

Jenny Hung and her present husband, Dr. Y.S. Zhiang, former presidential advisor and secretary of state in the Taipei government, had many important connections and considerable influence in both Taipei and Hong Kong. Dr. Zhiang was acclaimed as the father of Taiwanese agriculture. He held a PHD in Agronomy from the University of Minnesota, and, when the nationalist Chiang government came to Taiwan, introduced entirely new crops and farming techniques at differing altitudes, revolutionizing ag production of new and hardier plant species with much higher yields.

The Taiwanese were always short of nutritious food varieties under the Japanese occupation policy of confiscating the best foods to feed the Japanese population and the Japanese war machine.

In Korea, Taipei, and Hong Kong, connections were still critical. Powerful industrialists who had access to government favors and credit were a small connected circle, and T.Y., aunt Jenny, Tony, Michael, and Kyun Choi were within the circle of influence.

These connections went back to T.Y.'s home base, Ningbo, a suburb of Shanghai, noted for its concentration of business elite, including Y.C. Wong, who built the worldwide Formosa Plastics nylon and polyester empire from the Taipei base. In Taipei, T.Y. and his sons had well-established entrée into the growing industrial base which had been built during Japanese occupation and then left for the locals when war ended. In Ningbo, T.Y.'s father had been a banker of some wealth, which assured T.Y. of a degree of influence when he fled the mainland with the Chiang government to Taiwan.

Lion Woo, and old friend of T.Y., had come from Ningbo to Taipei as a laborer/refugee, and now was the patriarch of an empire which included the country's largest bank, the largest insurance company, the Taipei electric utility, and later, the tallest skyscraper in Taipei. The family holdings, now managed by sons Tony and Thomas, both American educated at the University of Southern California, included large interests in textile spinning and knitting. As such, they were large buyers of our acrylic fiber, a relationship personally overseen by T.Y.

Back in Korea, Chairman Y.D. Kim, a former government official, had acquired, through government credit, the spinning, and knitting assets of Kukje company. K. Choi of Cheong-On knew fibers processing, and maintained a close relationship with K.S. Chung, Chairman Kim's brother-in-law and purchasing manager for Kukje, as well as Tiger Jun, Kukje's operations manager. These contacts required lots of smoozing, but their mills were standardized on Monsanto acrylic fiber as a result.

Intermediate chemicals not requiring technical knowledge of processing were handled through the regular Monsanto entity in Seoul, headed by D.S. Kim, an expert in Korean agriculture and former war hero, and his sales manager, J.K. Kim. AN bulk sales went through the Monsanto entity to the Kukje fiber producing enterprise who, in order to focus on fiber making, had sold its downstream textile operations to Chairman Kim. Each calendar quarter, we held AN negotiations with Kukje on price and tonnage. The largest known AN spot sale ever was made to this customer, totaling 20,000 metric tons, delivery to occur over the ensuing three months. The world of AN sales and product movement is a tight circle and there are no secrets, therefore, this block sale was known around world within a matter of days, and served to set the market price for the commodity for the next contract period. As someone directly involved in negotiating the large sale, I suddenly became a contact point for AN interests around the world.

Business in Korea or Taiwan or the mainland is preceded and followed by lots of eating, drinking, toasting, and gift exchanging. Non-drinkers may choose to do business elsewhere! A two or three day stopover in Seoul will always have an elaborate dinner built into the schedule. Chairman Kim and his staff will be situated on one side of the table, on floor pillows, while agent staff and Monsanto personnel are seated opposite. Private restaurants set up for this purpose are standard venues.

Food and liquor service is handled by a restaurant staff of attentive young women, each assigned to look after a particular guest. After toasts all around, and continuous food service, a group of musicians perform and guests are expected to take turns singing, and, or dancing with the hostesses until the evening finally ends with drivers taking everyone home in an inebriated state. We endured several such parties on our trip there in 1984, but soon realized that the ritual would be followed on all subsequent visits.

Over the course of the next 18 years, during which I travelled to Korea on business more than 30 times, these parties were a consistent feature of Korean hospitality; a ritual considered necessary to getting business done. No matter how many visits or who from Monsanto happened to be with me, the routine was the same. Business discussions and agreement, followed evenings by dinner parties and drinking, and Koreans smoking incessantly. It was Korean industry supporting Korean restaurants and upholding the traditions of Korean hospitality, almost as if following a national policy.

The ritualistic aspects of entertaining suppliers and/or customers is expected and highly regarded all over Asia, with minor variations. In

Taiwan, designated drinkers at dinner repeatedly toasts guests with a Taiwanese rice wine. On the mainland, the toasting drink is Mao-tai, a lethal colorless vodka-like high proof alcohol. The quaint concept is to get acquainted and form a bond with guests in a relaxed setting aided by drink interspersed with food snacks. Mostly, it works as intended, but the guest must recognize the game and direct his private attendant to dispose of the most of the alcohol in favor of water or other appropriate toasting liquids.

Another dimension on entertaining in Korea is golf, and Koreans are justly proud of many fine golf resorts scattered across the country, used principally by wealthy businessmen and tourists. Chairman Y.D. Kim invited us on one occasion to a round of golf at his club, which began with his limo picking us up at 7:00 AM for the trip to the resort in the country. There, we had breakfast and watched the pouring rain come down in a heavy fog, limiting visibility to perhaps 50 or 75 yards.

We had coffee and waited for our game to be cancelled because of weather. We were shocked and amazed when the tee time arrived to hear Chairman Kim tell us we were should now go to the first tee. We realized that this was no joke!! He had no thought of cancelling the game. We were given rain gear head to foot, dressed, and teed off right on schedule. We had individual girl caddies, who, from experience, could locate our ball after each stroke even though we could not see it after a few yards and had no idea about the golf course terrain. We slogged through ankle deep water on some holes, and, in Korean tradition, stopped after each six holes for refreshments and rest, then quickly resumed our round.

The rain never stopped, and we saw our shots only a few times the entire day. It was tantamount to night golf, but without lights. Finally, soaking wet and exhausted, but never admitting fatigue, we got back to the clubhouse and immediately stripped for the hot soaking baths and cold plunges. This was far and away the most pleasant part of the day.

Korean hot springs baths are truly very hot, perhaps 105 to 110 degrees, and are followed immediately by a sudden dip in ice cold water, then back to the hot tub, and again to the cold plunge, and so forth until the exquisite torture ends with showers, shaves, and dry clothes. Then another meal with drinks before loading into the limo for the hour-long trip back to the hotel, and immediate bed.

The Chairman and his staff had obviously done all this before and were unfazed by it all. As I said, Koreans are tough and determined and will not be deterred by small things from keeping their appointed rounds. I never again went to golf with Koreans expecting the game to be cancelled for any reason short of sudden death.

Kolon and Dongbang were large Korean nylon producers, and bought our type 66 polymers for this purpose. Cheong-On also handled these sales, with Kyun Choi the point man. Choi was a veteran of the Korean war, and had from childhood lived under the yoke of hated Japanese occupation. With all rice confiscated by the Japanese, his family lived entirely on potatoes and kimchi during that time. He told me that he would never in his life eat another potato.

His compensation, I was told, was a percentage of the commissions earned by Cheong-On, and my belief is that he did well financially. His wife also worked as a statistician for the government, and enjoyed a good income while facilitating government connections. Together, they had paid for college educations for two sons, both serving, at that time, their mandatory two years in the Korean (ROK) army. Choi's sales expenses had to be high, given the amount of entertaining he did, but his arrangement with Cheong-On appeared to work smoothly.

Choi was a chain smoker of Korean made cigarettes, a habit he could not modify even on trips to the United States. In the midst of business meetings here, he would excuse himself several times to go out for a cigarette. It was a habit which eventually killed him with lung cancer, but we had long since enjoyed a mutually beneficial and close friendship.

On trips to St. Louis, Choi would always visit our home with gifts and Joan and I enjoyed his company at all times.

At various times over the years, Joan or Scott or Jon accompanied me as I made the Asian circle. Korea was always a favored stop, both because of the friendships there, and for the great hospitality extended us by Choi, Chairman Kim, K.S. Chung, and T.Y. Hung and his sons. On one such trip, J.K. Kim of Monsanto Korea took Joan, Jon, and me to visit Cheju Island, off Pusan on the Southern Coast. Cheju is a volcanic rock island formed entirely by lava, rising out of the sea perhaps a hundred miles offshore. Its sheer lava cliffs and resort accommodations have made this former penal colony and prisoner-of-war camp an international tourist destination. Hyatt has an impressive hotel there, connected to casino where only foreign tourists are allowed to enter. Koreans are not permitted in the casino.

We golfed with J.K. and his wife and enjoyed dinners and hiking with them over the weekend, before flying back to Seoul on Sunday evening. We tried to return this hospitality when any of them visited the States, organizing dinners with Monsanto hierarchy and technical experts, arranging special hotel accommodations through Monsanto connections in St. Louis, and presenting them with suitable gifts.

I asked Earl Brasfield, Managing Director, John Mackie, technical Director, and Bruce English, Acrilan General Manager, to make a couple of these trips with me, expressing their appreciation to these valued customers and agency personnel and Monsanto entities for their contributions over the years. These cross-cultural meetings were memorable, and provided insights into our ex U.S. business.

Like most of the world outside the U.S., business relationships in Asia, and to a lesser extent in Europe, are cemented after the requisite introductions, polite hospitable discussions of indirect subjects which may or may not bear on the business at hand. The point is to gain some understanding of each other as individuals; to perhaps explore mutual acquaintances; to establish rapport and sincerity; to allow the host and guest to take the measure of each other. This is valuable time well spent, often not well understood by those accustomed to the straightforward American approach.

D.S. Kim and J.K. Kim of Monsanto Korea were often included in these agent/customer meetings, even though they took no part in any negotiations. D.S. had responsibility for total Korea, so it was important for him to be informed. He had deep respect for Cheong-On and T.Y. Hung, and the key role they played in selling into the Korean textile industry. On visits to Korea, my time was split between the agent and the entity, getting updates from each on the outlook in Korea, and reviewing our position with the range of customers.

During a visit a few years later, Chairman Y.D. Kim insisted I visit his new spinning plant in Shenyang, in Northeastern Manchuria, for its opening day ribbon cutting ceremony. The plant had been constructed there with incentive loans from Liaoning province and the city of Shenyang, to bring employment to the city for its large Korean population. These were Koreans who had fled North Korea to China after being stranded in the North by the artificial division of Korea in 1945. In Shenyang, Koreans in Koreatown constituted one of the city's largest ethnic groups. They retained their culture and language and operated prosperous shops and Korean restaurants, assisted by capital investments from the South such as Chairman Kim's.

Shenyang proper had a population of 4 million, with 7 million in its metropolitan area, yet few Westerners know much about this Chicago sized metropolis. Unwilling to return to North Korea and unable to go to South Korea after two generations in exile, the displaced Koreans now view Shenyang as their permanent home. Shenyang and Manchurian Northeast China, a province now called Dongbei, are close to Japan and were invaded in 1931 by the Japanese army on the pretext that China had sabotaged the

Manchurian railroad in Korea, which the Japanese controlled. Manchuria was brutally occupied by the Japanese throughout the war.

We flew on Korean Air to the west of North Korea, landing in Shenyang after the two-hour flight from Seoul. A fleet of limos with VIP flags met our entourage, and a police motorcycle escort lead us to our downtown American style hotel. An hour later, the same limos and escorts took us to the plant for the ceremony, well attended by local officials including the mayor of Shenyang and other luminaries.

Chairman Kim spoke Korean to the crowd, which included the plant workers, and introduced me as the American supplier who had come for this occasion, and the Cheong-On staff. A buffet of assorted Korean foods was served, followed by an hour long tour of the plant, which utilized spinning frames transplanted from one of the Chairman's Korean plants. Plant workers wore uniforms, and women had identical hairstyles. All stood at attention as we passed their work stations.

Cheong-On had arranged special gifts as ornaments and good luck symbols to the displayed at the plant. Local officials also brought plaques and gifts to commemorate the launch of the enterprise and bring it good fortune.

In early evening, we strolled through the large open street market, where most customers and vendors were dressed in familiar blue Moa uniforms from the revolutionary period. While selling colorful clothing in their stalls, they dressed themselves in bland Mao suits, symbols earlier mandated but seen less and less frequently in Beijing, Guangzhou, and other cities.

The evening restaurant was the site of still another dinner party, with ritual toasting and congratulations, identical to the cultural practices of Seoul and Taegu and Pusan and other cities where Korean businessmen gather.

In travels everywhere, one of my goals was to maintain a rigorous exercise regimen. Full days of meetings and late nights of eating and imbibing required an offset of physical activity. My schedule called for 6:30 wake-up, at least 30 minutes jogging on a treadmill in the hotel gym, some weight machines if available, shower, hot tub, steam, and shower/shave, in preparation for 8:00 breakfast and 9:00 AM meetings.

Dinners were usually over by 9 or 9:30 PM, so a decent night's sleep was possible. Without intense exercise, sleepiness and lethargy and fatigue would take over, so training habits were important. Fortunately, most hotels in major Asian cities have excellent health clubs with more space and better equipment than those found in U.S. and European hotels.

Leaving Korea and heading to Taiwan for the next leg, I felt good about what Korea had become since my army days there. The country had experienced a transformation from agrarian to urban, from rice farming to high tech industrialization, from squatter shacks to skyscrapers, from destroyed infrastructure to one of the most modern in the world, from extreme poverty to large middle-class wealth, from erratic and questionable leadership to solid American-style capitalism and democracy. Leading businessmen and Industrial conglomerates still depended on close connections in the government for their financing and permits, much the same as those in this country.

Proximity to the North no longer seemed to generate the kind of paranoia about infiltrators and sneak attacks so prevalent soon after the war. The fast growing economy gave confidence to the people and the government that they no longer need fear invasion as they once had, but nevertheless retained a large and well trained armed force just in case. And the U.S. kept a large force of "advisors" to back them up if needed. U.S. forces were now more in the background, and had given up the prized real estate in Seoul which had earlier been 8th Army headquarters. On a personal level, I was glad to have the opportunity to reconnect with Koreans who had seen this transformation first hand and remembered conditions from 30 years ago, and were now among the leaders in their fields. Tracing both our paths over the years since then strengthened the admiration I have always felt for the Korean people.

TAIWAN

Chiang Kai Shek became the sole leader of the nationalist Koumantang party after the death of Sun Yat-Sen in 1925, and went on to defeat the Chinese Imperial government and unify the nation in 1928, with himself as Chairman of the Republic of China. Mao and his communist followers joined forces with Chiang and the Allies to finally defeat the Japanese, but reverted to fighting each other as soon as the Japanese were gone.

Mao's forces finally got the upper hand. Chiang and his ROC government went to Taiwan in 1949 to escape the communist advance. With aid from the U.S., Chiang built a strong economy on the remnants of the Japanese occupation, who had hurriedly fled what was then called Formosa. Chiang Kai Shek was accorded a status equal to Roosevelt, Stalin, and Churchill for his leadership in helping defeat the Japanese, and became President of the Republic of China in exile, serving from 1950 until his death in 1975.

He is revered in Taiwan, and his reputation is being elevated on the mainland as the true liberator of China from Imperial warlords. The Chiang white marble memorial and park are the centerpieces of Taipei's attractions, ranking with the famed national museum at the top of the country's destinations.

Taiwan has 22 million people, with 2.5 million in Taipei at the Northern end of the island. Taipei is city of fast moving motor-scooters, and trucks, dense with pollution, busy with commerce. A subway system took many years to construct under established roadways, and with many delays and great controversy. Wealthy Taiwanese industrialists invested early and heavily in production facilities on the mainland, where 1.2 billion people supply unlimited cheap labor relative to scarce and expensive labor in Taiwan. Following the money, political leaders once militantly against the mainland's claims to Taiwan now want warm relations and stronger business ties. For the mainland, Taiwan is an important source of investment capital, from an island culturally and linguistically compatible.

Taiwan's location off the mainland Southeast coast places it directly in the path of typhoons, which often do great damage but provide Taiwan with its fresh water. On one occasion, my Cathay Pacific flight took off Chiang Kai Shek airport in a blinding rainstorm just ahead of the full force of an incoming typhoon. The turbulence was severe and nerve wracking until we reached altitude above the storm, while conditions in Hong Kong, and hour and a half to the Southwest, were perfect.

Taipei is a city of elegant eateries catering to business groups. Formosa Plastics hosted a private banquet for us in one such restaurant, where guests were treated to musicians performing Chinese classical music on ancient instruments, a chef making and drawing noodles from simple dough, and artists constructing intricate ice-sculptures with chain saws. In room preparation and service of more than a dozen exotic Chinese dishes never seen in American Chinese restaurants, was a rare and special treat. Examples: Chickens feet, boiled and seasoned, from which gelatin was sucked, and fish heads, with each part being savored, including the eyes. Aunt Jenny was quick to tutor us on the proper way to eat both these delicacies.

T.Y. Hung's favorite hotel was the Taipei Sheraton, where he had a special arrangement through connection with the manger. Breakfasts there were strictly Chinese, with a variety of special congee soups and rice and egg specialties. The hotel's entire top floor housed a health facility among the best in Asia. Guests and members could exercise, experience hot tubs and cold plunges, get expert pedicures, and a "rub-back" treatment, which is a one-minute wet rubdown from a trained male masseuse, all in one visit.

Rounds with Cheong-On in Taipei included Aunt Jenny and, in some instances, Dr. Zhiang. The two day schedule outlined meetings with Y.C Wong and his son Winston Wong of Formosa Plastics, Lion Woo, head of the Woo empire and sons Tony and Thomas, a meeting with Monsanto Taiwan, a start-up nylon hosiery producer headed by Scott Wang and his Korean born wife, who utilized our polymers, and a couple of independent acrylic spinners and knitters.

On this get-acquainted tour, details of our shipments to these customers and related issues were left to the agent, who, in any event, would not be discussing them with prestige figures such as Wong and Woo. Discussions were about broad economic issues, or maybe the political landscape, and projections for the year to come. In 1984, direct flights to and communications the mainland were still routed through Hong Kong, and there was much give-and-take on what the mainland government was thinking and doing.

President Nixon in 1972 had officially recognized Beijing as the capital of China, and transferred the U.S. diplomacy effort from Taipei to Beijing. In 1984, President Reagan affirmed this during his diplomatic and trade visit to Beijing, and was told by Chinese leader Ding Xiaoping that the U.S. should not interfere with China's efforts toward reunification. Still, the U.S. continued to supply arms and aid to Taiwan, and there was considerable anxiety on the part of Taiwan business about the role the U.S. would continue playing in support of Taiwan.

Chiang Kai Shek's son, Chiang Ching-Kuo, was President of ROC in Taiwan in 1984. His government took a hard line against reunification and built large defenses against a possible invasion. He would be succeeded by Lee Teng-Hiu, a close ally and friend of Aunt Jenny and Dr. Zhiang. Lee was to take a more pragmatic and softer line encouraging direct opening with the mainland, consistent with the interests of Taiwan business.

Fascinating to me were Y.C. Wong and Lion Woo, two of the most powerful men in Asia, both former laborers on the mainland, delivering sacks of rice on their backs, and now heading huge worldwide enterprises. Wong was especially interesting. Formosa plastics had spread over much of Asia, including the mainland, and the U.S. and Europe, producing a variety of synthetic fibers and plastics for many end uses. Both Wong and Woo were in their mid-seventies in 1984, and transitioning power to their sons in the Chinese tradition. Wong's mother was still living, in her 90's, with her son atop one of his apartment buildings. Aunt Jenny and Dr. Zhiang were close friends of both Wong and Woo, a relationship reaching back to Chungking and Chiang Kai Shek on the mainland.

On future trips, Woo's son Thomas and Tony, both Americanized by their California educations, insisted on hosting golf at their elegant club. After one golf outing, Thomas gave me a lesson on the proper way to eat hot noodles, which was sucking the noodles in quickly while enveloping and surrounding them in a blanket of cooling air. In this manner, the full flavor and aroma of the noodles is retained, and the lips and mouth are protected from burning. Useful, but loud slurping sounds may go unappreciated in public places in the U.S..

Before departing Taiwan, T.Y. Hung, an amateur but excellent calligrapher by all accounts, scheduled a guided tour of the national museum of art. On display here were the most important historical artifacts and fine art and calligraphy from the mainland, crated and shipped from China with Chiang Kai Shek. Mao's government claimed ownership, but nothing was ever returned to the mainland.

Only a fraction of these treasures could be displayed at one time, with the rest stored in temperature and humidity controlled underground vaults, exhibited thematically for short periods, then returned to storage. A complete tour of the museum exhibits would take several days, according to T.Y. We had only about three hours to spend here, but enough to appreciate the depth and breadth of at least part of China's history and art. T.Y. Hung honored me with gifts of several of his caligraphies.

CHINA BEFORE NEW CAPITALISM: HONG KONG

L anding in questionable weather at the Kowloon airport was always a thrill. 747 jets on final approach were obliged to fly just over the rooftops of rows of residential buildings to utilize the full runway. Passengers on either side of the plane could easily view families having dinner. During Monsoon season, Hong Kong would be inundated with heavy rains and lightning, but the airlines seemed undeterred. After 12-14 hour international flights, fuel considerations restrict possible alternative landing sights, so the incentive is to find an opening suitable for landing rather than diverting. Whether this results in safety issues is open to debate.

Hong Kong was and is one of the most cosmopolitan and densely populated cities in the world, up from the ashes of Japanese attack and occupation during the war. Joan remembers flying there with Pan American in the 1956-58 period, when Hong Kong was experiencing great poverty during recovery, complete with children street beggars and entire mini-cities of boat people who never came ashore. There are still floating sampan communities today, but they are there by choice. Hong Kong, Kowloon, and the New Territories have over 7 million people, with one of the highest living standards in the world, in spite of having been officially returned to China in 1997 after 150 years of British rule.

The agreement was made in 1984, at the time of my first visit there, It permitted Hong Kong self-government and its own constitution with

Western style civil rights and court systems, with Beijing directing only foreign affairs, and defense. The document created "an island of capitalism within a communist state", noting that there would be one party, but two systems. On December 1, 1997, Prince Charles and Hong Kong governor Chris Patten, sailed away from the Island on the Royal Yacht Britiania, signaling a formal turnover of the island to the Chinese.

The Regent hotel in Kowloon is one of the finest in Honk Kong, overlooking the bay with a view of Hong Kong city center, the harbor teaming with ferries, junks, sampans, and commercial vessels. The view is one of the most incredible in the world. The hotel is alongside the 40 ft wide pedestrian causeway extending a mile or more along the waterfront and hotel row. The walkway is a favorite walk exercise/jogging way for residents and tourists, filled with families at all hours. It is one of the best places to people watch in all Kowloon. Three round-trips early each morning filled my six-mile jogging quota for the day, followed by a plate of fruit and congee to start the business day.

Cheong-On's T.Y. and Tony Hung led tours of Kowloon, where ordinary Chinese families shop, and central Hong Kong with its fancy brand name clothing and handbag and jewelry stores, filled mostly by avid Japanese shoppers. As today, the Yen was very strong vs. the Hong Kong dollar, and goods in Hong Kong were much less expensive than those same goods in Japan. Shoppers were lined up to buy Louis Vuitton luggage and Rolex watchers and designer bags and shoes. The Mandarin Oriental hotel was in center city, while Kowloon boasted the famous Peninsula hotel along with the Regent and other international hotel brands.

Shopping for anything and everything, at all price points, is possible in Hong Kong and Kowloon. German and Japanese cars, coop apartments, custom suits and dresses and shoes, exotic jewelry and designer brands, cheap but good value textiles from the mainland, fine art, sculpture. Any good or service or food is available in one neighborhood or the other, just for the asking. Hong Kong shopping is like Seoul shopping magnified. On the mezzanine of the Peninsula hotel, I had two custom suits and two pairs of custom alligator shoes made within one 24 hour period.

The Star Ferry from Kowloon to Hong Kong and back is the preferred and quickest way to travel between the two points. There is an auto tunnel under the harbor, but the trip takes longer due to congested roadways. Ferry terminals are convenient walks from the Regent and the Peninsula, and offload at center city in the heart of the shopping district.

Monsanto's entity was headed by Richard Flederer, a longtime chemical veteran. Dick and his wife lived in a large apartment in one of Hong Kong's most prestigious high rise buildings, company paid, reportedly for huge dollar rents each month, with a three year lease. Plans were being drawn for an office in Beijing, primarily in support of the ag chemicals business, but in 1984, the mainland office had not been opened. Like many American multinationals, Monsanto was looking at a long term strategy of whether and how much to invest in China, and whether and with whom to joint venture. At the time, the trade and diplomatic future between the two countries was still uncertain. Chinese communist rules for investing and repatriation of profits were not well defined or quite strict, so going slowly seemed to be the most prudent course. Monsanto could see a lot of potential, but was still in a fact-finding phase. Meanwhile, simply exporting to China was the main avenue of business there.

T.Y. took great pride in choosing restaurants for both lunch and dinner. Dinner ordering was a protracted negotiation between Mr. Hung and the maitre de, and dishes came in a particular order prepared exactly as T.Y. stipulated. I learned that the skin of the Peking duck is the choicest part, anointed with a delicate sauce, while the actual meat of the duck was simply avoided. Ground pigeon meat in lettuce wraps, lightly fried emerald green spinach, several soup and rice and fish dishes, were T.Y. favorites. Another evening, we took a launch out to the floating fish restaurant, where T.Y. chose the live fish to be cooked for our dinner. In Hong Kong and the mainland, dishes were presented which were rarely seen in any U.S. Chinese restaurant.

Later, in Ghaungzhou, a two hour train ride inland, the tastiest vegetables and fruits and fish dishes were served at a banquet hosted by Chinatex. As in much of the West, food in Asia is art, and group meals at the better restaurants are art appreciation experiences.

The tram ride up Hong Kong's highest peak ends with a remarkable view over the city's skyscrapers to the New Territories. These magnificent edifices were designed by the world's leading architects, always with careful attention to orientation, height, and design aspects to bring good Fung Shui to every structure. Fung Shui is the integrated application of Chinese astrology, Yin and Yang, five elements, numerology, geography, magnetic fields, interior/exterior design, and their effects on people's living.

Fung Shui is said to bring energy, luck, health, and wealth. Corporations hire Fung Shui consultants to help them earn more money and keep their employees happy. The rules of Fung Shui are detailed, and no architect will ignore these rules when building in China. The guidelines are the same whether building skyscrapers or residences. Virtually all Chinese embrace the art of Fung Shui, meaning wind and water, and insist that it be followed in every day design and decorating.

Some years later, Cheong-On took Joan and me by high-speed ferry to the Portuguese Island of Macau, about an hour away. Macau is an international gambling mecca, since relinquished to the Chinese, appealing to very wealthy Japanese and European tourists and gamblers as the Las Vegas of the East. Architecture in the small colony is entirely European, as were restaurants and hotels. We stayed overnight and took a tour of the casinos, where gamblers were placing huge bets on each role of the dice or the next card.

It was a time of conspicuous Japanese wealth, with $50,000 and

$100,000 gold tablet bets being laid on the gaming tables with regularity. It was said that private charters delivered plane loads of Japanese to Macau daily, for gambling and "sex tours", returning them to Japan a couple of days later. This same custom delivery of gamblers and tourists was also true to some extent in Korea, and for the same reasons. Outside Japan, these big spenders could be ostentatious and flashy, whereas in Japan, such showiness would have been looked down upon as being in bad taste.

Preparing to go to Guangzhou, we toured a cut and sew operation in Kowloon belonging to a friend of T.Y.'s. Perhaps five hundred women on the second floor of a warehouse type structure were at work over sewing machines, putting together shirt and blouse panels brought to them by dozens of runners, who, after the sewing, took away the panels to the next station for additional finishing such as button hole making and hemming. The production line hummed constantly, turning out tens of thousands of finished garments daily, at very low labor cost.

This was a true sweat-shop in the U.S. meaning of the word, but in Kowloon, it was eagerly sought employment and relatively well paid. Later, most cut and sew operations moved to Guangzhou and still cheaper labor, while Hong Kong retained ownership and managerial and financing skills. Hong Kong and The Pear River Delta region became the distribution and shipping point for garments fabricated on the mainland.

GUANGZHOU: THE PEARL RIVER DELTA.

A brief stop-over in Guangzhou led to my first meeting with Chinatex officials, the textile goods purchasing arm of the PRC. In this third largest city in China, with more than 10 million people in its metro area, we met Mr. Wong and Madam Wong, no relation, who were considered the two most powerful purchasing executives in Chinatex. During Mso's red guards re-education program, Mr. Wong had been sent to a labor camp for five years to the "retrained" as a chef, but had since come to play an important role in rebuilding China's textile industry.

Madam Wong was married and had a family, and presumably was a party loyalist who had held bookkeeping positions in the government before being assigned to Chinatex. The assumption was that she detailed all agreements and kept Mr. Wong honest. John Tung had known them since the mid-seventies, after the Nixon era opening and the beginning of inter-country trade.

A word about the historical significance of Guangzhou, one of China's most important cities, and formerly recognized as one of the top three cities in the world It was earlier known as Canton, a name given it by Portuguese explorers who arrived by sea in 1517 and controlled virtually all trade out of Guangdong province until the Dutch arrived in the early 17th century and pushed the Portuguese to the colony of Macau, to the West. The city was founded in 213 BC, annexed by the Han Dynasty in 111 BC, and was fought over by various dynasties and Persian and Arab pirates until Europeans arrived in the 16th century. Located at the mouth of the Pearl river, in Southern Guangdong Province, the area is part of the giant and prosperous Pearl river delta which accounts for 9% of China's total GDP. The Delta region has a population of almost 50 million, and is responsible for 34% of all mainland exports. More importantly, most investments there are private, not government . The Canton export and import fair, held twice annually, is considered vitally important for those hoping to do business with China. Shenzhen, another major city in the Delta, and an important manufacturing base for Hong Kong enterprises, is to the Southeast of Guangzhou, closer to Hong Kong.

The British captured Canton in March, 1841, during the First Opium War, and controlled it along with Hong Kong until the Japanese bombed and occupied it from 1938 to 1945. Communist forces took the city in May 1949. The city is sub-tropical and humid, with a monsoon season from April through September. The city is easily accessible from Hong Kong by rail, bus, and ferry, as well as air.

In both Shenzhen and Guangzhou, giant construction cranes dot the landscapes. Commercial buildings and high rise apartments and infrastructure to serve them command large resources including labor. Guangzhou alone adds more than 150,000 people each year as migrants from the North come south and farmers on the broad delta come to the urban center for work.

As a textile center, Guangzhou is close to the market and vital distribution, and, along with Hong Kong and Shenzhen, speaking mostly Cantonese, making communications easy between the three centers. Mr. Wong and Madam Wong have come to Guangzhou to meet us precisely because the city is the consumer of a large percentage of their fiber purchases, particularly acrylic fibers used in sweaters, socks, children's wear, knitting yarns, embroidery. At our dinner meeting together, we present small gifts to them, observe the toasting ritual, get acquainted, and discuss their projections for purchasing our fibers. At this point in time, China had almost no acrylic fiber production capacity. Cotton grown in China is a key commodity, and, until recent years had met China's simple clothing demands, but the demand had now greatly outgrown cotton supply as China increasingly became clothing manufacturer to the world.

China's acrylic imports from the U.S., Japan, and Europe now totaled as much as 100,000 tons, and had tightened world supply and firmed prices as a result. Excess capacity in the world was now being taken up by China, and they wanted even more. At the same time, cotton supply was plentiful in the world, so acrylics had to compete on price with this interchangeable commodity, and cotton/polyester blends were a factor, with polyester staple also cheap and oversupplied.

We reviewed all these factors with Chinatex, without specific negotiations on volume or price, but it was clear that John Tung's relationship with the two Wongs was excellent, and that we would be asked to bid on all their acrylic purchases.

Next day we briefly toured the mountainous city, which is filled with parks, museums, and monuments, one dedicated to Sun Yat-Sen. The Sacred Heart Cathedral, dating to Portuguese colonization, is also a tourist draw. In the afternoon, we departed for Beijing, together with Mr. and Mrs. Wong

BEIJING:

The Peking hotel was an old, rambling, and comfortable landmark in the center of old Beijing. A wave of new modern hotels was soon to follow to accommodate the onslaught of business people and tourists coming to the new China. In 1984, bicycles were the most prevalent transportation mode, followed by official government cars, mostly Japanese made. Western dress was allowed and being adopted, but with little sense of color or style coordination. Women wore bland fitted tops with unmatched flowery brightly colored skirts, and flip-flops or high heels or boots. Nothing seemed to go with anything else, but important individual expression was made in the clothing choices, with no apparent concern for color or pattern matching. Mao jackets or pants were to be seen with patterned peddle-pushers or ruffled blouses. Eclectic choices were obviously not an issue.

Tiananmen square, night or day, was filled with tourists, mostly Chinese, who come to see the crystal coffin enclosed body of Mao Zedong, embalmed and on display there in spite of his wish to be cremated. The square is the largest public square in the world, designed to hold 500 thousand, and is next to the gate to the Forbidden City. Tiananmen square was the site of large student protests in 1989, covered by international television, which led to the massacre by the army of several hundred protestors in the square. As usual, we were accompanied to Mao's mausoleum and the viewing by Mr. Wong and Madam Wong, and, in this case, by John Tung's younger brother, a resident of Beijing.

Dinner at the Peking hotel with the Wongs, the Hungs, and John Tung and his brother brought still new and different Chinese foods, Sea cucumbers among them. These creatures are slimy sea slugs, eaten whole, with supposedly many health benefits. The first reflex is to gag, but with a little soy sauce, they go down and stay down.

Next day, the obligatory tour of the Great Wall, an hour outside Beijing by official government car and driver, with a lady guide who spoke some English apologetically. We spent about three hours walking the wall, with many ups and downs, with very many rough sections under reconstruction. The weather in late Spring was humid and hot, and there were frequent stops for refreshments. Beijing is in Northeastern China, with the full range of seasonal weather, and, on the edge of the Gobi desert spanning Mongolia and Northern China, subject to high winds and sandstorms.

Even in 1984, Beijing and most large cities in China were seeing rapid growth of industrial and automotive and truck pollution. Coal remained the major heating and industrial fuel, and its haze hung everywhere over the city. Rapid growth of Beijing's population was evident, a result of both government expansion in the capitol and urbanization of formerly agrarian communities seeking steady employment in the big city.

In the next 20 years, Beijing's population would exceed 20 million, a number far greater than forecast, and well beyond the capacity of its infrastructure to supply water, electricity, transportation, housing, and essential services such as medical needs. Urbanization continues at a rapid pace throughout China, with over 40% now living in cities in 2010 compared to 18% a decade earlier. This has lead China to an internal passport system which identifies every citizen and his home area. He or she cannot move to a city permanently until an official government permit is issued, and these are increasingly difficult to get.

Between meals and discussions with Chinatex, we also toured the Summer Palace and the Forbidden city. At these attractions, we saw few of the foreign tours or American groups who were later to come in very large numbers. Most visitors were Chinese families on holiday. Tourism was to become an important industry in China, but the mid-eighties had not yet seen the building of western style hotels and structures needed to serve non-Asians.

An example were the Chinese style public toilets which required squatting and were often not segregated. Foreign visitors and tours were still officially guided by government overseers and directed to publicly "approved" destinations only, a policy which had to change if large-scale tourism was to be encouraged. Some dozen years later, Joan and I visited a different Beijing, with new hotels, more private cars, more taxis, wider thoroughfares, name restaurants, and many more western tourists and businessmen as a result.

SHANGHAI

Some 800 miles to the Southeast of Beijing, Shanghai is the largest and arguably the most polluted city in China and its most international in terms of trade, finance, culture, and the arts. At the mouth of the Yangtze river delta, the British, French, and Russians have long had trade interests and influence in the region. More foreigners live in Shanghai than in any other Chinese city, dating back to the Opium wars of the 1840's which gave Britian control of the port for several decades. Subsequently, Jewish and Russian refugees settled in

Shanghai in the 1930's to escape the turmoil in Europe.

Shanghainese, not Mandarin, is the local language, but Mandarin in increasingly spoken for business as the population grows from outside. The Shanghai skyline features many skyscrapers, among them the soon to be completed Shanghai Towers, the tallest in the world. A high speed railway is nearing completion to connect Shanghai to Beijing, covering the 800 miles in just four hours.

In 1984, we stayed at the old Peace hotel, directly overlooking the riverfront, with its miles of walkways for residents and tourists who stroll there day and night. We were guided around the city by Mr. Jiang, the local Chinatex representative. This stopover is intended as simply an introduction to the city, with no real business agenda.

After a later solo trip to Shanghai, my scheduled flight to Beijing was delayed, and I needed to reschedule to an earlier flight to keep an appointment. This presented a real problem, since all flight postings at the airport were in Chinese, and I could not find anyone at the service counters who spoke English. After a half hour of searching, a young woman with minimal English skills was sent out to meet me, and succeeded in putting me aboard a Russian built jet to Beijing. I knew this particular plane, which had four engines in the rear, had a bad safety reputation, so the flight was not at all pleasant, in addition to being unusually noisy, but thankfully uneventful.

XIAN

Part of the tour was the requisite visit to Xian and to the tomb of the terra cotta soldiers. A two hour flight to the Northwest on China Air, and we approached landing over large fields of cotton, the key crop in this particularly suitable climate. Xian's climate is hot in growing season, and not too wet or humid, which can cause cotton to rot in the fields. On the other hand, too little water also leads to poor yields and supply fluctuations, which causes China to import large tonnage of cotton when the domestic crop falters.

More importantly, Xian is known as the walled city and former Imperial capitol of China, home of the elaborate tomb of Emperor Qin, credited with conquering the warring kingdoms of China and uniting the country in 221 B.C. This sounds a great deal like what Chiang Kai Shek was supposed to have done in the 1920's. Nevertheless, Emperor Qin's greatest legacy is the thousands of buried terra cotta soldiers, created in larger than life detail, complete with horses and chariots, as part of his tomb. This great attraction is being unearthed one section at a time, with careful restoration by experts, soldier by soldier, and, it is said, there are thousands more still buried.

We stayed in a very old hotel, the best in Xian at the time, in a suite which had been occupied by Jimmy and Roselyn Carter during their visit. In the center of the living room stood an old refrigerator with a single bottle of Mao Tai liquor inside. There was no shower, and limited water for bathing in a large iron tub, but we had to manage. Mr. Jiang had arranged for us to tour the city and the sight of the buried soldiers, which, at that time, were covered by a large inflated reinforced plastic bubble, climate and temperature controlled.

It was my only visit to Xian, so I have only heard about the transformation of the farm city of 8 million to the modern international tourism mecca Xian has become today. Tom and Christine Chiang, friends who recently went to Xian, report that it is now able to comfortably take care of large numbers of world tourists, affluent Chinese among them.

Conspicuously absent from the streets of a city of 8 million were automobiles. Public buses, bicycles, taxis, black government cars, and a few diplomatic limos were prominent, but private cars were still unaffordable to most Chinese. The important underground metro lines later to become vital people carriers in cities such as Shanghai, Beijing, and Guangzhou, had not begun to be constructed in Xian.

City streets throughout Xian and in most China cities are lined with beautiful trees, all planted in careful rows as part of a beautification program under Mao. Residents of larger cities complain that their neighborhoods are ugly, dirty from constant and polluting construction. Tree planting is one attempt to offset these complaints, but, with the pressing need for more living spaces, noise and dirt and ugliness will persist until urbanization and modernization slows.

INDOCHINA: BANGKOK

Back through Hong Kong, and a flight to Bangkok, and a meeting with Monsanto Thailand. Historically, Monsanto had sold acrylic fiber to a few customers in the city. Normally, these were overseen by John Tung working with the local Monsanto staff. The Mandarin Oriental was the top hotel at the time, since eclipsed by newer brands, but classic Thai in its friendliness. Bangkok's 10 million people survive in one of the most congested and polluted environments in the world, with solid air particles dwarfing those anywhere in China.

On day one appointments, traffic snarls at major intersections could stop traffic up to an hour, with idling diesel trucks and soot spewing motor scooters creating unbearable breathing conditions. While waiting for traffic to clear, drivers and passengers would exit and walk around their vehicles, smoking all the while. We were due at a famous fish market restaurant to meet local Manager Suan and his staff, and were an hour and a half late, to nobody's surprise. The hot tropical climate added to the discomfort, but there was no time to go back to the hotel for a shower before dinner.

The restaurant was unlike anything I had experienced before. The routine involves filling a super market shopping cart with fresh fish and vegetables and other foods of your choice, then to the market checkout line. There, a chef and waiter meet you and get your instructions on how you want everything prepared, backed, fried, boiled, sautéed, poached, or steamed. You take your number to a nearby restaurant table, and wait for the food to appear, prepared exactly as you have requested. Thailand has perhaps the best seafood in the world, taken from the Gulf of Thailand's salt water, and from many fresh water lakes and canals criss-crossing the country.

The concept of a continuous chain of selection, preparation, and consumption, under one roof, has not, to my knowledge, been popular in the U.S. My guess is that health regulations require separation of the two businesses, but from the consumer viewpoint, this coupling could work very well here.

Thailand has developed championship golf courses to build its tourism bonafides, and Jim Everett and Suan arranged for us to play one of them the following day. Its design compares favorably with the best in the U.S., but tropical heat, like Florida in August, is a distraction.

That evening, we toured the massive public market, identical in character to such markets in all Asian cities. Families shop here for all their basics, unlike the shopping experience at home, where discreet businesses sell specific lines of merchandise and foods, requiring shoppers to make many stops. In these large public markets, one trip can satisfy every need, from food, to hardware, to clothing, to scooter parts, and kitchen appliances and furniture and bedding.

On to an evening classical Thai performance with nuances perhaps best understood by Thai audiences. The costumes were ornate, the movements symbolic, somewhat like classical Japanese Kabuki, which can be entertaining but repetitive and sometimes tedious to those unfamiliar with local theatrical art and history. This is a cultural must see performance, but too long for jet lagged Westerners with full stomachs.

There was a long and unpleasant bus trip next day to an historic Thai country village two hours from Bangkok. Fumes from the diesel permeated the inside of the bus, and, coupled with a bout of motion sickness from all the bouncing around, made me determined to say no the next time someone proposed a side trip such as this. I learned to be willing to risk ruffled feathers and political incorrectness when a trip for the "culture" is suggested. I found I could say no directly and still have credibility with my hosts, who I suspect were relieved to skip a site they had already seen dozens of times.

During the day-long trip to the country, we witnessed the classic must-see battle between Cobra and its natural predator, the rat-like Mongoose. The mammal is dropped into the Cobra's cage, and the Cobra prepares to strike. As he does, the faster Mongoose intercepts the Cobra in mid-air and proceeds to kill the snake by flinging it side-to-side violently, then pecking it to death. It seems an unfair fight, because the faster Mongoose always wins, but visual proof is still required to verify what everybody already knows.

To sustain this kill ratio, there must be many more Cobras born, or, their encounters with Mongoose must be avoided. Thailand, along with India, is noted as the land of many Cobras and snake charmers. The Mongoose, meanwhile, have their own predators including other mongooses, chetah, wild dogs, pythons, and eagles.

Thailand is an ancient Siamese Buddhist Kingdom culture with the volatile political and military history of Indochina, while retaining its image of peaceful friendliness. Its floating river markets and silk and textile merchants attract large numbers of tourists, as does its sex trade, which, like Macao, attracts Japanese men by charter plane loads. Thailand is highly export dependent, mostly rice and seafood, but rapidly shifting to electronics and automotive parts. It is the anchor economy for Myanmar

(Burma), Laos, and Cambodia, and is the second largest economy in the region behind Indonesia.

The Thai cuisine is one of the most popular in the world, with spicy soups and seafood and noodle and duck and beef dishes mixed with strong sauces and very fresh vegetables. A dinner party in Thailand is focused on food far more than drink. Western tourists and business people seem to prefer Thai food over most other cuisines in the region.

Thailand borders tiny Laos, which borders Vietnam, and the air route from Hong Kong overflies the country where some 60 thousand Americans died for a cause not well understood then or considered worthy even today. Looking down on the recent killing fields of Vietnam, Laos, and Cambodia from an altitude of 30 thousand feet, imagining the many who died there in the name of some domino theory of communist advance we now suspect was never valid, is an eerie and sobering experience. The time lapse since the Vietnam war confirms even more clearly that governments run by fallable political leaders are capable of monumental errors of strategy and judgment, leading to the needless sacrifice of ever-obedient military. Today's Afghan war risks repeating the same mistakes.

SINGAPORE

The British colonial footprint in Asia and India and Africa, controlled and managed from a tiny island empire by a small cadre of professional British military officers and diplomats, is unparalleled in history except perhaps by conquests of the Romans. Singapore was colonized when Sir Stamford Raffles opened a British port there is 1813, with no apparent resistance, and it flourished as an important trading center until conquered by the Japanese in 1942 and occupied by them until war's end.

Like India, English became the language of commerce and education. Singapore was given its independence voluntarily by the British, in stages, and, in 1965, it became in independent city/nation when it quit or was ejected from a Malaysian consortium of states. The U.S. and Singapore have an established free trade agreement assuring protection of intellectual property, and low tax rates on investments. Attractive financial incentives, a stable political and banking system, an educated labor force not subject to strikes, religious freedom, good transportation and a high living standard with stable currency, make it an appealing location for regional headquarters for American multinationals and expatriates.

Its population of almost 5 million is some 70% Chinese and Buddhist, but its 15% Malay component is Muslim. Indian, Thai, Japanese, and European and American expats comprise the balance, with all major religions represented. By reputation, Singapore is the cleanest city in Asia, and the toughest on crime.

We had arrived in Singapore via Thai Airlines, flying South down the Malay peninsula. Some years later, aboard a Singapore airlines 747 out of Osaka, I was invited to ride in the cockpit with the flight crew, where I stayed the several hours of the trip. On landing through rain clouds in Singapore, the nose-up attitude of the plane prevented any visibility of the ground or runway, and the crew depended entirely on instruments all the way through touchdown. I was told by the British captain that this was the standard landing attitude of all 747's, all the time.

We paid a courtesy call on Stu Daniels, Asia Pacific Vice-President, and his staff, reviewing the scope of our business throughout his region. In turn, old Monsanto friend Charlie Hobbs briefed us on total Monsanto in Asia Pacific. Discussion centered on our use of agents in the region, and we assured Stu that all local country entities would be kept informed. In the evening, we were hosted to Singapore slings on the veranda of the luxurious Raffles hotel Long bar, made famous in literature and movies.

Somerset Maugham, Rudyard Kipling, Joseph Conrad, and Charlie Chaplin were among its regulars. Raffles hotel dates to 1887, and symbolizes British influence in the former colony. My good friend, Mike Miller, became head of the Asia/Pacific region when Daniels retired, but Mike never relocated to Singapore, remaining at St. Louis headquarters.

Early the following morning, a Sheraton hotel bus delivered me to the wonderland of Singapore's botanical gardens, some 20 minutes away, where I did my morning jog in extreme heat and humidity. Singapore is just above the equator, with only small variations in its hot and muggy climate, but the plant varieties thriving in this moist, hot environment are delights to even casual horticulturists.

We were driven an hour away to Kuala Lumpur, the capitol of Malaysia and its largest city. The short day trip involved a border crossing and showing of passports, lunch in the large Chinatown market, and some discussion about the budding textile and manufacturing industries there. Like Singapore, KL is equatorial and uncomfortable, made habitable and industrial by air conditioning technology, much like parts of the American South. Unlike Singapore, KL is entirely Islamic, and many commercial structures reflect Islamic design influence.

INDONESIA: JAKARTA

A short flight on Singapore air delivers us to Jakarta, capitol of Indonesia, the largest officially Muslim country. Since the Japanese were driven out and the Dutch colonialists returned at the end of the war, Indonesia has experienced many violent government disruptions, beginning with Sukarno, who led a nationalist uprising which forced the Dutch to offer independence in 1949.

Sukarno embraced communist principles in achieving a "guided democracy", and was elected president for life in 1966, shortly before an attempted military coup. Suharto, Chief of staff of the army, put down the coup and his forces massacred hundreds of thousands of communists in taking control as dictator in 1967. Suharto remained in charge for the next 32 years. He was finally arrested on corruption charges, rare in Indonesia because of the wide latitude politicians have in rewarding supporters, and the general tolerance of corruption there. Suharto died before coming to trial. Indonesia now has a directly elected president, with Islamic representation below 20%, and aggressively prosecutes terrorists.

The archipelago consists of 17,000 islands arrayed along the equator, some with their own language, some sparsely inhabited, and with many still following ancient tribal rituals of animal sacrifice, or "cuttings", in celebrations of weddings or funerals. Only a few of the islands, principally Sumatra and Java, are considered to be a part of the economy.

The string of islands is known as the "ring of fire" due to its large number of active volcanoes and violent earthquakes, which in the past have led to large scale destruction, and devastating tsunamis which most recently killed over 200 thousand. Indonesia has oil, which is what attracted the Japanese, and spices, which attracted the Dutch in the 16th century. Jakarta, with 13 million people, is the country's largest, most industrialized, and most polluted city.

In the mid-80's, large office buildings were being erected, with Japanese trading companies as the largest tenants, and wealthy Chinese as the owners. Japanese are still hated here, but their enabling technology has brought many factories and jobs to the country. Chinese from Taiwan and the mainland have been large investors and control much of the economy, a fact which led to riots in the 90's in attempts to reduce Chinese influence.

John Tung and T.Y. Hung are longtime friends with Mr. Lim, another mainland Chinese who settled in Taiwan, and is now heavily invested in Indonesia. Mr. Lim's holdings include office buildings, car dealerships, oil refining, and textile factories, which are managed by his sons in the

Chinese tradition. We met Mr. Lim for dinner and to discuss his purchases of Monsanto fiber, and his long-term desire to build acrylic and nylon fiber producing capacity in the country.

He openly explained that getting government permission and permits for particular businesses in the country required close relationships with the President and his staff, and implied that donations of money were the key. In some of his businesses, members of the President's extended family are public shareholders. Mr. Lim saw this fair exchange for monopoly control of a business segment.

Indonesia's culture of open corruption among the powerful, is not understood in the context of western values. The circle of influence surrounding power has an understood right to share the spoils of power and success. It is a requirement for getting and holding power, and is regarded by the general public as a small price to pay for government, which, on balance, tries to do the right thing. Mr. Lim is simply confirming actual known practice which students of local business and politics understand well. American corporate and union practices of money in support of candidates and pet causes are not too different, only more circuitous. Indonesia donors go direct, and are rewarded more directly.

Many Asian, Middle Eastern, Latin American, and African countries share similar attitudes toward sharing the spoils of power. We see it as transparent graft, bribery, kickbacks, and general corruption. They view recipients of political favors not as criminals, but as beneficiaries fortunate enough to be close to the centers of power.

Heads of state of newly independent nations in Asia often chartered airliners for their state visits. This was the practice before each emerging nation established its own national flag carrier to enhance its national identity and prestige, as well as earn more foreign exchange through tourism. Indonesia started Garuda airlines, totally government owned, in 1949, but long-range passenger jets were not added to its fleet until 1965.

Post world war two and the emergence of formerly subjugated nations, a new national airline became a requisite first step in building a new identity for each nation, and political leaders quickly understood how important this symbol of power could become in employing people and building national pride.

Over time, the practice spelled the doom of Pan American World airways, which was U.S. government restricted to international routes only. As new national airlines came on line, Pan Am was relegated to minor status with the national carrier given preferred status. As stated earlier, the Pan Am case is perhaps the clearest example on record of the negative consequences of government meddling and regulation of what should have been free market capitalism decisions. Unable to get FAA approval for domestic routes, and facing subsidized international competition from every country, Pan Am effectively became extinct in the 1980's. One of the world's great airlines was forced by government fiat to ground itself.

Before this happened, Joan recalls three Pan American charters with President Sukarno for state visits starting in 1961, for which she was chosen as one of the crew. Pan Am 707 jets, staffed by Pan Am crew, ferried Sukarno and his entourage of 40 to Washington, New York, Paris, Venice, and Belgrade, in the former Yugoslavia, now Serbia and Montenegro. The five female cabin crew consisted of one American, Joan, one German, one Japanese, one Greek/Chinese, and one American male purser, all hand picked by Sukarno personally or his immediate staff. The cockpit crew were all Americans.

The cabin crew would be invited to accompany Sukarno to state dinners, such as with Marshall Tito in the Presidential palace, and on his private yacht. They also accompanied him on a tour of the private Vatican gardens, and to other public sites. Sukarno wanted attractive women on these tours, and actually proposed marriage to the Greek/Chinese flight attendant. She declined to become his fourth wife, acceptable practice in the Islamic faith of Sukarno.

During stops of several days, the plane and cockpit crew departed, but the cabin crew stayed in hotels with the entourage and press. A different 707 crew and plane would return to continue Sukarno's journey. Security concerns today would never see a head of state travelling on diplomatic missions with such lax precautions, but air security around the world in the early 1960's involved no airport screening gates or luggage searches. Terrorism concerns had not yet surfaced. Mechanical malfunction was a much more important issue. Security of heads of state changed radically when JFK was killed in an open convertible in Dallas in 1963.

At the end of one of the charters, Sukarno rewarded the crew with a week's vacation in Bali, Indonesia's best-known resort. Later, Bali's tourism sank after terrorist attacks there in 2004. Sukarno presented each crew member with gifts of antique gongs suspended in ornamental wood frames, and exquisite batique fabric, which Joan still has. Pan Am also received letters of commendation for Joan. She was invited to serve as crew for a fourth charter, but declined because she was resigning to get married.

Joan was also picked as crew when President Carlos Garcia of the Phillipines chartered Pan American aircraft, and she has letters of appreciation from the President and his staff.

AUSTRALIA

One two-thousand mile leg on Quantas took us from Jakarta to Perth and a new continent, then a long night flight Southeast across the sparsely settled inlands to Sydney and its famous harbor and opera house. We were in the country to see a nylon polymer and adipic customer in Melbourne, and to pay a visit to Wayne Lorenz, Monsanto country manager, and Robin Garnsworthy, marketing director.

John Tung left us in Jakarta to go back to the states, as did T.Y., Michael, and Tony Hung. Our limited sales in Australia were handled through our own entity. The customer in this case had multiple interests beyond nylon 66 filament production, the only such producer in the country. Mining, commercial buildings including hotels, a financial business, and gemstones were also parts of the family owned portfolio.

Even contorted Aussie English as a first language was comfortable to hear after three weeks of deciphering it as spoken by Japanese, Chinese, Thais, Koreans, Singaporeans, and Indonesians. With some 20 million people spread across an area just slightly smaller than the U.S., Australia is almost 90% urbanized, focused in Sydney, Melbourne, and Perth. The interior of the country holds only about 2 people per square kilometer, and is of little value for farming.

A brief tour of Sidney, then a flight South to Melbourne, over Canberra and what looked like millions of grazing sheep below. Melbourne is the location of Monsanto headquarters in the country. Garnsworthy met us and settled us in the Hyatt, and made the customer call with us in the afternoon. The next morning was invested in a tour of Australian nylon spinners plant, producing yarns for tire cord, specialty industrial uses, and carpets.

While Canberra is the capitol, located on a line between Sydney and Melbourne, the latter is an influential business and financial hub. Competition between Melbourne and Sydney to become the capitol led to the entirely planned capitol, populated by mostly civil servants. Melbourne is recognized as having the finest restaurants and seafood cuisine. Lorenz hosted us at one of Melbourne's best in seafood.

Like America and much of Asia and Africa, Australia was colonized by the British in the 18th century. White settlers treatment of the aboriginal peoples was similar, in many respects, to the genocide or forced relocation of the American Indian tribes who resisted encroachment and confiscation of their tribal hunting grounds. As at home, the controversy in Australia continues to this day, when the aborigines account for less than 2% of Australia's population. Australia is monitored closely by the United Nations for human rights violations and discrimination against the native inhabitants, to the resentment of the government, which claims payment of reparations and fair treatment of the reclusive aborigines, who confine themselves to "bush" areas of the country visited most often by foreign tourists.

Next day took us in reverse and again across the vast middle of the country to Perth, on the West coast, where we had a six-hour window until the overnight flight to Durban, South Africa. I called the Royal Perth Yacht Club and asked permission to visit as a representative of the Riverside Yacht Club, and was told to come and be welcomed.

The club had recently won the Americas Cup and had the Cup trophy on display in the center of their large trophy room. It was Saturday and race day at the club, and the Commodore and club officers were dressed in their whites. The taxi dropped me at the entrance where I was met by three club officers and escorted inside to a private room and lunch with the Commodore and his officers. The reception was a surprise for me, but fortunately, I was dressed in blazer and tie appropriate for the visit. The lunch was delicious and the conversation cordial, with lots of questions about Riverside Yacht club as well as Americas Cup and their own race day. After lunch, the Commodore toured me through the club and its excellent facilities and marina.

I wrote to Miles McDonald, Commodore of RYC, reporting on the visit in some detail, and sent him the Royal Perth burgee which had been presented to me. The Royal Perth extended reciprocal privileges to RYC members and their guests. I had hoped to simply visit the club and maybe have lunch. Instead, I got a formal welcome and grand reception never anticipated. Then it was back to the airport and make ready for one of the longest flights I can remember. We boarded the British airways 747 and headed west across the vast Indian ocean, to yet another continent.

AFRICA

A distance of 5,000 miles plus headwinds forced a refueling stop in the Mauritius islands, tiny specks of land east of Madagascar. The stop was in darkness, with only airport runway lights visible. There seemed to be no town or structures beyond the landing strip. We stayed aboard for the hour needed to load on fuel, then another two hours to Durban, South Africa, just as daylight was breaking. Altogether, twelve hours had elapsed since our departure from Perth, and the time went by slowly. Landing on South Africa's east coast, we could see the white sand beaches of Durban and a number of golf courses laid out along the ocean.

South Africa was still living under the rules of Apartheid law which would remain in effect for another six years. Facilities were totally segregated, legislated by early Dutch settlers and colonizers going back to the 16th century. Over time, Dutch, German, and French immigrants intermingled with slaves and "coloreds", resulting in the multi-toned Afrikaner race, all speaking a language blended of Dutch, French, and German with distinctive accents. Still, there were clear class separations between white Afrikaners and dark Afrikaners.

With the discovery of gold in the Transvaal, British immigrants invaded Afrikaner territories and armed conflict resulted, first with the British being defeated temporarily, then victorious in the Boer War of 1899, after which Afrikaner lands were annexed under control of the British. The Afrikaner culture survived and strengthened, particularly in inland areas, but the British government and military ruled. While slavery was no longer permitted, Apartheid continued in place until countrywide protests by the African National Congress forced its negotiated end in 1991, and the return of Nelson Mandela three years later.

We were met by Arthur Schroeder, our agent, who lived in Durban, and, first things first, had a round of golf in the afternoon. The game's unique gallery, lining each fairway and looking on interestedly, consisted of hundreds of well-mannered monkeys. I expected them to swarm the fairways and make off with our golf balls, but they stayed politely on the side as if they had been trained to this purpose. But their chatter never stopped. I jogged early next morning along a path by the course, and this time, monkeys filled trees on either side, hissing and chattering as I went passed. I was later cautioned about jogging alone in areas like this, where monkeys have been known to assault people.

After breakfast, a two-hour drive North to visit the agent's farm and get a look at the countryside. Toll roads along the way were manned by blacks, who our agent addressed as "boy", a condescension neither Afrikaner agent or "boy" seemed aware of. "Boy" had been the lifelong form of address for whites speaking to blacks. To Americans, "boy" was the equivalent of the N word, even in 1984. Farther north, in Zimbabwe, Afrikaners owned most of the farms and employed essentially slave labor.

This would change radically under the socialist dictator Robert Mugabe, who confiscated these productive farms, broke them into small plots, assigned them to former slaves, and generally turned the country into one of mass poverty in the name of restoring the land to its "rightful" owners.

Later in the day, South African airways to the town of East London, an hour and a half away, also on the East coast, where an acrylic fiber buyer and yarn spinning factory were located. Overnight in the non-descript town, and an early flight out to Port Elizabeth further south down the coast, to another factory belonging to the same owner.

Wednesday noon we landed in Capetown, a lovely city at the junction of the Indian and Atlantic oceans, in the shadow of Table Mountain. We stayed at the classic old British hotel, the Mount Nelson, in oversized rooms with very high ceilings and expensive décor, a refuge in a city still separated by race, but dependent on black Africans for all the service jobs essential to operating hotels and restaurants, and shops.

The Mount Nelson was situated in elegantly groomed gardens within a large park, with white guests from Europe, Asia, and the U.S., none black but served only by blacks. Downtown, Capetown at the time was a modest village of souvenir and trinket shops geared to tourists. I jogged through the Mount Nelson grounds and through the downtown business section, drawing stares from locals, and was later again encouraged to use caution in jogging or walking alone outside the gates of the hotel grounds.

Capetown is known for excellent seafood and local high quality white wines, and our customer, South Africa nylon spinners, owned mostly by Imperial Chemical Industries of England, treated us to a warm welcome and dinner. The executive staff of SANS were all British expats, with lifestyles luxurious in the expected mode of expats on foreign assignment. Touring the large plant facility the next morning, the workforce was a mix of white engineers and black and Indian machine operators, with obvious respect both ways between boss and subordinate on the plant floor. Discussion focused on raw materials costs in the months ahead, including diamine and adipic, and their end markets, most of which were in Northern Europe and England.

The Brits talked openly about the coming end of Apartheid, which was clearly on the horizon, and did not see nationalization or open hostility toward them resulting. The consensus was that a government run by the ANC would operate with a constitution respecting private property, and would still want investment and employment to remain prosperous. This pattern, if it came to pass, would be contrary to most other African nations freed from colonial rule.

Nelson Mandela became South Africa's first black President on May 10, 1994, and pledged to continue building the country and do nothing to harm it, seeming to live up to the promises made by F.W. deKlerk, the last white President of the Republic. The transition was peaceful and orderly, and Mandela used his prestige as a world respected leader to continue the unification of South Africa.

With almost 50 million people currently, 80% blacks, a life expectancy of under 50 years, over 20% of blacks having no education at all, high unemployment, and a shrinking white population due to high crime rates and affirmative action policies of the government, the long term prospects of South Africa are open to debate. In spite of negative trends, South Africa remains democratic and relatively much wealthier than it neighbors, and continues to attract émigrés from countries like Zimbabwe, for example, where government policies have driven many citizens out of the country.

Mineral resources are South Africa's greatest source of wealth. Mining of platinum, gold, manganese, chromium, and diamonds represents a key industry and biggest employer in the country. SA is the world's third largest producer of gold, with 40% of world supply, and produces almost 80% of the world's platinum. Investments by world-scale mining companies are being made in downstream value added industries to refine metals. These will add employment and bring in needed foreign exchange. The world's biggest mining names operate here, including BHP Billiton, Anglo American, Rio Tinto, Tata steel, and diamond miner De Beers.

The unstinting march of western European nations and the British to explore and arbitrarily claim new lands and their resources led to colonizing much of Africa, much as America was claimed by England and France, Mexico by Spain, and Indonesia by the Dutch. Several wars and three or four centuries were needed to unwind these claims, but the good and bad residue of the conquerors is ingrained in the culture, languages, political systems, and economies of nations emerging from hundreds of years of foreign rule.

Western Europe was next on our agenda, and in intermediate stop in Johannesburg, the capitol, connected us with a Lufthansa overnight flight back across the equator to the Northern hemisphere, and to Frankfurt, West Germany.

ON FAMILY

A seminal decision leading to at least the possibility of happiness and prosperity is the selection of one's embryonic environment. Far more critical than any potential genius inherent in sperm and egg is the location, location, location of their host carrier. Choose carefully to avoid fetal maternal nourishment from a Somali pirate, an HIV infected North African tribal member, a polygamist jihadist incestuous Middle Eastern Islamist, a polyandrous Indian Hindu caste slave, an illiterate Chinese peasant on the edge of the Gobi desert, or a Siberian banished political outcast.

Your selfish genes will matter little if your "drop" zone is inhospitable or even hostile, like a UPS package of diamonds bounced of the truck in drug cartel infested Juarez or Tijuana, or Sharia law controlled Teheran, or in a tribe of South American jungle aborigines.

Monogamy is a man-made construct of recent history, now weakened considerably by modern attitudes which embrace no formal commitment as prelude to child bearing or cohabitation. In many cultures, the options of polygamy or polyandry have depended on imbalances in the populations of a given region or country, or on tribal status or bloodlines or religious interpretations. Our own country historically stigmatizes these options based on puritan Christian concepts, with a high divorce rate and a succession of marriages as one likely result.

Our parents, like most Americans, still lived with the traditional concepts of the new-testament and Puritanism, even though the inherited Judeo-Christian social order was evolving into a more informal and secular arrangement. Today, single parent births are more common and accepted. So is parenting by gay and lesbian couples. Fewer people now make negative moral judgments about these newer, non-standard approaches to family formation.

The Garrett/Savage, Morris/Grimes, Johnson/Henderson unions were definitely traditional and colonial protestant, with monogamy as the only understood and absolute rule governing families, going back to the founding of the country. When grandfathers Garrett and Morris and Johnson and Henderson married, the ceremony was formal, modest, and very public. Frank and Dillie may have been married in the rumble seat of a model T Ford, but the ceremony itself was classically formal and publicly known by everyone in the community. Alice and Ed Henderson recited the same Christian vows, exchanged rings, and announced their union in the Oakland Tribune.

Our Texas farm parents had seven children over a long span, and Joan's urban California parents produced just two children, but each family behaved in responsible ways as expected by their communities, fulfilling their debt obligations and providing food and material goods and moral and ethical guidance. In this very ordinary American way, our traditional families progressed over time from modest beginnings to increasingly better living standards and some status in the community.

For us, their children and grandchildren, their most important contributions to our lives were the locations or "drop zones" where they happened to be when we entered the picture alive. In this unique location, the concepts of equality of opportunity and wealth creation happened to be embraced by law, generally free of religious fanaticism or dogma. Education for both sexes was an integral part of the value system of this environment. The accident of our place of birth has led us to follow the same traditionalist path to marriage and children, education, and career.

SIBLINGS

My two older brothers, Cal and Raby, and four younger sisters, Shirley, Norma, Dora, and Sharon, benefitted from the same birth circumstances, and went on to diverse careers, while staying close geographically. Cal became an engineer/ golf professional. Raby and Dad owned their own real estate business. Shirley earned a masters degree and a career teaching and counseling. Norma became a bank VP and Trust officer. Dora had a career in school administration. Sharon became an entrepreneur. Each married and had children and grandchildren who made them proud. Equally important are the warm and loving relationships they have with Joan and me and with each other. I know of no other family who have remained so close with so little divisiveness over such a long period of time.

They and their spouses are all reserved, with even temperament, supportive, caring, thoughtful, sharing, and eager to get together for annual reunions and special family days, to share stories and pictures of their children and their grandchildren. These attributes and love of family come directly from Frank and Dillie, who provided a loving home, valuable counsel, and occasional help of a more tangible nature. They, in turn, adopted these traits from their parents and siblings, and several generations of cousins and second cousins and third cousins and their mates still populate West Texas, just as my siblings do. Anywhere west of Dallas, no GPS is needed to find one or more of our relations, and their doors are always open to each other.

Joan and Scott and Jon are miracles to me, and I often reflect on how different my life might have been had I taken a different road when many alternate courses of action presented themselves. I will write more about the paths chosen later, but suffice to say that any number of decisions I might have made would have led to my never meeting Joan in New York, and, obviously, there would not have been a Scott or Jon or Terry, or Jack and Audrey in my life. The thought is depressing but could have easily become a reality, in which case, my imagination is not rich enough to conjure the picture of what life would be like without them.

Having them as my life was not pre-destined, and neither is a formula for being a great husband or father. There is not a spouse or father or mother alive who does not live with some regrets, inevitable because there is no moment-to- moment blueprint for exactly right. An unkind word, a careless remark, a wrong decision on discipline, a severe restriction, a damaging expression which cannot be withdrawn, inattention or impatience, a bad example, a failure to coach or teach, are but a few parental shortcomings and errors of commission or omission which haunt parents and cause them to question themselves.

Yet we learn to forgive ourselves enough to carry on with these life-giving relationships, and hope that our spouse and children come to understand that human foibles plague every human every day, and that they, in turn, will most likely make the same errors of emotion and judgment which lead to debilitating guilt unless they forgive themselves and are forgiven by those offended.

Errors are made the other way as well. I have made comments and committed deeds which brought anguish to my dear parents, I am sure, but they did not react to them with anything but forgiveness. Still, I wish I could have expressed myself more clearly to them, yet did not have the sensitivity and good sense to apologize and more openly express my love for them.

My business career was a top priority for 40 years, I think because financial security and continuity of employment had to come first in my mind. This meant risking unconsciously placing Joan and the boys second, although not less important, but second in the order of things which had to have attention. In the course of that career, I travelled away from home an estimated one third of the time, the equivalent of thirteen years on the road. But that is not the real story. Deducting 12 hours per day five days per week, 50 weeks per year that I would have been away from family in any event because of normal office hours, the net time totally away from family totaled seven and one quarter years.

I could not have been more absent if I had been in prison or overseas on military duty for the same period of time. I was absent from my children's lives and Joan's life during critical moments of their growing up and needing counsel and a father's presence. Joan was effectively a single parent during these times, making the same mistakes both of us would have made in any event, but at least she was there for them, trying to do the best she could, having to make decisions which weren't always popular or obeyed.

Neither Scott nor Jon seem resentful of the time I missed during their growing-up years, which is remarkable and generous of them. In fairness, I did take them with me, one at a time, on some trips to Asia, where we spent quality time. We also took family vacations to Colorado ski resorts, to Acapulco, to Disneyworld, and to the British Virgin islands. These were great opportunities to be together as a family, and perhaps offset some of their roughest growing up moments, exacerbated by several Monsanto relocations to new cities and new schools, and new acquaintances and adjustments.

When Scott graduated college, he and I went on a ten-day golf trip to courses in California and Las Vegas. Jon and I rafted with a group down the Colorado river beginning in Green River, Utah. So there were moments of bonding which will always be with us, hopefully with good memories forever. Joan also went with me on some Asian and European trips, while the boys held down the fort at home.

The lessons of family and parenting and bonding and communicating are the best lessons of life, and I can only hope that my relationships with my sons and my wife are treasured equally by all of us. No doubt about it, Joan, Scott, Jon, Terry, Jack and Audrey are the fruits of life, the components of living that are its reward; the aspects of being human that have made being on this earth worthwhile.

The cliché that grandparents have a second chance to get it right is clearly true. The perspective of time and years of opportunity to reflect on one's effectiveness as a parent brings a degree of wisdom to the process. Grandparents can be useful sounding boards for grandchildren's questions on many of life's issues, including their relationships with their parents. Grandparents serve as insurance backstops and trusted advisors to help smooth over rough periods in the phases of growing up, even while parents remain primary in all decisions, with all their uncertainty.

Perhaps a compelling aspect of the grandparent/grandchild dynamic and the underlying reason grandparents are so proud of their grandchildren is the fact that grandchildren are the conduit to the future of the family genome. They insure grandparents that their selfish, immortality-seeking genes have been expressed in still another generation, and the chance for generational continuity of the grandparent's characteristics is still alive and moving forward.

Another clarity with age is the truism that friends become family away from home. We are lucky to have maintained many warm friendships in Texas, Connecticut, Atlanta, St. Louis, California, Asia, Europe, and all over the world. Friends from high school, college, the Harvard experience, Washington University, and work at Monsanto, and thoughtful neighbors wherever we have lived, are all part of our extended friendship family. My brothers Cal and Raby, and pals John Roughan and John Long have been close to my heart most of my life. Some friends remain closer than others, but none are forgotten.

We laugh and learn from each of our friends, share many wonderful memories, and never want to loose them. Perhaps the Facebook social network premise that we all crave and are dependent on an array of interactive friends is correct. Their pictures need not be posted on the internet to remain vivid in the photo albums in our minds.

WESTERN EUROPE AND EGYPT

Over the course of the first week of June, 1984, Frankfurt, Cairo, Munich, Salzburg, Paris, Lyon, Brussels, and London were on the schedule. I had been to London and to the textiles fair, but this was my first time to the continent and North Africa.

A significant polymer customer in Cairo extruded hosiery yarns for sale to middle-east markets, and he insisted on our visit to reciprocate for his recent trip to St. Louis. He and his vice-president, a glamorous lady said to be married to an Egyptian army officer, hosted Jim Everett and me on tours of their plants and excursions in and around Cairo. On a side trip to the edge of the city to visit the pyramids of Giza, all traffic stopped while a herd of camels slowly marched up both outbound lanes of the four-lane highway. This fifteen-minute delay seemed to disturb no one, and the camel driver made no attempt to hurry things along.

The pyramids and the sphinx were surprisingly open and unguarded. Locals and tourists milled around the base of both structures and left litter and debris behind. June is a big month for visitors from everywhere, and hot and humid, but locals were wisely swathed in traditional full dress which kept out the sun.

Cairo's infrastructure was being rebuilt. The Aga Khan Trust had just appropriated money for a new 75 acre center city park, as part of the huge effort to modernize Cairo and its roadways. It seemed that every street and bridge was being torn up or torn down, excavated, widened, and reshaped. So were many high-rise office and residential buildings. As a result, the city was as polluted as Bangkok or Shanghai, but with a fraction of the truck and automotive traffic. Some of the disruption related to the beginning of construction on a new metro system.

Cairo is densely populated with around eight million people, the largest city in Africa, and with the highest economic standard in the middle east, with per capita income of about $25 thousand dollars equivalent. Still, by west European and U.S. standards, the city and the country are poor. Mosques are ubiquitous, serving an Sunni Islamic population of over 90%. [5]

Jogging in a three mile radius of the Cairo Hilton drew lots of amused stares from the street laborers, many of whom were wearing masks to guard against pollution. These were the days before apparent Islamic extremists, so I had no real safety concern, although I would have second thoughts today. Anwar Sadat, was killed by extremists, but suicidal terrorists acts were uncommon in 1984, especially in Egypt. Yet, as I write this, in February 2011, Egypt is caught up in violence, with thousands of demonstrators roaming the streets of Cairo succeeded in the removal of Hosni Mubarak as President, after thirty years.

As of 2/11/11, Mubarak has resigned, and the military has claimed control of the government. It seems clear that a Muslim fundamentalist group, the Muslim Brotherhood, will want a stake in any new government. The Muslim Brotherhood is committed to a religious Islamist state, with Sharia law, anathema to the U.S. and the West. Up to now, the group has

---

5. Some historical information and most updated demographic data on cities in Asia and Africa comes from Wikipedia on-line.

been outlawed, and, unless great care is taken, Egypt could evolve into another extremist state in the Middle East, run by Mullahs dedicated to the destruction of the West. Egypt has been our predictable ally in the Middle East, other than Israel.

Our hosts took us to shop in the local Cairo bizarre in the evening. Like major Asian cities, this enormous public street market had booths featuring rugs, foods, appliances, hardware, and gadgets of every description. We sampled local foods, but my main interest was in the swarm of humanity.

On leaving Cairo on TWA airlines the next morning, old friends Ron and Noreen Ronholm and daughter Beth were in the check-in line in front of us. Ron was at the time a TWA captain, taking his family on vacation. Neither of us had any idea that the other was in Cairo, an affirmation that wherever you go, be sure to be on your best behavior, because friends are everywhere and capable of surprise.

BACK IN EUROPE

The rest of Europe was a high-speed sprint to visit customers and Monsanto offices and plants. Frankfurt to Munich, to Salsburg, Paris, Brussels, London, and Northern England to visit Imperial Chemicals Industries, then Italy to visit Montedison. Monsanto in-country people made these trips with us. Mogens Anderson in Germany and France, Ian MacDonald in England, and Belgium. Our country manager invited us to his home in Brussels to taste his variety of red wines, each in its distinctive bottle, then took us to his cellar where he stored red wine in bulk and bottled and corked it himself. All the wines were exactly the same, which surprised one of our party who had graded each wine differently based on his long experience and "expertise".

Paris in June is lively, and I had time to walk and jog alongside the Seine and around Notre Dame cathedral, tour the Louvre, and sample excellent foods and wines. And we met with Rhone Poulanc officials to discuss the worldwide adipic acid and acrylic fibers markets.

The flight to London was aboard a British Air Trident. Bad weather in London led to a fully automated landing in rain and fog, a fact announced after we had safely taxied off the landing strip. A formal dinner in London sponsored by Monsanto found us in rented tuxedos, and an evening to get acquainted with many who would later become good friends. Ian and Silvia MacDonald's son, William, visited us years later at our home in Connecticut, and stayed several days.

In Milan, Ernst Morhenn of Monsanto met and stayed with us during our meeting with Montedison to talk about acrylics and intermediates, our technology which they licensed. I had worked with Ernst in Monsanto International in St. Louis before he was transferred back to Europe. It the last time I would see Ernst alive. He committed suicide a year later.

Outside of Milan, on Lago Maggiore, we were guests in the country estate of one of polymer customers, who were Swiss but with business headquarters in Milan. It was here on the lake that Adrian Brennar, the customer, rolled his pontoon equipped ultra light airplane out of the garage, bolted it together, and took me for a flight all around the lake, allowing me to take the controls once we had treetop altitude. The gossamer winged craft was powered by a snowmobile engine, and had side-by-side plastic bucket seats for pilot and co-pilot. We each wore football helmets in case of a crash.

On to nearby Venice by train as our final stop on this tour, and we were met there by T.Y. Hung and Tony and Michael, who had come from Hong Kong and were interested in working a deal to import Montedison acrylic fiber to China and Taiwan.

The best seafood can be found in Venice, as can some of the world's most unique scenery. Marco Polo was known to have brought home many of China's culinary secrets, and T.Y. recognized China's influences in the excellent foods served us in Venice.

After Venice, we headed back home via the Milan airport, arriving New York early morning to see a fog enshrouded Empire State building visible above the clouds. This concluded my zip trip around the globe, excluding only Russia, Indian, and Eastern Europe. I was anxious to be back home.

In St. Louis, Joan met me at Lindbergh field. The boys were scattered with their friends, so I immediately dealt with the fatigue of jet lag and unpacking, and would see the boys later in the day with an assortment of souvenirs.

The trip was transformative. I had, through business, luck, and mentoring, made the leap from the edge of civilization in rural Texas to the mega-cities of the world and their corporate and international business cultures. Dealing with governments and world-class businesses, representing a fine company with complex products and processes which delivered great value to them, negotiating contracts, analyzing and discussing world market shares and competitive forces on several continents, was a heady experience. A background of diverse assignments helped in these bargaining sessions. I was fortunate to develop friendships which would last for many years, helping me to embrace the people, mores, customs, and foods of many countries and cultures.

Channeled from Flomot and Plainview by circumstances and timing, with the good fortune to be encouraged and mentored by many good people, feeling my way through a series of jobs, selecting from multiple choices the paths which led me to a larger world, I tried to think about what conclusions I could draw.

• I did not have life or career goals in mind at any stage of the journey—just the thought to be as prepared as I could and do the best I could in every assignment given me.

• This value framework was the legacy of my family. Their guidance was "always do your best, be honest, work hard, take pride in your work, and treat your fellow man with respect." These directions have been more important and relevant in my life to date than any ancient writings or commandments.

• Traversing the world of commerce from Amarillo to New York and all the major business and population centers of this country and the world, I have had unique chances to observe diverse societies at work, to associate with some of the most respected and educated business people on the planet, in all major cultures and belief systems.

• I have been fortunate to hopefully understand through these exposures and through readings of history, the human dynamic and basic strivings of civilizations in Asia, Africa, Europe, Latin America, and here at home.

• I have had a chance to look at the lowest rungs of laborers in factories and in mines and on farms and construction projects, in their back-breaking day-after-day grueling and exhausting effort to obtain the basics of life. Having experienced farm labor first hand, I could identify. Having served in the military in a war-ravaged country, I saw poverty and depravity and was able to place these curses in context.

• I have sat with those at the top of society; the top of the food chain, and observed their thinking and work as chief executive officers, owners, investors, directors, Wall streeters, and those in ivory towers of academia who write and teach. I have seen those who live lavishly and think it a right, and perhaps for them it has been earned and is an entitlement.

• I have lived in a time of transformation of much of Africa, Asia, and Eastern Europe, of horrible wars and genocide, of brutal dictatorships, and of the end of colonialism. I have seen the spread of capitalism, with all its inequities, as the only economic system with hope for feeding and clothing and prospering humanity.

• I have come to believe that, over time, all governments become selfish, bloated, corrupted; that each has a life cycle, and that ingrained patronage, privilege and corruption will lead to change, peaceful or violent, but tantamount to revolution in either case. History says that this is so, that governments are dynamic, never static, always in flux, and this includes our own government. Just this very day, Egypt proved this point. And Libya is now in the throes of revolution.

• I have learned to my satisfaction that the majority of the world's people, religious extremists and fanatics excepted, have the same wants and desires, and the same mentality and emotional make-up as citizens of Flomot and Plainview, and that they identify themselves as being close to the same place in the spectrum of humanity.

• I have learned that to this majority, faith belief systems as a comforting force supersede science and reality, often delusional but nonetheless real to them. In hopelessness, survival depends of the idea that somehow, even if it is in the next life, there will be less despair for them and their children. Religion delivers transparently false hope, but it is balm some cling to in the absence of any other.

• In summary, the years and experiences had come together to allow me to "escape" my Flomot and Plainview roots and values, only to discover that the farther away geographically I moved from them, the closer I came to grasping the concept that these roots and values are universally sought and prized.

For now, the pleasure was coming home and being with family, and starting a routine which would be repeated over and over for the next five and one half years

KNOWING ST. LOUIS.

St. Louis is one of the oldest cities in the country, and one of the most ethnically diverse. It began as a French fur-trading center, founded by Pierre Laclede, and still is heavily influenced by its French origins.

At the time of the 1904 world's fair, it was the fourth largest city in the country and a key inland port for the movement of goods to and from the West. Today, at the confluence of the Mississippi and Missouri rivers, the city is less than half its former size due to white flight to the suburbs, but still influential in the country's commerce and home to many large corporations. The metro area is also well known for its fine educational institutions and medical facilities, with Washington University medical school ranked # 5 in the country.

Mark Twain, Scott Joplin, Joseph Pulitzer, Stan Musial, Sheryl Crow, and Yogi Berra all hail from St. Louis. Blues musicians came up the Mississippi from New Orleans at the beginning of the twentieth century to establish the city's reputation in blues music, beer brewers came from Germany, refugees came from all over Europe during the first and second world wars. The St. Louis Cardinals baseball teams, the Rams football team, and St. Louis Blues hockey have built the city's reputation as a center of professional sports.

The city and suburbs boasts fine parks, art museums, cultural centers, an excellent symphony, a world recognized zoo, and a superb botanical garden. St. Louis has 40% of the state's GDP. All things considered, St. Louis is an attractive place to live and raise a family, weather extremes excepted. Its landmark Arch on the west bank of the Mississippi is within the Jefferson Park memorial, and is known as the gateway to the West.

The second half of the 80's saw our family settle in to the St. Louis suburban routine. Scott had finished two years at the University of Colorado in Boulder, and transferred to St. Louis University, working summers at a geo-engineering firm, where he met the lovely Terry Bowers, his future wife.

He graduated pre-law in 89, after which we took our father/son flying golf tour of the west coast and Las Vegas, ten courses in ten days. At Pebble Beach lodge, we bumped into my cousin Ed Garrett and his wife Nancy, and celebrated New Year's eve memorably with them touring various pubs in nearby Monterrey.

Jon was still in Horton Watkins high, but would graduate in 86, give college a try, then elect to take time off in Colorado before deciding his future. In Boulder, he worked in restaurants, and for a year or so toured with a rock band, Roshambo as their sound man. He later worked at a ski resort in Ketstone, worked a summer on long lines fishing boats in Sitka, Alaska, became an entrepreneur in San Diego and Key West. He travelled around the world at the invitation and expense of a Australian woman friend, ending in western Australia, before heading back to the states. His variety of life experiences is worthy of its own book, which he is capable of writing.

We experienced the usual growing pains as our boys matured and experimented with life's temptations, and had several close but injury free encounters with their "trainer" automobiles. Scott rolled a Nissan 280Z into a field and landed upside down, producing an anxious night or two. Jon rear-ended another car after falling asleep while driving back from Cape Girardeau, but was uninjured and detained only one night while law enforcement sorted it out.

Joan was busy doing interior design work for Hal's Interiors in Clayton, and had good success with many clients, most of whom became her friends.

Our house at 7 Conway Lane in Ladue happened to be in a flood zone, so declared because of a small creek behind our property which was clogged with trash and tree limbs, and would quickly overflow during heavy rains. This happened a few times before we installed a new concrete drainage basin at the end of our driveway.

While we were at it, I decided to build a new three car garage, and did so with the guidance and help of a carpenter, Charlie, who I served as helper. Charlie and I erected the sidewall framing and sheathed it with particle board after the foundation had been poured, then I installed the clapboard siding myself on weekends. Jon and I ended up putting shingles on the roof, with Jon doing most of the work because I chickened out on the steep 12 pitch roof.

I learned that 12 pitch means the roof rises 12 feet in a 12 ft. span. This was indeed very steep, but needed because of snow accumulation in St. Louis. A separate horizontal single garage in the rear, with its own entrance. ran across the two stalls in front, and gave us lots of extra storage room.

The previous owners of the house had 10 children. It happened that the sliding door closets in the upstairs hallway were large enough to sleep kids, and those two big closets served as beds for at least two of their children.

There were eleven different levels in the house. The lowest level was therefore hard to heat even with a nice fireplace in that room. But it was nice and cool in Summer. A spiral staircase led from that family room to Jon's large bedroom and bath immediately above it. Trouble was that he did not have much privacy since there was no door at the top of the stairwell.

At the South end of the upper level of the house were three small bedrooms with a step up from bedroom two to bedroom three. I took a sledge hammer to the wall between these rooms and made a two-room suite, then added a bath across the hall. This suite became Scott's private quarters. Out the bathroom door we constructed a wooden porch deck, with a long wooden stairway leading down to the ground. Scott could come and go in privacy, and both boys learned to use this entrance if they came home late at night. The stairs were a little creaky, so we had clues as to when they came home.

I bought a used Honda motorcycle from one of Jon's friends and rode it on weekends. But I never got completely comfortable with it or joined a riding group, and sold it after one season. Jon was into small motorcycle racing on tracks, and soon owned one. We had to haul it on a trailer about 20 miles out of West county to reach a track, but he had many good hours with it until he took a nasty spill and decided to give it up.

Scott, meanwhile, had hockey injuries which required arthroscopic surgery on both knees. A few days on crutches and some rehab, and he was as good as new.

Joan suffered a slipped vertebrae, and underwent a experimental pineapple extract injection in her spine at Barnes Hospital which put her in shock. There were tense moments until the antidote was administered and kicked in and lowered her extreme blood pressure and heart rate spike. She spent several days at home recovering fully, some of it while I was out of town, with her friend Mary Pat from work helping to nurse her back to health.

As a family, we had many good social gatherings with our friends Bruce and Barbara English and Don and Petie McKinley. We met Don and Petie through a neighbor in Connecticut who had been Petie's roommate at Northwestern University. Christmas Eves were spent with our family going to church with Bruce and Barbara and their son Robert and daughter Patricia. Jon and Patricia have remained friends over the ensuing years. She is married with two children and living in Montana.

My work routine became predictable, with one three-week trip each calendar quarter to Asia, or Europe, and occasionally Australia or Africa. The Monsanto campus was just two miles North of our home, and I sometimes walked or biked to work, but this was awkward with a briefcase, and because people I knew kept offering me rides. I continued my jogging program most weekday mornings and took six mile runs on weekends. I joined the JCCA gym for workouts with weights.

On the road, Japan was almost always first stop, followed by Korea, then Taiwan, and ending in Hong Kong, with infrequent side trips to Beijing, Shanghai, Bankok, and Singapore In each country, I worked with country managers or our agent, Cheong-On, to review business progress with key customers, and meet face-to-face with the most important ones.

Hotels came to know me. The Okura or Imperial hotel in Tokyo, a Ryokan in Kyoto or Osaka, the Lotte or Hyatt in Seoul, the Sheraton or Hyatt in Taipei, and the Regent or Grand Hyatt in Hong Kong. After the initial visits in 84, little time was spent sight-seeing, but golf played an important role in customer relations, particularly in Japan and Korea. The Japanese trading companies, Mitsui, Mitsubishi, and Itochu invariably had pre-arranged outings at some excellent course in the Mt. Fuji area, a full day outing including dinner and gifts. Escalators carried golfers up steep inclines to the higher tee boxes, a feature unique in golf course design.

Korea was always a homecoming with K. Choi, T.Y.Hung, Michael and Tony Hung, as well as J.K.Kim and D.S. Kim of Monsanto Korea. Time there was productive and enjoyable. The spirit of friendship , cordiality, and individuality among Koreans brought a lot of pleasure to these visits, abetted occasionally by a brief trip to again visit the new AFKN radio and TV facilities, where I had served on active duty in the middle 50's.

The same was true of Taiwan customers and friends who welcomed me each time, even though our negotiations were sometimes intense. That was expected.

Hong Kong and the Regent hotel was the usual last stop and port of departure for the trip back home, with non-stop flights of 14 hours the standard, but far better than an intermediate stopover. Cathay Pacific was my favorite airline for the region, but Korean Air and Japan Air were also excellent. United was adequate but I ranked it fourth. On one flight over the Pacific, a young JAL flight attendant woke me in the middle of the night to view Haley's comet in the sky to our left, clearly more visible from 38 thousand ft. than from the surface.

Each trip involved adjusting to the 10-12 hour time change, easy on the outgoing leg but impossible to conquer when coming back home. I found that a full two weeks were needed to begin to feel normal and productive again, and family and office staff learned to tolerate me with kindness during these periods. Watching television and reading in the middle of the night for a few hours, was the dreaded penalty for three weeks away on the other side of the world, with clock's upside down.

On a pleasure trip abroad, adjustment is relatively easier because the concentration required and day and night schedule can be individual choice. Business meetings involving many people cannot be postponed on a whim, whether in the region or back in home office. I learned to just buck up and bear it, but not without chagrin.

In between, there were quick trips to Europe, two from New York to Paris and back on the now grounded Concorde supersonic craft. The three-hour flight across the Atlantic to Paris was cramped but quick, and at an altitude of 60 thousand feet, there is no discernable landscape below, and only darkness above. The Concorde was abandoned after a fatal crash on take-off from Paris, and poor economic performance because of high ticket prices and limited capacity. Passenger seating only accommodated about 100 people, smaller than a medium range jet in the states.

Side trips to London, Milan, Frankfurt, and down to Capetown, South Africa would follow once a year. From Milan, I elected to spend a layover weekend in Rome, and stayed at a hotel at the top of the Spanish steps, touring Roman ruins and the Vatican and other sights during the days. It was late September and hurricane season in the states. Our house in Old Greenwich, then rented, was in the path of one approaching New York, and I spent an hour one day talking to Lee and Verne Westerberg on Lucas Point about hurricane preparations. Fortunately, there was no damage.

On the trip from Johannesburg to Capetown on South African Airways, I was invited to sit in the cockpit with the British crew, and they answered my questions about African history as we looked down at various regions of the country.

Mixed in with international travel was domestic travel to attend task-force meetings or meet customers in New York, or the plants in the South, or in California. Chairman Kim and his wife from Kukje, our big acrylic customer, chose to vacation in California one year. His staff made all arrangements, including golf. With my special Hyatt green courtesy card, I reserved a private bungalow for the Chairman and Mrs. Kim at the Grand Hyatt in Indian Wells, and Bruce and Barbara English and Joan and I flew to Palm Springs to host them for a weekend. We dined at excellent restaurants and played the championship Indian Wells golf courses. They were impressed, but no more so than we had been with Kukje's hosting of us when visiting Korea.

One of Chairman Kim's key executives, President Lee, had a daughter at Harvard, and Chairman Kim's own daughters were on schedule to attend Universities in the States. Like China and India, Korea's national examination system rewards only the hardest working and brightest students with entry to university, which explains why Asian parents push their children so hard to make excellent grades in science and math.

Asian parents, especially Chinese and Korean, are not afraid of damaging their children's self-esteem in insisting on straight A academic records. The students are drilled for hours on end until they completely master the lesson at hand, unlike American parents who often let their children slide by. There is no restriction on who goes to college, the differentiation being just which colleges will admit students with mediocre records.

A tragedy of our educational system is that every student, regardless of ability, is led to believe that four years of college are the only route to success and a happy working life. Even Harvard University now states that many if not most students should not attend traditional college, but enter specialized occupational training right out of high school. Why the U.S. has taken so long to come to this realization is a mystery and an indictment.

Industrialist Andrew Carnegie had contempt for college as life preparation, saying, "While the college student has been learning a little about the barbarous and petty squabbles of a far-distant past, or trying to master languages which are dead, the future captain of industry is hotly engaged in the school of experience, obtaining the very knowledge required for his future triumphs."[6] This argues for a return of the apprenticeship system as a means of integrating young people into society in respected trades.

A MASTERS AT WASHINGTON UNIVERSITY

I decided to enroll in Washington University graduate school of business to earn a Masters degree in International studies. Classes were mostly nights and weekends, and were rigorous in their requirements for research papers and testing. I had last been enrolled in a regular curriculum in 1955, but had a more recent exposure at Harvard Business school. The Profs were seasoned international pros, teaching sociology, law, foreign language, history, contracts, government structures, and business cultures around the world. Most instructors held doctorates. Faculty for International Affairs was drawn from across

6. Wall Street Journal, February 11, 2011, p. D-9.

various specialties in the Graduate school. Blue book testing within time constraints was standard with every course.

I was able to do some first hand research as a part of my travels, and ended the program writing my thesis on the " Economic, Political, and Cultural future of Koreans in Manchuria and Shenyang, China". The thesis had to be reviewed by an academic board of the Graduate school, then defended in front of the committee.

The ethnic Koreans had been stranded in Manchuria by the defeat of the Japanese, and the division of Korea at the end of world war two. They could not return to North or South Korea, and constituted a large and growing foreign labor force in Shenyang, basically forming their own city. Tapping this Korean speaking labor pool in Shenyang was the motivation for Chairman Kim locating his spinning plant there.

A degree requirement was completion of a year of foreign language. I chose Japanese, having already had three years of one-on-one Spanish tutoring in my office. We learned Japanese language structure, vocabulary, pronunciation, prefixes and suffixes and aspects of culture imbedded in language. Tests were oral and written, involving translations from English to Japanese and back, and conversations with the Japanese instructor and with classmates.

Clora, my secretary, volunteered to type my papers without complaint, each of which ran 15 to 25 pages, with footnotes and references, and the thesis, which scaled over 100 pages. Over the two years, plus thesis prep, Clora typed and proofed some 50 of these documents.

Washington University has high standards for graduate work (and undergraduate). I remember coasting through undergrad at West Texas A&M some 35 years earlier, but this was a different time with much higher expectations from the faculty, and the fact that I was in my fifties and older than many tenured faculty meant nothing to them. A's and B's were acceptable, nothing less. Like a Chinese mother breathing down my neck, I knew it had to be done right. I remain very proud of my MA in International Affairs, which helped me land a couple of seats on Boards of Directors later on.

LOSS OF DAD

My parents came to visit from Texas, their first trip East since their visit to Connecticut, long ago, and one trip to Atlanta when we lived there. They spent several days with us in 1987, driving themselves from Texas and back. None of us realized at the time that Dad was in rapidly declining health. He seemed to enjoy himself, as did Mom. In early March 1988, my Dad suffered a lethal stoke in their living room at home, and never regained consciousness. I will forever remember getting the call from my brother Raby. We were next door at the Hellmuth's for a social hour, and one of the boys came to get me. Dad was 82.

Joan and I and the boys (now men), drove two cars to Texas to his funeral, and stayed a couple of days with family. My mother was surrounded by my siblings, so we knew she would be OK. We left on the third day and the family dropped me at the Tulsa, Oklahoma airport, where I took a plane to our plant in Alabama for a task force meeting. It was the end of an era for the Garrett clan, and left a void in the family which remains to this day. My mother lived on for another 17 years, to age 99, where she died in the Prairie House nursing home in Plainview, surrounded by her children and grandchildren.

Our time in St. Louis was filled with hard work, the growing up of our children, family skiing vacations with the English's and McKinley's, a number of trips to Texas for reunions, business travel, and lots of fun dinner and parties with old friends.

I joined a golf club in 1985, and the clubhouse burned on the day

I was accepted by the admissions committee. A new clubhouse involved assessing the members, and it was built but was not completed until our last full year in St. Louis, which was 1989. My oldest brother Cal flew to St. Louis twice to play as my guest in the club annual member/guest tournament. We had a great time together but didn't win anything, and I treasure these memories with my older brother. Cal was the retired golf professional at Hereford at the time.

Jimmy Dean came to town on business and visited us at the house for dinner with friends the English's and McKinley's. We stayed up late, he played the piano and sang, and we laughed until the wee hours. It was this evening when he opened the subject of me becoming president of his sausage company, but I knew booze was doing some talking. In any event, I could not consider it because it would have meant taking sides against his brother Don, who was a good friend. We didn't discuss it again.

Our sweet and loyal dog Chumley, age 17, finally gave in to old age. Ladue did not have a leash law and she was free to go outside by herself, which she needed to do often because of incontinence. The humane thing would have been for us to put her down, but none of us could bring ourselves to seriously consider it, especially Scott and Jon. The boys found her by the side of the road in front of our house, unmarked, but presumably brushed by a car. I was out of town at the time, but Joan and the boys clearly had a traumatic experience picking her up and delivering her to the vet.

Chumley had been a mainstay in our family since the boys were very little. The tiny boys she had brought joy to were now gone forever, a sadness Joan and I still feel, but Chumley represented continuity and a link back to those times which are the most precious for parents. Today, 22 years later, Chumley is still vivid in our memories. We speak about her with love, remember her as a new puppy, picture our boys holding and loving her as they sat on the rope swing in our backyard. Chumley will always be with us, and them, no matter how many other pets might follow.

By this time, I was beginning to feel burn-out on the job, from travel and repetition. Age, I knew realistically, blocked further steps up the hierarchy. Human resource facts of life, and my own experience supervising significant numbers of people with the guidance of personnel planning specialists, told me that step-ups within the senior management ranks are rare at age 55 or older, a plateau I had reached in 1988.

Younger managers with high potential were beginning to infuse the organization, and they rightfully deserved shots at the key positions. Older managers may hang on and mentor and play important roles, but are unlikely to progress higher. Big public corporations, unlike small businesses, plan exhaustively for succession, and regular reviews of personnel to select the next generation of leadership is a big part of the responsibility of Boards of Directors.

I consulted with Joan and made a decision to give my one-year notice of retirement on April 1, 1989. A one-year notice was required in order to be eligible to collect a lump sum pension payment, discounted to present value, upon retirement. I figured the lump sum, invested, would allow me to control our destiny far better than monthly payments over my remaining life expectancy. Monsanto accepted my plan, and began thinking in terms of organization to replace me effective April 1, 1990.

Meanwhile, I continued performing the job, travelling to the usual places, waiting for change when it occurred. That never happened.

Two months before my retirement date, Earl Brasfield asked me to continue heading the International effort of the Division, but as an independent contractor. They simply had no replacement who knew the business well enough to step in and take over. I agreed to a three-year contract with full expenses and higher income (since I would no longer receive fringe benefits except medical), and with the provision that I could perform the assignment out of my office in Connecticut. Brasfield agreed, and the deal was on. I also had the latitude to take outside clients provided there was no conflict of interest with Monsanto's business. It was a dream contract, from my point of view.

Joan has drawn detailed plans for remodeling our house in Old Greenwich, and had actually moved back to the house in the Fall of 89 to supervise the work with our contractor. Our house at 7 Conway Lane was sold on favorable terms, and I rented a bedroom and kitchenette from a widow lady nearby, living there for several months before my retirement date kicked in. Her now dead husband had spent the last months of his life in an adjustable hospital bed, which became the bed in my rented room. The realization kicked in that you don't have to be sick to enjoy the push-button flexibility offered by a hospital bed. Changing the configuration of the bed, at will, in the middle of a sleepless night, can work wonders. The arrangement could not have worked out better.

I flew down to Connecticut on some weekends to see work in progress. Bill Cameron and his crew took out walls, installed a completely new kitchen, put in air conditioning ducts and a new gas furnace. We installed a new stairwell from the living room to upstairs, recessed lighting, a fantastic new master bath with marble floors and counter tops and Jacuzzi tub and new marbled shower.

I installed an office at the top of the stairs in an 8 x 12 space which was adequate for desk, computer, fax, printer, storage, and telephones, and, yes, my framed academic diplomas. A second phone line was installed for business, listed as WORLDLINK Ltd., the name of my new S Corporation. At the time, there was still no internet and international business was still done with dark ages technology of fax, telex, mail, and international calling, with broken connections. The Internet would soon revolutionize and increase productivity of international businesses in a big way.

Joan's color scheme was perfect, and the furniture we had accumulated in St. Louis through her design shop was all with an eye to eventually taking it back to our Connecticut house. We put new shingle siding on the house and installed larger triple pane casement windows throughout. A wall was opened connecting the master bedroom to a large sitting and entertainment room, and leaving enough space for a larger dining room. All hardwood floors were refinished to a natural varnished state. In all, we invested some $400 thousand dollars in the remodel, not counting a new two car garage and new enlarged deck and elaborate landscaping and fencing which came a little later.

Joan created the showplace of the neighborhood at the time, although later new buyers in Lucas Point began tearing down older homes and building mega-mansions far more expensively appointed and spacious than ours. While supervising the remodel, Joan slept upstairs on a rented rollaway bed but had only a working shower and toilet there. She had to use the kitchen sink in the early mornings to brush her teeth, and be out of the way before contractors arrived for the day's work. During this period of several months, she made only one trip back to St. Louis, and stayed with me in my rented room, sleeping on a fold out cot smaller than a twin bed.

We were so excited about the new look of the house and the move back East that we overlooked any inconvenience the move might have caused. It was a time of renewal and start of a new chapter in our lives.

Customers and agents and country entities were notified of the new arrangement between Monsanto and me, without a ripple. Surprisingly, and very happily, inquiries started coming at me from a number of directions and countries about whether I would consider consulting arrangements with them, independent of Monsanto. I was elated with this response, and formed TRADELINK LTD. to accommodate new clients and contracts. I hired an accounting firm in Westport, and an attorney in Greenwich to draw up the papers of incorporation, registered the S Corp with the state of Connecticut, and began gathering up new business.

HOT BUTTON: POLITICS AND THE ELECTORAL PROCESS

T he treatise below is ethereal and so surreal it is humorous, but should it be? There are three curable maladies which are defying common sense while putting our form of representative democracy on a clear downward slope. I have no illusions that politicians will move to cure them voluntarily, and am not naïve enough to think that our constitution can be amended quickly enough to avoid calamity. But I do believe that most thinking citizens would agree that, absent reforms, the current system is terminally ill. Thinking hopefully and wishfully, the major issues are:

- The absence of strict term limits.
- The acceptance of donations from special interests lobbies
- The corrosive effects of the existing prolonged electoral process.

1. Citizen legislators who serve the public interest altruistically, and then return to their civilian status outside of government, ala George Washington, are rare. Gaining and holding power at any state or federal level becomes the goal. Elected officials convince themselves that they are indispensable, that they must be returned to power to provide continuity; to see their pet programs through to fruition; to provide security for the sycophants surrounding them, or to further the larger ideological causes of their party.

As these views take hold, politicians immediately become compromised and morally corruptible, precisely because they must make commitments and promises to myriad interests in order to be reelected, or even nominated by party machinery.

2. Seeking to sway power, special interests of left, right, or center spectrum push, with money, quid pro quo arrangements, pledging their support to candidates who pledge them their votes. The legislator rationalizes this as simply a part of give and take democracy, necessary to serve his larger purpose, as a trade-off essential to his use of his power for the "common good."

In these two insidious steps, taken over time, he has explicitly corrupted himself and the process. He cannot be objective on any issue, but must place each within the spectrum of promises made to his benefactors. Altruism has left the scene at this point. The general public interest, and even the interests of his particular district, have become subordinated.[7]

3. Having built the campaign war chest with special interest payments, he or she must now immediately begin building his specific media brand, claiming dubious accomplishments , developing rationales and arguments in support of the narrow themes he has pledged to his sponsors to represent. The process is expensive and exhausting, and corrupts completely during a two-year phony populist circus leading to actual party nominations and elections.

A current example is the announcement by the Obama reelection team that One billion dollars will be needed, over a two-year span of dispensing propaganda and hyperbole at media staged "campaign" stops tailor-made for TV sound bites. These events are insulting to the electorate and a waste of the country's resources, void of virtue and full of vice.

In return for pledges of money necessary to run the media and travel and staff machinery, he or she promises entitlements, amnesty, roads, bridges, medical care, retirement benefits, higher union wages, populist rhetoric blaming the rich, or Wall street, resistance to free trade, and special benefits to "minority" ethnicities, using all the demagogic messages his tax-paid speechwriters can conjure, and, if implemented, add enormously to the already ruinous national debt.

The repetitious and empty populist evangelical rhetoric coming

7. The movie, Casino Jack, while overdrawn for story purposes, accurately depicts Washington corruption of legislators, fed large sums of money by lobbyists for special interests. The Jack Abramoff story is real and on-going.

from all forms of traditional and new internet media, will be eulogized by the ad hungry print and broadcast world, while driving the electorate wild with boredom and disbelief. And it is consciously designed to be vague and obfuscating, not educating and enlightening.

Candidates seeking new terms in office have signed on to the adage that "politicians will never go wrong underestimating the intelligence of their audiences."

The corruption deepens, and power has corrupted to the point that the candidate cannot even remember altruism, but thinks only of demographics, polls, ethnicities, welfare and unemployment benefits recipients, soliciting donations from unions, leveraging one group or the other for more funds. The process comes full circle, with the powerful thinking of themselves increasingly as invincible, reinforced by the adoration of minions who live in the shadows of power. The Axelrod's and strategy and media consultants and pollsters will enrich themselves as they sell their souls, but that assumes they started the process with souls.

Our constitution enshrines free speech, but does it enshrine transparently corrupting and false populism which brings harm to the republic as surely as shouting fire in a crowded theatre brings harm?

Is free speech that is made possible only by corrupting monetary contributions, made with the intention of buying specific votes on specific issues, to be encouraged under the first amendment, if the amendment is interpreted in this light? Is prolonged false speech, paid for with the loss of integrity and respect for the electoral process, and by gullible contributors and cynical and calculating self-seekers, to be given an open field without limits in a society which says it wants honesty and morality and ethics from its representatives?

In the context of honest and meaningful elections, is all of this really an abuse of free speech? Common sense and a long-term interest in upholding the values of the republic, say that it is, and should and, in fact, be corrected.

Governments, including our own, have life cycles. All fail over time because they overextend and lose the support and respect of the governed. Colonial powers, dictatorships, imperial dynasties, kingships, democracies, all are dynamic with traceable life spans throughout history. Ours is no exception, and many now believe that our own inactions in controlling corrupted spending have put us well along the downside of the cycle. Eventually, actions will be taken, peaceful or violent, to purge corruption and modify government institutions to restore integrity.

Enlightened free speech and media should have the effect of educating and encouraging peaceful reforms, and preventing collapse, but rigidity in reading the founding documents, together with rampant excesses and blatant opportunism of those in power, make overdue reform very unlikely.

These reforms, among others, could be:

• Strict terms limits for both houses of congress, perhaps six years and out, with no chance of future election to the same legislative branch. No retirement or other fringe benefits accrue to the representative during his tenure or as a result of his tenure. Term limited representatives and their families prevented from serving as lobbyists for a period of ten years after their term has ended.

• Strict prohibition on acceptance of any funds, favors, meals, transportation, tips, or gifts from any group or individual, and no advance commitment to any group or individual. This restriction would apply to immediate and extended family.

• One national primary, with a one-month campaign time limit, strictly enforced. One national election day, with a one-month campaign time limit, strictly enforced. Domestic campaigning only, with ads vetted by a non-political jury.

• Elections paid for from the general federal fund, strictly limited and audited, with no closed campaign rallies, no promises to constituents, no meaningless debates with media moderators. No "packing" of campaign events; no exit or publicly announced results of polling; no push polling; no surrogates and consultants espousing talking points for candidate views during the black-out periods.

- In effect, a "lock-down" two month sterile period, void of pundits and purged of transparent nonsense, would encourage truth and enlightenment from the candidates on issues, and restore belief to the now fragile system.

- Each campaign event begin with a disclaimer that all government programs discussed will be carried out within budgeted limits, without undermining the financial integrity of the country, and breaching this pledge, short of all out declared war, will lead to automatic impeachment and removal.

- Until neuroimaging can tell us in real time whether a politician is lying(the presumption is always), each political ad might be preceded by the disclaimer, "What you are about to see has not been vetted for truth, reason, or sanity." And the ad should be followed by, "Possible negative side effects could include false promises of new entitlements, higher taxes and national indebtedness, questionable statements about global warming, and platitudes promising health care for all at no cost."

- A constitutional convention, called by 35 state governors, could ask for ratification of an amendment specifically to allow for conducting elections in the manner specified. The convention could codify and ask for ratification of amendments modifying Federal and state governments powers, change the make-up of congress in light of modern communications obviating arcane and outdated structures. Do we really need this number of royalty in the house of representatives, and all these demi-gods in the Senate, when we have the internet, Skype, and tools of modern communication which allow the taking of each voters views on every issue in one millisecond? We have a horse and buggy set-up in congress, and the bodies behave exactly that way. Secure vetting and electronic voting, from the comfort of home, could reflect the will of the people far more accurately, and save the country hundreds of billions of dollars.

These changes, or changes like them, will be necessary to rescue us from our current down cycle, and preserve the republic as we know it. Of course, nobody believes that these things could actually happen, given our current view of the religious sanctity of the first amendment, but even rank and file general public see that these things must happen in order to avoid the tragedy of government suicide.

Of course, all these steps are wishful thinking! They could never actually happen in real life! Our electorate is not smart enough to see the advantages and insist that they be made reality!. Or is it?

REFLECTIONS ON 60 YEARS OF HUMAN INTERACTION

Morality, ethics, and belief systems develop not from the God of Abraham, who did not imagine a world without slavery, but from the growth of awareness through a lifetime of interaction, of the vulnerability of all humans, and of the consequent desire to do them no harm.[8]

Societies know instinctively that babies need to be held and rocked and soothed by human touch. But so do adults, and for all their lives. Innate insecurities inborn in all humans, with the possible exception of psychopaths, need touch and kindness, and caressing and warmth, and they never outgrow these needs.

But these realizations are taught to new generations with great

8: Sam Harris, in his new book, The Moral Landscape, makes the case that values of morality and ethics could not possible come from the Old or New Testaments, because of their numerous contradictions and inconsistencies, including mass genocides.

difficulty. This wisdom is not received from elders, but accumulates from becoming wise elders ourselves, honed by insights gained from many individual and group relationships. Inexperienced youth, acting out as surrogates for testosterone and genome directives, inadvertently do unkind, emotionally harmful deeds in the course of their interactions with the opposite or same sexes. That these wounds have been inflicted may become apparent only with the passage of time and understanding.

But the irony of youth is that it needs to be lived raucously, irreverently, loudly, and without somebody else's boundaries. Youth is too inexperienced to really appreciate regret. It needs singing and high kicking, and running hard, and bouncing off all walls, and trying everything that is legal, and maybe some things that are borderline, all the while keeping the left-brain engaged in achieving balance and focus in academic and social matters for the sake of the future. Have fun, but don't lose sight of bedrock responsibility to yourself and others while having your fling.

Too heavy a conscience weighs youth down; too much dogma impedes its development; too much restraint brought by convention slows the learning process. The point is to get in the arena and butt heads, play or get off the field, get back up when hit hard, whether in romance or in sport, in friendships or on the job.

This is the time the individual relearns age-old truths and defines himself and his own ethics and morality, through error and over-correction, another error and another course correction, building his own dogma through time. Like laying down a field of fire, many rounds are required to zero in on the target and get things right. Youth takes practice to learn to stay away from sharp elbows and hairpin turns and dangerous associations and wild horses, all metaphors for addictions, dishonesty, and anti-social outcomes.

My own youth and those of my contemporaries was no exception. Part of the passage is doing and doing over again, getting kicked and knocked down, being coached by people who care, and getting up again and attacking. Psychiatrist Carl Jung , in recognizing distinct phases of life, was quoted as saying ,"We cannot live the afternoon of life according to the program of the morning, for what was great in the morning will be little at evening, and what in the morning was true will in the evening have become a lie." Certainly, the program of youth is more vividly understood to be unique and exploratory, as age steepens wisdom.

As a young single man, on my own, I knew quite a few women, and dated some of them. These relationships were light-hearted, fun, and mostly innocent. We laughed, partied, danced, and enjoyed each other's company until we parted, mostly amicably, but sometimes with a tinge of sadness, or the realization that our personalities were not a match. We bounced off each other and moved on, each taking something from the experience.

Looking back on that period of life as an adventure in maturing and learning, our conduct was not always exemplary nor our impulses pure, and our words or deeds did not always meet standards of respect or right and wrong. Put another way, we made mistakes which limited experience prevented us from articulating at the time, but which, some years after the facts, can be clearly identified as insensitive and harmful.

In the course of living and laughing and striving, I have disappointed many, including myself; made some laugh, caused some anxiety and brought some pleasure, and made and lost friendships, while testing boundaries and building my arsenal of knowledge about how life might be lived better. I was fortunate to be young when nicotine became my only addiction, when hard drugs were not a part of the scene, when boot-legged alcohol was available at parties but not generally elsewhere.

Those who drank excessively drugged their senses and interrupted their learning and maturing. In college, I worked in radio and TV, and the requirement of constant sobriety kept me away from heavy involvement with booze. But for these restraints, I most certainly would have become part of the herd and overindulged in everything available.

I quit smoking the day the U.S. Surgeon General announced it to be harmful, and have heard that experts name it as the most addictive drug. My experience with smoking nightmares over five years bears this out, but I never smoked again.

In youth, as in parenting, there is no perfect decision or outcome, and prolonged guilt is a wasted emotion when compared to the resolve to do better in the future. Keep trying to get it right even if not always successful.

In delicate situations involving feelings and potential resentment, I have often come up short due to simple abject ignorance of youth. An example is a promotion I got in late 1969, which overnight pushed me two rungs up the hierarchy, over the level that one day before had been my organizational superiors. I no doubt felt empowered by the sudden recognition and advancement, and had the urge to immediately take charge; to assert new ideas and programs; to establish myself as the new boss on a mission.

What I badly needed was a wiser head to counsel me to talk one-on-one with each of my new reports, soliciting their support, understanding their feelings at being passed-over, assuring them of the value of their counsel and emotional support, expressing my appreciation of them, and pledging to do my best for each of them.

Instead, I came across as hardened, ambitious, even as someone to be feared. Such lessons are clear in the rear view mirror, and I was embarrassed to have handled the opportunity inappropriately and narcissistically. Over time, I repaired some of the damage, but the damage was needlessly self-inflicted. The moment was gone, and could not be retracted. I thought I would never make the same error again. As always, one error is not a lesson learned.

In Atlanta, as a new Business Group Director, I wanted to know every issue with every customer, and there were many of them. I asked to be copied with every sales and technical service call report, and each night went home with an inch thick notebook to study the notes of fifty people. I scribbled questions and suggestions, even instructions on a great many reports, and they were sent back to the writers each morning.

Before long, my reputation as a micro-manager was being well earned, second-guessing staff with long experience. An older head took me aside and squared things up with me. He said I should back off and trust the organization or change it, but stop looking over everybody's shoulder every day. He suggested I ask for reports on the intractable issues of greatest importance which actually required my attention to help resolve, otherwise, let the men and women do their jobs, and show my respect. What a great friend this man turned out to be! In fact, without this advice his advice, I would never have had my next promotion.

Travelling abroad through the years, my thoughts on my relationships with Joan and Scott and Jon sometimes bordered on regret or sadness. I might be 10 thousand miles from home, alone in my hotel, and think suddenly of the inattention I had shown them, needing to talk with them and to hear their voices. I felt the need at these times to have been a better listener to their concerns, to have been a better counselor, to have simply been present when they needed me.

But guilt and regret serves no purpose in the end except to say, "Be better every time you have the chance. Live so there are no regrets. Be there for your children." And remember Bob Sparacino's words to me from long ago, when he was dying. He said this, "Try never to refuse your children." The living need not wait for such a threat to receive and practice this wisdom.

One last example of a lesson learned from real life which could never have come from a textbook. As a young man fresh out of the army, and in

TV time sales, I was asked by Don Curphey of the First National Bank's ad agency in Amarillo, to be the on-air talent for the bank's TV commercials. But the elephant in the room was the fact that Bob "Pappy" Watson, station manager and my long time mentor, had been doing the bank's commercials for years, inside the nightly news. But the bank wanted a change and the change involved a fresh face….me.!

In a typically youthful act of gross stupidity, I went to Pappy's office and announced this fact to him as if it were business as usual, as if it were some routine to be expected, with no emotional component to my actions. This gentleman had done me many kindnesses, and in that moment, he had to wonder about his investment in me and about my character.

He took the news stoically, but I immediately knew my mistake and apologized and made embarrassing excuses. A brash, rude, green kid had come into his office and demeaned him. How could I have been so out of tune with reality? Why didn't I recognize the pitfalls, and leave the job to Curphey or wiser heads. My irrationality was that Pappy would want to hear it from me. Wrong again!!

Bob Watson and I remained friends, but only because of his magnanimity in rising above my bad manners. He and his wife, Dixie, coached and touted me whenever they could, and continued to help mold my character. This episode was part of learning the hard way that every human being needs to be held and touched, and treasured.

Part of being hugged and rocked and cradled is knowing that your voice is heard. Listening intently to someone, acknowledging but not judging or countering, asking for more information, honestly trying to absorb what is being said, is perhaps the most prized social trait anyone can perfect. Really listening to and hearing someone is exactly the same as soothing and touching that person, treasuring them as human. Subordinate yourself in favor of listening to others, and your value will go up in any social setting. My good friend John Roughan is just such a listener, and I learned much observing him.

Each of us is a tiny pile of cells making a small island in a sea of humanity. Each of us is vulnerable to disease, violence, and accidents. One simple puncture could be the end of us. Is it any wonder that our survival is contingent on approval, touch, and reaffirmation, consciously or unconsciously?

Extrapolating experiences, I see that almost every person I meet is smarter than me in some ways. He or she may have better developed brain cells for calculus, or physics, or anatomy, comprehending this subject or that. On the other hand, I have concluded that I may be smarter in other areas such as linguistic ability, music, or social comprehension.

The rudimentary lesson is that each person is unique and valuable, and that each carries useful information and perspectives. A current friend and I share great conversations on many subjects. He is an avowed socialist to my right of center conservatism. We learn much from each other.

There are geniuses to be appreciated, for sure, but genius is almost always focused narrowly, and the genius, if his mind will allow him, can learn from every other human. It is not necessary to think of one's self as being superior or inferior to any other human, only to think of yourself and that other human as "unique", with differences to be treasured. .

OBSERVATIONS ON RACE

A perfect conundrum is what we say about race in our country, versus what we actually do about race on a daily basis. We say that "human race", without distinctions of color, is what we want. We want to be judged on the content of our character rather then the colors of our skins. We attack anyone who invokes race in public comments, even inferentially, as racist himself, and shame that person until he apologizes publicly. The invocation of race within the context of the civil rights movement of the 50's and Dr. Martin Luther King, is understandable, but as a country we now have laws and attitudes repelling those biases,.... unless we refuse to let them go. And we do refuse to let them go, for very selfish reasons.

Today's reality on the ground is that we live with self-inflicted apartheid, made more prominent and divisive everyday by all forms of media, government actions, political tracking, demographic groupings, and allocations of taxpayer funds. We track and report the racial composition of our Supreme court, our congress, sports teams, in specialty magazines, in neighborhoods, in our news analysis, in our TV shows, and in our motion pictures. We allocate special places and exceptions for "people of color". We breach our own values and pronouncements while hypocritically insisting that we don't.

The United States census wants to know your exact race, even if you are multiracial and uncertain, the number of children you have, your income , your education, your employment, your street address, whether you own or rent, and your social security number. Our own census is far more intrusive than social networking sites like Facebook or My Space, which we correctly accuse of invading and violating our privacy.

The federal department of education is adamant in its search to know the "race" of each student or potential student. College admissions boards insist of knowing the "race" of each applicant.

Sportscasters identify the rise of "black" quarterbacks in the NFL, or at the college level. Examples are Cam Newton of Auburn, and Michael Vick of the Philadelphia Eagles. Do we need to know that Vick deserves a second chance because his is black, or that Newton is the "black" winner of the Heisman?

Is it important for media consultants to shout that "blacks will always support Obama", because he is black? Support based on race undermines every precept of true choice in a government structured as an educated democracy.

Do we need to know the racial make-up of the Supreme Court, as we are reminded daily? Do we not think that the Congressional Black Caucus actually makes us more aware of the color differences between us? Does the NAACP erase the color line by hawking an overtly racist agenda? Would a white counterpart organization ever be tolerated? Profiting from race baiting is apparently lucrative, as at least two black racial activists have proven. My personal role model in a rainbow world is Condelezza Rice, who lives the example to strive for in achieving high status without any reference to color or race-based excuses.

There are dozens of ethnically focused magazines and TV shows. Hispanic versions and black versions openly promote and track successes within these communities, not simply translating into Spanish or other languages, but being cheerleaders for these ethnic groups, while continuing to emphasize their separation from a common culture and color blind society.

Rap music and Ebonics are just fine culturally, but why is it necessary to take the next step and identify them as black? Are violinists identified as white or Asian? Are musicians just music-makers, or are they black musicians? Why would any thinking society seeking racial harmony choose to institutionalize "African-American", when 98% of blacks in the U.S. have no blood connection with Africa greater than any descendant of Noah, if you believe in Noah? Archeologists, geneticists, sociologists, anthropologists, neurologists tell us we all came from Africa originally, so what's the big deal.

Blacks in this country have had no direct connection to Africa in perhaps a dozen generations. Like most Americans, they were born in Savannah, Detroit, New York, Chicago, Los Angeles, Dallas, Indianapolis, Charlotte, many into segregation and ghettos, but does that make them

"African? Are whites known daily as "Anglo-Americans", or European-Americans", or "Swedish-Americans"? What is the benefit is linking any of us to some remote continental genetic ancestry when we no longer have any need for such linkage. Why can't we be "human Americans?"

We persist in retaining racism as a definition of tribe because that is how human beings learn. Collecting data and sorting and categorizing information, and making judgments about such data, is a huge industry in this country, precisely because it has a large constituency. We slice and dice the data and hire demographers, and pollsters, and sociologists to tell us how these groups and sub-groups think and act, and in so doing, continue the divide of color separation that we hear in our national dialogue every day, while saying that we don't really want to hear it.

We live a total contradiction, refusing to adopt "human" as an adequate term for who we are as a race. Until we do; until this becomes a national theme of goodness, until we stop counting and grouping people by color, until we stop eulogizing "black" or "white" or "Asian" accomplishments or defeats, we and the world will remain racist and hypocritical, with self-inflicted wounds. The conundrum lives on!!

BOOK EIGHT
Connecticut And New/Old Beginnings

CONNECTICUT AND SELF-EMPLOYMENT

In her book, Silent Spring, marine biologist Rachael Carson describes the changing face of the sea in Spring. As on land, Spring is a time for renewal of life in the sea, with deep warm waters rising to the surface with a rich supply of minerals ready for use by new forms of life. Salmon and Shad return from the open sea to their birthplaces to begin the cycle of life once again.[9]

This metaphor accurately describes our return to the headwaters of Greenwich Cove, to our home on Lucas Point, surrounded by the sea, to begin our new life in our newly modernized home, with feelings of hope and optimism for good things ahead. Joan had supervised the entire beautification job with outstanding results, and directed the movers on

9. Silent Spring became the environmentalist's screed against pesticides, and DDT in particular. DDT was subsequently banned, resulting in the deaths of millions of people around the world from mosquito-borne malaria.

placement of the furniture, while I wound up my Monsanto career with a couple of goodbye events with my coworkers in St. Louis . Scott was in law school, while Jon elected to come home from Colorado and try Greenwich living.

From a business viewpoint, New York was optimal. All the Japanese trading companies U.S. headquarters were in New York, and meetings with them involved only an hour's commute into the city. Koga and Yabuta at Mitsubishi, Haruke at Itochu, were regular lunches, as were key people from Mitsui and Marubeni. I had soon negotiated consulting contracts with three of these companies of two years each, open to renewal and extension. These related to market intelligence, chemical and fiber sourcing, and possible M and A candidates.

My primary responsibilities to Monsanto took me to St. Louis often, where I reported to Bruce English for acrylics, John Hunter for nylon products, and Graham Wildsmith for chemical intermediates. My international travel pattern, now confined mostly to Asia, remained about the same as before, but direct flights from New York to Tokyo or Hong Kong were easier to arrange. Monsanto executives visited New York frequently, and our meetings in Monsanto's New York office made more sense than still another trip to St. Louis.

Chinatex was also based in New York, and negotiations quicker and easier when Mr. Wong came to the city, compared to seeing him in Beijing or Hong Kong. Cheong-On personnel liked to visit New York from time to time, obviating some trips to Korea and Taipei. K. Choi, from Korea, had many friends and contacts in New York, related to his non-Monsanto business, and getting together with him was now easier.

So the new location quickly made more sense from the standpoints of travel and time usage. This was especially true when trips to Europe became necessary to see Rhone Poulanc in Paris, and Montedison in Milan.

Settling in with old Connecticut friends and renewal of social bonds

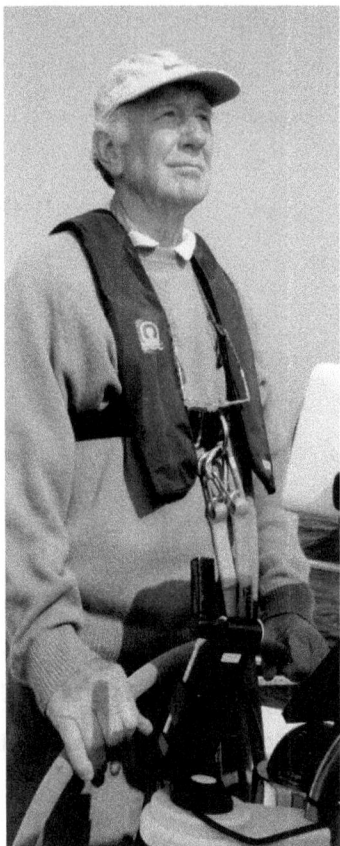

Photo 30.   Me, at helm of Moon
Potato, in auto-inflatable life jacket,
beginning our cruise in 1995.

naturally brought us back to Riverside Yacht Club, and my aim was to jump into boating, specifically sailing. On counsel of Bill King, a Nonsuch Cat boat owner, I negotiated with attorney Bob Barnum to buy his Nonsuch 30, and began refurbishing it at a boatyard in Essex, CT. The vessel had a single large sail of over 700 sq. ft, was 30 feet overall in length, had a 12 ft beam, four bunks, a head with toilet and shower, and a propane fed two-burner stove with oven. The power auxiliary was a 23 horsepower Volvo diesel which could propel the hull at 6 knots, slower than under full sail with a decent breeze, but enough to get to the next harbor and mooring.

The boat also had a wall-mounted propane cabin heater which warmed the cabin within minutes, and an ice box for food storage. A bank of oversized batteries fed by a generator kept us in engine-cranking power, as well as cabin and navigation lights, cell phone, radio, GPS, and radar power. A sophisticated breaker panel beneath the companionway stairs allowed us to select exactly the instruments we wanted to power, while conserving power to all other appliances and gadgets.

We had the marina install new charting GPS color plotter at the cockpit wheel, an autopilot with remote control, an electric power winch to hoist the heavy mainsail, new rigging lines, new lifelines, new throttle and gear controls, and a new color scheme for the hull and interiors. Joan chose the colors and the new upholstery, the red stripping separating the freeboard hull from the black five- foot underwater keel, and beige for cabin pillows. The name was changed to Moon Potato, a translation from skimiemo, meaning mountain potato in Japanese. This name was a parody on serious small boat names at the yacht club, many adopted from well know vessels in history or intent on capturing some essence of the sea. We decided to lighten up the naming trend, and Scott and Jon both had a hand in the unanimous decision selecting Moon Potato.

Above the cabin fold-down dining table was rigged a kerosene burning marine chandelier , and the forward cabin had new over-the-bunks reading lamps, and a small television set with antenna halfway up the mast. Joan used her most artistic Isabel O'Niell finishes to sketch and paint a replica of Moon Potato's stern and rigging to decorate the top of the table, and this art drew raves from the yacht club visitors.

The cockpit featured a fold out teak table, and the stern rail held a barbecue as well as fold-away life raft for emergency release, plus various electronic antennas. We had ship to shore radio capability, and early versions of cell phones which worked well over water. Navigation planning was done on paper charts, taking careful note of tidal swings of 8 feet or more, and swift currents on the Sound. Way points chosen were then programmed into the GPS, and could easily be tracked and monitored sequentially. The leather wrapped wheel was 36 inches in diameter, and all electronics except radar could be monitored and controlled without leaving the wheel.

The boat weighed seven tons and was stiff in heavy seas. Cabin and cockpit storage bins were stuffed with extra lines, an extra anchor, safety equipment such as life vests, foul weather gear, emergency medical kit, and spare parts including an extra prop assembly. Fully provisioned for cruising, with 25 gallons of diesel, we probably weighed between eight or nine tons, and squatted low in the water.

As a local runabout and fishing boat, we bought an 18 ft. Boston

Photo 31. Joan and me sailing in Vineyard Sound, approaching Menemsha Bite on Martha's Vineyard, on our last cruise aboard Moon Potato. This picture taken by Lee Westerberg aboard Kristen.

Whaler, with 85 horse outboard gasoline engine, named her Spud after our Moon Potato, and used her a lot for blue and bass fishing in local waters. We also water skied and tubed behind her. Scott and Jon preferred the whaler most times because moving at 25 knots is often a lot more fun than plodding along at 6 knots or less.

Each summer, beginning in June, 1990, for the next ten years, Joan and I cruised Moon Potato and lived aboard for at least four weeks, gunkholing the entire coast lines of New England states Connecticut, Rhode Island, and Massachusetts, as well as all stops on the New York side of Long Island Sound, down to New York harbor and the Statue Of Liberty, on to Redbank, New Jersey.

Additionally, we went long distance cruising at least a week each summer with the large Riverside yacht club fleet, racing against other club vessels along the way, rafting together at moorings or parking at slips each night for social hours and dinners.

Typically, when cruising alone, we would provision for a week, then resupply when in port. Going Northeast up the Coast, we might choose Essex on the Connecticut River as our first stop, reserving a mooring at the Essex Yacht Club. While there, we would dinghy ashore with our 10 ft. inflatable dinghy, which we towed under sail, assisted by a three horse gasoline kicker, stored on the stern rail while underway, or row ashore if the distance to be covered was small. We shopped local markets for fresh foods and ice, refueled if necessary, and usually had breakfast and dinners aboard the boat. Most marinas delivered ice to the boat, and offered fresh water to fill our two-forty gallon fresh water tanks.

Second stop might be Mystic Seaport or Stonington, CT. On one early trip, we were overtaken by a heavy fog bank, and had to navigate blind into Mystic harbor with charts and radar, a treacherous passage because the harbor channel is narrow and protected by large rocky outcroppings. Joan manned the radar in the cabin below while I steered and followed the chart plotter. We eased our way through at one/two knots, pausing after we cleared each rocky point, finally breaking out of fog when well into the harbor, surrounded there by dozens of moored vessels. Moon Potato's keel extended five feet below the water line, and a depth finder indicated less than a foot of bottom clearance at some points. The successful effort was nerve wracking, but confidence building at the same time.

Photo 32. A view of Menemsha Bite, on the west end of Martha's Vineyard. This was our favorite harbor on MV. That's me in the dinghy going ashore. The following summer, we rented the little house with the triangular roof line to my upper left, together with Verne and Lee Westerberg.

Photo 33. Joan and me with Verne and Lee Westerberg, our friends and neighbors from Lucas Point. We sometimes cruised together, they on "Kristen", and us on "Moon Potato"

At Stonington, we would pick up a mooring belonging to our friend Verne Westerberg, and stay a day or two before hoisting sail and heading East to Newport or Block Island, Rhode Island. Exploring ashore in villages like Mystic, Stonington, Block Island, and towns on Martha's Vineyard like Vineyard Haven, Edgartown, and Menemsha, and on out to Nantucket, made these trips fascinating and enjoyable, while stretching our sea legs.

Life on the water in New England reveals the true character of people of the region. At every mooring or slip in every harbor of every village and town, we found helpful, warm, outgoing sailors eager to exchange information about their passage and their families. Sailing and salt water bring out the best in people's nature. Borrowing a spice or tool from a neighboring boat, or lending a bottle of wine or discussing mutual friends or boat performance or a passage just completed, is a way of life on the water. The same people, rushing about their lives on the land, would never have crossed our paths.

SUMMER CRUISING IN NEW ENGLAND

The Summer of 1995 is chosen as an example of how our lives had changed. The business routine was set, my contract with Monsanto had been extended for another three year term. I had found that working for myself, in my own company, had its time and financial benefits. Contracts with various trading companies required spurts of intensive research and work followed by periods of discretionary time. As we had each Summer, we planned a one month cruise aboard Moon Potato, June 15 to July 13, to cover the New England coasts of Connecticut, Rhode Island, Massachusetts, and New York, on both sides of Long Island Sound and beyond.

What follows are actual entries from the daily log of this cruise.

This cruise is memorialized as symbolic of our cruising life for the ten years we owned the Moon Potato.

THURSDAY, JUNE 15, 1995

Departed Riverside Yacht club 8:30 AM bound ultimately for Martha's Vineyard and Nantucket, with stops in between. Scott and Jonathan saw us off. Sunny day with West wind building to 22 knots by early afternoon. A perfect 7-8 knot run under full sail, arriving Old Saybrook at mouth of Connecticut River 4 PM. Motor sailed upriver against strong current. Called Essex Yacht Club waterfront and reserved mooring for the night. Took launch ashore, had drinks at famed Griswald Inn before dinner aboard.

FRIDAY, JUNE 16

Dropped mooring at 8 AM heading downriver before tidal swing. Reached entrance to LI Sound and headed East just as flood tide beginning at the "race". (The race is a narrow inlet from the Atlantic through which ocean waters flood in and out of Long Island Sound. Flood tide occurs when the Sound is being refilled by the ocean. Slack tide occurs when the Sound empties back into the Atlantic.)

First 1 and ½ hours against the race current meant slow going, but strong west wind kept us at 4 and ½ knots over the ground. Relaxing sail to Stonington, arriving, 1:30 PM. Joan picked up the mooring line for Westerberg mooring inside Stonington breakwater, took the launch ashore to meet Gene Connett at his home on Water Street for showers and drinks and dinner with old friend. Our dear friend, Effie, Gene's wife, had died suddenly a few weeks before. Gene seemed in good spirits under the circumstances.

Moon Potato performed flawlessly first two days.- no sign of trouble.

SATURDAY, JUNE 17

Left Stonington 7 AM for a perfect 3 and ½ hour sail to Block Island, Rhode Island across open ocean. Very windy on arrival in Great Salt Pond, but waters protected. Picked up town mooring. Lunch aboard. Took our dinghy ashore and walked the town in afternoon. Block Island filled with tourists, already crowded for the short New England season. Block Island is a favorite for day sailers from the mainland and for second homes for the season. Plenty of restaurants and shops and nightlife for those so inclined. Bought fresh seafood for delicious dinner aboard.

Good weather forecast for Sunday sail to Menemsha Bite on Martha's Vineyard. Plotted waypoints to the Vineyard and entered coordinates in Chart Plotter GPS.

SUNDAY, JUNE 18

Left Great Salt Pond at daybreak and made first waypoint G-1 at North end of Block in 45 minutes. Motor sailing with strong west wind of 20 knots on our port beam. Rounding G-1 and heading east, our engine quit, and I could not restart it in spite of bleeding air from fuel line repeatedly. Joan took the helm while I checked all other possibilities but engine would not restart. Made decision to continue on under full sail with course set to Martha's Vineyard 30 miles of open sea to the east.

Had intended Mememsha port, but guidebooks indicated mechanical services only at Vineyard Haven, 10 miles further east, at the opposite end of the island. Twenty knot west wind continued steady all day and following sea was rough but boat speed was excellent and boat performing well. Called ahead on cell (a must)to harbor master for mooring assignment, explaining our situation, and he gave me engine mechanic's phone.   At 3 PM, we rounded up and tacked west into VH harbor, maneuvering by sail only, tacking port and starboard, inside the stone breakwater and through the mooring field.

We had to tack back and forth quickly to avoid hitting boats on the densely placed moorings. Kept boat speed down in the high wind by shortening sail and doing short tacks. We had only one chance to pick up the mooring buoy and put the loop over the bow post, otherwise, a miss would have sent us backwards through the mooring field, no doubt damaging several boats including our own.

Joan caught the mooring line perfectly just as our forward motion stopped, and brought the marker and line aboard and over the mooring post to secure us. We were now inside safe harbor, and we could relax after the day's wild ride and little room for error at the end of the day.

Called the mechanic at Maciel Marine ashore, and he came out right away to diagnose our problems. Late in the day on Sunday, and more diagnostic work would have to be done on Monday morning. Nothing more to be done, so we relaxed and went ashore to explore VH, a large community with attractive shops and restaurants. We ate at the "Black Dog", a haunt known throughout New England, and a favorite of yachtsmen.

MONDAY, JUNE 19.

Maciel marine called early to say a mechanic would come at 11:00 AM, so back we went ashore to the Black Dog for breakfast and a long walk. George, the mechanic, came and found that our injector pumps had failed and new ones were needed. Fuel injector pumps for a 23 horsepower Volvo deisel engine cost $900. And would have to be flown in, entailing extra charges. George brought Steve, the head mechanic back to verify his diagnosis, and Steve added a new fuel pump to our needs.

Dinner aboard. Weather hot but clear. Good thing to have check book and credit cards.

TUESDAY, JUNE 20.

Fuel pump installed but injector pumps will not arrive from Virginia until late tomorrow. Injector pumps removed with great effort because of limited space in the engine compartment. Engine access had been improved earlier, fortunately, when I had cut access panels from the port and starboard quarter berths the season before. We had dinner aboard, after late day visit by taxi to nearby Oak Bluffs harbor, and a look at the quaint "doll houses" surrounding the huge religious revivalist structure in the center. Religious camps and tent meetings had been the original core settlement of Oak Bluffs. Oak Bluffs was recognized as the center of the black community on Martha's Vineyard. Joan did our accumulated laundry in the Oak Bluffs.

JUNE 21, WEDNESDAY

Another "Black Dog" breakfast ashore and a long shopping walk awaiting arrival of new engine parts. By 4 PM , all parts installed and engine up and running, sounding great. I dutifully paid the $2100. Bill which included 16 hours of labor at $55. Per hour, a hard lesson about the need for preventive maintenance, but don't know how this could have been foreseen. George and Steve said injector pump failures are one in 10,000, so I made a note to seek redress from Volvo if possible.

Refilled fresh water tanks and motored out of VH for Oak Bluffs harbor, around the corner, poorer but not much wiser, thankful that we had had the perfect sailing wind from Block to VH, otherwise we might have been in serious trouble anywhere along this open ocean. Town mooring in OB harbor.

THURSDAY, JUNE 22

Dinghed ashore for groceries, ice, then on before noon to Edgartown harbor, arriving about 1 PM. First of six nights in this very pretty harbor, days spent ashore, walking the village, shopping and exploring, nights aboard for dinner, news and movie on TV. TV and cell phone as AM/FM music important links for us staying in touch. Cell has been especially useful in working through mechanical issues and talking with family, making mooring and dinner reservations, and calls from and to Korea, Japan, St. Louis, for example. Cell phones were relatively bulky at the time.

Breakfast at Edgartown Inn, where Ted Kennedy spent the night after accident at Chappaquiddick, Dinner at Daggett house. Long hike around Chappaquiddick island was good exercise one foggy day, and we walked over the rebuilt bridge which Teddy Kennedy drove off, killing Mary Jo Kopeckne 23 years earlier. Charming streets and weathered clapboard houses in Edgartown, many of them historic, but noted the lack of town services to transient yachtsmen. No showers, restrooms, or laundry facilities, strange for a community dependent on tourism and especially boaters.

We finally snuck into showers and used laundry facilities intended for Boston Commons apartments, but nobody questioned us. Edgartown is more upscale but similar in character to VH, both very commercial with day transients and limited services. Great scenery everywhere. Weather marginal 3 of 6 days with fog and drizzle, but no heavy rain.

WEDNESDAY, JUNE 28

Slipped our mooring at Edgartown 7:30 AM, headed for Nantucket Island, motoring directly into 15-20 knot east wind and building seas for first hour and a half. After rounding waypoint buoy 21, mid-channel, we sailed on heading of 135 degrees at 7 knots and seas smoothed out. Weather clear and sailing better after rounding Tuckernuck Shoal buoy, and a heading of 165 degrees gave us a fast beam reach all the way past Brant light and into Nantucket harbor, arriving 11:05 AM, ahead of planned schedule.

Nantucket harbor is large, scenic with luxurious yachts, and protected. Spent first night in reserved slip in Nantucket boat basin marina, charged everything up, re-provisioned food, ice, water, fuel, and explored the historic village. Nantucket, the former national port for whaling vessels and whale oil, is clearly a cut above anything we saw on Martha's Vineyard, with tasteful, well maintained historic homes with strictly uniformed/weathered shingle exteriors. Houses often flower covered with small gardens.

Dinner at Yoshi's Japanese restaurant on East Chestnut street, a small eatery with no liquor or beer license owned by two gay men, one American, the other Japanese. A guest offered me free beer and the American owner provided free saki, gratefully accepted. As a non-drinker for many years, Joan endured.

THURSDAY, JUNE 29

Moved from the slip to mooring L-1, mid harbor, surrounded by very large sailing and power vessels, including "Gleam, and "Philanderer", the former 125 ft in length, and the latter 150 ft. or more. These monsters were elaborate and showy in terms of special gear, fittings, and crew, with unlimited luxury. Equally large power yachts, among them "Mystique", about 150 ft., "Silver Shalin", 130 feet, and "Lady Valarie", a feedship of about 120 ft. Discretionary wealth of this magnitude is unimaginable. Maintenance costs of hardware and electronics together with permanent crew and operating expenses, are mind-staggering.

FRIDAY JUNE 30

We spent the day ashore, finding Nantucket shops and galleries much higher quality and services plentiful, albeit expensive. Cobblestone streets were authentic and attractive. The entire village better kept than MV or Block Island. Restaurants and Inns appear excellent. Clientele more permanent and less day trippy. Short season and high taste levels mean

Nantucket delivers high quality at high prices, no apologies.

We reserved "Company of the Cauldron" for dinner on the night of July 4, my 62nd birthday, and anticipate big fireworks in the harbor on the 4th. Lots of fog every morning so far.

SATURDAY, JULY 1

Rented bicycles and rode 6 miles to the west end of the island, which was fog shrouded with almost no visibility when we arrived, but good and essential exercise.

SUNDAY, JULY 2

Rain all day, with heavy fog. Stayed aboard and read…..and ate.

MONDAY AND TUESDAY, JULY 3 AND 4

Both perfect weather days, and we repeated ourselves on the 3rd, going back to some village shops seen earlier. The whaling and native American histories of Nantucket hold great interest to tourists. The Wampanoag Indians were original occupants, devastated by disease and servitude when the English claimed the island and gave it by grant to merchants on Martha's Vineyard. At one time, Nantucket was the third most important port in the United States, behind New York and Boston. With the demise of whaling and whale oil, Nantucket lost 60% of its population by 1850.

Famous authors Herman Melville and Nethaniel Philbrick wrote books about Nantucket.[10] Well known artists from around the world have painted Nantucket scenes and sold them in the many art galleries there.

On July 4, my birthday, we had boiled lobster dinner in the cockpit,

___
10. Melville wrote the classic "Moby Dick", and Philbrick wrote "In the Heart of the Sea", the latter the story of the whaling ship Essex, and about Nantucket as the port for Whaling vessels and whale oil.

under oil lamp rigged off the boom, and watched fireworks on Brant Point. A fitting and beautiful end to a full week on Nantucket.

WEDNESDAY, JULY 5

Departed Nantucket 5 AM for passage around MV and up Vineyard Sound to the small harbor of Menemsha on the western end of MV. There to meet Lee and Verne Westerberg, our neighbors and friends on Lucas Point, who left the same hour from Stonington, CT. on their Sabre 38, named Kristen.

Nantucket sound was placid, contrasted to the rough trip inbound. We motor sailed, and with favorable tides, arrived off Menemsha early, fished for awhile under sail, and entered Menemsha Bite just after noon.

Westerberg's arrived on schedule at 2:30 PM and we rafted together, on a mooring, for the next four nights, until Sunday, July 9.

We went ashore to the great Home Port restaurant twice, and, on a third night, went to the Beach Plum restaurant and Outpost Inn near Gayhead light. The restaurant and Inn are owned and operated by Hugh Taylor and wife, Jeannie. Hugh is the brother of James Taylor, the well known singer. The Taylor family is said to own lots of land on MV. Hugh dropped out of high school in North Carolina at age 15 to come to MV and work as a carpenter. He now owns the Inn, a catamaran day sail business, still does construction, and sails the boat to the Bahamas during the off season. Hugh sings at David's in Oak Bluffs every Thursday night.

With Lee and Verne, we have many laughs and lots of gin rummy, as always. Every day, we would row about 75 yards to the dock side clam shell restaurant, have at least a dozen cherrystones on the half shell, take boiled fresh lobster back to the boats with us, and feast. Verne is the retired publisher of Vogue, House and Garden, and Gourmet magazines, and most recently, he and Lee did a three year stint in Sydney for the magazines. Later, we rented a dockside house overlooking the bite, with the Westerbergs, had many laughs, and ate lots of watermelon.

SUNDAY, JULY 9

Kristen departed Menemsha 6 AM for Edgartown, and we left the mooring 8:30 AM on course for Block Island. Strong head winds and very rough breaking seas on our bow forced us to alter course to Newport, R.I., fifteen miles North. We arrived safely and spent the night on a mooring in Newport harbor. Did not go ashore this time. We had explored Newport and its many mansions before. On one July 4 weekend in Newport, rafted with the Westerbergs, we stayed in the great old New York Yacht Club at the head of the harbor. There, a total stranger with a great operatic voice sang happy birthday to a very surprised me, in front of a crowd of over 500 celebrating the 4th with an elegant picnic on the lawn.

MONDAY, JULY 10

Passage from Newport to Stonington uneventful, in sight of land, arriving Stonington 10:30 AM. Re-provisioned fuel, water, and ice, and had lunch by chance with Gene Connett and two friends. Napped aboard in PM, followed by a great swordfish dinner.

TUESDAY, JULY 11

Eager to head West toward home, we got an early start for Mystic but bypassed it because of rain and heavy fog in favor of the Connecticut river and Essex. Visibility limited, but forecast was for some clearing later, so we pressed on.

The village of Essex, as noted earlier, is five miles North up the Connecticut river, itself a life source for many towns and villages along its path from the Sound to Hartford. The river is a major marine and wild fowl habitat. Osprey nest on flashing buoys, and close-up views are possible. A little past Essex is the fresh water harbor of Hamburg Cove, where once, while at anchor and we were in the cabin below, I rushed up the companionway to investigate a sudden loud noise, only to slam my head into the closed hatch. Significant blood and bandages later, I was thankful not to have been a hemophiliac.

In Essex, after lunch at Griswald Inn, we cleaned Moon Potato and asked a local yacht broker, Jim Wallis, to estimate her trade-in value on a Nonsuch 33, as a lark. He promised to write us his estimate. Dinner of pizza aboard, with homemade topping on Boboli crust.

THURSDAY, JULY 12

Left Essex 5:00 AM to catch favorable currents and caught a perfect sunrise just as we reached the mouth of the river and entered Long Island Sound, entering the Sound on a due West heading. Northwest flood at the race began at 5:56 AM and we timed it just right. This meant a 2 and ½ knot tidal assist for the first two hours on a course to the North of Faulkner's island, in the middle of the Sound, and a 1 and ½ knot assist for the next three hours on a 257 degree course to just South of Stratford Shoal, 23 miles away. In spite of low visibility and the threat of rain, the Sound was eerily calm for most of the day, with barely a ripple all morning.

We rounded Stratford Shoal at 11:00 AM and set a course for Green's Ledge and Zeigler's Cove, planning an overnight moorage and the finale to our cruise. After a tuna salad lunch and a rest, we elected to continue west to our home port of Greenwich Cove and our own mooring there. Arrived Greenwich Cove 5:30 PM and had banquet night aboard in one of the most scenic harbors on the east coast, our own harbor. Interestingly, bird life here is more prevalent than anyplace we saw on our cruise. Blue heron, white egrets, Osprey, gulls, are all plentiful, along with ducks, geese, and cormorants. This abundance is possibly due to the wide 7-10 ft tidal swings here, the widest range of any harbor we visited. This swing affords better fishing for birds.

THURSDAY, JULY 13

Reflecting on this month long trip, we learned that we can sail safely and confidently to almost any east coast destination, with good planning and safety first in mind. Navigating to the Vineyard and Nantucket and back home had been easy. We found favorite moorings and anchorages, restaurants, where to do laundry and sneak showers, even though we could have had all showers on board, but chose to conserve fresh water whenever possible.

Joan did laundry mostly in commercial machines ashore, but also on board a couple of times with fresh water and soap on deck, laying clothes on deck and over the boom to dry. She also did great meal planning, and our very best meals were on board in the comfort of our own cabin, while swinging on a mooring.

We also learned that the boat was reliable and safe, the Vineyard Haven breakdown the one exception, and that we could live together in harmony in very tight quarters, each playing his role. Joan kept us shipshape , and with great meals and clean clothes, and was a great first mate underway. I did the trip planning and navigating and steering. We both shopped for food and enjoyed walks, bike rides and sightseeing, while avoiding organized tours of any kind.

A valuable lesson in hindsight is the clear need to stay physically fit while on an extended cruise of this type. This will not be done unless planned and committed to. At least two hours per day when in port, with many brisk walks, some of which might be slow jogs. Sit-ups and stretches can be done aboard, and hand weights are essential for upper body conditioning. The tendency aboard is become lethargic, eating carelessly and minimizing movement, although trimming sails, adjusting lines, moving about the boat while it is heeling at a sharp angle, stresses a lot of muscles. Good discipline in exercise routine and healthy eating is the key.

Also useful aboard is a big box of baby wipes, half diaper sized pads for "dry bathing" when showers are not available or convenient. One box lasted us the month, and are a great aid for personal hygiene.

Aside from engine repairs of $2100., we were trouble free, had varied but mostly good weather, met interesting people on some incredible boats in beautiful harbors. We never encountered discourtesy.

FRIDAY, JULY 14, END OF THE CRUISE

At noon, we pulled alongside Riverside Yacht Club docks and offloaded our gear and remaining food, completing a perfect vacation. We cleaned the boat, put the sail cover on, put her back on her mooring, and arrived our house on Lucas Point just ahead of the first major heat wave of the summer.

Over the ten years we owned Moon Potato, we embarked each summer on similar adventures, sailing alone or alongside friends on their boats, traversing the South Shore of Long Island Sound to Port Jefferson and points East to the Hamptons and Sag Harbor and Montauk, and all stops West, all the way to Manhattan. We came to understand and appreciate and respect the Sound and the Atlantic beyond, from our small vessel, in ways we could never have experienced from the decks of cruise ships.

Complimenting our large boat was our 18 ft. Boston whaler tender, SPUD, our essential runabout for fishing and transporting ourselves and our sons around Greenwich Cove and Greenwich and Portchester, N.Y. harbors.

Finally, we decided it was time to sell our boats because we committed to still another new interest, the California Desert. Jim Read had recently built a magnificent home in Riverside, near the Yacht club, and needed a sailboat as an entry ticket for the membership committee.

We made a deal with Jim, one of the finest gentlemen anywhere, and the boat was gone within a week, together with the whaler, which I sold to friend Verne Westerberg. The end of boat ownership was bitter-sweet. Jim insisted we use Moon Potato as long as we wanted, whenever we wanted, which we continued to do for several summers afterward.

Jim and Pattie went on to buy a second boat, this one 38 ft. with twin screws, naming it Sweet Potato. We had assumed he would quickly change Moon Potato to a name of his choice, but he loved the name and refused to part with it. A man with very good tastes.

Ashore, we vacationed in Tuscany with our friends Conrad and Adele Teitell, hiking most of the ancient villages along the Mediterranean making up the Chinque Terre region along the coast. Walled villages, wonderful food, local culture of these small walled towns, plus a tour of Florence, provided us with lasting memories of a purely personal two-week visit.

BOOK NINE
California Years

INTRODUCTION TO THE WESTERN DESERT

Our friends Halsey and Sharon Burke, of Burke Industries in San Jose, CA., owned a second home in the Southern California desert community of Indian Wells, near Palm Springs. In 1991, they invited us to fly out for a visit. Joan and I had both been to Palm Springs before. She and her parents and brother Bob vacationed there in the early 1940's, driving down from Oakland. She remembers the desert as primitive, with narrow, two lane roads connecting Palm Springs to the La Quinta hotel toward the east end of the Coachella valley, and almost nothing in between but orange groves.

The Coachella valley, and Palm Springs in particular, had been a playground for movie stars seeking a get-away from Hollywood, with exclusive tennis and golf club catering to the very wealthy. After the war, developers went into action and transformed the valley into large-scale housing developments, exploiting the water resources of the huge aquifer just below the desert floor. Whole new towns sprang up and became prosperous, built around heavily-watered golf resorts and gated enclaves accommodating both middle class and rich in search of second homes in dependable weather and scenic settings.

The Santa Rosa mountains to the south and west, the 10,000 ft. San Jacinto pass to the west toward Los Angeles, the Little San Bernadino mountains to the east, offered protection to the sea level agricultural valley below. The setting was a developers dream. Cheap land, plentiful water, perfect weather, and spectacular scenery combined to set off one of the biggest building booms in the country. Palm Springs saw big growth, as did formerly sleepy towns to the east such as Rancho Mirage, Palm Desert, Indian Wells, La Quinta, and Indio. Golf courses and gated communities sprang up everywhere, in a building frenzy that would last for almost 60 years. From a town

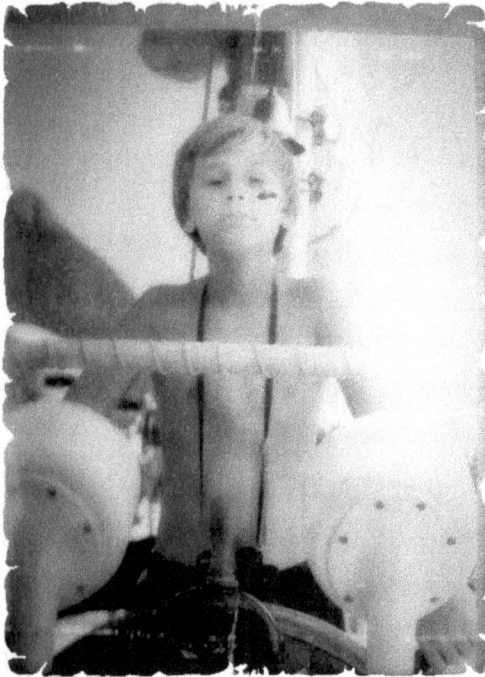

Photo 34. *Jon at the wheel of Halsey Burke's 65 foot yawl, in Desolation Sound, off Vancouver, B. C. We vacationed with the Burkes two weeks, visiting various ports along the west coast of the U.S. and Canada.*

of a few thousand people, the Valley grew to half a million people by 2006, with fine housing, shopping, restaurants, galleries, educational institutions, parks, and attractions for tourists seeking warmth and relaxation.

We stayed three days with Halsey and Sharon, and fell in love with the desert. We looked around at real estate but decided to rent awhile before making a decision to buy.

The next two winters, we rented condos for a month at the Palm

Valley Country club in Palm Desert, played golf, explored the area and our options. The third winter we tried a rental in a different club, and remained impressed. In 1995, 96 and 97, we rented for three winter months at PGA West in La Quinta, from Dick Settle, a law professor from the University of Washington, who Scott and I met by chance while playing the famed Pete Dye Stadium Course. Dick had never rented his house, but agreed to rent to us, and the relationship became friendship.

During this period, our friend Halsey Burke passed away, having declined slowly from a number of maladies. Sharon asked me to speak at his Memorial service at Desert Horizons Country Club, which I was honored to do, recalling our sailing times and family vacations together with our sons and their daughter Michelle on Desolation Sound and the Columbia River in Canada aboard his 65 ft. yawl.

Halsey had been a great and loyal friend, starting from a customer/ supplier relationship, sharing common interests in sailing and golfing and business. He had been the youngest captain of a Liberty Ship during the war, ferrying troops to the European theatre, dodging German U-boats. He was a first class and honorable gentleman. We have stayed in touch with Sharon, his widow, who has now remarried, this time to Jack Wolter, a retired W.R. Grace executive, and they live in Palm Desert at Ironwood Country club.

In 1998, we rented three winter months from Kathy Wallen, who had a house identical to Dick's, just down the street , also at PGA West. By this time, we were convinced that a second home in the desert was the right choice for us. We put money down and made a lot selection next to a neighborhood pool at 80126 Merion, on the Nicklaus private golf course, and kept a distant eye on construction through 1999, visiting the site a couple of times. Joan came out alone for a week and picked all finishes, paints, window treatments and furniture, and we closed on the house in October 1999 and moved into our Ryder One model, with three bedrooms, three baths, a garage for two cars plus golf cart, next door to what turned out to be our nearly private pool, since nobody else used it much.

We continued to go back and forth between the California and Connecticut houses for the next two years, flying out of White Plains airport, connecting in Chicago directly to Palm Springs. In late 2001, having sold Moon Potato to our friend Jim Read, we took the plunge and put the Connecticut house on the market. As it happened, the open house was scheduled for 9/11. As told earlier, Verne Westerberg and I sat on the deck of the Riverside Yacht Club and watched the twin towers burn that same day.

Everything stopped, the housing market in particular, and during the next two weeks, the realtor brought only one potential buyer to the house. We expected nothing to come from it, and neither did the realtor, but a near full price offer soon arrived from Hennis and Marquitz, the European retailer of inexpensive women's fashions. H&M wanted to purchase the house for their U.S. Managing Director, who was in the process of moving to the States to open the chain in this country.

We bought the CT. house in 1976, and kept it rented while in St. Louis for ten years, and sold it in late 2001, 25 years later for ten times our purchase price. We had invested in remodeling the house, but the margin over cost was still very gratifying. We were mortgage free years earlier, so bought the California house free of debt. We closed the sale in late November and started driving west to our new home, with stops in Texas to see family.

By Thanksgiving, we were moved in, and our first visitors were family. Scott, Terry, and three month old Jack came for Christmas, a true house warming for us. We had bought a second car for use in California from Sharon Burke, a well-used Cadillac sedan, but soon began having mechanical issues, and ended up giving the car to a local charity for the tax deduction.

We joined PGA West club, with its six championship courses designed by Arnold Palmer, Jack Nicklaus, Tom Weiskopf, Pete Dye, and Greg Norman. I bought a golf cart and began golf in earnest, while Joan dabbled in golf lightly before pursuing jewelry making from jacaranda pods, and other interests. I joined the men's golf club and began playing in their regular weekly tournaments, and met new friends. Joan and I ate some dinners and lunches at the club, but avoided the party curcuit. As non-drinkers, we remained pretty private in our social lives, eating out with the Burkes and a few others, but mostly keeping golf and social lives apart. I met good friend Ray Shaffer on the golf course, and we have stayed close all these years. Ray is 84 in 2011, and going strong every day. Brother Cal and wife Jan became regular visitors from Texas, and we enjoyed many good times and golf together, along with gin rummy. John and Annette Long, for whom I had served as best man almost 58 years ago, came from Odessa for a week each year until John's Parkinson's disease no longer permitted it.

Friends from Connecticut included John and Harriet Roughan and Harriet's sister Elaine, who lived in Los Angeles. Dear Elaine passed away on 2/12/11 after a twelve year battle with cancer. Miles and Pat McDonald, Bobby and Rich Hopkins, and Tom and Christine Chang visited from Connecticut, and Don and Petie McKinley from St. Louis. Jerry and Billye Jones, friends from Dallas, also came, as did Joan's college friend Marilyn Johnson. And, of course, Scott and Terry and Jack and Audrey, and Jon.

I began a regular routine a the fitness center, which I have continued all the years since, doing some aerobic warm-up, then 500 repetitions of various weight machines, 50 each at ten different stations, with at least 100 lbs of weight on each. This I do at least three times weekly, even while we are away for summers, when I join a health club wherever we are. I read recently that weight lifting helps brain cell renewal, scientists believe, and I hope its true. Joan also enjoyed the fitness center, but prefers walking regularly and gardening to weight-based exercise.

Summers we continued to visit Connecticut, renting houses or house-sitting houses for friends the Geismars, while they went to Maine to their summer home. It was an excellent arrangement, and we reciprocated by inviting our hosts to use our house for periods during the cold CT winters, while we travelled the west coast from San Francisco down to San Diego. On several occasions in CT., Jim Read insisted that we stay aboard and cruise Moon Potato, just as if we still owned her, a very generous offer which we accepted. Other times, we stayed at the Roughan house or the Chang house while they were away vacationing elsewhere.

Scott and Terry gave us our first grandchild, John Scott (Jack) on

August 26, 1999, and our granddaughter Audrey Joan, on September 26, 2000, both born in Stamford, CT. hospital. In early 2001, Scott joined Husch and Eppenberger, a large law firm based in Springfield, MO.,

Photo 35. Son Scott and me on the golf course at PGA West.

and moved his family there. Springfield became a stop over on our trips back and forth across country, and we rented a penthouse one summer while looking for property there. We ended up buying a three-bedroom condo in the Chesterfield area of the city, in a lovely setting with park and public pool nearby, and Joan was able to use most of our furniture from the CT house in the new Springfield condo. The condo was about five miles away from Scott and Terry and Jack and Audrey, so we saw lots of our grandkids, just the way it was planned.

Jon was now living and working in San Diego, so we had an easy trip over the mountains from our home in La Quinta to see him, and he often drove over and spent time with us. He and a partner had a computer generated name badge business, doing caricatures of guests at conventions,

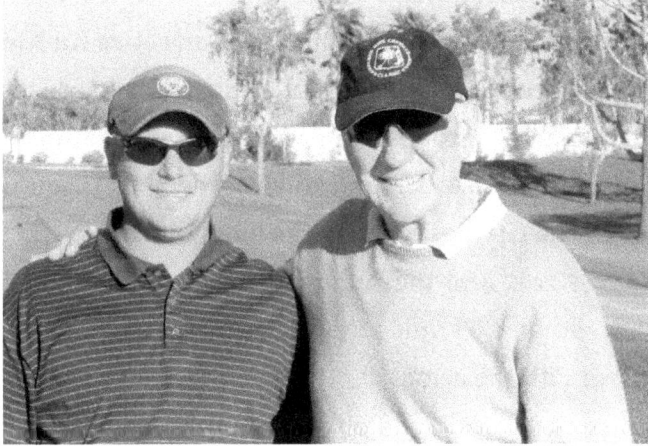

Photo 36. Jon and me on the golf course, the same day. Playing golf with sons is the best.

among other endeavors. Still single, but with a few near misses in romance, he later moved to Key West, Florida, and worked there for several years before being flooded out by hurricane Wilma, and decamping to Peidmont, Missouri, where he lives today.

We kept juggling cars until all seemed right. Joan bought her dream convertible, a 380 SL Mercedes, which we shipped to California. I had purchased a new E-420 Mercedes in Greenwich in 1997, and, in Springfield, we replaced it with a new E-500 and sold the 97 model to Scott. He, in turn, gave us back our older E-300 which we had given him when we bought the 97. In Springfield, we used it as our condo car and left it garaged there when we went back to California . On subsequent trips to Springfield, including Christmas, we flew there and had ready transportation.

Springfield , in Southwest Missouri, is a university town of 150 thousand, including 25 thousand students. It is a convenient distribution point to most of the country, and a favorite home base of trucking firms, warehousing, and some manufacturing. Homes and buildings are attractive, with old town largely bypassed in favor of widespread sprawl and many strip and indoor shopping malls. The terrain is appealing, on the edge of the Ozarks, with the country music town of Branson just a few miles away. Joan and I felt Springfield was an inviting, friendly town with full amenities, reasonable real estate values, and the vibrations of a young college town in terms of its restaurants and nightlife.

Pre civil war, the town developed a reputation as an active Ku Klux Klan center, an image long since shed. But even today, there are few blacks in the town, while other minority groups are growing steadily, attracted by the university of Southwest Missouri, and town leadership intent on building sustainable jobs. The city has many parks and golf courses open to the public, a world class zoo, and the full range of services found in much larger cities like St. Louis, 200 miles to the Northeast. Springfield's most famous native is Brad Pitt, the actor.

Nearing the end of the first decade of the new century, California desert life had become a well-established routine. Our ingredients were lots of golf, good books, internet tracking of family and good friends, visits from our family as they sought to get a break from the extreme cold of Milwaukee and Missouri. We took short trips to San Francisco, Santa Cruz, Monterrey, Santa Barbara, Carmel, San Diego, and occasionally to Las Vegas.

After Springfield, Scott and Terry had moved to Peoria, where Scott joined Caterpillar as litigation manager. We rented an apartment near their home there for one summer, and enjoyed every minute with Jack and Audrey and the family. Jon came up from Missouri and we celebrated birthdays and holidays together. Three years later, in 2008, Scott became head of litigation for A.O. Smith Corporation in Milwaukee, and we began renting apartments there for three summer months each year. Milwaukee climate in summer is ideal, while the California desert is unbearably hot,with temperatures reaching to as high as 115 degrees in July and August.

Scott attended a charity dinner and won a silent auction bid on a day's sail, with captain and crew, on a 63 foot mahogany sloop. He took the

Photo 37. Captain Jerry Sullivan at the tiller of his 63 foot Swedish mahogany sloop, on lake Michigan. Scott won the sloop, with crew, for a day sail, and our whole family was aboard. Joan and Terry in the foreground. Summer, 09

whole family sailing on lake Michigan. The captain/ owner, Jerry Sullivan, about 80 years old, told me that racing ocean-going sailboats is all he had ever done. He said he was a trust fund baby, and that his father owned the largest shipping line on the Great lakes, and he was always able to indulge his hobby. Jerry seemed completely unspoiled by wealth. His life's work had been working hard at winning the Trans Pac and Atlantic races, and philanthropy.

LOSSES

In October 2005, our dear Mother Dillie Dean Morris Garrett died at age 99, the last of eleven siblings and spouses to go. She had been a great and generous lady, a loving mother and wife, and a wonderful grandmother and great-grandmother. We had seen here only a month before as we passed through Plainview going west to California, and knew she didn't have long to live. Still, returning to Texas for her funeral, 17 years after Frank had died, brought back many memories, thinking over her long life and legacy to her children.

In 2008, my oldest brother Cal died after suffering a subdural hematoma a month earlier, the cause unknown, but he had been through heart surgery seven years earlier to repair a leaky valve, and had since been kept on Coumadin, a blood thinner known to cause bleeding unless very carefully regulated. We all speculated that Coumadin was a contributing factor. In any event, the death of our oldest sibling and a brother we all looked up to was a big shock to the entire family, and we think about him and miss him every day.

Cal was a retired golf club professional, and we organized annual memorial tournaments to honor him, and created a golf scholarship in his memory at West Texas A&M University, in Canyon, Texas. Cal's widow Jan and his daughters, Lynn and Lisa, and his grandchildren, all continue to live in and around the Hereford/Canyon Texas area.

Old friend Bruce English died suddenly in 2007 in his living room in St. Louis. Bruce and Barbara and Joan and I and their kids and ours had spent many hours together in Atlanta and St. Louis, and on the road for business. Bruce and I had talked about many of life's issues over the years, and had a lasting and close friendship. I was honored to give a eulogy to

Bruce at his memorial.

And old friend and neighbor Eugene Connett passed away in the summer of 2009, after several years of suffering dementia in an assisted living facility in Connecticut. Joan and I regarded Gene and Effie and their five kids as our second family. We lived next door to them, and saw them several times each week socially in addition to working together in New York city.

Great friendships deserve a chapter of their own. They are one of life's rewards, and the ability to make and hold fast, loyal, honest friends, has to be regarded as a gift. We have been so fortunate to have and hold good friends, and I was pleased to be asked to speak at Halsey's, Bruce's, Cal's, and Gene's memorials. To be chosen to offer eulogies to these friends and my dear brother is a signal honor.

Traversing the country California to Milwaukee and back each summer, we began accepting the invitations each Fall from Travis and Millie Goree, old high school friends, to join a group of 20 other high school classmates at the spectacular Goree ranch, known as the T-Bone, in Valera, Texas, each September. Travis had done well in his career selling potash to the oil exploration and drilling industry in and around Midland/Odessa, and had invested some of his wealth in this 5,000 acre showplace, stocked with exotic African animals for show. He designed his magnificent main ranch house, and restored several other historic houses on the property, making it perfect to house and entertain a couple of dozen friends.

We toured the ranch to view the animals, ate great food, had special entertainment, but, most of all, enjoyed conversations and memories with friends of 60 years ago when we were high school teenagers. Most of these friends had not changed during all that time. They were strong of character, smart, fun, and had chosen wonderful and agreeable spouses. We see this group only once a year, but the gathering is a highlight of the Fall for us.

Photo 38.   Travis and Millie Goree, at their T-Bone ranch in Valera, Texas, where 20 high school friends are invited each Fall. The weekend is filled with memories, laughter, and good food, courtesy Travis and Millie and their ranch staff.

RETIREMENT?

A t home, we wonder about the definition of retirement. We seem to be more active but less regimented, more reflective and analytical, more conversational, and more bookish, perhaps because we have time to be. We choose to be politically less vocal, but still marvel at a few highly educated people we meet who believe that this time, disregarding all of history, the socialist welfare state model will work.

We both try to practice good health in physical activity and in eating the right foods. We enjoy action movies while abhorring slanted political documentaries, and we like eating out with our friends Ray Shaffer, Mary Lou and Dennis Green, Mike and Eleanor Miller, and several of Joan's women friends. Dr. Alex Korn and I enjoy frank conversation over lunch every couple of weeks. Dr. Paul Chavin and I debate over tea once every week or so, and learn from each other.

I play golf some with Ray, but not obsessively, in fact, I play less and less, but go to the gym more. Joan makes jewelry, has many lunches with friends, does some desert hiking, and joined a book club and Bunco group, and is active in her own causes.

I attend occasional lectures and classes at our local Cal State University campus. We are living the dream of choosing exactly how we want to spend our hours, invest them toward a larger goal or waste them without guilt. We are mostly serene and less material, with less striving toward goals, with not much interest in acquiring things or repeating our many years of travelling abroad, or any form of group regimentation. We both stopped drinking alcohol years ago, and our lives are better having done so. Our sons followed our example in this regard, and we are especially proud of them for their decision.

We miss our children and grandchildren and wish every day that we could be with them more, yet moving to Milwaukee or Missouri does not suit us at this moment in our lives. A small but great pleasure is exchanging emails with our grandson Jack, and granddaughter Audrey, and receiving Skyped calls several times each week from Scott or Jon. The internet is perhaps man's greatest discovery, and its potential is just beginning to be realized. We think it will obsolete traditional network media, with its timed shows and fixed schedules, laced with commercials. Very soon, we think, most all news and programs will be on demand, with pop up ads only, void of the irksome interruptions to which we have been habituated. Long term, the networks will be content providers only, and local media outlets may be programming local material only, while national media will be demand based only.

THE ROAD LESS TRAVELLED

Robert Frost's most famous poem, "The Road Not Taken", ends like this:

"Two roads diverged in a wood, and I—
I took the one less travelled by
And that has made all the difference."

The "what if" game is tempting to play. Each of us comes to crossroads...decision points in our lives and careers, and choices, sometimes fateful, have to be made. We may not know at the moment that our decision will lead to great new adventures, or to great disappointments. We know only that we have set sail on a new tack, to new destinations, to new expectations, and that had we chosen the other path offered, it would have led to a wholly different life, with different career ladders and influences, different friends, spouses, locations, children, and grandchildren. Each of us would have become decidedly altered human beings in a different play on an unknown stage.

The paths I chose at seven critical diverging points have made all the difference. An offer of a music scholarship led me to choose West Texas A&M university over Texas Tech or North Texas State, or perhaps the University of Texas in Austin.

A chance speech class in college led to Dr. Jack Walker, who recommended me for my first job in radio. This led to valuable experience in television, in front of the camera, and on the business side. In turn, I was offered and accepted the job to go to New York and open a sales office for FM Associates. In the interim, a chance meeting in Tokyo with Major

Joseph Gigandet of Armed Forces Network Korea landed me the spot with AFKN Seoul. From this platform, I was selected to go to Tokyo's Far East Network as writer/producer for "Salute To You", the show of Commanding General I.D. White. I turned down an offer from FEN Tokyo to remain there as a civilian, which would have defined a very different life.

At a decision point in New York, I chose to accept a job with a trade association rather than reverse the decision, when I had the chance, and join WQXR FM, the New York Times station in New York. Had I done so, and remained in media, life would have taken an entirely new course.

A chance introduction to Joan Henderson when she was in the city on vacation led to our marriage a couple of years later, leading to Scott and Jonathan, and Terry, and Jack and Audrey, all the most important people in my life, all there through a fateful chain of decisions which might easily never have been.

My association with Gene Connett led us to chose our first home in Connecticut rather than New Jersey or another borough of the City. Connecticut became the bedrock of our social lives and friendships for the next forty years, and the real starting point for our son's lives.

When it was time to move on from the trade association, I had a choice of Monsanto or Beaunit, and chose Monsanto, leading me on a career path of promotions and opportunities and friendships I could never have imagined. What if I had gone the other way? Beaunit was out of business within a few years. Monsanto led onward to Atlanta, back to New York and Connecticut, to headquarters in St. Louis, to years of studying Spanish and travelling in Latin America, and finally, to years of travelling to the capitols of civilizations, making lasting friends, and getting acquainted with diverse cultures from Asia, to Europe to Africa.

These experiences inspired the study of International Affairs at Washington University, and to applying that knowledge in my Monsanto travels and negotiations, and to my own business, started after retirement from Monsanto.

Our friendship with Halsey Burke influenced our decision to buy a second home in California rather than Florida or Texas, or the Carolinas, which might have been viable options. In making this choice, our path was laid for our retirement lives.

In each instance, options had to be considered and pros and cons weighed, and finally, decisions made which would lead to still new paths and choices, and, perhaps, new roads less travelled.

The course of world history hinges on just such choices, and the outcomes would be radically different if divergent paths had been selected. What if the Romans had not crucified Jesus? Jesus was an itinerant preacher defying Roman authority. Would there be Christianity if Jesus had simply been allowed to continue preaching and had been ignored by Pontius Pilate?

What if Harry Truman and Winston Churchill had not supported the reformation of Israel on Palestinian lands in 1948, and instead encouraged the Jewish diaspora to assimilate around the earth where they were scattered? Would there be cause for the unending conflict and war between the Jews and Arabs?

What if King George has granted independence to the American colonies without resorting to war? Chances are good that British loyalists would have continued to hold great power and land assets, and that our colonial founding Fathers and General George Washington would have remained forever obscure. There may never have been the need for the Declaration of Independence or the Constitution, and the shape of our country would not resemble today's. And, by the way, tens of thousand of lives would not have ended prematurely.

What if we had treated the native Americans as equals, kept our treaties with them, perhaps purchased rather than taking land and goods from them? What if we had not come armed with an almighty sense of right to take whatever we wanted in the name of manifest or God-guided destiny, with its concurrent right to commit genocide and lie and cheat and abrogate agreements, and had not been so quick to see all disputes in terms of having military solutions?

Could we have lived together as diverse human beings and avoided cloistering Indians in prison-like reservations, neatly provisioned with all the conditions of poverty and addiction? Would great swaths of the West still be Indian territory, and the inhabitants self-sufficient instead of welfare and casino dependent?

What if Napoleon had rejected Thomas Jefferson's offer to buy the center of our country, and the territory had evolved into a separate nation, rather than what we know as the Louisiana Purchase?

What if Mexico had put up a real fight and won the Mexican/ American war? What if the Comanche Indians and other tribes had not worn down the fighting spirit and ability of the Mexicans to the point that they were an easy target for the small American army? Would much of the western half of the country remain part of Mexico, as it was before the war? And as it is becoming again, through illegal and legal immigration from Mexico.

What if the South had simply been allowed to secede from the union and form a separate nation, without a devastating Civil War? Could this have resulted in a more manageable North American continent, not balkanized or Europeanized into fragments, but two major and viable countries cooperating as equals? Millions of lives could have been saved and our gene pool altered in a major way. And slavery would have run it course over time, just as it had in Europe.

What if there had been an eye witness to Mohammed's encounters with the angel Gabriel. These miracles, alone in cave, resulted in the Koran, the governing document for more than one billion humans today. Could eye witnesses have come out of the cave with a different story, conflicting and contradictory, which could have changed the course of civilization? Mohammed was, after all, illiterate, and his story had to be transcribed by others, and over many years and wives. Did God and Gabriel literally condone the subjugation and stoning to death of women and the barbarism of sharia law? A third party may have edited a different Koran!

It may be useful to note that almost all religious commandments, of all faiths, are based on a single individual communing with God, so claimed, in a setting removed from any witnesses, with only the claimant, thereafter known as prophets, to verify the substance of what revelations God gave. Also useful is the knowledge that each year, hundreds if not thousands of persons claim themselves to be new prophets, with the ability to commune with God, who has anointed them with divinity. Rational humans look for evidence corroborating such claims, but none is ever given, yet gullible cults form around them and support them with gifts and money.

What if Abraham or Moses had invited a committee of elders to listen as God spoke to them? Would the story have been different? Would God have been interpreted as being so vengeful that he was willing to let Abraham sacrifice his son? Would the ten commandments have had a different twist or two if others eyes and ears could have been privy to God's voice? Would the Old Testament look at all the same? Would God have threatened death to anyone who chose not to love him, or to worship another God of choice, if many had been invited into the tent to listen?

Circumstance is a key player in the life-forming elections of humans as they feel their way along, hesitating, faltering, analyzing, and finally selecting the ways to go from many roads available. Choosing left or right or center has consequences and molds life differently from that day forward. We read history as heroic or dastardly, without an examination of civilization changing outcomes had alternate roads been taken.

ON OTHER MATTERS

A truthful examination of a life must contain some understanding of the subject's philosophy; his value system; his ethics and morals, settled upon consciously after being forged through experience and reflection. Nietzsche said that a philosophy is valid only if it can be lived. It is fine to be an esthete, an activist idealist, a religious dogmatist or an entitlement socialist, so long as all the consequences can be lived with. Walking the walk and talking the talk is proof of the validity or failure of the philosophy. As an example, would a socialist give away his own wealth directly to the poor or less privileged, or would he rely on other taxpayers and governments to do this job? If the latter is true, he is not living his philosophy. Would Bill Gates or Warren Buffett hand out money directly to poor people rather than donating their wealth to family foundations which they control, while enjoying tax benefits for those donations?

Some may choose personal behavioral rules more stringent and demanding than rules laid down by society, themselves subject to whimsical change by governments, courts, or evolving standards.

Laws may legalize drugs, capital punishment, abortion, wartime killings, eating animal meats, etc., but individuals may reject these social norms on the basis of principle or conscience.

Legislated ethics and morals, therefore, do not work for everyone. Nihilists think there is no truth, no human purpose, no verifiable meaning, and that man-made laws are simply responses to temporary exigencies. There may indeed be no human purpose unless individuals decide to construct their own usefulness by intelligent free will, leading to philosophy with a purpose, followed by actions to live the chosen code. Individuals can willfully choose positive goals, and reject the notion that life is random, and that it cycles and disappears without a residue of consequence.

Within the context that it is possible for individuals to shape their own identities and lives, it is important to accept that narcissism is the steady state of humanity. Altruism is halting and easily spoken of but hard to live by. Self-preservation is gene driven. Few would elect to sacrifice their own lives if doing so would save the lives of ten strangers, if that were the stark moral choice.

Against that heavy backdrop, below are the key tenants of philosophically driven ethics and morals which my brain embraces, at age 78. The framework is my early environment, seasoned by study and observations and conclusions drawn from adult life and experiences around the world. Nowhere are these represented to be the "right" ethics or morals or convictions, but are those that are correct for me at this moment in my evolution.

I am a social libertarian and a fiscal conservative. Any political leader who governs along these lines is someone I could support. I am personally convinced that the legalization, control, and taxation of all drugs would be a net positive for society, while emptying half our prisons and reducing the need for prison guards, police forces, clogged courts, and their attendant expenses. Organized drug cartels, gang murders related to territory, and broken families and lives should decline as the appeal of illicit substances recedes. Drugs are ubiquitous today in every corner of society, distributed by killer criminal gangs. Legalization could only lead to better outcomes. As stated earlier, the ultimate gateway drugs are nicotine and alcohol, and society has learned from them valuable lessons applicable to the regulation of all such substances.

*Keynesian economic policies favoring top down government spending have been completely discredited, yet a cadre of idealists and academicians persist in propagating these outmoded models. Government stimulus programs, administered by self-interested politicians interested in prolonging power, amount to redistribution of wealth with politically chosen priorities. The evidence is that they are always a waste of money and time, but to admit failure would mean loss of control and power. Those in powerful positions will commit almost any dishonest act to get and retain power.

Society works best when individuals take responsibility for themselves and the environment or family they have created. Each should strive to be self-sufficient in physical and financial health, resorting to any safety net only temporarily. Consequences for choices made are part of responsibility. Addiction, obesity, large numbers of children, debt, recklessness, fall as a responsibility on the person or persons who made those selections. They should and must work through their problems, with no expectation of help from anyone or anything but private charity, freely given. Governments should stay out of this picture.

Not for goodness sake or religious reasons, but for the practical functioning of societies and cultures, cheating, lying, stealing, and subterfuge of any sort should be avoided. Civilizations much older than Christianity have known and practiced these restraints long before the Ten commandments were set in stone by God himself, according to the old testament. Contracts are best when balanced and fair, and are not sustainable when either party is disadvantaged.

Individuals who seek and work within their level of competence to sustain themselves and their families, are to be admired. Levels of competence can move up with experience and time. A component of this concept is the realization that not everyone is suited to higher academic education, and should, as is common in many cultures, advance in academia on merit alone. Those souls whose competence is more practically oriented should go to specialty or trade schools, and graduate with skills society will reward.

Avoid self-delusion above all else. In this connection, I happen to be an athiest, coming down on the side of Richard Dawkins, Sam Harris, Christopher Hitchins and H.L. Mencken all in opposition to religious dogma. Like Bertrand Russell, I have not been shown evidence to overcome disbelief.

The vengeful, genocidal, slave holding , favorites-playing, polygamist endorsing, child sacrificing God of the Old testament, and the God of original sin who causes innocent little children to ask to be forgiven, and who promises death in hell fire if they do not love him above all other Gods, is not my idea of enlightenment. If the stories of Noah and the battle of Jericho correctly represent a God, count me out. I count genes as my higher power, behind my compulsions and impulses.

• I do not foresee an afterlife, and, if I am wrong, I would say, in my defense, as Hitchins did, that I came by my position honestly by using the powers of reason and intelligence my genes gave me; that the best scientific evidence was used, and hypocrisy rejected.

• If there is a God of any kind, he/she cannot be benevolent and protective. Read the Bible for proof. And the ultimate and unanswerable question, who/what made God?

• And what could be more suspect than the popular concept of mindless heaven, floating in forever clean white robes eternally on a cloud. What's for dinner and who is the chef, are there golf or card games? Evening cocktails: What God-approved game or conversation would be acceptable? How could mere eternal humans get by with no sin inspired tensions to make life interesting? [11]

• I note here that my grandchildren, Jack and Audrey, are being steeped in Catholic beliefs and dogma as part of their parochial schooling, and that is consistent with Terry's wonderful upbringing and wonderful

11. "Letter to a Christian Nation", by Sam Harris, is the best and most concise documentation of the many dangers and distortions of dogma I have read. It convincingly dispatches all religious dogma, based on reason and solid science.

for them. They have had first communions. Their value systems in terms of helping others and community service are being honed. Their lives will be better as they grow and put religious teachings in perspective. The fact that I was not introduced to dogma at an early age accounts for my inability to accept dogma as an adult, but that in no way disrespects their training or their lasting beliefs. If not introduced to dogma at an early age, say, before age 13, then the powers of observation and reason will almost surely reject it. And even those stepped in dogma reject it at some point.

• I mourn the loss of apprenticeship as a means of transitioning young people into society, treating them as worthy workers and rewarding them with respect and money. This critically important dimension of youth education has tragically been taken away by child labor laws prompted by labor unions, sometimes with good intent to stop the exploitation of children, but more often to simply stop young people from taking meaningful jobs. Institutions of higher learning are starting to come around to this view, but our national obsessive embrace of traditional four-year college educations is tragically skewed away from the reality of our needs as a country.

• Having come this far in this narrative, it is no surprise that I would favor a constitutional convention to rebalance power between central government and states, between the executive and legislative branches, to strictly limit terms of service of elected officials, to restrict or eliminate lobbying during election cycles, to carve out a section of the first amendment on free speech to apply to our electoral process, restricting transparently populist and false speech as harmful to the Republic. Our current system is as corrupt as almost any in the world, but in perhaps more subtle ways. Our slippery down slope will accelerate without a revolutionary course correction, peaceful or violent.

• Unimpeded free enterprise, minimally regulated by power hungry politicians, is the best economic system yet devised, with its many faults. Periodically, the system must be purged of dynastic tendencies, of hangers-on to power and status, in order to continue to function. Currently, in 2011, I believe we are close to the point institutional breakdown, brought to this point by demagogues who are given the platforms of national media, aided by a gullible, uninformed electorate.

• I favor charity for the truly needy and permanently disabled or disadvantaged, provided the charity is privately funded. Everyone should be charitable except federal or state governments, who have no constitutional charge to give away other people's money in support of charities selected by politicians. Yet governments persist in budgeting huge amounts of give-aways to unsupervised users of these funds, with the rationale that the unfortunate or the organized minorities in our society should be given subsidies by the government, many of them permanent. In so doing, the dependency is enabled and becomes institutionalized and socially accepted, exactly the opposite of actions governments should be taking. And the most virulent form of racism is perpetuated by our own representatives who publicly mouth platitudes against racism.

• Freedom of religion is rational, so long as the dogma of that religion does not seek to kill me or my family for not believing. No religious dogma should trump civil laws of the host country. And church owned property, other than the property of the worship site itself, should be taxed as any other property. Many grandstand churches operate much like organized criminal ponzi schemes, with most funds enriching the church staff or suspect causes, or paying off legal fees for the sins committed by their ministers and priests. In Afghanistan, we fight for and support a backward regime embracing Sharia law, which subjugates and stones women, and sentences to death those who commit apostasy, the conversion from Islam to another religion. For this reason alone, we should be out of Afghanistan tomorrow. If we defeat the Taliban, we have nothing better in its place.

• In this connection, political correctness prevents us from using the most obvious tool we have to seek out radical Islamic terrorists, which is profiling. We must get over this brain-dead approach to fighting radicalism, or we will go on failing.

• I am for a color blind society, banning the collection of data about race, insisting that specific ethnicities end their racist platforms, ending any allocation of government money according to "needs" of minorities. Pollsters who track voter attitudes by race insure separation by race. Politicians who act on their data are dishonest hypocrites.

The list could be substantially longer, but my conservatism is obvious at this point. I have found a substantial divide between philosophies of those from small towns versus those from urban settings. Urbanites in high density industrialized setting live the experience curve of associations and relationships much faster than rural dwellers, due mainly to density and proximity. They see large scale poverty in ghetto-like tribal settings which small town inhabitants don't. They sometimes conclude that the only way out for urban poor is government assistance. Rural people say, "move out of the ghetto and stand on your own two feet and find a job." I side with farm dwellers, in the belief that anything else perpetuates ghetto and bario poverty, breaks down the family structure with welfare payments and food stamps, and enables inaction on the part of the welfare recipients.

AT THIS PLATEAU

Nearing my 78th birthday, almost each day brings some new evidence of impending mortality, although I continue to be among the healthiest of my friends. It would be silly and superstitious to ignore age and the end of life, because that would be delusional and childlike, as well as an admission of ignorance of the cycle of life. Older age must be embraced as a time of reflection and wisdom seeking and sharing. It is a time to help others, to observe the workings of humanity, of participating in every event to the end, and making careful plans for one's end.

I am comfortable with my choices in life. I have forgiven myself many youthful mistakes and stupidities. I have fixed my attitude toward religions and dogmas, and am completely comfortable with my convictions.

I have been extremely fortunate in my choice of life mate, and grateful for our sons and their lives, and Jack and Audrey, and Terry. I am grateful for my siblings and the love they have given me and my family. I salute my mentors.

I have developed my opinions about life thoughtfully and with evidence, while accepting that others will have different opinions based on their studies and experiences. I continue to learn from them. I have few regrets, knowing with certainty that I might have done some better, but also knowing that I did my best.

Our little house in La Quinta, California is hardly a dot in the Garrett/ Savage, Morris/Grimes, Henderson/Johnson galaxy. Just five generations downstream from Joan's and my grandparents are several hundred of their progeny. In two or three more generations, they will number in the thousands, and within 20 generations of the colonial era of this country, their genes will infuse literally millions. This seems proof that the selfish gene truly is the ultimate survivor in this evolutionary epoch.

What a treasure of insight and knowledge if Alexander Shakespeare Morris, or his wife, Lillie Grimes, or his father, James Morris, or perhaps Henry Garrett, veteran of George Washington's army of the Potomac, had passed onto us some written legacy of their actions, feelings, motives, and understandings. We have wondered many times about the lives of Dora Savage Garrett, and Joan's large Johnson family heritage from Sweden.

We know the general outline of their lives, but know nothing about their thinking. We have not a single vignette, a signature, a poem. We don't even know if they were literate!

Men and women of the time lived from one inconvenience and crisis to another, and had no time for frivolity. Fighting disease with primitive remedies, nursing too many children, going here or there on horseback or with a wagon team, grubbing stumps, clearing small plots for planting, harvesting, canning, sewing, tending animals, heating the house with coal or wood, cooking, searching for potable water, home schooling, reading by oil lamp light. Daily survival took all available hours, with no time to record life or reflect on it or contemplate its meaning. Such contemplation was better left to preachers and higher powers, who presumably were better equipped to deal with philosophical issues. For many, there is a certain safety and security in wisdom received from anointed wise men, ministers, and holy books. Regrettably, some turn out to be con men and opportunists.

Men heads of households of the time could not give in to sentiment or emotion. They had to face each hard day head-on, with no excuses. Weakness was seen in sensitive men. In my own father, love was an unspoken yet certainly felt emotion. Annette Wright Long correctly thought her father, T. L. Wright, emotionally uninvested when he signed letters to his children, "Sincerely, T.L. Wright". But every depression, dust bowl family man we knew was much the same. A hug or kiss or expression of love in public was to admit an emotional and less stoic nature, and that was not acceptable.

Our generation has no such easy excuses. Freed from life's earlier drudgeries, aided by computers and publishing software, informed by pictures from around the world on the hourly news channels, tracked by cell phones and I-Pads and Blackberries, and social networking sights, we now have time, precious time, to think about and record our memories, analyze and try to make some sense of them, look at how the pieces of the puzzle might fit together, and think about how life with chosen purpose can really work.

I decided to take my turn at writing in order to leave for Jack and Audrey and their children what our own ancestors did not; a sense of what is in the genes that are now inside of them; that they might know and understand themselves better, so they don't have to wonder what life was like for Mimi and Pop Pop. I hope I have succeeded.

Perhaps they will tell me face to face when they are married and have children, and I am lucky.

Meanwhile, I will be working on my next book.

JBG, 2/4/11 LA QUINTA, CALIFORNIA

ADDENDUM

As *TOMATO HEAD* went to print, we received word that our oldest son, Scott Edwin, 46, was diagnosed with AML Leukemia on June 7, 2011. He has now undergone intensive chemotherapy at Froedtert hospital in

Milwaukee, Wisconsin. He will be hospitalized for at least until July 11, but perhaps longer, depending on the results of two bone marrow biopsies which will show whether or not the chemo has achieved remission.

If the result is positive, the most likely follow on treatment with the best chance of achieving a lasting cure is a Bone marrow transplant, which will require another month of hospitalization after the surgery, and an estimated year of recovery, during which time he will be out of work and under close monitoring through visits to the hospital every other day. Testing of possible matching donors is beginning, and his younger brother, Jonathan, has volunteered to be the first tested. Others, including my siblings, have also asked to be tested, and expressed the desire to donate marrow. Such is the mettle of the Garrett clan when one of their own is in need.

We have learned that the odds of a sibling match are only 25%, while the probability of finding a match from the International bone marrow bank, is 80%. Fifteen million people have donated bone marrow to the bank. News of the existence of the bank comes as a surprise to almost everyone who hears of it. We also learned from the head of Scott's medical team, that marrow cannot be donated across ethnic lines, and that minorities, therefore, have the greatest risk of not achieving a match.

In September, we learned that a single 10 of 10 perfect match had been found from the computer registry, and a transplant is tentatively set for mid October. The whereabouts of the donor are unknown, but could be almost anywhere in the world. When actually donated, the marrow will be transported by courier directly to the marrow transplant wing at Froedtert Hospital in Milwaukee, and transplanted under the supervision of Dr. Jeanne Palmer and her team specializing in this procedure.

News of Scott's sudden illness was stunning and surreal. He has been a high energy and very athletic personality all his life. His legal career and personal goals will now have to be reset. The lives of his wife

Terry, and his children, Jack, 11, and Audrey, 10, will also take new and different paths. As his parents, we have had occasion to examine the depths of our love for him and his family, and for our son Jon. Our humility and humanity and compassion have been deepened and broadened by this experience, confirming, as it has once again, the precariousness of suddenly changeable human life.

ON JUNE 8, 2011 we got word that my dear sister NORMA JEAN, had died of liver cancer, after a short illness, in Amarillo, Texas. Her death was expected, but a sad and great loss to her remaining five siblings, her husband Ronald Phinny, son Brad, and daughter Gina, and her grandchildren. Our rush to Scott's side prevented us from attending her service on June 13, but we will miss her forever.

Update

"On December 14, 2011, our dear son Scott died of complications from Bone Marrow Transplant, 187 days after his AML leukemia diagnosis. Initial remission was achieved through chemotherapy, but subsequent intensive chemo to suppress his immune system so it would not reject new bone marrow basically destroyed his liver, and caused his death. He was 47. We can never recover from his loss. Our lives are forever diminished.

--JBG

.

www.ingramcontent.com/pod-product-compliance
Lightning Source LLC
Chambersburg PA
CBHW060746100426
42813CB00032B/3412/J